The Kingdom and the Republic

AMERICA IN THE NINETEENTH CENTURY

Series editors:
Brian DeLay, Steven Hahn, Amy Dru Stanley

America in the Nineteenth Century proposes a rigorous
rethinking of this most formative period in US history. Books
in the series will be wide-ranging and eclectic, with an interest
in politics at all levels, culture and capitalism, race and slavery,
law, gender, and the environment, and regional and transnational
history. The series aims to expand the scope of nineteenth-century
historiography by bringing classic questions into dialogue with
innovative perspectives, approaches, and methodologies.

THE
KINGDOM
AND THE
REPUBLIC

Sovereign Hawai'i
and the Early United States

NOELANI ARISTA

PENN

UNIVERSITY OF PENNSYLVANIA PRESS

PHILADELPHIA

Published by
University of Pennsylvania Press
Philadelphia, Pennsylvania 19104-4112
www.upenn.edu/pennpress

Printed in the United States of America
on acid-free paper
1 3 5 7 9 10 8 6 4 2

Library of Congress Cataloging-in-Publication Data

Names: Arista, Noelani, author.
Title: The kingdom and the republic: sovereign Hawai'i and the early United States / Noelani
  Arista.
Other titles: America in the nineteenth century.
Description: 1st edition. | Philadelphia: University of Pennsylvania Press, [2019] | Series: America
  in the nineteenth century | Includes bibliographical references and index.
Identifiers: LCCN 2018022539 | ISBN 9780812250732 (hardcopy: alk. paper)
Subjects: LCSH: Hawaii—Politics and government—To 1893. | Hawaii—Foreign
  relations—United States—19th century. | United States—Foreign relations—Hawaii—19th
  century.
Classification: LCC DU627.1 .A75 2019 | DDC 327.730969/0904—dc23
LC record available at https://lccn.loc.gov/2018022539

For my father, Vicente Arista, and my mother, Rose Marie Arista
No kuʻu kāne ʻo Chad Hashimoto a me nā lei a kāua
Hiʻiakalehuakaulei lāua ʻo Kaʻulawena
No ke aloha.

CONTENTS

INTRODUCTION

He Ao ʻŌlelo

A World of Words

I ka ʻōlelo nō ke ola, i ka ʻōlelo nō ka make

In speech there is life, in speech death.
—On the mana that inheres in chiefly oral pronouncement

This is a study of a world of words, world-making words, and how historians have written—or not—about them. We begin right in the middle of a dramatic expansion of this world. It is December 1827. An *ʻaha ʻōlelo*, a Hawaiian chiefly council, has met for several days on the matter of an American missionary, Rev. William Richards, accused of libel by a British whaleship captain, William Buckle, and the British consul, Richard Charlton. Rev. William Richards, according to the British men, had libeled Captain Buckle when he wrote back to the home office of the American Board of Commissioners for Foreign Missions (ABCFM) in Boston, Massachusetts, describing the captain's "purchase" in 1825 of a Hawaiian woman named Leoiki. Excerpts of this letter and others like it were then published in various missionary and American newspapers as a public airing of the violations of Christian morality occurring between American and European sailors and Hawaiian women.

It wasn't Christian morality that had British consul Charlton and Captain Buckle concerned. It was, instead, the accusation that Captain Buckle had bought the Hawaiian woman, Leoiki. Such a claim opened Captain Buckle to charges of trading in slaves, a violation of Britain's 1807 Slave Trade Act. Thus, words about a Hawaiian woman, written in a letter from Hawaiʻi, edited and rewritten in New England, printed in American newspapers, and read in England, brought the British, American, and Hawaiian legal worlds into collision.

On this day in 1827, a group of American Congregationalist missionaries was summoned from their new settlements across the archipelago by the *ali'i* (chiefs) to appear before them on O'ahu. In this 'aha 'ōlelo, spoken words carried the force of law. And *words* were the central issue in this dispute. While the British men chose to focus on the parts of Richards' letter that told of Leoiki's sale, for Richards, what was far more important about the letter and other reports like it from the mission were their detailed accounts of the "outrages" or attacks on mission stations by British sailors and whalers over a *kapu* (chiefly legal pronouncement) that prohibited Hawaiian women from traveling to ships. Serving as his own defense, Rev. Richards gave a verbal performance illustrating his already ripe capacity for political expression in the Hawaiian language, though he had lived in the islands a mere four years: "It is for you to deliver us over to such hands as you see proper, for you are our chiefs. We have left our own country and can not now receive the protection of its laws. . . . If I am a bad man or have broken the laws of your country, it is for you to try, and acquit or condemn me—you alone are my judges—it is for you to send me from your shores, or protect me here. *With you is my life, and with you is my death.* The whole is with you."[1]

Richards' speech is striking because of the forcefulness with which it recognizes Hawaiian structures of legal authority, although "laws," "acquit," and "condemn" were concepts that Richards imported from other legal traditions. Richards begins by recognizing the political authority of the ali'i, repeatedly stating that the American missionaries stationed in the island were now *subjects* of the ali'i—"for you are our chiefs." He then emphasizes the distance of New England and its laws from Hawai'i. He asserts that his behavior and words should be judged by Hawaiian law, posing it thus: if I have broken the laws of your country, "you alone are my judges." British and American laws had no primacy in this matter, for Hawaiian chiefly authority was the only rule of law in the islands.

Richards made clear to the 'aha 'ōlelo and any outside observers that he considered himself subject to the rule of the chiefs, but a more important aspect of his verbal performance gives us insight into how persuasive Richards might have appeared, and how his precise choice of words may have moved the ali'i. Although Richards *wrote* about these proceedings in English, his *speech* cannot be understood or interpreted only in English. A correct apprehension of Richards' words as a performance within a chiefly parliament requires that one also have an ear for the kinds of Hawaiian phrases and terms that were native to Hawaiian law and politics before the arrival of foreigners in the islands and into the nineteenth century. With such an ear, we can hear a phrase that clamors for chiefly attention: "It is for you to send me from your shores, or protect me here. *With you is my life, and with you is my death.* The whole is with you."

With these words, Richards revealed an aptitude for understanding Hawaiian political discourse that had thus far not been widely evinced among his missionary counterparts.[2] The Hawaiian phrase *I ka ʻōlelo nō ke ola, i ka ʻōlelo nō ka make* (In speech there is life, in speech there is death) may appear to indicate Richards' abject submission to the chiefs. But instead, his repurposing of the phrase and its cadence demonstrated his cultural intelligence, as he played a rhetorical game of power in Hawaiian. The Hawaiian phrase is a precept descriptive of the authority of chiefly speech, which could determine the life or death of a person according to the degree to which a kapu had been flouted.[3] By taking this Hawaiian precept and turning it slightly to point toward his own life, Richards attempted a moment of Hawaiian political theater. He chose the perfect moment to invoke the *mana* (power) inherent in chiefly speech.[4] And he deftly reminded the aliʻi that it was their responsibility as pronouncers of kapu to judge the words he wrote about Leoiki in relationship to precedent, to past chiefly judgments of similar behavior.

Richards' rhetorical and political performance at the ʻaha ʻōlelo of late 1827 pushes us to rethink many aspects of writing a history of late eighteenth- and early nineteenth-century Hawaiian law and governance. First, his condition at that moment—when a British consul and sea captain demanded that he, an American, face British justice for writing about an incident that happened in the Hawaiian Islands—foregrounds the fact that early nineteenth-century Hawaiʻi was not a colony of either America or Britain. Second, that an ʻaha ʻōlelo was called to deliberate what to do with Richards in the face of British demands reminds us that Hawaiian governance and legal practices were strong and viable; the aliʻi were asked to deliberate about how to deal with foreigners in the islands. And finally, the rhetorical skill with which Richards asserted Hawaiian rule and jurisdiction over his body and conduct not only gives us insight into an important evolution in Hawaiian governance (is he a foreign or domestic subject?). In Richards' speech, we can also observe how languages and epistemes might engage one another deeply. When systems of meaning-making intersect, we see not a "missionary perspective" or a "native perspective." Instead, we find a coalescence of different worlds of words, expanding their reach and salience. And Richards offers us a window into what one must be able to hear, to know, and to interpret to be a successful teller of how meanings and histories are made at the confluence of languages and cultures.

This book is about Hawaiian governance and law at the moment of this coalescence, about the forces both internal and external that contributed to this coalescence, and about how we correct the imbalance in the historiography of Hawai'i by revealing what colonial histories of Hawai'i have left out: a story of continuing and evolving Hawaiian governance and law conducted in the Hawaiian language.

*   *   *

Readers of past historical narratives of Hawai'i may feel *kama'āina* (familiar, at ease) with a history that starts in 1778 and ends in 1898. In these accounts, Hawaiian historical time begins with Captain Cook's "discovery" of the Hawaiian Islands, the remotest place in the vast northern Pacific Ocean. Many histories relate that Hawaiians lived isolated and unknowing of the greater world outside their islands, amazed at the foreigners with large ships they called floating islands. Cook's deification was inevitable, yet the natives killed him when he did not live up to that status—or so the story goes. After this initial contact with the British, the islands were laid open to visitors from across the globe. A young chief from the island of Hawai'i named Kamehameha used foreign advisers and weapons to aid in his quest to conquer all the archipelago's islands. His wars succeeded in consolidating a unified kingdom. But tragically, mere months after his death in 1819, his two closest wives and his heir, Liholiho, struck down an entire system of laws and regulations called the *'ai kapu*, ordering temples destroyed and images burned. This historical narrative leads us to a conclusion: the old religion is cast down, and in its wake is left a vacuum—no law, no religion—that begged to be filled by civilization.

This narrative continues. Serendipitously, mere months after this cataclysmic break with the past, a new kind of *haole* arrived in the islands. American missionaries from southern New England brought Christianity and implements for planting a new civilization. They brought the Bible, printing presses, and the religious traditions and teachings of their God.

Upon landing, these missionaries viewed Hawaiian governance structures in terms of the feudal lordships and social relations that their own Old World English ancestors had escaped.

The story usually told of the 1820s in Hawaiʻi begins with this missionary settlement as the primary stimulus of a decade of radical transformations in Hawaiian life, especially in governance and law. Now-cemented relationships between Boston merchants and certain Hawaiian aliʻi produced the first large-scale harvest and export of *ʻiliahi* (sandalwood). This sandalwood trade with China, according to the narrative, fed avaricious chiefs who tyrannically exploited their *makaʻāinana* (non-aliʻi) subjects. As the makaʻāinana were forced to go to the mountains to harvest a tree for outsiders, they had to leave their agricultural work; without growing more food for the people to eat, makaʻāinana were pushed along a path of disease and malnourishment that had begun with the introduction of diseases by sailors a generation before. With sex and sandalwood threatening Hawaiian makaʻāinana, the American missionaries tried to intervene, seeking to redirect Hawaiians away from vices like drinking and engaging in sex with foreigners.[5] This narrative codifies the missionaries' role in the 1820s as the bringers of law and order, the champions of enlightened civilization and salvation—both physical and spiritual—on behalf of the Hawaiian people. And this role continues to unfold in histories of Hawaiian governance, as the Christian conversion of ruling aliʻi like Kaʻahumanu and Kauikeaouli, and of King Kamehameha III result in a missionary-driven move to a Western system of land use, laws, and constitutional monarchy in the 1830s and 1840s. The emergence of a modern Hawaiian nation-state, designed and impelled through the guidance of men like Rev. William Richards, drew upon the examples of America and Britain. It signaled that civilization and Christianity had surely taken root in Hawaiian soil, banishing any memory of the void that had come before. Thus the start of Hawaiian history is its discovery by British foreigners, and Hawaiian governance and law arise from American missionaries' settlement.

Most historical studies of Hawaiʻi are profoundly shaped by this narrative. And they rely upon two premises: one, that Hawaiian leaders and their people were incapable of self-governance, and two, that the 1819 abolition of the ʻai kapu left *kānaka maoli* (Hawaiian people) without law, government, and religion. The errors of both these premises and the narrative of American colonization as *the* history of governance and law in Hawaiʻi are what this book corrects. For while historians have rightly identified the

1820s as a crucial period of political, legal, and social change in Hawaiian history, the nature of that transformation merits further study.

This dominant version of Hawai'i's history has not gone unchallenged, and revisionist narratives have attempted to address this problem from the contact period through annexation. These interventions have sought to rebalance the unequal measure of Hawaiian history by illuminating possible Hawaiian worldviews, made visible through abundant Hawaiian oral and written texts, and by focusing on the agency of native Hawaiian historical actors. Indeed, Hawai'i may arguably have the largest native-language historical and literature archive in the Pacific, and perhaps all of native North America, exceeding one million pages of printed text, a staggering 125,000 of which were Hawaiian-language newspapers published between 1834 and 1948.[6] It is because of Hawai'i's relatively late Western "discovery" toward the end of the eighteenth century that the textual legacies of cross-cultural relationships in the islands are markedly different from those of other indigenous peoples in North and South America, Africa, and the Pacific. Due to the missionary introduction of printing presses to early nineteenth-century Hawai'i and chiefly commands to their people that they become educated and literate, Hawaiians began to write and publish Hawaiian histories, genealogies, and "traditions" during the 1820s. As a result, continuity in the transmission of Hawaiian oral, historical, and cultural "traditions" into writing and print may be unparalleled in the historiography of native peoples.

In the first real attempt to correct the historiography through Hawaiian-language sources, Hawaiian historian Lilikalā Kame'eleihiwa illustrated the power of metaphors framed out of deep literacy in Hawaiian language. Using these metaphors to expand our understanding of Hawaiian governance through the concept of *pono* (correctness), her work provided an important corrective to the argument that avaricious ali'i facilitated the spread of western institutions to the detriment of their native subjects.[7] At the same time, Hawaiian-language expert Puakea Nogelmeier forcefully argued that generations of scholarly work on Hawai'i were profoundly limited by the sole use of English translations of four major nineteenth-century Hawaiian intellectuals and writers.[8] Nogelmeier challenged this four-text canon, calling its enshrinement a "discourse of sufficiency."[9] Thus Nogelmeier put the onus on scholars to go beyond an impoverished canon of sources and draw upon the numerous extant sources in Hawaiian.

Political scientist Noenoe Silva has continued Kame'eleihiwa's work with Hawaiian-language sources, arguing that kānaka maoli were not passive victims of colonialism; instead, her work restored the *leo o ka lāhui* (the voice of the people) to Hawaiian histories of the Overthrow and Annexation periods.[10] To do so, Silva presents, translates, and interprets numerous late nineteenth-century written protests against American seizure of Hawaiʻi. Petitions, newspaper editorials, and chanted and sung protestations against the overthrow and annexation counterbalance the unequal settler colonial histories of this critical moment.[11] The most recent works by geographer Kamanamaikalani Beamer and literary scholar Marie Alohalani Brown illustrate that new scholarship on nineteenth-century Hawaiian history is no longer apologetic about engaging Hawaiian-language source material. Beamer's work rejects the "fatal impact" thesis that imagined a passive native capitulation to foreign influence. In his historical narrative of Hawaiian governance, the aliʻi are portrayed through *ʻōiwi* (native) optics as having "agency" in selectively appropriating western ideas and technologies to augment traditional Hawaiian governance.[12]

In these attempts to rebalance the unequal measure of colonial histories of Hawaiʻi with a native history of Hawaiʻi grounded in the Hawaiian-language archive, these scholars have made essential interventions, especially in their attempts to illuminate Hawaiian historiographic concepts, paradigms, and tropes through culturally literate interpretation of Hawaiian-language sources. But this revisionist work's emphasis on restoring "agency" to Hawaiian historical actors carries another risk: the unreflective use of Western historiographical paradigms, tropes, and plots in telling histories of culturally Othered peoples. As the historical anthropologist Marshall Sahlins argues, any history of first contact in Hawaiʻi, let alone a history of contemporary Hawaiʻi, can easily be trapped in its own Western cultural paradigms unless we rigorously recognize how "our" paradigms and tropes replicate them, working instead to respect and seek the cultural differences that make all the difference.[13]

Revisionist projects' use of "agency," then, is an effect of the historiographic distortion introduced into Hawaiian histories as part of a colonial historical narrative, fundamentally based in Enlightenment definitions of places and peoples, of modern political subjects defined by their self-agency, and of primitive naturals with passive natures. In other words, natives with agency have been created out of necessity to combat historiographic narratives that have made natives historical objects rather than subjects.[14] But this revisionist work has left uncritiqued the fundamental binarism embedded in settler colonial historiography.

This book takes seriously Sahlins' warning, critiquing the premises to which colonial historiography of Hawai'i has bound us by deepening the revisionist dive into Hawaiian-language sources to reveal and employ Hawaiian-language-based "ideas, actions, and ontologies" in historical interpretation. Different languages let us see different historiographies. This is the heart of correcting histories of unequal measure: we must seek an understanding of a multilingual and epistemologically diverse Pacific World, full of many kinds of exchanges. We need to attempt an integration of the methodological and intellectual practices of both Hawaiian and American histories. And the foundation of this necessary correction to imbalanced power and priorities in our distinct and converging historiographies is an unwavering insistence upon including disparate worlds of words that met in early nineteenth-century Hawai'i.

From this perspective, the political and legal transformations of the 1820s—transformations of vital importance to Hawai'i's modern history—were Hawaiian responses to "colonial" disorder, rather than well-organized colonial impositions upon Hawaiian disorder.[15] This work maps the political, economic, and religious intercourse between Hawaiians and foreigners from 1810 to 1828. In doing so, I argue that Hawaiian governance and law enter into a moment of global modernity, marked by the expansion of chiefly governance to now include kānāwai, or printed laws. This legal change in the 1820s marks a clearer distinction between Hawaiian political subjects under chiefly kapu, American and British political subjects, and foreigners who sought political existence under the chiefs. This mixed world of words came together in a Hawai'i still ruled by the ali'i and governed by long-standing council and legal practices. From this view, we can see a new Hawaiian history.

In this new history, Hawaiians were not waiting to be civilized, rather they were experiencing a series of dramatic social and political upheavals marked most significantly by Kamehameha's unification of the islands. This long-term military campaign flattened the political structure of rule by eradicating rival ali'i, collapsing lines of genealogical succession, and subsuming religious leadership under his rule. Unification was aided by the incorporation of haole expertise and munitions, and hastened by new diseases that struck warring factions indiscriminately. It was this complex religio-political contest that American merchants and missionaries encountered. Thus Hawai'i in the 1820s was shaped by a heterogeneity of value systems, in which each group of people brought their own ways of making decisions to their engagements with each other. The entry of Hawai'i into the global sandalwood trade occurred through an alliance between certain chiefs and American merchants. In this alliance, different ideas of obligation and debt held by chiefs and merchants made for a necessary evolution of economic thinking in Hawai'i and laid the foundation for a modern Hawaiian national debt in the mid-nineteenth century. As increasing numbers of whalers arrived in the islands, sexual encounters between Hawaiian women and foreign men brought the ali'i, foreign sailors, ship captains, merchants, and American missionaries into serious conflict beginning in 1825, resulting in the pronouncement of legal restrictions (kapu) by the ali'i that sought to regulate foreigners' access to Hawaiian women. Disturbances escalated, driven by foreign sailors' refusal to accept this kapu, and this phenomenon, I argue, caused Hawaiian law to evolve a new written form; the first kānāwai were issued by the ali'i, printed and distributed in 1823 and 1825. This book highlights the political deliberations between ali'i over the sale of a Hawaiian woman to a British ship captain in 1825, and the fallout from three attacks on mission stations by whalers and sailors angered over the ban. The misplaced blame of the sailors further illustrates their mistaken apprehension that missionaries rather than Hawaiian chiefs were the source of law. This new history also reconsiders the arrival of American Christian missionaries in 1820 by looking back at the experiences and narrative productions of Hawaiians in New England. By looking at the continuity of missionary contact with Hawai'i through the production of narratives of native converts, before their actual arrival in the islands, this book illuminates New England missionaries' discursive preparations and justifications for their settlement project.

* * *

My view of missionary work in 1820s Hawai'i argues against previous historians' insistence that the ABCFM missionaries brought a vigorous colonial endeavor to the islands.[16] In this respect it is both inspired by and in dialogue with important new work in native and indigenous studies, most importantly Jean M. O'Brien's *Firsting and Lasting*.[17] O'Brien has written a history of the birth of a new American discourse, a proliferation of local histories that firmly fixed non-Indian settlers and their descendants in the landscape of the new nation by repeatedly pronouncing the absence of Indians from early nineteenth-century America.[18] Her work focuses specifically

on the local histories written and circulated in southern New England, the
same region from which the Sandwich Island Mission came. These southern New England histories "made the boldest claims to 'firsting,'" which
O'Brien describes as an assertion by non-Indians that they were "the first
people to erect the proper institutions of a social order worthy of notice."
In order for that narrative to address the obvious pre-existence of Indians
on the land that became southern New England, those histories also had to
assert that the last of those Indians had come and gone. Indian disappearance left the land unencumbered of past names and meaningfulness; the
histories of non-Indians' new nation could be built upon clean ground.

Even though the Sandwich Islands Mission emerged from this same
home, such a discourse of "firsting" and "lasting" could find no purchase
in the Hawaiian Islands of the 1820s. Instead, missionary letters and publications circulated throughout America and beyond were full of descriptions
of Hawai'i and Hawaiians, made for foreign consumption. This textual production of Hawai'i far exceeded the writings of explorers, "discoverers,"
ship captains, and merchants combined. But it did not perhaps exceed the
writings and oral literature of kānaka maoli themselves, written and published *ma ka 'ōlelo Hawai'i* (in the Hawaiian language) over the next century after the mission arrived.[19] The 1820s is an important period when, for
kānaka maoli, the production of the history of Hawai'i was moving between
oral/aural production and performance, writing, and print, while at the
same time the creation and circulation of non-Hawaiian views of Hawai'i
and its natives was increasing in volume.

This book is also in conversation with histories of encounter, especially
those written about Indian and non-Indian, *maoli* (Hawaiian, indigenous)
and haole first contacts.[20] Encounters are important points of engagement,
meeting, and coming together. But the paradigm of encounter tends to reify
a homogeneity of "encounter culture," which the parties encountering each
other must unequivocally represent. Thus histories of encounter tend to
emphasize fatal impacts, worlds colliding, with contention and conflict
defining the interpretations of events. This book seeks a different approach,
one more akin to the confluence of worlds, where the mixing of numerous
languages, social practices, and ways of defining life works fluidly. It highlights what occurs when people from different meaning-making systems
engage with one another; moments of understanding and misunderstand-
ing become constitutive of historical outcomes. Concentrating on negotiations and deliberations at the confluence of worlds of words, rather than

always emphasizing conflict and clashing, helps us see Hawaiian governing practices and transformations in Hawaiian law *in context*, a critical correction of previous histories' characterization of Hawaiian rule through distant and deeply ideological concepts like feudalism, despotism, and tyranny.

Early chapters examine little-known interactions between the aliʻi, merchants, and ship captains in the sandalwood trade, who each have their own, often differing concepts of debt and obligation, as well as important moments in New England missionary efforts to plan and plant a mission in the Hawaiian Islands. Highlighting these moments reveals the ubiquity of Hawaiian self-governance in the 1820s, as well as its characteristics and underlying principles. Later chapters on changes in Hawaiian law during this period examine the critical addition of written laws (kānāwai) to enhance chiefly kapu. These chapters also argue that the unruly behavior of foreigners in the islands—men who were not subjects of kapu—forced the chiefs to extend their jurisdiction over foreigners. As increasing numbers of whalers arrived at the islands, sexual encounters between Hawaiian women and foreign men would bring the aliʻi, foreign sailors, ship captains, merchants, and American missionaries into serious conflict beginning in 1825, resulting in the pronouncement of kapu by the aliʻi that sought to limit foreigners' access to Hawaiian women. I follow the discussions that aliʻi had in the ʻaha ʻōlelo, or chiefly council, over whether their pronouncements should also apply to foreigners or to Hawaiian people exclusively. The result is a more accurate history of Hawaiian politics, the evolution of Hawaiian law, and the extension of chiefly rule over foreigners.

My research seeks to clear a space for understanding different value systems borne by different groups in my history. By incorporating different approaches, methods, and ways of reading sources in Hawaiian and English, I seek to narrate a more nuanced account of the story of settlement, one that illustrates the centrality of indigenous-language sources to writing histories of encounter. The challenge in writing this history has been communicating a robust Hawaiian language and sign base during the moment when these sources were just beginning to be produced, making room for Hawaiian disciplinary paradigms of historical thinking and praxis alongside powerful legitimated Euro-American narratives. Thus this work utilizes methodological and interpretive techniques that may be applied in other histories of colonial settlement, especially where native-language sources are available.

The distance between Hawaiʻi and the American and European worlds was not just one of nautical miles; it was an imaginative space enlarged by the projection and production of Hawai'i and Hawaiians as objects of knowledge by New England merchants, missionaries, visiting transient explorers, and ship captains. Alongside that production of Hawai'i, this book deliberately places the actions and words of maoli *and* haole in cultural contexts in ways that resonate with how Hawaiians of this period deliberated and acted in relation to their own constructions of the past. Numerous histories have been written detailing the background of the missionaries and merchants that came to Hawai'i, mapping the historical trajectory of their journeys.[21] This work argues that the actions and choices of Hawaiians cannot be interpreted unless scholars take into account Hawaiian understandings of the past and their material (embodied) relationships to that past. Hawaiians in this period under study were people to whom the past mattered. And like other people who had rigorous criteria, pedagogies, and rules for the "scripting," maintenance, and use of that past, they made decisions—especially political and legal decisions—in reference to that past. Framing present actions with historical thought and justification ensured that the past gave meaning and a sense of order and continuity to governance in the present.

In his theoretical piece on "the concept of language" in the historian's work, J. G. A. Pocock warned historians seeking to study "languages of political thought" that "we wish to study the languages in which utterances were performed, rather than the utterances which were performed in them." [22] While Pocock addressed historians working with languages of political thought in early modern Europe, his theoretical piece is vital for informing this study. Like early modern European historians, Hawai'i and Pacific historians, especially Māori and Maoli historians, are engaged in the deep study of "idioms, rhetorics, specialized vocabularies and grammars, modes of discourse or ways of talking about politics which have been created and diffused, but far more importantly employed in political discourse " in native languages.[23] How to identify these hallmarks of authoritative speech—the idioms, rhetorics, and so forth, that Pocock wrote of—is one of many challenges facing scholars who read and interpret non-Western language sources that have yet to be valued as sound evidence in Western historiography.By uncovering Hawaiian modalities of political discourse, this work also aims to "find language as context, and not text."[24]

To do so, this book pays close attention to the writings of chiefs and chiefly advisers, studying the usage of particular words or rhetorical turns of phrase that arose when the ali'i or their advisers were engaged in political discussions. I do this so that I can get closer to understanding the fabric of Hawaiian political discourse and how power was shaped by the perform-ance of words in these situations. Understanding of early nineteenth-century Hawaiian political thought can be found not only in important concepts, such as kapu and mana, but also by paying attention to the lan-guage that historical actors used in their interactions with one another. Speech is the primary mode through which the aliʻi secured rule and gov-erned, as it was also central to the construction and maintenance of *moʻolelo* (history and past-history as precedent) and the proclamation of kapu (oral law) and kānāwai (published law). Rather than being elusive, authoritative speech and Hawaiian patterns of discourse can be tracked across numerous written and published sources in Hawaiian, in translation, and even when transferred by fluent Hawaiian speakers into English.[25]

To accomplish this kind of recovery of Hawaiian political language and thought, this book must alleviate the tensions between orality and text as well as speech and writing. This project illustrates how people in this history moved between orality and writing, choosing in different instances to draw on the authority of written legal instruments, oaths sworn verbally, chiefly pronouncement (kapu), or the word of God, depending on their situation. Casting aside the colonial privileging of written texts over oral genres not only opens the door to a fuller Hawaiian-language source-base; it also reminds us that British and American historical actors in this period brought with them oral genres and rhetorical performances that structured their interactions with people at home as well as with Hawaiians.

The use of a term like "oral tradition" is problematic. I use the phrase sparingly to refer to genres in Hawaiian that were performed and passed on via networks and institutions that rigorously trained people to memorize materials, maintain their form and genre, and pass them on. A prevailing assumption in the use of "oral tradition" is that it predates the introduction of literacy to native communities and that orally expressed information represents "authentic, traditional knowledge's, legends and tales." Categori-cally, such traditions are relegated to "memory"—a body of knowledge reproduced uncritically and without analysis. The turn to the textual, in contrast, demarcates the inauguration of history, where texted materials are considered valid and "true." At the inception of the written production of Hawaiian history, minister and professor Sheldon Dibble denigrated Hawaiian traditions as unverifiable because they were oral and not writ-ten.[26] There is no compelling equivalent in our scholarly discourse for the way that print reproduces consensus arguments, research questions, and tropes uncritically as part of Euro-American discursive "written traditions," and yet it is possible now using sorting search engines to reproduce the way discourse reproduces itself across scholarly works for generations.

How to construct rules for formulating contexts and deciding what evidence is applicable is one of the challenges this book offers; it suggests several avenues to continue the Hawaiian practice of mobilizing "precedent" from oral texts, as well as aids to their proper interpretation. Thus this book juxtaposes diverse worlds of words and the histories they carry to illustrate the vital importance of oral, oral-to-textual, and textual sources, especially in Hawaiian but also in American and British accounts of 1820s Hawai'i.

This book also draws upon a wide range of source material generated by the American Board of Commissioners for Foreign Missions (ABCFM). The mission was a quintessential record keeping and generating enterprise that produced written and published works to convert native peoples and to promote its good works in order to fund future missionary endeavors in the islands and in other mission fields. The ABCFM corpus includes letters of candidacy, personal correspondence between missionaries in the field and families at home, official mission station reports, and journals, as well as the letters and official pronouncements to the Sandwich Islands missionaries from the Boston headquarters. The *Missionary Herald* was the monthly official magazine that kept home-based supporters apprised of the various foreign and domestic missions.

Missionaries also generated a lot of published material directed at native Hawaiians, including language materials to teach them how to read and write and translations of the Bible in the Hawaiian language. The mission also published other religious tracts while working to publish the Bible in Hawaiian as a means to further Christian instruction. In considering the relations between Hawaiian women and foreign men, as well as the ali'i and transient and settled foreigners, I have used a previously untapped corpus of legal documents written in Hawaiian: published laws and depositions and firsthand accounts of the "outrages" that were generated during the investigation of Leoiki's sale to Captain William Buckle.

Although many of these mission sources were composed in the Hawaiian language, it is important to note for our purposes that textual correspondence and mission reports in English incorporated quotes and glosses of Hawaiian words and phrases designated for an Atlantic audience. In order to identify important Hawaiian phrases in English-language sources, or in an English translation of a Hawaiian-language text, scholars need to be familiar with Hawaiian generic conventions—with Hawaiian modes of memorializing and representing the past.

These Hawaiian genres constitutive of Hawaiian historical thinking go beyond what has been labeled moʻolelo. What kinds of historical paradigms and historiographic methods must we consider in a world of chant and oral "texts"? Narratives structured by chronological time are most at home in worlds of writing and print.[27] Hawaiian historical paradigms before and during this period demand a different approach to writing this history than our usual orientation toward modern, strict chronological ordering of events and source uses. What kinds of historical thought emerge from a fundamental intellectual organizing genre/practice like the *helu*—the stacking or listing words and texts?

Recognizing the helu's centrality in Hawaiian conceptual structures pushes us to recognize its role in constructing historical contexts, which make possible interpretations of events or other texts.[28] Because words and certain rhetorical phrases gain power from their repetition and reiteration in particular contexts (*ka mea i ʻōlelo mua ʻia*), these phrases and words can be researched in chronologically later writings to offer clues to past, multiple meanings. In addition, when they are used and by whom also provides clues to the weight of those key phrases and terms. Hawaiians who wrote and published also recorded older oral texts in writing. Even as I consult materials that were published later, events and concepts found in these sources may predate their recording.[29] To write this kind of history, I draw upon a vast corpus of writings produced by Hawaiians writing after 1825 in Hawaiian-language newspapers, personal manuscripts, letters and correspondence, and legal documents.[30]

What kind of history is conceived in *moʻokūʻauhau* (genealogies) or *koihonua*, the chanted Hawaiian genealogies that entwined lineages of aliʻi with the birth or appearance of islands? The koihonua's contents are often structured as name lists of ancestors that sometimes offer descriptions of their importance, such as the kind of kapu each chief bore and the mana exemplified in their words and deeds.[31] While sometimes the helu or list serves simply as a mnemonic device for the chanter that opens out to other avenues of story and song, that only one trained to knowing could recapitulate. Some koihonua were also constructed as chants of emergence and navigation between the islands.[32] A close-reading of an excerpt of a koihonua give us access to fundamental definitions of places and people and their relationships in time.

The chant "Ea Mai Hawai'inuiākea" narrates the emergence of islands as seen from the ocean.

> Ea mai Hawai'inuiākea, Eia mai loko mai o ka pō
> Puka mai ka moku, ka 'āina
> ka lālani 'āina 'o Nu'umea
> ka pae 'āina o i kūkulu o Tahiti [33]

> Here is Hawai'inuiākea,
> There it is come from the deep, dark ocean
> The island emerges, the land
> the string of islands of Nu'umea
> the Archipelago, the border of this edge of Tahiti.

The Hawaiian islands appear out of the darkness (pō) of the ocean depths. This pō is most likely connected to lipo, the blue-black oceanic band stretching to the horizon, marking out the extremity of the ocean south at Kahiki moe. The pō of this chant brings to mind the Kumulipo, or origin in deep darkness—a Hawaiian genealogical chant in which all creatures and plants in existence are born. First among all things born in the world is the coral polyp, spawning in the ocean. The chant moves through successive generations of plants and animals, gods, chiefs, and people, ending with the naming of stars and the genealogies' penultimate chief, Lonoikamakahiki. This darkness of origin, this pō, especially when connected to chiefs in Hawaiian and Polynesian conceptualization, is a positive, profound, and sacred expression of the ancient origin of a chief's lineage and mana.[34]

As each island appears over the curve of the horizon, the sight of the islands set out in a row (lālani) becomes clear to the navigator: an archipelago set out as one border of the known world—Hawai'inuiākea, large, widespread, and fertile Hawai'i. The word, lālani, that describes the position of islands set out in a row is a word also used to describe ranks of soldiers, as well as lines of ali'i (chiefs) arrayed by kapu and rank, perhaps while assembled for heiau (temple) ritual, or on formal speaking occasions or other public gatherings, including celebrations, folding both island and people into one evocative word image.

From Kahiki in the south to Hawai'i in the north, future Hawaiians followed an oceanic map traversed by stars. Hawaiian ancestors preserved the way between island homes in oral genealogical chants and verbal maps linking seemingly isolated islands and people across vast ocean spaces. The chant's orientation toward Hawaiʻi binds together the emergence of islands in a line of sight—out of the deep ocean—with the emergence of genealogical lines of chiefs, grounded in language for emphasis.

> Hānau ʻo Maui, he moku, he ʻāina, Na Kama o Kamalalawalu e
>   noho,

> Born is Maui, an island, that Kama of Kamalalawalu ruled.

It is not a random set of islands, nor a random set of chiefs; rather, it is an intertwined genealogy, a history relating the emergence of islands to lineages of chiefs. In this discourse, we see the inextricable interconnection of island home and generations of Hawaiian people. Perhaps more than anything, this genre of chant and maoli interpretations of it provide us with one kind of textual example that tracks closest to what a kānaka maoli formulation would be for the English language term native—one that is not predicated upon concepts of "firsting" or blood discourse, but upon bone, birth, movement, and deep knowledge of home place: of islands, stars, and seas.

CHAPTER 1

The Political Economy of *Mana*

Obligation, Debt, and Trade

Tamaahmaah: King of the Sandwich Islands. This Indian
Prince, illustrious for his magnanimity, his love of
civilization, and his great abilities, was one of nature's great
men who led the van of the age in which he lived. . . . He
was the hero and conqueror of that cluster of islands in the
Pacific Ocean (excepting Onehooi and Atooi,) of which
Owhyhee is the principal . . . the Sandwich Islands from the
exuberant fertility of the soil, their situation directly
between Asia and America, their native and intelligent
population; but above all from the noble character of their
king, have become the most important groupe, inhabited
merely by savages, in the known world.

On New Years' Day 1820, readers of American newspapers in Boston, New
York, and Connecticut enjoyed a lengthy reflection about the life of Kamehameha soon after news of his death in Kailua, Hawai'i, reached the United
States. The timely essay may have been especially interesting since a group
of missionaries sent by the American Board of Commissioners for Foreign
Missions (ABCFM) had left Boston a few months earlier and were at that
moment en route to the islands to plant the first American mission field in
the Pacific. Hence, readers in America were recipients of the news of the
great chief's passing before the missionaries themselves, who would not
learn of Kamehameha's death until they arrived in Hawai'i some three
months later.

While lauding the chief's "love of civilization," the article also dwelt upon the importance of the Sandwich Islands to American and British commerce. In terms of their geographic situation, the islands provided ships in the China trade with a perfect stopping place between the markets of China and the northwest coast of America. But its placement as way station between ports did not diminish the importance of the islands to beleaguered ships in need of repair, and crews and captains that longed for respite from the regimented discipline of shipboard life. The excellent soil of the islands promised fresh fruit and vegetables aplenty. All long trading voyages depended on water, fresh meat, and salt to cure it, all found in abundance in Hawai'i. The Sandwich Islands were indispensable to the expansion of Euro-American commerce in the early nineteenth-century Pacific.

In American and British newspapers, Kamehameha was dubbed an "Indian Prince," another "Bonaparte or Peter the Great conjoined in one." The image of a savage who could conquer several island kingdoms while engaging in international commerce and employing foreign labor in service of his oceanic empire struck Euro-Americans as impressive.[1] What these articles shared in common was the conviction that Kamehameha had transformed himself from a savage into a civilized ruler by engaging in mutually beneficial trade relations with Euro-Americans, building his own fleet of ships, and employing foreigners as advisers and skilled laborers.

Newspapers from the period (1805–1813) reported with something like wonder that since British captain George Vancouver had built a ship for Kamehameha in 1792, by 1805 the Hawaiian chief had amassed a fleet of twenty vessels of different sizes of "20 or 30 tons," some with gleaming copper bottoms.[2] Kamehameha, according to these accounts, also encouraged the settlement of Europeans in his islands, "provided they be industrious," in a surprising role reversal that bolstered the presumption that Kamehameha had been civilized by way of his newly cultivated value for "industry" and that overseeing foreign labor to manufacture Euro-American goods such as ships made him a noble ruler. His imperial triumphs were also impressive to Euro-Americans. As "proof" that his savage nature had been transformed, Kamehameha brokered a trade monopoly with New England ship captains. As a visionary, Kamehameha built ships of Hawaiian manufacture, such as the brig *Kaahumanu* (named after one of his wives), stocked it with sandalwood, and sent the cargo to Chinese markets in order to cut out the European middleman.[3]

Not only was Kamehameha interested in trade and ship building, he also reportedly knew how to drive a hard bargain: "He is not only a great warrior and politician, but a very acute trader, and a match for any European in driving a bargain. He is well acquainted with the different weights and measures, and the value which all articles ought to bear in exchange with each other; and is ever ready to take advantage of the necessities of those who apply to him or his people for supplies."[4] Civilization, argued these narratives, was *the* main product of Euro-American trading interaction with Hawaiians. Euro-American narratives of the emergence of capitalism in the islands cannot be divorced from stories of the ambitious and bold leadership of Kamehameha as he propelled his people toward "civilization."

The myth of Kamehameha as a "great man" had been enshrined in American narratives about Hawaiians, serving to entice early trade between New England and Hawai'i.[5] In addition to his acuity at trade, American narratives portrayed Kamehameha as a visionary leader because he was capable of uniting all the islands under his singular rule. This admiration of his political and military abilities to conquer—like a Bonaparte or Peter the Great—set Kamehameha within a global historical context of leadership, even as such praise ironically lauded a model of governance Americans of the new republic had so recently cast off. Hawai'i under Kamehameha's rule became a place of curiosity and potential opportunity for American merchants and missionaries.

The distance between New England and Hawai'i was not only physical and temporal but cultural as well. The novelty of the king and his new, unified kingdom stirred the hearts and minds of a postrevolutionary generation of the Early Republic. But for Hawaiians, the phenomenon of Kamehameha's rise to power was an older form of conquest conducted at a much larger scale than in the past. Hawaiian histories (mo'olelo) remember Kamehameha's harnessing of spiritual power (mana) with a warrior's strength and grace. These histories dwell on the unusual circumstances of his birth, prophecies of his rise to power, and his training and prowess as a *koa* (warrior). They also provide stunning detail about Kamehameha's campaigns, his individual battles, and the words and chants of ali'i and their *kāhuna* (priests, experts).[6]

These histories of Kamehameha provide extensive genealogical information, revelatory of Kamehameha's exceptional character and suitability for rule as defined *within* and *against* a larger web of male and female chiefs,

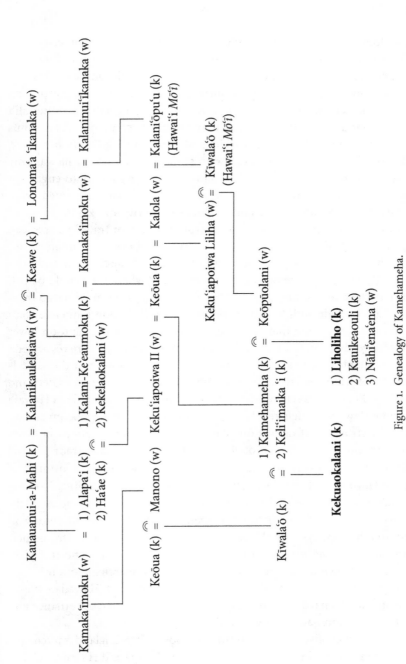

Figure 1. Genealogy of Kamehameha.

counselors, and priests. These moʻolelo thus illustrate Kamehameha's central position within a dense network of alliance and family connection. His greatness was impossible, according to the moʻolelo, without many historical actors, members of an extended social and familial network, positioning him for rule. Genealogical connection was present in every encounter aliʻi had with one another. It was the sinew and bone of every story, the calculus that makes evident the inner workings of Hawaiian legitimation, power, and authority—a national politics always in motion. Kamehameha was only as great a man as those around him allowed.[7] And his ability to engage in trade of Hawaiian resources with foreign merchants was predicated upon the healthy functioning of systematic chiefly authority and kapu.

Hawaiian harvesting of sandalwood from Hawaiʻi for trade by American merchants in China marked Hawaiʻi's entry into global trade interactions. When it was begun under Kamehameha I's rule, he exercised his authority as *mōʻī* (king) to regulate through kapu when and where trees could be cut. This had the effect of preventing lesser chiefs around the archipelago from entering into trade with foreigners on their own. But upon Kamehameha's death in 1819, the kapu that he pronounced—including the kapu on lower chiefs harvesting and trading sandalwood with foreigners—were rescinded.[8]

This chapter focuses on the development and evolution of the sandalwood trade from the late 1810s and into the 1820s in order to understand how New England merchants navigated the complexities of trade in Hawaiʻi and how Hawaiian chiefs regulated sandalwood trade through kapu and an authority structure of obligation. These early economic relations between New England and Hawaiʻi through the sandalwood and ship trade became a key enabler of American trading success in China. Previous histories of the sandalwood trade have used merchant and missionary writings to portray this trade as one-sided in Hawaiian life: greedy and avaricious chiefs, hungry to trade with foreigners for luxury goods that end up rotting in their storehouses, tyrannically sent the common people away from their farms and into the upland to cut and haul sandalwood to be traded in China.[9] The previous historiography's emphasis on merchant and missionaries' portrayal of the social and political structures of Hawaiian life as somehow feudal have obscured a history of how Hawaiian governance and law functioned in nascent global trade.

This chapter gives a fuller history of both New England merchants' attempts to operate in the Hawaiian sandalwood trade and Hawaiian chiefs' interests and activities seen as part of Hawaiian governance and social structures. It focuses on the disparate understandings of debt and obligation between chiefs and merchants by supplying nuanced contextual information about Hawaiian sandalwood use and the way mana was maintained through genealogy, which set up relationships of obligation and debt. Rather than avaricious chiefs who are opportunistic or confused about trade, what emerges is the way in which chiefs used their networks of relationship, deliberation in the 'aha 'ōlelo, and kapu to achieve the upper hand in negotiations with New England merchants for goods desired. They also used kapu to punish traders who attempted to cheat the ali'i in a manner that restricted the traders' access to sandalwood and Hawaiian labor. Finally, what this chapter suggests is that while traders after Kamehameha I's death sought to assign debt to individual chiefs across the islands, his successors in rule—specifically Kālaimoku—sought a way to have that debt made collective. This debt then becomes the debt of the kingdom that is established in 1840.

'Iliahi: The Hawaiian Sandalwood Trade

The trade in 'iliahi, Hawaiian sandalwood, began when the wood was "discovered" by sailors working for the ill-fated captain John Kendrick of the *Lady Washington*. Kendrick had left several sailors on one of the islands, and they informed him of the presence of sandalwood.[10] This would become an important find, since European and American ships had been accustomed to ranging as far east as India, or far to the west and south into the Pacific, to Fiji and the Marquesas, to obtain the much-sought-after wood. The Sandwich Islands could now provide a highly desirable commodity to offer Americans besides provisions, salt, and women.

Trade in 'iliahi between New England and Hawai'i began with Kamehameha, who chose to deal only with American ship captains Jonathan and Nathaniel Winship and William Heath Davis, who worked for the Boston firm of J. and T. H. Perkins. These ship captains enjoyed a short-lived monopoly, from 1809 until the War of 1812 slowed New England ship visits to the islands to a trickle. It is also surmised that Kamehameha's new alliance with Great Britain further put this trade relationship on hold.[11] After his death in 1819, the kapu (restriction) forbidding others to cut down trees and therefore to engage in this kind of trade was rescinded, and throughout the islands the most prominent ali'i began to engage in trade with relish.

'Iliahi grew and was collected by merchants on all the settled islands in the archipelago. Trees and shrubs could grow in dry areas, and on ridges and slopes in moist or wet forests, at an elevation anywhere from six hundred feet on Kaua'i, to five thousand feet on the slopes of Mauna Loa on Hawai'i. There are four species of sandalwood trees on the islands, and they vary in size. The *Santalum pyrularium* found on Kaua'i grew from sixteen to forty feet in height, while *S. ellipticum* could purportedly grow up to eighty feet high, its trunk three feet in diameter. The coveted fragrance of the sandalwood increased with age; its intoxicating scent hides in the heartwood of the tree, which reaches full maturity after thirty years.[12]

Mustering the labor for the collection of trees was relatively easy for the ali'i, but long absences took a toll on workers' families, taro, and sweet potato fields, as well as fishing. Hawaiian ali'i had been leading designated groups of sandalwood cutters into the mountains since Kamehameha's reign.[13] Sandalwood required intense bouts of labor. Work parties walked and climbed up into the mountains, bringing along their food and supplies. Trees were cut and bundled and hauled back down to portside storehouses. These periodic bursts of effort could be undertaken at any time of the year, except perhaps the rainy season, or *ho'oilo*, between November and March.

Historians have argued that the sandalwood trade had devastating effects upon the forests and the people, frequently conflating the collapse of the tree population with the harm it inflicted upon Hawaiian sensibilities or proscriptions about *mālama 'āina*, caring for the land. This confusion on the part of historians results in the argument that the collateral damage of the sandalwood trade was the further decline/degeneration of Hawaiian culture and values.[14] What this argument misses in nuance and context-based examples it makes up for in sentimentalism—since mālama 'āina is, in fact, a value rooted as always in practice and, therefore, in the exercise of the practical. The word *mālama* means *to watch over, preserve, or care for*—sandalwood, however, did not necessitate any care on the part of Hawaiians, and neither did its disappearance affect any facet of the Hawaiian way of life, save for constricting the ability of individuals and chiefs to engage in further trade.

Sandalwood was not a tree cultivated by Hawaiians; it simply grew in the uplands. Furthermore, it was not a wood much utilized by Hawaiian people. It had no known ceremonial usage; it was not the *kinolau*, or sacred body form, of any *akua* (god or goddess). Hawaiians did not carve *akua ki'i* (god images) out of its wood. While the wood of 'iliahi was worked into a form suitable to scent fine *kapa* (mulberry cloth) for the ali'i and may have been used sparsely for medicinal purposes, its conspicuous absence from poetry, song, and legend means that sandalwood was not particularly significant in the everyday lives of Hawaiian people in the 1820s, during the height of the sandalwood mania, the drive to collect wood in exchange for goods delivered.[15] Harvesting sandalwood and turning it over to merchants must have been, for the chiefs, akin to acquiring a lot of something for little or next to nothing.

Politically, this kind of widespread trade by the lesser chiefs was overseen by the chiefs who ruled as Kamehameha's successors: Liholiho, his son and heir; Ka'ahumanu, his wife and *kuhina nui* (the chiefess who shares rule with the *mō'i*); and William Pitt Kālaimoku, his chief counselor who held the king's purse and who inventoried and distributed land to chiefs.[16] In the sandalwood trade, it was Kālaimoku who was the chief whose importance rose as American merchants pursued as many tons of sandalwood from as many chiefs as possible. His management of this merchant free-for-all after Kamehameha I's death elevated Kālaimoku in the eyes of the merchants as the chief to trust in approving contractual relations with the lower chiefs.

A portrait of Kālaimoku, the chief, was sketched by English artist Robert Dampier on his visit to the islands in 1825. In the sketch, Kālaimoku's hair appears shorn, handsomely so, and sideburns in European style are cut close to his face, framing his cheekbones. He is wearing a loose-fitting white shirt of European manufacture, finely made, along with a jacket. The chief is older, with a receding hairline and lines etched into his forehead—no doubt a legacy of the many responsibilities he has had to take on over the years. His expression is direct, yet in the moment that has been captured, there is nothing harsh that appears in that gaze, which is measured and wise. According to many foreign accounts, Kālaimoku's character seems to match what the artist's hand sought to portray. Charles Hammatt first met Kālaimoku in the house of Liholiho, Kamehameha II, on May 12, 1823, two days after Hammatt's arrival in Honolulu. That afternoon, the chiefly residence was full, some "fifty or sixty" people in attendance; Kālaimoku stood apart amid the assembled crowd, "a lively intelligent looking old man, & seemed to be full of thought."[17]

Kamakau, the famed Hawaiian historian of the mid-nineteenth century, penned the only obituary for Kālaimoku written in Hawaiian, which began,

"I ka make ana o Kalanimoku, ua moku ke kaula hao o keaupuni i paa ai" (At the death of Kalanimoku, the iron cable that held fast the nation was severed).[18] Kālaimoku, Kamehameha's kuhina nui (high-ranking counselor), was a favorite (*punahele*) of Kamehameha, and he served as tax collector (*pu'ukū nui*) and carver of lands (*kālaimoku*). He was also an *'alihikaua*, a skilled warrior and general.

The shifting political terrain of chiefly authority was opaque to outsiders who came to the islands seeking bountiful provisions, access to women, or, in the case of missionaries, minds to educate and hearts to convert. Merchants and missionaries came to the islands with their own agendas; they learned enough about chiefly politics and relations of power to achieve their own ends. In the management of mercantile and spiritual economies, the goal was not to understand the intricacies of relation among the ali'i; instead, it was to locate the individual chief or chiefs who held power at any given time in order to ingratiate oneself so as to get what one needed.

After Kamehameha's death, Kālaimoku ruled jointly with Ka'ahumanu and Liholiho, who was acknowledged as the king of the Sandwich Islands—although in truth, his elder relatives seem to have taken on the massive responsibility of dealing with foreign vessels, their personnel, and merchant agents in the islands.[19] When foreign traders opened their showrooms aboard vessels or in portside stores, they dealt with a coterie of chiefs of diverse rank and whose administration of lands and resources portended different levels of purchasing power. Merchant agents were stationed at Kaua'i and Honolulu, reflecting the still acknowledged and pronounced division of chiefdoms between those ali'i who served Kamehameha, who ruled over the islands of Hawai'i, Maui, Lāna'i, Kaho'olawe and O'ahu, while Kaua'i and Ni'ihau were still largely left to the rule of Kaumuali'i. The paramount chiefs of the intertwined families of Ka'ahumanu and Kamehameha were those who traded most frequently with merchant agents and ship captains. From their reports, it appears that Kālaimoku was instrumental in consolidating the debt of the chiefs and was efficient at mobilizing both ali'i and maka'āinana as laborers to collect the massive amounts of sandalwood that were sent to Canton at the end of the season in 1821. As debt collector and administrator of resources, the chief innovated upon his role due to the necessity of having to deal with the influx of foreigners into Hawaiian society, which steadily increased each year after the death of the great chief Kamehameha in May 1819.

The Politics of *Mana*

Kālaimoku's abilities and capacity to manage trade and subsequent debt during this period must be examined within a larger understanding of how mana underpinned chiefly authority. Without understanding mana as the basis of chiefly authority, we cannot understand how a chief could mobilize entire populations to harvest sandalwood and engage in trade with American merchants. Hawaiian engagement in this global trade was predicated upon the politics of mana, and these politics evolved and adapted to address what the sandalwood trade brought to the islands.

Simultaneous with the tales of chiefly heroism and rule are stories, far more complex, about relationships set in bone (*'iwi*): of mo'okū'auhau (genealogy), the carefully manipulated couplings between chiefs, a politics of debt, obligation, and exchange.[20] Hawaiian chiefs possessed sophisticated ideas about debt and obligation coincident with, but quite separate from, those brought by New England traders. The most excellent example of the formulation of debt and obligation occurred, however, with respect to the circulation of chiefly bodies (both male and female), kapu, and mana (spiritual power) in an engineered system of genealogical connection, an economy of mana.

Excavating the term *mo'okū'auhau* (genealogy) and uncovering its layers is an excellent starting point for our investigation into Hawaiian conceptualizations of relation, obligation, and connection. The oldest published definition of *kū'auhau* is supplied by American missionary lexicographer Lorrin Andrews in his 1865 *Dictionary of the Hawaiian Language*. *Kū*, to be set fast, is added to *'auhau*, or tax, hence *kū'auhau*, by Andrews' reckoning, is to "be recorded in genealogy, in history or tradition."[21] A later dictionary produced by Samuel Elbert and Mary Kawena Pukui, the most prominent genealogist, ethnographer, lexicographer, and translator of her generation, offered another definition of *'auhau*: "femur and humerous [*sic*] bones of the human skeleton." The polysemy of the word *'auhau* furnishes another layer of understanding—genealogical connection as bred into bone. The layered meaning of words leads one to consider the ritualized practice of the ceremonial stripping away of the flesh of a chief after his or her death in order to preserve the bones, which are the repository of mana. Hence, *'auhau* can be an accounting in word; it can point to connection through sexual intercourse, and birth, and is physically manifested in ritual practice and in the careful caring for the bones of the ali'i. Finally, a third way to parse the word *mo'okū'auhau* is to consider the word as made up of three constitutive parts: *mo'o, kū'au,* meaning stem, shaft, or stalk, and *hau (Hibiscus tiliaceus)*.[22] The *hau* tree is a low-lying tree whose branches form a tangle of impenetrable thickets. The plant "has a highly spreading, near surface, lateral root system, often comprised of only a few main roots."[23] This perhaps is the closest visual, somatic, and metaphoric inspiration to the genealogies of ali'i—entangled branchings that spread copiously emergent from a few main roots.[24]

Plumbing these semiotic depths is important because Hawaiian chiefs of Kamehameha's time did not think genealogically *on paper*, but through word, act, engagement, and interpretation. Moving from ruminations over the concept "mo'okū'auhau," it is important to see how these webs of chiefly interrelationship create both stable outcomes, such as arranged "marriages" or sexual couplings, *and* the opening up of unstable, dynamic *multiple possibilities* for leadership, counsel, reproduction, and sacrifice. Genealogy as a system of accounting thus also becomes a system of account*ability*, as relationships between chiefs include measurements of closeness/distance (in sibling groups, in spousal groups, or in generational successions, for example) that are foundational for understanding how the chiefs perceived their distinct yet interlocking ambits of authority, of action, and of responsibility to each other. This genealogical accountability between chiefs is the first place to look to begin to understand what debt was to the chiefs in the early nineteenth century.

Perhaps more importantly, perceiving and analyzing chiefly genealogies is essential for understanding the basis for political action and the authoritative (one could almost say legally binding) qualities of chiefly utterances. Mana (authority, power) is rooted in the couplings of chiefs and chiefesses, winding through generations of calculations of physically embodied concentrations of power. But while mo'okū'auhau is the basis of Hawaiian chiefly position and politics, mana could also be acquired, lost, or destroyed through a leader's behavior and actions. Thus the politics of mana—let alone its definition (it is both in the bones and in the behavior of a chief)—is a shifting energy, playing out through dynamic chiefly interactions along family lines. Mana is therefore not just genealogically but also socially constructed.

Perhaps it is not without cause that American merchants, engaging in ventures in the Hawaiian Islands, found themselves lacking in a clear understanding of exactly how politics and economic interrelationships between chiefs might function, given the deep and complex foundation of those chiefly relationships in moʻokūʻauhau and mana. On top of this incompatibility, merchant agents found themselves also dealing with a more general incompatibility between American businessmen and agents and the entire environment of the Hawaiian Islands. What seemed to be required to establish successful and thriving business in the islands seemed quite undercut by the characters, ignorance, and even ineptitude of the men who came to try their hands at economic ventures in Hawaiʻi.

New England Agents in Hawaiʻi

> I do not know of one man that has a correct idea of the
> trade in the North Pacific or how to carry it on to
> advantage—we have got the advantage of the whole and I
> mean to keep it if possible, I have cut them all this year,
> most of the agents at the Sandwich Islands divide the 24
> hours into three parts, Drinking, Gambling and Sleeping.
> The one I have discharged is among the number, if we are
> not capable of selecting better agents than the last we must
> both have guardians . . . there is no witchcraft necessary in
> carrying on the Trade at the Islands all we want is sober,
> honest, industrious men, if we cannot have our
> establishment placed on a more respectable footing than it
> has been I think I shall set fire and burn all together—on
> my arrival at the Islands.[25]

Captain Dixey Wildes' estimation of the chaotic and unpredictable nature of trade in the North Pacific in this letter to business partner Josiah Marshall comes as somewhat of a surprise, as Wildes was no stranger to trade. He had served as a sailor and then captain in the Pacific—sailing between New England, the Northwest Coast, Hawaiʻi, and China—for twenty-five years, since 1800. Wildes' letter comes at the trough of cycles of boom and bust, when merchants employed by rival houses were increasingly anxious about the debts owed to their businesses by Hawaiian chiefs. The merchant's critique is lodged against his fellow Americans who were inattentive to their work and remiss in looking out for the "establishment" settled in the islands. According to Wildes, agents simply lacked the traits that most men of business in America should have cultivated: "sobriety, honesty and industry," traits essential to making a profit. Wildes was also probably sick of the bellyaching and complaining that filled the letters of agents and ship captains about the difficulty of conducting their business with Hawaiian chiefs.

In Hawai'i, sailors and merchants met with unfamiliar rhythms of time discipline. While ships arrived at prescribed seasons during the year, docking, landing goods, staying to obtain provisions, repair ships, and collect sandalwood, the lull that struck after the bustling business of arrival and departure threatened boredom. Pleasure-seeking had not only become an avocation among sailors and captains, but also for some merchants, contributing much to the legend of Hawai'i as paradise. Men longing for the bustle of home established public institutions and entertainments, and the rhythm of steady employment and diverse social interaction of their home-lands were especially susceptible to acting out or, on the contrary, failing to act at all.[26]

Pleasure-seeking, even in *paradise*, could not only become tedious—it could seriously harm a business concern's prospects for trade. Merchant agents and captains were rightly concerned with employees' inability to adjust to island living, since indolence and a lack of industry were poor generators of profit. The agents tasked with overseeing business were often left to their own devices when trade was not brisk or steady. With no regular work structuring the days, weeks, and months spent waiting for ships or wood to arrive, rival merchants found themselves in common society, which meant that they often swapped stories, while attempting to elicit information from rivals about the current status of their business. "It will be for your interest as well as ours, to be on good terms with as many of the white men at the islands as possible. Your usual deportment will neither invite nor provoke hostility among the agents, & we are confident you possess the address to get on with them without attesting to all your communications. We have no fears of you falling into any of the vices you will find at the Islands, but it may be well to reflect on them, to be better prepared to reside in a society where indolence, intemperance, debauchery and gambling are so fashionable."[27]

This warning did not flow from the pen of a missionary, although in its assessment of the degenerative power of society in the Sandwich Islands, its authors had much in common with them. This statement was part of the contractual terms of employment and instruction that the supercargo

Charles Hammatt of the ship *Champion* affixed his signature to, perhaps in the well-ordered and busy offices of merchants Bryant and Sturgis, located at 47 Central Wharf, Boston. Hammatt's employers had been sending ships out to the Pacific for five years before the first company of missionaries to the Sandwich Islands departed in 1819. Their mercantile concern directed ships trading goods around the world, and like the other oceans it operated in, in the Pacific it employed a cadre of vessels and captains. These floating storehouses routinely plied their wares between the Northwest Coast, the Sandwich Islands, and China, while filling up the ships' ever-emptying holds with the bounty of Hawaiian and Indian lands and the surrounding seas. However, New England merchants had little enough to tempt Chinese consumers until the discovery of furs on the Northwest Coast and sandalwood in Hawai'i created greater trading opportunities in Canton, as these goods were both highly sought after.

The primary business of New England traders in the islands in the decade after the death of Kamehameha in 1819 was the collection of debt owed to them by Hawaiian chiefs. Debt collection developed into the number one priority of New England traders and ship captains, and was the source of consternation and constant anxiety that fueled intense, sometimes bitter rivalries between merchant houses based in Honolulu and the ship captains engaged in the business of trade and collecting debt. Before investigating the relationship between Hawaiian chiefs, transient ship captains, and agents from New England settled in the islands, it might be useful to take a closer look at the sandalwood trade to get an idea of the rudiments of this point of commerce.

In order to conduct business on outbound voyages to the Pacific, New England merchant houses employed supercargoes like Charles Hammatt, who not only oversaw the inventory and monies belonging to the voyage, but also haggled with local distributors in South American ports for the lowest priced baubles and goods that could be sold at inflated prices to natives on the Northwest Coast and Hawaiians. In addition to his duties as supercargo, Hammatt was to be left in Honolulu after the *Champion*'s arrival and was stationed there as Bryant and Sturgis' agent, charged with the responsibility to sell more goods to the ali'i and people and to collect debts that were owed by the ali'i for goods previously delivered, preferably in sandalwood.

When Hammatt arrived in 1823, he was in good company. John Coffin Jones was the resident agent employed by rival concern Marshall and

Wildes. The twenty-five-year-old Jones had arrived in the islands two years before, on May 20, 1821, with an additional appointment from President James Monroe to serve as agent for commerce and seamen at Oʻahu. As US commercial agent, Jones was in charge of keeping a record of American ships arriving and departing from Hawaiian ports. Jones was also responsible for seeing to the care of sick sailors and ship captains and finding them passage home upon recovery or arranging burial in case of death. As agent for Marshall and Wildes, Jones was assisted by Mr. Babcock, who had been in the islands longer than he had and who purportedly had more influence with the aliʻi than did any other trader in the islands.[28]

These Hawaiʻi-based agents would oversee shops and storehouses that contained fancy and mundane trade goods, as well as provisions that were left at the islands by arriving ships, as even space on a ship was a commodity one could sell. Provisions stored in the islands would be retrieved at a later date for use on a ship's return journey home. Voyages to the North Pacific could last anywhere from three to five years, so the agents, officers, and ship captains involved in the trade were relatively familiar with the people in the ports they frequented if they managed more than one voyage, which many ship captains did.

As agents in the islands, men like Hammatt, Jones, and Babcock were charged not only with selling goods to Hawaiian people and aliʻi, but also with increasing people's desire for goods. Once merchants had spent time taking orders and drumming up interest in new, more extravagant wares, they would write letters to the home office that included long lists of goods for the Hawaiian market. Trade in the Pacific was about managing risk, since ships could be dispatched from New England before a letter from an agent based in the islands requesting the latest fashion or indispensable new item had arrived. By the time another ship came out with the requested goods, a year might have passed, along with the desire for that item, which had been filled by goods brought ashore by a competitor.

Promised goods long looked for and not delivered could destroy the reputation of the agency conducting trade, and a reputation worthy of trust in the business of credit and debt was important to employers and chiefly clients. John C. Jones had been unable to fulfill his promises to chiefs on numerous occasions. When a Captain Masters failed to show up in May 1821 with ship and cargo that Jones had chatted up to the aliʻi Kaumualiʻi, the king of Kauaʻi, to Jones' dismay, purchased a ship "of inferior quality" for 3,500 piculs of sandalwood from rival ship captain John Suter, who worked for Bryant and Sturgis. On another occasion, Jones, who had "secured the friendship of several powerful chiefs," persuaded them not to purchase any ships until the *Paragon* arrived. A number of chiefs had wood to spend, and Jones projected his hope that an excellent trade could be made across several letters beginning in January and ending in August 1823, when his hopes were finally dashed.

Instead of the very fine elegant goods he had enjoined his employers to send in his letters, the *Paragon* carried "no merchandise for this place, save a quantity of sour wine, tin pots, lanthorns, frying pans, miserable Spanish brandy, mouldy cherries, cask of honey and last though not least brick bats."[29] These were not even pickings—the dull thud of the motley assortment spoke volumes about Jones' own deflated hopes, of consumer dreams dashed. The chiefs, including Kālaimoku, were not at all interested in the poor cargo and objected to its landing, which further irritated Jones. Consider Jones' enthusiasm and optimism for this moment of trade in a letter he had penned two and a half months before the *Paragon*'s arrival. "A small quantity of superfine broadcloth, a large quantity of cambric prints . . . also first quality calicoes, white cambrick muslin, Irish linen, ladies shoes large sizes, white stockings, silk and button, black silks hats, women's bonnets must be different patterns large size and of good 60 or 100 would sell well, ladies dresses large and small sizes made of 1" quality of materials and showy would command a good price."[30] The list has an almost melodic quality to it, veritably singing off the page. The list is illustrative of merchants' personal investment in setting up the best goods that would bring the highest prices at market.

In this letter Jones also reiterated the belief that like their famous chief Kamehameha, the Hawaiian people were being civilized through their consumption of Euro-American goods:

A cargo should consist of an assortment of every thing no great quantity of any one Article, were I at home myself I could select an outfit that would do well—Ox teams, Light wagons, handcarts, wheelbarrows, carriages, and one or two of those vehicles Called barouches [covered carriages], two or three chaises you might be surprised that such articles Would sell but you would be more surprised to see how fast these people are advancing towards civilization, only two days since Mr. Pitt asked me to send for three carriages And have them adorned with gold, every thing new and elegant will sell and at good Profit, coarse articles are of no use.[31]

Jones here imagines that Hawaiian chiefly consumers demand wheeled vehicles, and he says that "Mr. Pitt," Kālaimoku himself, has asked him to send three carriages to the islands. He uses this purported desire for vehicles that move faster than walking as a metaphor for his claim that Hawaiians are "fast . . . advancing towards civilization."

Distance from the home office, the source of all potential goods desired, made desiring subjects of not only the aliʻi but also of the merchant agents themselves. Though the aliʻi may have wanted these goods, what merchants consumed greedily (or were consumed by) was not only the actual point of sale or trade but the raised expectation of seeing whether or not their orders would be fulfilled by the timely arrival of cargo that they had personally requested. Lulls between seasons of selling, accounting, and ingratiating themselves to chiefs while wheeling and dealing were spent scheming against rivals. Lengthy lists of goods and services, bordering on the obscene, did not originate with the "devouring" or "avaricious" chiefs. Instead, they first originated with the agents who dreamed them up out of their own longing for profits and their desires to beat the competition at the profit-making game.

Moku (Forests) for *Moku* (Boats)

The most extravagant purchase any aliʻi could make was to buy a ship (moku) in exchange for forests (moku) of sandalwood. Ships were the highest-priced items traded between chiefs and New England merchants and therefore accounted for a disproportionate amount of the debt ascribed to chiefs by individual merchant concerns.[32] Rather than fetishizing the detrimental effects of trade upon "Hawaiian tradition," in this section I ask what effect trade and debt had upon Hawaiian chiefly relations. Far from being the ravenous and idle consumers that fill merchant narratives, Hawaiian chiefs were active participants in commerce, often setting the terms of trade and payment according to scales of value foreign to New England agents and ship captains.[33] The chiefs Kālaimoku, Keʻeaumoku, and Kaʻahumanu worked strenuously to organize other aliʻi to pay off debts owed to merchants. Kālaimoku, along with several other chiefs, also sought to curb the buying practices of individuals among them, whose excessive purchases threatened to turn all Hawaiians, including chiefs, into laborers working off the debt.

Providing a better view of the way the business of trade was managed by the ali'i also casts doubt upon the immensity of the debt American merchants claimed was owed by Hawaiians. While the chiefs and people were enthusiastic consumers, the prices traders set for large items like ships and houses, as well as dry goods like cloth and luxury items like rum and wine, often included a significant markup. Meeting in council, the ali'i deliberated and deployed kapu restricting the ability of certain ali'i to purchase ships from certain captains who sold rotten ships.

Merchant concerns Marshall and Wildes and Bryant and Sturgis managed several trading voyages in the China–Northwest Coast–Sandwich Islands trade during any given season. Merchant agents stationed in the islands working for both concerns were routinely given instructions to sell any ship touching at the islands if the ali'i appeared interested in making a purchase. The cost of ships fluctuated depending on the number of ships ali'i owned, the state of their wear, and competition between rival merchants and chiefs in any given area.

In the two years preceding Hammatt's voyage, 1819–1821, the chiefs purchased between four and six ships, one frame house, and several cargoes full of trade goods, accruing new "debt" of 29,760 piculs of sandalwood to Marshall and Wildes and Bryant and Sturgis combined.[34] Ali'i owning ships was also perhaps a matter of scale, as high-ranking ali'i also had *peleleu*, single- and double-hull canoes, in their employ in order to pursue war and send messages and goods between the islands. The ability to mobilize a labor force to build canoes and propel them was also a measure of the power of the ali'i and his wealth. Acquisition and ownership of Euro-American ships differed from Hawaiian canoes in matters of scale, and also because there were neither enough ship carpenters to go around nor large wood suitable enough to build these types of vessels on each island, making the ready-made ships of the merchants a bargain, considering all that they wanted in exchange were useless sandalwood trees. The ali'i Kamehameha popularized the fashion among chiefs of owning ships purchased from New England merchants a decade earlier. The desire to own ships and the knowledge and materials with which to build, maintain, and sail them was pragmatic, as building a fleet also coincided with Kamehameha's campaigns to take over different island chiefdoms.

By March of 1821, American missionaries in the island observed that Liholiho had amassed his own fleet of ships, which were employed by all of the ali'i to sail between the islands. Liholiho's fleet included *Cleopatra's*

Barge, Thaddeus, Neo, Columbia, Bordeaux Packet, and the Kauaʻi schooner *Eos*. Ships afforded the aliʻi a measure of independence, allowing them to come and go as they pleased, to engage with pesky foreign agents or depart for familiar places devoid of foreign presence. They were also very visible signs of the wealth and power of the aliʻi.

The most famous ship to be sold to Hawaiian chiefs also turned out to be the most infamous trade of this Hawaiian age of sail/sale. The Bryant and Sturgis pleasure craft *Cleopatra's Barge* had enjoyed an entirely different life, having been built on October 21, 1816, for the wealthy Salem, Massachusetts, merchant George Crowninshield, costing him a reported $50,000.[35] Apparently the barge lived up to its name, delighting Hawaiians so much that John Coffin Jones complained that it was "so superior" to any ships offered for sale by Marshall and Wildes that the chiefs would "scarce look at them." Liholiho had agreed to purchase the eighty-three-foot-long, 191-ton brig that had sailed into Honolulu under the direction of Capt. John Suter on November 16, 1820.[36]

Bryant and Sturgis agent Charles Bullard returned to the islands on March 24, 1821, expecting to collect payment for the barge and reap the additional benefits that resulted from the king's continued goodwill toward his concern for selling him such a beautiful ship. After meeting with Liholiho, Bullard found that the best lots of wood had been cut, expecting that these would soon be delivered in payment for the vessel. Unfortunately, Kaʻahumanu was very sick, so the business was postponed. In the meantime, Liholiho went with Bullard to examine the cargo of goods recently arrived and "appeared much pleased with them." The cargo was of such quality that according to Bullard, "a taboo was put on the trade in order that he and the Head chiefs might have first choice."[37]

The king and chiefs placed kapu setting the terms of buying and selling—*who* could purchase certain cargo and at *what time*. April was a busy month for trade on Oʻahu. Kaʻahumanu's prolonged illness, the large numbers of whaleships visiting the port (approximately sixty), and two vessels from New Holland, one of which proved to be a present from the king of England to Liholiho, all conspired, to Bullard's irritation, to "take up so much attention of the 'court'" preventing his making a "prompt" sale. "Until April 18th," Bullard wrote in his letter, "my business was in the best possible terms," when to his consternation, carpenters "overhauling the Barge" reported it was "rotten." This was a charge that Bullard was reluctant to believe, but which upon examination he found was "too true."

In describing the damage to his employers, he spared no words, "from the main chains aft above the water, She was a complete mass of dry rot." Bullard's hopes for making a good voyage had moldered along with the barge. The response of the ali'i to his concern was immediate and harsh. "Their [the chiefs'] disappointment was great in proportion to their previous expectations—When I went to Court where I before received every attention I found nothing but frowns—I saw at once that my voyage was nearly done up, If not quite ruined."[38]

To make matters worse, the chiefs in council reportedly told Bullard that his partner, Captain John Suter, had promised them that the barge was a "first rate vessel, nearly new and guaranteed she would wear ten years without repair."[39] As criticism, the ali'i deployed the words of rival merchant agents to stinging effect; "the concern" they accused, "were a set of liars and villains," who had sent the barge out "on purpose to deceive them."[40]

Bullard, his high aspirations dashed, reported that a "grand consultation of chiefs was held," at which the chiefs decided not to pay any more wood. After three weeks of negotiation with various chiefs, Bullard succeeded in persuading a "majority" in his favor, who allowed the collection of 1,984 piculs on the price owed. Remaining in Honolulu harbor through May 30, Bullard, at the "request of some chiefs," decided it was best to make a trip around the island to collect more wood. But Bullard had yet to feel the strength of the king's resentment against him and his concern. "I was aware that opposition would follow me and was not in the least disappointed," he wrote. "The ship was no sooner under way, than messengers were sent to every part of the island, forbidding (in the name of the King) the sale of any wood—but notwithstanding his Majesty's taboo, I succeeded in obtaining over 1400 piculs."[41]

*   *   *

Another detail of trade emerges here in Bullard's letter. Ships obtaining permission to collect sandalwood in payment were dispatched from port cities to areas on the island that were sandalwood collection sites. If a merchant or captain incurred the displeasure of the high chiefs, messengers would be dispatched and a kapu placed on trading with particular individuals. Bullard was savvy enough to understand that he had to keep his relationship with the chiefs on the best possible terms if he wanted to collect on previous accounts owed and also purchase wood for his concern: "The animosity of the King's party and some others is so great on account of the Barge, that they are determined if possible that I shall not buy any wood; and I am obliged to keep on as good terms as possible with them on account of old debts."[42]

Three months later, Charles Bullard was still attempting to collect san-dalwood as payment for the rotten *Cleopatra's Barge*, reporting in his letter to his employers that Captain Thomas Meek, who worked for Marshall and Wildes, had been contracted to "bring timber and plank from Norfolk sound" to repair the damage; begrudgingly, he observed that "he (Meek) will probably make a profitable job of it."[43] Bullard had just come from an intimate audience with Liholiho, who offered to show him a "house of wood" provided that Bullard would simply "take the whole"—an incredu-lous Bullard declined. Liholiho's offer came with a justification: since the long-awaited barge had been guaranteed for ten years but was rotten, Lihol-iho was only willing to pay in sandalwood pieces he deemed suitable for the balance of the transaction. The offer provoked from Bullard an early version of a soon-to-be familiar merchant complaint about chiefly author-ity in the islands: "The fact is, there is no Government here at present—all the chiefs have more [or] less to say, and some of them have used their influence from the first not to pay any thing."[44]

Charles Bullard's disenchantment with Captain John Suter's divergent approach to trade in the islands meant that he was inclined to believe the chief's claim that the vessel had been guaranteed to "wear ten years without repair."[45] While admitting as much in his letters to his employers, Bullard still blamed the chiefs for the dissolution of the once promising transaction. Hammatt and Bullard's employers, Bryant and Sturgis, were not apprised of the situation regarding *Cleopatra's Barge* when they wrote Hammatt's contract three months later, advising him on the proper way to sell ships to ali'i. Charles Hammatt's instructions of 1822 directed him to get as much sandalwood from the chiefs as possible by selling the ship he sailed in on, the *Champion*. He was also directed to sell the ship *Lascar*, another of Bry-ant and Sturgis' ships working in the Pacific: "To effect the sale of the ships, we should advise you on arrival to avoid making it known that it was contemplated. You will soon perceive it, would they take a fancy to her and should they, then will be the time for making a bargain."[46] By the next year, Charles Hammatt was still seeking 480 piculs, the balance of the 2,000 piculs agreed upon as its price, which Liholiho refused to pay since the

Cleopatra's Barge had proved "rotten." The chiefs, incensed at being sold poor goods, refused to deliver the balance of the wood, sending it instead to rival agent John Coffin Jones.[47]

What is clear from Bullard's engagement with the chiefs over the course of the *Cleopatra's Barge* debacle of 1821–1822 is that although the sale of the ship was to Liholiho, all the chiefs worked together to protect their common interest. When Bullard would not accept the terms they offered him in the midst of an 'aha 'ōlelo or chiefly council, they placed kapu barring sales of wood to him, significantly reducing his ability to function and remain competitive in the marketplace. The ali'i were not simply thoughtless consumers who "devoured all before them," as the writings of Stephen Reynolds and John C. Jones suggest. Instead, they set the terms for trade and refused to buy from merchants who they felt were trying to cheat them. This example is one among many that illustrate that merchant claims about a lack of governance and authority on the part of chiefs frequently arose from the frustrated aspirations of merchants to make successful sales. Incendiary language about governance masked merchant failures, directing attention and responsibility away from those who managed trade for New England merchant houses in the islands and casting scrutiny upon Hawaiian chiefs.[48]

Debt and *Pono*

Beyond the issue of merchants' disparagement of Hawaiian chiefs' governance and conduct in the sandalwood and ship trades, problems that arose from the differences between New England and Hawaiian conceptions of "debt" and obligation—and the values of good governance and trade—are not to be underestimated. In order to understand how the chiefs of the 1820s navigated their engagement with the merchants, we have to look back at the final *kauoha* (order) Kamehameha I speaks to his chiefs about his legacy and the possible relationships and responsibilities that the chiefs might have with their islands.

Just before the death of Kamehameha in May of 1819, the chiefs Kālaimoku and Ke'eaumoku, who were on O'ahu overseeing the business of cutting sandalwood, were recalled to Hawai'i to the side of their ali'i. After all avenues of curing the illness were exhausted, the chiefs arrayed around the body of their dying ali'i spoke, saying: "Here we all are, your younger

siblings, and your chiefs and your foreigners. Leave a word for us." The aliʻi
were asking Kamehameha for his kauoha, a directive or command, which
quite possibly would be his last words to them. Kamehameha replied, "For
what purpose?" Kaikioʻewa answered, "As a word for us."[49] Kamehameha
said, "E ʻoni wale nō ʻoukou i kuʻu pono ʻaʻole e pau" (Enjoy the good
which I have provided, for it is not finished).[50] Several hours later in the
early morning, the mōʻī Kamehameha would die. This would be his final
command to them, and it weighed heavily upon the chiefs who were left
behind.

The "good" of any aliʻi was expressed in Hawaiian by the word pono—
the pono of the chief encompassed the nature of his rule, his protection
of the people, and his ability to maintain healthy balance in the world
through the proper administration of lands and resources, through the ven-
eration of the akua (gods). What was the nature of government and governance? Was it peaceful and just, or marked by cruelty and war?

Kamehameha's rule was novel, as his vision of uniting all the islands
under his administration was both ambitious and relatively unheard of in
Hawaiian experience; there had been other aliʻi who sought to craft one
aupuni—one unified government out of separate islands or district aupuni.
Aliʻi had charge of moku, or districts, or entire islands, sometimes two or
three in proximity, but no aliʻi had successfully prosecuted a campaign,
harnessing resources, and mobilizing mana, men, and munitions to bring
all the islands under the rule of one aliʻi nui (high chief) and his circle of
chiefs. Kamehameha's success depended in no small part on his mastery of
trade with foreigners, in which he successfully wooed away or captured
British and American sailors who provided him with skilled laborers and
advice during the years of his conquest of the islands, and after, greatly
assisted him in achieving his vision.

Pono also has a moral dimension. Aliʻi were disciplined in their deportment and behavior; in their relations with others, there were agreed-upon
norms governed by religio-political and social expectation. Pono, therefore,
was not only indicative of the nature of a chief's rule, but it also referred
to his or her moral character. For example, nearly two hundred years after
his death, Kamehameha is remembered as a aliʻi pono, one who enacted
kānāwai (laws) that protected the welfare of the common people. This des-
ignation also bespoke the excellent relations the chief maintained with
the aliʻi around him—his supporters as well as his enemies. Within the
compass of what Hawaiians considered "right action," there were definite

indicators that showed whether the aliʻi and his approach to the people and land was pono.

But the pono of Kamehameha was not bound by traditional ideas of "right action," as it also included new indicators of wealth, well-being, and prosperity. While the health of the land and its people were formerly prime indicators of the pono of an aliʻi, during Kamehameha's time, he and his chiefly supporters were becoming accustomed to a different kind of wealth—namely, fine and fancy goods, new clothing, housing and furnishings, and ships brought to the islands by New England merchants.

The aliʻi of the 1820s, left bereft by the death of Kamehameha, had much to consider. In what ways would they strive to uphold the pono of their chief, Kamehameha? Who would carry the burden of this responsibility, and in what ways would they be able to consolidate their rule against multiple adversaries, Hawaiian and foreign? The chief Kālaimoku—along with Kamehameha's powerful widow, Kaʻahumanu—would strive to do as Kamehameha commanded: "E ʻoni wale nō ʻoukou nō i kuʻu pono ʻaʻole e pau" (Enjoy the pono which I have provided, for it is not finished). And it was this pono established by his rule over this new unified kingdom that they were enjoined to take up and continue.

The *Aliʻi* and Trade

The traditional roles of the chiefs and the relationships they had to one another were not completely clear to traders. The key to any successful trading venture in the islands was knowledge. Supercargoes like Hammatt, along with most ship captains, were directed in contracts and periodic letters from the merchant house to ascertain the political, economic, and social climate in the Hawaiian Islands as soon as they arrived. Merchants warned agents to be on the lookout for signs of political unrest, change, and transformation that would affect trade. Information about the current state of Hawaiian chiefly politics would give their concern the edge over competing firms who also had agents stationed at Honolulu and ships circulating between Boston and Hawaiʻi. This was the first time that Hammatt ventured into the Pacific as supercargo, although he had come out previously as one of the mates on the *Thaddeus*, Captain Blanchard's ship, which brought the first missionaries to Hawaiʻi. Hammatt's contract included the following instructions from his employers Bryant and Sturgis:

You must look for information as to the condition of the Islands, their disposition for trade, and in particular their ability to pay, for they have never shown any reluctance to making purchases—You are aware that we have always feared some changes in the Govt. that might endanger property on the islands. Should you find all quiet and business going on as it has done for some years past, it will give encouragement to trade boldly.[51]

John C. Jones wrote frequent letters to his employers about the movement of the chiefs and the progress of sandalwood collection, fulfilling his duty to inform his employers of developments which might affect trade positively or adversely. In Jones' letter to his proprietors in October 1821, he supplied his judgment of the immediate political situation among the chiefs. The letter also revealed Jones' frustration at trying to figure out the web of power relations and politics in play among the ali'i.

I was present when Tamoree [Kaumuali'i] gave everything he possessed to Rheo Rheo [Liholiho] and acknowledged him to be his king. . . . Rheo Rheo returned a few days since in the Cleopatra's Barge, and has brought up Tamoree with him, for what purpose we no not, some say he will never return, I do not think so myself. Tamoree is fast growing old, and I think, is not long for this world, should he pass off I tremble for the consequences. Pit [Kalaimoku] is here [O'ahu], he returned yesterday from the mountains where he has been cutting wood for the last five months, he is almost worn out, Cox has charge of Atooi [Kaua'i], John Adams [Kuakini] is at Owhyhee, Carhamano [Ka'ahumanu] is at the leeward part of the island. She and Pit are the only persons we put any dependence on they have some sense of propriety and integrity.[52]

Both Cox and Adams were brothers of the chiefess Ka'ahumanu, whose father, Ke'eaumoku, had warned of Ka'ahumanu's desire for and rise to power. But what is clear from Jones' letter and what troubled him most were the developments between Liholiho and Kaumuali'i, which he could not make out. Jones considered Kaumuali'i an honorable trading partner and hardly a credit risk. Kaumuali'i appears in Jones' letters, as in the writings of Hawaiian historian Kamakau, as being an excellent provider and welcoming host, having "received" Jones as he had Kamehameha's emissaries with "every attention and honour." Clearly Jones was being interpolated into Kaumuali'i's circle of allies and associates in ways consonant with Hawaiian chiefly practice, but which perhaps eluded Jones' awareness as such.[53]

Jones' reports show that he considered the ali'i belonging to the generations preceding Liholiho—that of Kaumuali'i, Ka'ahumanu, and Kālaimoku—to be "honest"; these ali'i had a "sense of propriety" and "integrity." These character sketches of the chiefs were set in contrast to Jones' damning view of the highest ruling ali'i Liholiho Kamehameha II in the same letter: "King Rheo Rheo is only a boy, pleased with the rattle tickled with a straw, rum is his god, scarce have I seen him sober, he is flying from one island to another, devouring all before him."[54]

Liholiho's drunkenness was a frequent obstacle to trade that all agents faced. According to Jones, Liholiho's frequent "frolicks" and "rounds of dissipation" would "put a stop to all business" wherever he was. On this particular occasion, Jones noted bitterly that "every man was recalled from cutting wood."[55]

In October 1821, as Hammatt was signing his orders in Boston, Liholiho traveled to Kaua'i on what appeared to outsiders like John C. Jones as yet another one of his "frolicks," a drunken parade wending its way between the islands that drew all the chiefs along in its train. When this frolick was done, however, the result was that Kaumuali'i had made public cession of his kingdom of Kaua'i, Ni'ihau, and Ka'ula to Liholiho. He offered his guns, his lands, and the men who served him to Kamehameha II, a gesture which Liholiho gracefully declined while also affirming the superiority of Kaumuali'i's rank and age. Kaumuali'i's cession to Liholiho was a repetition of an early diplomatic exchange between himself and Liholiho's father. Through this act, Kaumuali'i conferred upon Liholiho the deference and honor that he had previously bestowed upon Kamehameha I.

While not publicly proclaiming that he was taking possession of the lands, Liholiho accompanied Kaumuali'i in a circuit of Kaua'i, taking powerful symbolic charge of the lands, resources, and people of the island.[56] Taking over administration of the island for the time being would be Kahekili Ke'eaumoku, or Gov. Cox as he was called by foreigners, one of Ka'ahumanu's brothers, who had been a trusted adviser of Kamehameha I. Kaumuali'i was taken to O'ahu for reasons none of the merchants could fathom. Though they were competitors, both Charles Hammatt's and John

C. Jones' letters to the home office noted that Kaumuali'i was one of their best chiefly customers, who they felt did not pose a credit risk until his change of situation altered their prospects.

Imagine their surprise when Kaumuali'i removed from Kaua'i to O'ahu and then married Ka'ahumanu in November. Through this connection, Ka'ahumanu had achieved what had eluded her former husband Kamehameha—namely, by allying herself directly with Kaumuali'i through marriage, she had effectively extended her governing reach and that of her circle of chiefs to Kaua'i and Ni'ihau, encompassing all of the main islands in the archipelago. Competing circles of ali'i continued to form alliances in order to solidify and extend particular claims and access to rule. While a male chief could produce social change through rebellion and war, or by taking care of the high-ranking male sons of other ali'i, the female ali'i could effect change in the social and political structure through marriage alliance and the birth or adoption of chiefly children. These political processes of genealogical elevation, succession, and alliance fell outside the knowledge of New England merchants, and missionaries as well. What Jones did know was that the political alliance between Ka'ahumanu and Kaumuali'i was "bad for business," as Kaumuali'i was made virtually a captive on O'ahu, unable to return to Kaua'i to organize his people and chiefs to cut and gather the sandalwood for Jones.

But the removal of Kaumuali'i to O'ahu and his subsequent important political marriage to Ka'ahumanu may have hidden another object of other prominent chiefs Kālaimoku, Kuakini, Ke'eaumoku, Kaikio'ewa, and Ka'ahumanu—namely, to prevent Kaumuali'i from entering deeper into debt with New England merchants. In a very anxious letter to his employers written on October 5, 1821, three days after the return of Liholiho and Kaumuali'i to Kaua'i, Jones noted that Kaumuali'i owed their concern some eight thousand plus piculs, and the forecast only darkened with the pronouncements of others who claimed that "he [Kaumuali'i] will never return," to his island. Jones concurred with this assessment, observing that "Tamoree [Kaumuali'i] is fast growing old, and I think, not long for this world." According to Jones' account book, Kaumuali'i owed Marshall and Wildes eight thousand piculs alone, whereas ten months later, Jones' catalog of debts owed by other chiefs showed that they owed much less than Kaumuali'i in comparison. "The King is owing 850, Cox about 800, Pitt about 60, John Adams [Kuakini] 130, these are the principal debts at this island. We have received no wood from Atooi [Kaua'i] since the ship sailed,

Tamoree [Kaumualiʻi] and consort have been at Owhyhee [Hawaiʻi Island] all summer . . . they intend paying about two thousand piculs of debt at this island."[57] By bringing Kaumualiʻi to Oʻahu, these chiefs were able to keep a watchful eye on his transactions and separate him from the source of his payment—namely, the labor and forests of Kauaʻi.

At the same time that Kaumualiʻi moved to Oʻahu, Kālaimoku himself had emerged from the uplands of Oʻahu after heading a labor force of two hundred men and women into the mountains five months before, in March 1821. He not only accompanied the people into the uplands, but he also made sure that provisions were made available for their use.[58] Kālaimoku, like Kamehameha I, saw to it that no important work was undertaken that he did not personally have a hand in.[59] By October, through the strenuous efforts of the aliʻi and people on different islands, an estimated thirty thousand piculs of sandalwood had shipped to Canton from Hawaiʻi, selling poorly due to the miscalculation of rival American agents who had all pressed the aliʻi to pay debts at the same time. Sandalwood that year glutted the market, driving down prices, resulting in significantly lower profits for merchants.[60]

The chiefs were clearly savvy customers who were not confused by trade and not completely given over to self-indulgence. They often worked together to set the terms of trade, deploying kapu in innovative ways. By compelling political alliance through marriage, they also effectively blocked the ability of Kaumualiʻi to plunge himself and the chiefs collectively into deeper debt. They also worked together to organize labor and provisions in an unprecedented attempt to deliver thirty thousand piculs of sandalwood in 1821 to pay down the debt they owed to New England merchants.

On the other hand, in their scramble for trade opportunities and collection of wood for debt, agents and ship captains from rival concerns engaged in vicious competition that threatened everyone's profits with unforeseen consequences. While worrying about the laziness of chiefs to pay, and foreseeing an eventual surfeit in wood, they had prosecuted their claims successfully with disastrous results. "Every foreigner in this country is ready to cut his neighbor's throat, truth is a stranger here," Jones wrote that month, "the sandalwood fever will deprive some of their reason."[61] And apparently the fever for wood and the competition that fanned its temperature would also cheat them all of their profits.

The boom of 1821, though an anomaly, affected the traders in the same way that hitting a jackpot affects a gambler: they simply wanted more.[62]

The problem lay not only in chiefly consumption or the way in which the well developed tastes of so-called savage rulers were off-putting to agents scrabbling over scraps of paper debt, who themselves could never hope to own such finery. It also lay in the distance between market and market-place, which stoked, chafed, and inflamed longing and desire on the part of agents for the next cargo of better goods that would secure a "good voyage" and, most importantly, help them to best the competition.

Fair Trade?

Agents and ship captains used their persuasive powers to cajole the chiefs into purchasing more goods. But another way to secure large profit was to inflate prices. Jones, like other agents, had developed a rapport with the chiefs. He had become used to offering gifts and throwing elegant dinners to whet the appetite of his royal clients.[63] On one occasion, Jones had attempted to sell a brig and cargo to Kaumuali'i, but he found to his cha-grin that Kaumuali'i had recently purchased another brig, the *Becket*, and its cargo from representatives of Bryant and Sturgis.

In order to dispose of his ship and cargo, Jones then turned to Liholiho, on O'ahu, who rebuffed his initial offer, saying that he wanted to buy no more ships: "I treated him with every attention and honour, made him handsome presents and gave him elegant dinners after much trouble and difficulty I succeeded in selling the Brig and cargo including the house for 7700 piculs of wood payable in one year the boat he has given me an obliga-tion to pay when she will be finished, per twice full."[64] Jones regularly inflated in excess the price of goods and ships, a problem enabled by the fact that there was no agreed-upon rate of exchange.[65] On another occasion, Jones asked his employers to send out a billiard table—"one that you might get for $200 would command at least $1500"—as Liholiho was "quite anx-ious for one."[66]

Unfortunately for the merchants, some of the ali'i were also getting excellent advice from the young Hawaiian men who had lived in New England for many years. "Our worst enemy at Atooi, I found to be Mr. George Tamoree [son of Kaumuali'i] he endeavored all in his power to prevent the sale of the Brig but fortunately he has no influence with his father, he has become a worthless dissipated fellow, of no advantage to anyone."[67] On numerous occasions Jones extended "credit" to Kaumuali'i in the form of goods delivered in exchange for promise of future pay. He also extended credit to the chief, who he referred to on occasion as "the King," by building up Kaumuali'i as a copartner in expediting the business of sandalwood in numerous letters sent to his employers.[68] This connection between father and long-lost son must have been a blow to Jones, as Kaumuali'i and he enjoyed a lively trading relationship. Jones must have felt awkward in this position, since he would have a hard time denying the younger Kaumuali'i's accusations of inflated prices for goods they both knew cost significantly less back home in New England. The Hawaiian missionary assistants who were educated at the Cornwall Foreign Mission School regularly counseled Liholiho and the chiefs on the costs of goods. Houses, they argued, were bought for $300 in America, and thereafter the chiefs offered only forty piculs for a house that might have fetched, under the trade expectations of New England agents, thousands of piculs earlier in the year.[69]

As trading became more difficult over the years, by 1823 merchants were beginning to direct their anger at the American missionaries who had arrived two years before and who by March were actively awaiting the second company to reinforce them in their labors. Stations had been set up on Kaua'i, O'ahu, and Hawai'i, but the mission had already lost a doctor and his wife, who had been excommunicated from the little church. Jones vented in a letter to his employers that the missionaries "from the Andover mill" were getting in the way of trade, because they "are continually telling the King and chiefs that the white people traders are cheating and imposing on them."[70] What really angered Jones was that the missionaries were, in his words, "blood suckers of the community, had much better be in their native country gaining their living by the sweat of their brow, than living like lords in this luxurious land, distracting the minds of these children of nature with the idea that they are to be eternally damned unless they think and act as they do."[71] Jones was bothered that while he earned an "honest" living working as a trader, his fellow Americans, the missionaries, were living like chiefs in Hawai'i, "the luxurious land." Jones was suffering from a class conflict, one that pitted himself against his fellow Americans, most of whom had come from farming backgrounds, but who were more adept apparently in garnering the attention and condescension of the chiefs. Jones even suggested a divine solution to the problem of the missionaries: "O that Providence would put a whip in every honest hand to lash such rascals naked through the world."[72]

Intense debates among the chiefs began to surface in the 'aha 'ōlelo, or Hawaiian chiefly council, by 1823 regarding large purchases made by individual chiefs. These discussions illustrate Hawaiian negotiations over power and status, and perhaps the recognition among ali'i that they must consolidate their power as a unified group against the would-be predations of merchant agents. The merchants, for their part, hoped to interject themselves into and sought to manipulate the relations between chiefs in order to promote their business.

Agents desperate to make sales would often seek a meeting with Liholiho, who was often inebriated. Therefore, agents were forced to negotiate with Kālaimoku. In May, just after Charles Hammatt arrived in the islands, he had a meeting with Kālaimoku, who had sent for him to discuss the king's plan to purchase a ship. Hammatt spotted Kālaimoku "sitting down on the grass before the King's house." The elder statesman offered eighty piculs of wood for the boat, but after a half-hour conversation, Hammatt became frustrated, telling the chief, "I would sooner burn her" than agree to this price. But Kalaimoku had made it known to the merchants that for anybody who trades with the king when he is drunk, "the bargain will not stand." According to Hammatt, Kālaimoku's say was "potential," meaning the final most powerful word.[73]

Hammatt would write with increasing frequency of the wise counsels of Kālaimoku, noting on several occasions that there was a rift developing between Liholiho Kamehameha II and Kālaimoku, Ka'ahumanu, and the rest of the high chiefs. It was the family of the minister, Hammatt claimed, "who in reality hold the sovereignty of the kingdom, and have rather permitted this man to be called King than considered him as such. They have now abandoned him to his own guidance, and if he does not soon kill himself, they may put him down by force. Under these circumstances I am afraid to trade with him, and certainly shall not do it, to any considerable amount, without the sanction of Krymakoo. The King cannot command a man, or obtain a stick of wood without the assistance of Pitt or some of his clan."[74]

A few months later, the chief Kaikio'ewa, who was guardian of Kauikeaouli, the youngest son of Kamehameha and Liholiho's younger brother, met with Charles Hammatt to discuss his purchase of the schooner *Ann*. According to the terms of their agreement, Kaikio'ewa would pay twelve hundred piculs over the course of five months, beginning on June 17, 1823. In August, the chief met with Hammatt again and reported that there had been a meeting of the chiefs and that Kālaimoku, Ka'ahumanu, Boki (Kālai-moku's brother), and Cox were all opposed to the purchase, largely because the ship was "old & rotten and good for nothing." Hammatt coolly played his hand, saying that he would take the ship back if that was what the chief wished. When Kaikio'ewa replied that he did not want to give the ship back, but pointed out repairs and supplies needed to get the ship under sail, Hammatt lost all patience, accusing the chief of breaking his contract and his word, a serious charge. When the chief remonstrated that Kālai-moku and Ka'ahumanu were both pressuring him to return the ship, Ham-matt asked provocatively if Kaikio'ewa was the servant of Kālaimoku and the old woman: "are you bound to obey their orders, or are you a chief at liberty to do as you please?" Kaikio'ewa protested vehemently that "he was a chief, would be a chief," and "would keep the vessel."

Hammatt won that round, but in the end, the wishes of Kaikio'ewa, Kālaimoku, Ka'ahumanu, and the other ali'i would prevail. Kaikio'ewa returned the schooner nineteen days later because it was leaky and needed new coppering, rigging, and planks, things which Hammatt simply could not supply. Though Hammatt fully expected this turn of events, since the *Ann* was not fitted properly for sail, and it was leaking, he still raged that it would be better to sell the ship on the coast than "to the damned scoundrels here, who are held by no contract, and who regard no promises."[75]

Hammatt's hard bargaining and coercive manipulation of Ka'ikioewa's sense of his authority in relation to the other ali'i was no match for the pressure that the high-ranking ali'i Ka'ahumanu and Kālaimoku could place upon any individual ali'i who did not comply with the wishes of the 'aha 'ōlelo. Hawaiian structures of power and authority could not be transposed effectively upon the merchant's ideal individual as consumer; indeed, Hawaiian ali'i clearly were engaging in trade on their own terms, following their own political agendas. When merchants attempted to cheat them by selling rotten or unfinished boats, chiefs refused to fulfill the agreed-upon terms of exchange by simply returning items they no longer found to their liking. The ali'i also listened to the advice of Hawaiians whose knowledge of the cost of goods and trade in American markets worked to their advantage. While claiming that they were being treated unfairly in business, merchant agents inflated prices and sold defective goods truly unfit for sale. Much of the anger and wrath of merchants directed at chiefs are also a direct result of their inability to successfully navigate the political intricacies of chiefly relations.

Studying the writings of merchants and agents, one is struck by the detailed descriptions Charles Bullard, John Coffin Jones, and Charles Hammatt generated regarding trade in the islands. Descriptions of the reliability of any aliʻi to trade, "follow through" on transactions, or pay debts provide a view of the anxiety agents struggled with on a daily basis concerning their success and their ability to deliver profits into the hands of their employers.[76] Present profits also ensured future gains—the reputation they built as successful men of business on Hawaiian shores would lay the foundation for their professional lives when they settled back home in New England. Rather than transparent descriptions of the behavior and shortcomings of aliʻi, the letters, reports, and journals kept by these men also illustrate the agents' difficulty in ascertaining the shifting loci of Hawaiian political power, whether it be invested in the person of a particular aliʻi, or as it was held by particular groups of chiefs against others. All in all, knowledge of the relationship between chiefs and political power was not an end unto itself; it was the necessary precondition that agents set for themselves in order to carry out successful trade.

Agents' insistence on pinpointing and projecting New England standards of proper character, deportment, and behavior belonging to "good consumers" or "good leaders" upon individual aliʻi was a vain endeavor. This individualization of the chiefs could not extricate an aliʻi from his or her embeddedness in the web of close genealogical ties, which were the foundation of their governing powers. Though attempting to ensnare individual chiefs in debt, traders consistently met with opposition from groups of chiefs. As happened also with missionaries, New England traders' assumptions completely missed Hawaiian ideas of debt, obligation, and exchange. Hawaiians had their own ideas about what constituted proper leadership in the form of the aliʻi pono. Yet merchants persisted in assigning debt to individual chiefs in a manner that their economic system required: one simply had to know who to send the bill to.

It is no wonder that the merchants in 1824 began to become more agitated about what was due to them, and when their ability to cheat, flatter, cajole, and insist that the chiefs pay their debts was exhausted, they called upon the United States to intervene on their behalf and collect the debt that was owed not to their employers, they insisted, but rather to the citizens of the United States.[77]

By 1825, Dixey Wildes was calling upon his partner to petition the government to send a US ship of war to the islands to press the aliʻi to pay their debts.[78] "The Islands are quite out of trade, our prospects are very fair. Lord Byron has been here in a frigate he has not been of any service to the American trade. Our government must send a frigate here. The interest of the United States require it. The Russians and English send ships of war, although their trade is small compared to ours. I think it would be well for you and others to make a strong representation to our government to send a ship here."[79]

This mode of running the business came screeching to a halt when, beginning in 1825, the merchant agents in the islands began to demand the transformation of individual chiefly debt into a new "national" debt. The steps toward this development, the significance of its occurrence for the groups involved, and how it affected the progress of Hawaiian governance will be the subject of a later chapter. But for now, it is important to emphasize that the emergence of a conception of "national" debt is something that converges complexly with chiefly political and economic reorganizations that come as a consequence of Kamehameha's unification of the different islands in the archipelago and of the final defeat, through religio-political changes and active suppression, of secessionist chiefs' ambitions.

CHAPTER 2

Creating an Island Imaginary

Hawai'i's American Origins

Long before American westward expansion and the growth of the United States into a global imperial power in the late nineteenth century, America found itself entangled with the Hawaiian Islands in ways that were far less self-assured, far more tentative, and far more curious than an anachronistic focus on colonialism, imperialism, and "nation" might suggest. Hawai'i became a place more prominent during the Early Republic, an opportune space through which American conceptions of the world and the United States' new place in it expanded. In looking closely at the entertainments that came to the Atlantic, made from narratives and material objects brought back from the Pacific, we can see the development of an American imaginary of the Hawaiian Islands and kānaka constructed as bountiful, full of alluring women and fierce warriors, ripe and open for the "influence" of great, civilizing European and American men. Americans' imagined Sandwich Islands were shaped by enterprising entertainment producers and curiosity collectors, who shaped the tastes of Americans eager to consume Hawaiian objects: pieces of information, material curiosities, and stories of paradise.

This chapter focuses on the self-interested efforts of the New England–based American Board of Commissioners for Foreign Missions (ABCFM) to raise money for a school in Connecticut and a series of missions to bring Christianity and its church to the Hawaiian Islands by producing narratives of the lives of young Hawaiian men living in New England. It examines the way in which these native men's stories were the ground in which settler origins were sown, and though these historical narrativizations were keenly opportunistic, when read against the grain, they illuminate a portion of the experience of the Hawaiian men living in New England at the time. American familiarity with an imagined Hawai'i is profoundly transformed with the advent of the ABCFM's Sandwich Island Mission in 1820. From that point onward, an avalanche of administrative and official reports and histories produced by the ABCFM reschooled American expectations about the islands. In this new light, Hawai'i became a field in which an American mission was planted to civilize and save Hawaiian souls.

A central component of the ABCFM mission was the narrative fashioning of native subjects suitable for conversion, the young male escaped from a pagan world of savagery. Before the Sandwich Islands Mission could come to fruition, the figure of the young Hawaiian male, freed from human sacrifice, became an ideal vessel for stirring public sentiment and stimulating financial support of the mission. The funds raised by the individual stories and testimonies of these men would facilitate the planting of an American mission church in Hawaiian soil, free from British and American authorities and the bitterness of church controversies and denominational competition that continued to roil the New England landscape. Reading through the surface to the more complex contradictions of these public productions of Hawaiian types—fierce and deadly warriors, the intensely desirable women whom men are always fighting for, the noble yet not yet civilized chief, and the earnest and skilled Hawaiian convert—we will find the basic bedrock of imaginary fantasies of Hawai'i that continue to be reproduced today. More immediately, the production of these types for late eighteenth- and early nineteenth-century Atlantic public consumption set the stage for increasingly intimate connections—both imaginary and material—between the young republic's people and an emerging Hawaiian nation. The disorderliness of a savage desire for women and things must, in these narratives, give way to the civilized orderliness of restraint and Christianity. And nothing was more likely to stir American desire to consume Hawaiian things than stories of sex, sacrifice, and death.

Ship captains returned home from the Pacific with souvenirs, and news of their contributions to American museums was published in the papers. In 1790, a "donation of curiosities" was deposited at the Museum at Cambridge by Boston-based ship captains James Magee (*Astrea*) and Joseph Ingraham (*Columbia*), showcasing materials from places along emergent maritime trade routes connecting New England, China, the Northwest Coast, the Sandwich Islands, and the Southern Pacific with which mariners were familiar. The skin of sea otters from Nootka and a bird of paradise from the Moluccas were "natural curiosities," while the shoes that bound the feet of Chinese women and mathematical instruments used by merchants were considered "artificial." From Hawai'i was collected "a great variety of cloths made of the bark of the mulberry tree, specimens of military weapons, domestic utensils, fishing tackle, musical instruments, dresses, ornaments, and idols."[1]

Whether artificial or natural, these items were artifacts of commerce, merchandise that circulated in exchange networks between Euro-Americans, Asians, and indigenous traders connecting the Pacific to the Atlantic. The items were "highly gratifying to the curious, who love to trace the operations of nature, and observe the progress of human ingenuity and industry in every part of the world."[2] Trade goods were collected by historical associations, maritime companies, and museums in Boston, which was just beginning to build its own national collections of cabinets of wonder in the decades following the American Revolution. Stripped of proper context and removed from their places of origin, items were rehistoricized as part of an enlightenment narrative that sought to distinguish nature from ingenuity and industry and that measured progress in the crude or artful distances between items of familiar Euro-American manufacture and those made by heathen hands.[3]

News from the Pacific was as desired a commodity as material objects. Commercial-minded Americans perusing the papers of the day could search through the shipping news to see the names of ship captains who were putting out to the Sandwich Islands, as well as lists of goods arriving in ports and sold in stores. News also circulated between the ships in the China–Northwest Coast–Sandwich Islands trade, and those returning brought back news about the present state of political affairs in the Sandwich Islands. Readers in America were kept up to date on the progress of Hawaiians toward "civilization" under Tamaahmaah (Kamehameha), along with the progress of his war against other ali'i, in which Euro-American ships and sailors also took sides. Keeping abreast of the political situation in Hawai'i, in order to keep investors at home informed, was good for the stability of business.

Burgeoning trade routes between New England, Hawai'i, China, and the Northwest Coast brought both native bodies and the material culture of their homes to American shores. Knowledge of the Sandwich Islands and Sandwich Islanders in the late eighteenth and early nineteenth centuries was readily available. Theater and print, exhibition and collection, exploration and merchant shipping—each venue provided different and very particular kinds of knowledge about Hawai'i that increased people's curiosity about the Sandwich Islands. They helped to shape specific images about Hawai'i and the Pacific as a seemingly *known*, albeit exotic, place.

But why did Hawai'i and the Pacific exotic become desirable? Was there some kind of fascination with Hawaiians because these were a people who killed Captain Cook, the man responsible for the torrent of print that came out of his many voyages—the maps, words, and meanings made silenced forever? The reasons why Americans were interested in Hawai'i were multifaceted, but what is clear is that the United States trade in the Pacific supplied goods, materials, stories, news, and bodies that circulated in the early American republic, feeding a growing desire for more information of this far-off yet increasingly interesting place.

The ships that hunted whales and brought Hawaiian wood to Chinese markets also carried Hawaiian sailors to New England, several of whom intended to stay. Upon their settlement in the States, these sailors, boys and young men, worked for and were supported by American ship captains, schoolmasters, and ministers. In some cases, they were forced by circumstances to make their own way and find employment and eventual passage home.

In 1802, a young Hawaiian boy of four or five years of age was sent to America for an education by his father, Kaumuali'i, the ali'i nui (high chief) of Kaua'i. Some Hawaiians who never left home had their own ideas about what they wanted from the ship captains, crews, and merchants who passed through or settled in their islands. Kaumuali'i, one of the last ruling ali'i to survive Kamehameha's conquest of the archipelago, never surrendered administration or rule of Kaua'i, his home island. Rather, Kaumuali'i gave his lands, men, and munitions over to the Hawai'i Island chief in 1795 in a symbolic cession which would reverberate through the next generation.

Kaumuali'i's gesture to Kamehameha meant that he could continue to rule over the island of Kaua'i and that he continued to manage his own commercial exchanges with visiting ships. In 1802, Kaumuali'i made an agreement with Captain James Rowan of the *Hazard*, sailing out of Providence, Rhode Island. In exchange for money and provisions, Rowan agreed to take Kaumuali'i's young son to New England to receive an American education. In this way, Kaumuali'i set in motion his design for a long-term plan to secure his rule over Kaua'i. Kaumuali'i's hope was that his American-educated son would one day return and assist him in making profitable and well-informed transactions with New England merchants and ship captains in the islands. Perhaps such a son could help him keep his island kingdom, or aid in the expansion of his rule beyond Kauaʻi's shores.

The boy accompanying Rowan moved a lot for the first decade of his residence in America. He lived in Providence, and in Boston and Worcester, where the property for his care ran out and he was placed in the care of Captain Samuel Cotting. With Cotting, he moved from Worcester to Fitchburg, and then back to Boston. Frustrated by his treatment and the impoverished situation of his various patrons, an underage "George Prince Tamoree" enlisted in the US Navy. He shipped out aboard the US sloop of war *Wasp*, and then was assigned to the brig *Enterprize*, where he was wounded in the side by a boarding pike when his ship engaged the British ship *Boxer* during the War of 1812. After the war, Tamoree was drafted aboard the USS *Guerrier* and traveled to the Mediterranean. On this voyage, he fought in a three-hour sea battle against Turks from Algiers. It was also on this cruise that Tamoree visited Tripoli, Naples, and Gibraltar. Upon his return to America, Tamoree supported himself by working for the purser at the Charlestown Naval Yard in Massachusetts while looking for a passage home.

By 1814, as Tamoree continued his employment in the US Navy, four other Hawaiian sailors who served on merchant vessels—Henry Obookiah (ʻŌpūkahaʻia), Thomas Hopoo (Hopu), William Tennooe (Kanui), and John Honoree (Honoliʻi)—had found their way to Connecticut, their living expenses and education supported by a circle of ministers, community and church leaders, and their families. But while this support of former Hawaiian sailors turned students sustained the men for a little while, soon enough, a group of Connecticut ministers would see in the presence of these Hawaiian men an opportunity to set their financial maintenance on firmer foundations, and a chance to develop and extend their Christian duties. New England pastors and parishioners thus discovered the power of promoting stories about the lives of these Hawaiian men living in Connecticut as part of a fund-raising push to raise monies for both the school and the broader American foreign mission movement.

A School for Hawaiians, for Heathen Youth in America

Samuel Mills was one of the young men who took part in the now-famed 1806 Haystack Prayer Meeting while he was a student at Williams College.

Mills, along with a few of his fellow classmates, believed that an American Foreign Mission Society should be created. The American Board of Commissioners for Foreign Missions (ABCFM) arose as a direct result of their queries and the debates that followed. The board had been formally incorporated and recognized by the Massachusetts legislature in 1810, thanks to the faith and efforts of these students, but it was not until Mills and a group of ministers and educators from neighboring Connecticut raised the question of educating and supporting several young men from the Sandwich Islands in 1814 that visions for the success of the mission began to coalesce around heathen youth, specifically these Hawaiian men. In meetings and correspondence, the subject of establishing a school for their education was raised.[4] Over several years of deliberation about the school and the education of the Hawaiian men, ideas developed about the important role that "heathen" youths would fill in raising the American public's awareness of foreign missions.[5] Heathen youth would be used not only to raise awareness, but also to raise funds for the school and the foreign mission movement. Finally, discussions about the role newly educated heathens would play in the foreign mission field of their homelands engendered discussions about the way in which the foreign missionary movement should be structured both in America and in the field.

Samuel Mills first began writing to the Prudential Committee of the ABCFM in 1814 for assistance in the education of Henry ʻŌpūkahaʻia, who had been under his educational guidance for at least four years. Mills was applying to the committee on behalf of ʻŌpūkahaʻia to see if they would consider providing financial support for the young Hawaiian's education.[6] Henry ʻŌpūkahaʻia was born around 1792 on the island of Hawaiʻi and arrived in New Haven, Connecticut, in 1810 along with another Hawaiian man, Thomas Hopu. ʻŌpūkahaʻia had been living initially with Captain Brintnall, whose ship he had arrived on, and when the opportunity to obtain an education presented itself, he moved in with the family of Yale president Timothy Dwight, with whom he lived until he met Samuel Mills. ʻŌpūkahaʻia went to live with Mills and his family in Torringford, Connecticut. He then moved with Mills in late 1810 to Andover, Massachusetts, when Mills went to undertake his studies at the recently opened Theological Seminary. Henry then went to nearby Branford Academy to pursue his own course of study for a few months. In all, Henry spent two years at Andover with Mills. However, between 1810 and 1816, Henry changed residences frequently, living in Torringford, Andover, Goshen, Litchfield, and Canaan,

Connecticut, either following Mills or removing to other situations in order to pursue an erratic course of study with local ministers and deacons, or hiring himself out to work in order to pay for his subsistence.[7]

It seems that nothing formal had been undertaken by the Boston-based board for the financial support of these men through May 1816, as can be seen by ʻŌpūkahaʻia's frequent movement between households. By this time, however, there were several youths from the Sandwich Islands who were also in Connecticut and whose educations, religious and otherwise, were being supported by the same circle of ministers, educators, and their families who had been helping to provide for ʻŌpūkahaʻia. That month, another letter to the board requested "provision for their support," asking whether or not a school was to be established for these men.[8] From the necessity of providing financially and spiritually for the five Hawaiians within their community, a larger vision for a Foreign Mission School to train native missionaries was born.

A meeting dedicated to the subject of patronizing the Hawaiian men had been held at New Haven in June of that year, wherein agents and trustees were appointed to "superintend the particular concerns of these young men."[9] The next month, the newly elected Board of Trust composed of Rev. Charles Prentice, Rev. Joseph Harvey, and James Morris met in Goshen to deliberate the "best method of conducting the education of these and other heathen youths." The young men from the Sandwich Islands, noted the trustees in a letter to the board, were sent to them by the hand of Providence in order to "draw the attention of the Christian public to those Islands, as an important missionary field; and also to point out the method of facilitating the introduction of missions to other parts of the heathen world."[10]

Hawaiians, with their frequently remarked-upon amiable dispositions and desire for knowledge, were not only the impetus behind the establishment of a school; their presence in New England spurred discussion and thought about the role "heathens" should play in spreading the gospel in foreign mission fields. Hawaiian men would be invaluable as assistants to missionaries, as "interpreters, schoolmasters, catechists and translators."[11] It was felt that if "properly trained," the natives would be more successful in discharging the "duties of these subordinate stations" with "much greater success than missionaries from foreign countries."[12] This developing American missionary theory about the place of natives in foreign mission fields held out the possibility that "natives" would do important work in their homes once educated properly.[13] Mission letters and pamphlets spoke of the desire of the Hawaiians to "carry the gospel to their perishing country men,"[14] and certainly, over the course of their studies, Hawaiian and other native men cultivated the expectation that they would bear some of the responsibility and pleasure of preaching among and converting their own people.

Discussion about the necessity of building a foreign mission school also engendered thinking about the best system for preparing New England missionaries for foreign mission fields. Missionaries sent to "heathen lands" usually had to spend precious time learning the local language, and once they become relatively accomplished, they would train "assistants," very often from among the people who taught them the language, to serve as translators and teachers. But the Connecticut trustees proposed that it would be best to establish a school in America, where "youths from different heathen countries may be collected and taught the rudiments of science, the necessary arts of civilized life, and the great principles of Christianity."[15] They argued for the comparative advantages of this model, since "heathen youths brought to this country and placed in a school, are at once under a regular government, and have their business systematized. They will of course be inured to habits of industry and regularity, they will learn the art of government and subordination."[16] The school would also benefit American missionaries by affording them the opportunity to study "heathen languages" with their foreign classmates, spending a sufficient enough period that they would be prepared and "furnished with every facility to enter immediately on their work."[17]

Students from around the world had been provided to the mission free of charge, and the Connecticut trustees assured the board that as "commercial relations and enterprise increase, the number of these visitants will also increase." The trustees clearly had some knowledge of the commercial interests of the nation, since their vision of collecting students followed the Northwest Coast–Hawai'i–China merchant routes, "We suppose that young men of talents and influence might with little difficulty be obtained from China . . . from the islands of the sea, from Nootka Sound and the various tribes on the Western Coast of America, from South America."[18] While builders of missions depended upon merchant shipping to supply students to their schools, they would also find allies in commerce who would carry missionaries to foreign mission fields and facilitate the mission's progress by carrying letters, journals, and reports back to Boston, where they could be published in newspapers and religious magazines, reaching a large American readership. The trade routes that brought curiosities to American museums would supply students, who would also be placed on display and whose stories circulated through the Christian community. The men would eventually serve as examples of Christian progress—their newly civilized persons made a deeper impression when compared to the already established savage Hawaiian imaginary of print, and the museum.

As a cohort, the Sandwich Islanders embodied a lesson on the spectrum from "savage" to "civilized," since ʻŌpūkahaʻia was by all accounts the furthest along in his education, followed by Thomas Hopu and William Kanui, whereas John Honoliʻi could barely speak any English. The presence of the men in school, at public examinations, in community churches, and on fund-raising tours would, according to the committee, "bring heathen manners, as a living and impressive spectacle. It would afford a constant fund of interesting facts rendered weighty by their proximity, by which we may rouse the attention and call forth the resources of our country in the cause of missions."[19] While raising awareness, the students would also "call forth" funds for the school and foreign mission cause from the "resources" of the country. The mission school would generate more revenue than "many sermons," the trustees argued, if annual reports of the progress of the students were made public.[20] These observations, they said, came from their own experience with the Hawaiians: "Since the youths from the Sandwich Islands have been under our care, we have found the public greatly interested in their state and concerns. Many generous donations have, unsolicited, poured in upon us, and many have expressed a willingness and even a desire to aid, when their aid is needed."[21]

In their petitions to the American Board for assistance for the education of these Hawaiian men, the Connecticut group of ministers and community leaders developed ideas about how the mission should be structured both at home and abroad. Instead of focusing on the education of heathen youth in foreign lands, they would concentrate their energies and direct efforts in educating heathen youth in America.

The men from the Sandwich Islands were the impetus behind the establishment of the Foreign Mission School in Cornwall, Connecticut. The Hawaiians were the largest group of pupils hailing from one place in attendance in the school when it unofficially opened on May 1, 1816. By 1817, just one year later, the school housed seven pupils from the Sandwich Islands. As the agents for the school and the General Association of Connecticut were to find, their observations about cultivating the public's interest in the state, activities, and progress of the Hawaiians to successfully raise funds for the school and the broader cause of foreign missions would pay off handsomely.

The Lives of Men

Before they appeared as signs of Christian providence that inspired calls for the establishment of a school for heathen youth in America, before their names were popularized in newspaper articles or reports and sermons, Henry Obookiah ('Ōpūkaha'ia), Thomas Hopoo (Hopu), George Prince Tamoree (Kaumuali'i), William Tennooe (Kanui), John Honoree (Honoli'i), and George Sandwich worked as sailors or cabin boys on New England merchant ships. The many different paths which brought these Hawaiian men to the classrooms and dormitories of the Foreign Mission School were obscured by the ways in which the Connecticut Agents of the School and the ABCFM produced and then promoted them as objects of interest for the patronage of the Christian public. As native elites securing alliance and advantage at home, as sailors on ships or marines fighting in the war, as servants or farmers, the lives these men made alongside Americans were barely fleshed out. What was of supreme significance to the mission press was the distance they managed to put between themselves and their heathen pasts through their residence in a civilized nation. What mattered was the promise of what could be done through these educated few once they received instruction paid for by Christian benevolence and once they were returned to their own homelands—within the confines of an American *foreign* mission.

The concern for Hawaiians in America was connected to the long colonial settler project of regenerating the heathen through Christian education and a process of civilization. This undertaking could claim ancestry in a deeper New England history that reached all the way back to John Eliot's work with the American Indians in the seventeenth century. However, this project never grew significantly in scope, nor did its nineteenth-century progeny often seem to reflect on the possible pasts of their present endeavor. Instead, news of these Hawaiian men in New England capitalized on the interest in the Sandwich Islands and the islands of the Pacific that had begun gradually with the first sales of the journals and logs from the voyages of Captain Cook, the much-performed pantomime of his death, and the ubiquitous commercial news that related the daily comings and goings of ships from New England to the Pacific. The new American foreign mission movement was progressive, future oriented, and aiming to convert natives in a far-removed field, but first they had to stoke the public's interest in their enterprise in order to raise the money to train teachers and send them halfway across the globe.

In 1816, the forty-four-page promotional pamphlet "A Narrative of Five Youth from the Sandwich Islands, Now Receiving an Education in This Country" would set the reader back twenty-five cents. For the first time the public could read in extended accounts about the lives and accomplishments of Henry Obookiah, Thomas Hopoo, William Tennooe John Honoree, and George Prince Tamoree.[22] Designed by the ABCFM for the consumption of a Christian audience, the narrative's purpose was to provide a "simple and authentic statement of facts" respecting the men, along with "specimens of their ability and improvement."[23] The production of the lives of these men made them into both fund-raising tool and product—they were embodied as produced by the mission while also serving as its ultimate outcome and aim. Obookiah was clearly made to appear as the outstanding pupil of the bunch and the star of this pamphlet, as its first twelve pages were devoted to him, his writing, his composition of prayers, and a listing of his phenomenal accomplishments in his educational endeavors.

That same year, the *Religious Intelligencer* ran an article entitled "Honourable Munificence" that was extensively reprinted in both secular and religious newspapers.[24] Those people who were unfamiliar with the progress of the men of Owhyhee were gently chided, since "the Christian public are extensively acquainted with the fact, that several young men, natives of the Owhyhee, are now in Connecticut," suggesting that the story of these Hawaiian men was widely covered and followed by many Americans. The Christian public would have become familiar with these Hawaiians through pulpit sermons, official published reports, Christian magazines and newspapers, and membership in the many auxiliary missionary societies that had begun to spring up in towns all throughout New England.[25]

The subject of "Honourable Munificence" was a woman from Savannah, Georgia, who mobilized a circle of her friends to raise funds for the education of the Hawaiian men. Brief information on the Hawaiian students studying at the Cornwall Foreign Mission School was provided, and the accomplishments of one Henry Obookiah, a sometime resident of Tor-ringford and Andover, where he was "instructed by the students of the Theological Seminary," were especially touted. Obookiah had "not only learned reading, writing, and arithmetic, but grammar and geography." However, what was of most importance was his familiarity with "the princi-ples and doctrines of Christian Religion."[26]

The accomplishments of ʻŌpūkahaʻia were set in contrast to the linger-ing heathen beliefs of his friend Thomas Hopoo (Hopu). Hopu had left Hawaiʻi at the age of fourteen and served as a cabin boy aboard the ship that brought ʻŌpūkahaʻia to New Haven. In a well-circulated story, Hopu fell overboard and was saved when a fellow sailor tossed a hen coop over-board for him to grasp. Struggling fiercely to catch up to the ship, Hopu promised his akua (gods)[27] that if his life were spared he would give them his most prized possession: a pea jacket that the captain had given him. When the ship turned around and he was plucked from the open sea still clutching the hen coop, Hopu had resolved to treat the pea jacket with the utmost care and respect. He never wore it again for the duration of the voyage, or allowed others to touch it, and it was "not until he became fully convinced" that his akua were "no God(s)" that he felt he could release himself from his vow. Even years after he had turned to the Lord, Hopu's past history of heathen devotion could still be used as a prod to the strug-gling Christian. "This instance of native conscientiousness in a heathen boy discharging his vow to an imaginary god, ought to raise a blush on the cheek of many a Christian, for his own neglect of paying his vows to the 'Lord that bought him.'"[28] The carefully chosen words of this admonish-ment might also inspire a guilt-ridden Christian to pay out a decent dona-tion. While the article lauded the accomplishments of the older Obookiah, who had "already begun a translation of a part of the New Testament into the language of Owhyhee,"[29] Hopu's story froze him in time as a fourteen-year-old lately arrived in the country. The distance between Obookiah and Hopu was now a pocket example of the progress that a heathen could make if subjected to the correct program of Christianization and civilization.

The woman from Savannah was persuaded by the poignancy of these stories; heathens could be educated, and they could use this education to carry the Christian message to the Sandwich Islands. In the fall of 1815, she visited her friends in New Haven and was transfixed by the story of these men, "particularly as the future missionaries of Owhyhee." On her return home, she enlisted the assistance of her female friends and collected $335, to be "given for the purpose of educating Henry, Thomas, and William, as missionaries to Owhyhee."[30] The authors of the essay urged readers to consider that "this example of Christian liberality is highly honourable to the citizens of Savannah; and ought to be known, that others may *go and do likewise.*"[31]

Answering the call, the ladies of Charleston, South Carolina, also "imitated" the example of their female counterparts from Savannah by contributing their own "liberal donation" to the effort of educating these men.[32] Whether through word of mouth, the press, or through networks of missionary societies, how the ladies from South Carolina got wind of the charity of the Georgia ladies may never be revealed. However, what is clear is that the mission's supporters held these men up as examples of their own work, a work that all American citizens should interest themselves in. "Honourable Munificence" connected the capacity of American women to do their Christian duty for young Hawaiian men currently residing in their country in the hopes that by giving monetary support to these prospective missionaries, Americans would both transform their own souls and those of an entire foreign people.[33]

For two years, until the death of Henry ʻŌpūkahaʻia, the activities of the Hawaiians were promoted by the American Board in order to raise the public's interest and concern for foreign missions. Stories of the educational progress of the men of Owhyhee, their internal struggles, and their speeches, prayers, and letters were produced and reproduced by the ABCFM and its supporters in both the secular and religious press. These stories were generated as a means to create a supportive public interested in the cause of missions. The ability of the men to stand before congregations and discourse on religion, to lead a prayer, and to speak before assemblies in both Hawaiian and English provided substantial, physical proof that heathens could be educated and Christianized. Stories of these men were generated in the hopes that Americans would be moved to donate money and materials to the foreign mission school and the mission to the Sandwich Islands. Americans needed to be converted to the idea through tangible examples and proof.

Christian benevolence paid for the education that hastened their conversions. The mission published stories to convince the public that once the transformation was initiated, through their financial intervention, the Hawaiian men would take it upon themselves to convert the other Hawaiians in their midst. Rev. William S. Vaill, who had taken in at least three Hawaiian students as boarders at his home in 1815, wrote to the editor of the *Religious Intelligencer* about Thomas Hopu's visit to John Honoliʻi, his benighted countryman who had arrived in the country in December 1815. Hopu reportedly came sixty miles on foot to visit Honoliʻi, who was at Rev. Vaill's home in North Guilford, Connecticut. Honoliʻi was joining William Kanui, who was already engaged as Vaill's pupil. Honoliʻi was "buried in all the senseless ignorance of a devotee to a *block* of *wood*,"[34] wrote Rev. Vaill. "Whatever ideas the more enlightened of his countrymen may have of God, or of the soul of man," Honoliʻi "had none." Honoliʻi's ignorance was placed in stark contrast to the newly acquired enlightenment of ʻŌpūka-haʻia and Hopu. "He could mutter over his unmeaning prayers; and previous to leaving his native place, had sacrificed a hog, as a preparatory step to becoming a priest in their filthy temples."[35] These scenes were constructed to shock the American public, to stoke their curiosity about the Hawaiian men, and to engage their imaginations by allowing individuals to place themselves as witnesses to such dreaded scenes. Relief at finding oneself, after these brief "imagination vacations," within the safety of the home or church, reinforced the distance between the civilized self and heathen Others. But while the imagination and actual encounter with Hawaiian men reinforced the distance between Owhyhees and Americans, plays like the *Pantomime of Captain Cook* offered audiences a secure space in which to experience the exotic, extending the viewer's comfort zone and slowly transforming the unknown exotic into the *familiar*. Thus imagination labored under a double process: one of confirming distance, while another supplied a comforting sense of superiority and condescension that grew out of the conviction of authentic *knowledge* of the savage. Cultivating the public's desire for authentic natives—as the theaters, waxworks, and museums promised—contributed to a cultivated and progressive knowing that inspired a spirit of generous giving that would in turn support the "spirit of missions."[36]

The difference between "heathen" beliefs and logic and those of the civilized ministers was exemplified in the discussion between Rev. Vaill and Honoliʻi about where the soul went after death. When asked by Rev. Vaill where he thought his dead mother had gone, Honoliʻi "pointed to the earth, and said, 'there.'" When asked if he thought she had gone to heaven, Honoliʻi shook his head and replied, "No heaven, Owhyhee."[37]

Conversion was supposed to be a painful experience for all Christians as the renunciation of one's past ignorance and sin for new birth. But cross-cultural conversion was painful for other reasons, as it was frequently impeded and by turns spurred on by the conviction of the American missionaries that they were possessed of Christian cultural superiority. Rev. Vaill had never been to the Sandwich Islands, nor was he ever likely to make the long voyage. Instead, he crafted a Hawaiian imaginary out of what he knew to be common characteristics of idolatrous heathens throughout the ages. Honoli'i was taught a bit about God and came to see, according to Rev. Vaill, "that our religion was better than theirs." One day, Honoli'i described Hawaiian "idols" as having hands and feet in a conversation with the minister. "I said, your God has hands, but he no *work*. He replied, with a smile of contempt, *No*. Your God has eyes; but he no see. He replied again, shaking his head in disdain, *No*."[38] "Communication" between Rev. Vaill and Honoli'i lay in Vaill's assumptions about what Honoli'i meant when he gestured, smiled, shook his head—in perhaps Vaill's broken knowledge of Hawaiian language. To the reading audience, however, who would not pick up on Vaill's inadequate knowledge of Hawaiian, it was his staged pidgin English that spoke volumes. The responsibility (*kuleana*) lay upon Kanui, a Hawaiian man better skilled at English, to be the translator and conveyor of meaning between the minister and his new charge. And yet, in all the accounts provided by missionary writers and the mission board themselves, there is no question about the missionaries' ability to authoritatively interpret the words, meanings, gestures—the hearts of Hawaiians—for a benevolent Christian public.

Hopu's approach to instruction was shown to be less painful, and yielded more progress: "He [Hopu] labored and prayed in their own tongue, and observed, that if his brethren had taught him in this way, he might have found Christ in one day."[39] The alienation of Hopu's individual soul from other Christians was made more acute because the words of God could not be expressed to him in a familiar tongue. Hawaiians far from home also found solace in each other's presence and shared memories from home as they lived a temporary life in the diaspora. Language may have facilitated bouts of homecoming reminiscence. Of those Hawaiians that were in New England, Hopu, 'Ōpūkaha'ia, and especially Honoli'i, were noted to have retained their native language.[40] Rev. Vaill hoped to persuade potential donors that the best thing for the conversion of Hawaiians would be to educate more of them and place them in the mission field. Why wouldn't this work in the Sandwich Islands? The experiment was already working in North Guilford.

George Prince Tamoree (Kaumuali‘i)

"I have the pleasure seen [sic] the young prince, at Charlestown," wrote Benjamin Carhoooa (Kalua), a Hawaiian man living in Boston, to Henry ‘Ōpūkaha‘ia on May 30, 1816. As vast as the land occupied by Americans was in 1816, Hawaiian men who arrived in the fledgling nation were possessed of an uncanny ability to find one another. Working and living far from home, Hawaiian men went to great lengths to keep in contact once they had become acquainted. The task of finding other displaced countrymen would have been aided by the newspapers, which carried information regarding the arrival of Hawaiian youth in the country on particular ships arriving at specific ports. Some of these men were passably literate and wrote to one another, sharing news from their area. "The Prince," Kalua wrote, was working in the purser's office at the Boston Navy Yard in Charlestown. He had forgotten how to speak Hawaiian, and he said that his father was the king of Attoi (Kaua‘i). When asked his father's name, the young man's reply to Kalua was "Tamaahmaah."[41] Of course, Kamehameha was not the ancestral ruling chief of Kaua‘i; indeed, he had been the opponent of this young Hawaiian man's father. Kamehameha was certainly not this young man's father, but since "the Prince" had been in America since he was about six years of age, it was understandable that his memories of home and family were blurred by the years he had spent in America and at sea.

Perhaps it was Kalua's letter that alerted the ABCFM to the presence of a Hawaiian of "royal" lineage living nearby in Charlestown. Four months later, the ABCFM held their seventh annual meeting in Hartford, Connecticut, where the petition to establish the school for heathen youth was presented, and the subject of educating the Sandwich Islands men, including the newly discovered "son of a king in one of the islands," was enthusiastically discussed.[42] Soon all of America would learn about Prince Tamoree (Kaumuali‘i), heir of the king of Atowy (Kaua‘i). The board had taken steps to get Kaumuali‘i discharged from the US Navy so that "he may be placed under advantage similar to those which his four countrymen enjoy."[43]

The school which Prince Kaumuali‘i, Henry ‘Ōpūkaha‘ia, and the other students would call "home" was settled in the town of Cornwall, Litchfield County, Connecticut. While revivals in religion led to the creation of the ABCFM in Boston, several towns in Litchfield exercised their religious fervor by supporting the Hawaiians and then petitioning the board for the education of heathen youth in America. The Cornwall Foreign Mission School was built on land good for farming. Farmers grew primarily wheat, but also raised oats, rye, and hay. Butter, and especially cheese, was manufactured for export, as well as beef, pork, and wool.

While hardworking, the people of Cornwall were also generous, supplying a forty-by-twenty-foot building for the school. Thirteen acres of woodland were also provided by the town, one part within a half mile of the school, and the rest within a mile's walking distance. The townspeople gave generously for the cause, subscribing in money and clothing "a considerable sum" of approximately "eleven to thirteen hundred dollars."[44]

The public's imagination had been ensnared by stories of the Hawaiian youth, more so than for the mission spirit in general. Hoping to capitalize on their newest charge, the ABCFM's writers emphasized Kaumuali'i's royal connections and his service in the navy on behalf of Americans. With these stories, the ABCFM inaugurated another phase of their promotion of the Hawaiian men for the Foreign Mission School. The mission also solidified their claim upon the Sandwich Islands as an American mission field. The ABCFM began to promote stories about Kaumuali'i that appeared first in religious newspapers and quickly spread to the secular press. Numerous newspaper notices about the life of Kaumuali'i were published from September 1816 through April 1817, appearing in newspapers in Massachusetts, Connecticut, New York, New Jersey, Washington, DC, Maryland, and Virginia. Two Philadelphia-based German-language newspapers also republished articles that had already appeared previously in English-language newspapers.

From the first, notices about Kaumuali'i were engineered to persuade the Christian public to be more liberal with their donations by publishing them alongside notices of the names of those who had already donated to the cause. Kaumuali'i's letter to a female benefactor, dated October 1, 1816, accomplished both these aims. The letter also revealed much about the lives of the young Hawaiian students in America and gave some glimpse into how the young "prince" related to home. Far from embodying the exemplary kinds of reports the American Board produced about the accomplished 'Ōpūkaha'ia, George's letter, published on October 29, 1816, in the *Boston Recorder*, appeared "not from any particular merit there is in it; but as the first essay of a child in knowledge."[45] By placing before the public the written production of their royal pupil, the ABCFM writers challenged readers to "judge for themselves, whether their charities bestowed on these interesting young men, will be lost or not."[46]

The young Kaumuali'i thanked his benefactor and related his progress in his studies with Rev. Vaill. Learning also occurred outside the confines of missionary prescribed subjects. For example, George wrote about living with John Honoli'i, who was teaching him how to speak Hawaiian, while George taught Honoli'i some English. The younger Kaumuali'i did not forget that education was the reason his father sent him to America, although it seems strange to think of the young "prince" as just having embarked on an educational path, considering the number of years he had spent in America and in the naval service abroad. Although he left home at a young age, Kaumuali'i remembered his father's imperative that he should acquire a good education, though opportunities had since arisen for him to return home. "I think it better for me and for my father to stay here and receive a good education than to go back in the situation I was going in," he wrote to his patron.[47] Reflecting on his island home at so far a distance probably made thinking in Christian terms of this life and "the next" readily accessible. The distance from God, as well as from home and family, weighed heavily upon the Hawaiian men, as they considered their own aspirations and kuleana they would bear when they finally returned home as part of the American mission. "I hope I shall be a benefit to my father if I should ever return. I hope it will be provided so that I may return again, but I must seek after God. He will help me through this world. I hope I may be prepared for another."[48]

No other symbol of the divide between this world, "America," and another, "Hawai'i," was so palpable as that which arose with the question of what Kaumuali'i should be called, now that he had been "called" to the mission. "Mr. Vaill has put an addition to my name, it is George Prince Kummooree that is my father's name, so I thought it would be proper enough. Obookiah thought it would be better for me to have the name of my father Kummooree and we thought if ever I should return back again it would be better for me to have my father's than to have an English name."[49] Renaming was a practice that missions frequently engaged in with their native converts. Giving a person a new name stripped them of their past associations and their familial contexts, but it also afforded missionary benefactors power over the newly named soul by dint of a name that was easily pronounced by them—and not necessarily easily pronounced by the one who was so named.[50] Mr. Vaill, Kaumuali'i's teacher, sought to improve on a name that struck New England tongues dumb ("Kummoorree" or "Tamoree") through the addition of "George" and "Prince." But while Mr.

Vaill made his additions, Henry ʻŌpūkahaʻia, in conversation with Kaumualiʻi, reminded him about the importance of keeping close ties of identification with one's aliʻi lineage. Besides learning how to speak Hawaiian from the other men, Kaumualiʻi must have spent many hours listening to them describe Hawaiʻi to him and the expectations that would be placed upon him as the returning son of the aliʻi of Kauaʻi.

News of Kaumualiʻi's father also appeared in the papers at the same time. The *Boston Recorder* published an account by Captain Edes, who had recently arrived in Boston from a visit to the Pacific. While at "Atooi" (Kauaʻi), Kaumualiʻi asked Captain Edes if he had any news of his son. Unfortunately, the captain had no information to give to the concerned chief. However, Edes was able to relate an "anecdote" about the aliʻi's treatment of Captain Ebbets that made it into the pages of the *Boston Recorder*. Ebbets, of the ship *Enterprise* of New York, was at Kauaʻi in February 1815 and had lost all but one of his anchors in a "violent gale." The ship had been spared only by the intervention of "King Tamoree," who sent a boat "at the height of the gale" to supply Ebbets with a large anchor that enabled the ship to withstand the storm.[51]

The story might have simply made the circuit between captains and sailors of ships in the China trade (through word of mouth, good news passed between ships about friendly chiefs and safe ports of call), but this story had gotten into the ears of someone at the ABCFM and was then published and mobilized in service of the mission. Occurrences oceans away were relevant to those at home, argued the writer, because "an American ship, and the lives of American seamen have thus been preserved by the humane exertions of King Tamoree. Let every American remember that Tamoree has a son in this country, that for several years past he has been enduring all the hardships attendant upon a life of a common sailor on board our frigates; that he fought in several of our battles during the late war, and was badly wounded."[52] Those unfamiliar with the recent developments of the mission were then told that Kaumualiʻi was under the "protection" of the ABCFM. Americans were called upon to do their duty by assisting a patriot, to honor the desire of a noble father, as well as the years lost to the wandering prince, who had been searching for an education in his adopted home in America for years. "We trust that when our countrymen are called upon to contribute for the education of Heathen Youth, these facts will not be forgotten."[53]

The mission plan was twofold: persuade the American public of the importance of supporting the school for heathen youth in America, and persuade them that these youth were indispensable to the opening of a mission in the Sandwich Islands. That there were so many men from Hawai'i being taught at the Connecticut Foreign Mission School was a seeming sign of Providence that an American mission belonged in Hawai'i. The American mission had successfully produced Kaumuali'i as an object of desire for public consumption, much like the curiosities and panto-mimes displayed and performed on both sides of the Atlantic. This production enabled their quite successful fund-raising efforts to build their school. But Kaumuali'i, especially, offered the ABCFM an opportunity to light New England imaginary fires with the possibility of funding this young, now-Christian chief's triumphant return home to Hawai'i as a bringer of new values and new leadership. The envisioned tableau of reuniting a chiefly son with his chiefly father, the king who had had enough foresight to send his son away for schooling, supplied another strong reason for the ABCFM's strenuous effort to go to the Hawaiian Islands. "How can we better manifest our gratitude to the father, than by restoring to him under such circumstances his long lost son?" they wrote. [54] It would be in the ABCFM's best interest to oversee Kaumuali'i's education in order to reap the benefits of returning him home.

In the ensuing months, biographical notices about the prince's astonishing years adrift at sea and in America would be published, along with speculation that Kaumuali'i may "at some future day, be King of Atooi, if not all the Sandwich Islands."[55] Letters the young man had written to the father he had not seen in over a decade and a half were also published. In these letters, he described to his father (and to a public privy to these letters through publication) what had transpired since Kaumuali'i's father had turned him over to the care of Captain James Rowan of the *Hazard*.

Considering that Kaumuali'i was "royalty," the tale that was told about his hard usage at the hands of Captain Rowan and Captain Samuel Cotting was tragic. Rowan, according to the young man, had spent the property Kaumuali'i's father had provided for his son's education. Kaumuali'i was then given into the care of his preceptor, Captain Samuel Cotting, whose slide into poverty left him unable to care for the youth.[56] Like some young American males at the time, Kaumuali'i was forced by poor financial circumstances to move around a lot and had to "shirk for himself." In his letter to his father dated October 19, 1816, Kaumuali'i provides a lengthy description of his travels around the world, the battles he fought, and the scars gained in war. "I hope I shall be a benefit to you," he wrote, echoing the phrase that had appeared in his previous letter to a charitable lady.[57]

Reading the very brief letters of Kaumuali'i, however, one is struck by other possibilities of meaning that were foreclosed by the mission's narrow characterization of the lives of these Hawaiian men as symbols for the progress of Christian reform and salvation. George Prince Kaumuali'i had been away from home for so long, he no longer remembered his native language and had to be retaught how to speak it. Separated from his family, he had lived a life of poverty and of service, adventure, and hard labor in the US Navy. He had adopted a new name, "George Prince," a mark that had translated him in appreciable linguistic terms for Americans as both indicative of title ("Prince") and as civilized and anglicized ("George"), the would-be king who was on his way to becoming a successful product of a missionary education. For most of his life, Kaumuali'i, the chief's son, had worked at many things. As a subject crafted to promote the heathen school, however, his life had been reduced to the role he could play for other people's aspirations—a character in another people's history that was profoundly uninterested in his own.

The prince's chiefly father was not immune to the narrative power of the mission press to shape character. Kaumuali'i, the elder chief, was lauded before American audiences in newspaper notices as a "generous, noble-minded man"[58] who could not, based on his treatment of Captain Ebbets, "be prevailed upon to accept of any thing without returning an equivalent." The ali'i Kaumuali'i was then set in contrast to Tamaamaah (Kamehameha), whom missionary writers painted as "an artful sagacious man and extremely avaricious."[59] Directly contradicting early reports that were published in the secular press, which praised Kamehameha's commercial prowess and civilized ways for employing English and American boat and sail makers and sending his own shipments of Hawaiian sandalwood to Chinese markets, the mission cast Kamehameha as a heathen whose ideas of exchange were not based upon any shared sense of equivalence, reciprocity, or care for his people, the maka'āinana. Instead, he could hardly practice restraint, because he "wanted every thing he sees."[60] Thus Kamehameha, the supposed conqueror and unifier of the Hawaiian Islands, was, according to missionary writers, a "usurper," an amoral businessman, and a poor Christian. By contrast, Kaumuali'i became in this mission narrative "the rightful sovereign of the Sandwich Islands," a hope for reform and Christian correction of Hawaiian society.[61] If Kamehameha was a "usurper," and Kaumuali'i the rightful sovereign of the islands, then, the mission surmised, "it appears not improbable that George, may, at some future day, be King of Atooi [Kaua'i], if not all the Sandwich Islands."[62] If the mission writers were correct about the young Kaumuali'i's future as ruler of all the islands, they sought to position themselves in a very important place as the restorers of the true "King" to his "Kingdom."

There were some facts, of course, that were correct in the account. Kamehameha had been unsuccessful in his attempts to invade Kaua'i. His fleet of canoes had been first repelled by storm; a second attack was put down when a fatal illness decimated his forces waiting for a good tide on the shores of O'ahu facing Kaua'i. Kaumuali'i, in order to preserve his reign, ceded the lands, his men, and munitions to Kamehameha. This much was true, but the way in which these stories were framed and constructed in order to meet the mission's needs twisted the narrative to their ends.

In its push to raise funds for the heathen school, and claiming the Sandwich Islands as its American foothold in the Pacific, the ABCFM set the power of the printing press in motion, placing news of Hawai'i in American hands long before any missionaries set foot in Hawai'i. Hawaiian history, politics, genealogies, and social relations, the very names and characters of people, were all available for fabrication. However inaccurate, these missionary stories were republished over and over again, and they were disseminated through newspapers to readers in far-flung corners and in important political and commercial centers of the American republic. History was a thing that could be crafted and honed as an instrument of the mission, used to stoke the already present desire of an American public for more news of the exotic, for new objects of curiosity. Desire for profits and goods had already impelled American ships to go east for the new nation. Soon, Americans would send other ships after a harvest of souls.

The mission's stories about the young Kaumuali'i's rise from poverty to piety did not go unquestioned. One astute reader, "T," sent a letter questioning Kaumuali'i's authorship of a letter that had been published. While not going so far as to accuse the mission of simple forgery, "T" (perhaps for "Truth"?) had noted that: "On perusing the production, I was a little surprised to find identified in it parts of several letters written in 1811, by the late Harriet Newell, (then Harriet Atwood) and printed in the Memoirs of the life of that amiable and truly pious woman."[63] If that was not enough of an observation, "T" also noted for those who chose to compare both texts themselves, "the different paragraphs of it, with but slight variation, may be found by reference to pages 31, 107, 75 and 123 of the fourth edition of the above work."[64] The reading public could be scrupulous, as is evidenced by T's close reading of the published texts about Kaumualiʻi. As a letter writer himself, T posed a few questions to his fellow citizens, and in his carefully worded, slippery prose, he intimated and accused the author of fabrication of the letter and of self. "With what design these have now assumed their present form, and novel pretentions [sic], and whether the plagiarism be chargable [sic] to Prince Tamoree, or his kind Connecticut friend, I leave the curious to conjecture, and the better information of that Correspondent to settle."[65] The mission, he suggested, had "a design," and had designed the present form of the letter. It had also crafted the character of the prince, who, caught in pretense, while asserting truth, was a pretender. These pretenses were "novel" in the sense of being completely brand new—that is, "fake"—while also being touted as the "news." But in the end, these novels, or narratives, quite simply belonged to the realm of fable, of fabrication, and of fiction.

Another writer who took the mission and George Prince to task for forging letters and for lying was Captain Samuel Cotting, George's former benefactor, who defended his own character and that of Captain James Rowan against Kaumualiʻi's published letters to his father (December 1816). Captain Cotting's letter to the editor of the *Massachusetts Spy or Worcester Gazette* argued that the prince could not have remembered any details of the transaction between his father and Captain Rowan, let alone accuse Captain Rowan of misspending funds, having been placed on board the ship at the age of four.[66] By the time Cotting had met the boy, when he was placed in his subscription school in Worcester, Kaumualiʻi was six years old, "having been two years on the water."[67] When they met, Cotting said, the boy could barely speak any English and retained nothing of his native language. As further proof, the former mate of the *Hazard*, a Captain Davis, also attested to the fact that Captain Rowan had not received any money for the boy's support, calling this claim in Kaumualiʻi's letter "a vulgar and idle tale."[68]

Cotting insisted that Kaumualiʻi's education and development was due to his and Captain Rowan's care and educational work. He wrote, "It is not true that George was 'very much neglected' by Capt. Rowan." Instead, according to Cotting, the death of Rowan's wife made him unable to care

for the boy. Cotting boldly took credit on behalf of himself and Captain
Rowan for Kaumuali'i's "plain legible hand" and his "specimen of composition."[69] These were, he noted, a product of the public schools in which they
enrolled him. Cotting obviously felt wounded by the published accounts
and wrote ironically, "His [Kaumuali'i's] friends in this quarter will be
pleased to hear that he has retained those virtuous habits and principles in
which he has been instructed in various families where he has been placed."
While Kaumuali'i's circumstances had admittedly "exited considerable
publick and individual attention," Cotting regretted that "his new friends
could have encouraged and aided him" in writing a letter that was "so
unfounded in many of its statements, and devoid of gratitude for a single
favor received during ten years of residence among a Christian people."[70]
Cotting then proceeded to bring to the public's attention all of the expenses
for education, physicians, and medicine he had incurred over the years of
caring for the prince. Cotting had even attempted to petition the Massachusetts state legislature in the spring of 1810 to take Kaumuali'i under their
patronage, a petition that had cost his friends some money to put together,
and which was wholly ignored.[71]

In addition to seeking redress for the public tarnishing of his reputation,
what Cotting's letter highlights is the reproduction of personal history as a
biased and self-interested narrative activity, linked strongly in the case of
these young Hawaiians with financial stakes. Writing is perhaps the most
powerful tool that the ABCFM deployed in its subsequent efforts to Christianize Hawaiians in the Sandwich Islands and heathens around the world,
but the written word could be both the instrument of salvation and a powerful tool used to manipulate, to tug at the heart and purse strings of the
readers of Christian journals and secular newspapers. In the long run, it
may have been Captain Cotting's reputation that suffered, as Kaumuali'i's
letters were more widely published than Cotting's single letter to the editor
that appeared in a handful of newspapers. Readers up and down the United
States found it hard to dispute the authority of an emerging mission press.

The Death of Henry 'Ōpūkaha'ia (and What It Gave Birth To)

"I shall never see Hawai'i again," Henry 'Ōpūkaha'ia said mournfully as
he turned to one of his Hawaiian friends on his deathbed the day before he
died. On the day of his death, February 17, 1818, barely able to speak, he

asked to see his fellow Hawaiian students. They filed into the room, taking seats around his bed, and he spoke with them ma ka 'ōlelo Hawai'i (in the Hawaiian language). In this intimate conversation in their own language, 'Ōpūkaha'ia reminded them of their "obligations to Christian friends who had done so much for them."[72] He continued, "In this country, you have neither father nor mother to take care of you, but you must make God your friend and you need not fear."[73] Though the particulars and hushed tones of this private conversation have been lost, what it must have meant for five Hawaiian men suffering the pinching ('iniki) cold of a New England winter to talk about family, obligation, and home when all were so far removed, and to have the elegant voice doing the speaking silenced forever before them, one can only imagine.

'Ōpūkaha'ia and Hopu had expected to leave New England as they had arrived—together on the same ship. When it became apparent that 'Ōpūkaha'ia would die of typhoid, Hopu admonished him, saying, "You will not go with me to Hawai'i now, and I cannot go alone." Henry put his hand before his eyes as if in prayer and "both burst into tears."[74] That there was anxiety and expectation among these Hawaiian men about returning home after a long absence seems to be lost on these writers, for all the scenes of grief and goodbye were fixed and interpreted in terms of the progress of the gospel, the providential plan of God for the American churches and people, and the mission's plans for the minds and souls of Hawaiians who remained as yet persons unfamiliar and unseen.

A little over two weeks after 'Ōpūkaha'ia's death, an obituary that was published in several newspapers concluded by soliciting information from any individuals who were acquainted with any important facts of 'Ōpūkaha'ia's life which had "never before been published."[75] It also asked that those who have "in their possession any interesting letters of his" to communicate them to Mr. Edwin W. Dwight, principal of the Foreign Mission School at Cornwall.[76] These bits of biography and proof of 'Ōpūkaha'ia's education were collected and published to raise funds for the future mission to the Sandwich Islands.

Reports of 'Ōpūkaha'ia's death, his deathbed profession of enduring faith in God, and the reward to which he was about to go, were published again and again in American newspapers. Americans in places as remote from one another as Middlebury, Vermont, and Chillicothe, Ohio, would read about the life and death of this interesting man. Although the hopes of the Christian public respecting this youth were "blasted" by his untimely death, the scene of his death became an instrument in the financial revitalization of the Foreign Mission School. More importantly, ʻŌpūkahaʻia had excited a great American interest "in favour of his country." As one poetess conceived it in her elegy entitled "Obookiah's Grave":

> But thine, Obookiah! Thy cold narrow bed!
> O'er the turf that enwraps it what lostre is shed?
> Tis the glory that beams from the STAR in the East,
> That breaks the deep night of the isles in the West?[77]

The "isles in the West," envisioned as temporarily held in the dark night of heathen ignorance, are, through Obookiah's death as a Christian convert, to be guided out of darkness by his deathbed pronouncements, which urged his countrymen to bring Christianity to the Hawaiian people. The arc of the star rising from the east painted by this poem traces ʻŌpūkahaʻia's exemplary rise from heathen origins to accomplished student and professor of faith, an arc played over and over again in these accounts of his death.

The moving elegy for ʻŌpūkahaʻia highlights the ways that women were especially interested in the lives of these Hawaiian men. A lady from Connecticut wrote a letter to her friend in Boston that was later published in the newspaper. She reported that a week before his death, ʻŌpūkahaʻia sent a note on the Sabbath "beseeching that he might be spared to carry the Gospel to Owhyhee, but that whether he lived or died, God might be glorified."[78] The woman also noted the close tie between Henry and Thomas Hopu, his "bosom companion." ʻŌpūkahaʻia's letters seemed to stimulate a sentimental attraction in female readers of the newspapers, so much so that over and over again letters about the young Hawaiian men poured in to newspaper editors up and down the United States.

Drawing on the public's sentiment and grief and the intense interest ʻŌpūkahaʻia's story generated, the ABCFM attempted to capitalize on this phenomenon in order to increase public financial support for the mission cause. Nine months after ʻŌpūkahaʻia's death, the ABCFM had written and produced *The Memoirs of Henry Obookiah*, available for purchase in December 1818 at the cost of fifty cents. Prospective buyers were assured that the neat, medium-sized octavo volume, which included sketches from his life as well as letters he had written to Christian friends and his fellow Hawaiians, would be "embellished with a handsome LIKENESS of Mr. OBOOKIAH."[79]

Also included in this work was the sermon delivered at his funeral by the distinguished Rev. Lyman Beecher and Mr. Daggett's inaugural address that was given at the opening of the Foreign Mission School.

The Memoirs of Henry Obookiah would inspire a rising generation of Christian youth to foreign missionary service. The vision of Obookiah after death inspired one young American to consider a life as a foreign missionary. Upon visiting the lamented Hawaiian's grave overlooking the Cornwall Foreign Mission School, he penned these words, which were published in the *Christian Watchmen and Baptist Register* and which placed ʻŌpūkahaʻia as the latest addition to an American genealogy of grace,

> Lamented Obookiah! Lo I stand,
> Lonely, in solemn sadness by thy grave . . .
> Let me but tread
> The path of my Saviour sanctified—the path
> Which Brainerd, Mills and Obookiah trod—
> The path of usefulness—then let me die,
> Or on the couch of lingering disease,
> Or by the stake of painful martyrdom,
> Or in some wilderness, with none to close
> My eyes, or watch my dying agony;
> Or in some place of solitude and peace,
> Or in the coral caves of ocean's bed,
> Or let my ashes be the sport of winds;
> Thus shall I strike with thee, lamented youth!
> "The high-toned harp of heaven"—thus shall stand
> Before the throne of glory, where the Lamb
> Beams happiness on all his followers.[80]

Whether they encountered them as performers upon the stage, in the museum, or on the printed page, Americans were becoming well acquainted with images of Hawaiʻi and Hawaiians that they themselves produced. The savage Koah or the civilized Obookiah were two popular images that rose out of America's Hawaiian imaginary. These images and the stories that accompanied them became the foundation of what Americans knew about Hawaiʻi, gradually solidifying into the bedrock of the historiographic record that we have inherited today. As stories and information of Hawaiʻi and Hawaiians were produced, published, and republished again and again for generations, the mission gained ground as the arbiter of all things Hawaiian.

The business of producing Hawaiian subjects—'Ōpūkaha'ia, Hopu, Honoli'i, and Kaumuali'i—was perfected by the American Board of Commissioners for Foreign Missions, contributing to and strengthening to a great degree the reach of the board at home. The stories of Hawaiian men and their progress under the interested largess of the ABCFM inspired the benevolent public to give donations of money and material that funded and sustained the first mission to the Sandwich Islands in 1819.

Lurking outside the safely prepackaged images of these young Hawaiian converts, however, was a vigorous public production of other Hawaiians—Hawaiians back in the islands, Hawaiians of rank and grandeur and importance. New England merchants pursuing enterprise in the China trade found themselves and their ships intimately interacting with ali'i (chiefs and chiefesses) as well as countless maka'āinana (commoners) in their work. And just as the ABCFM developed narratives advantageous to their projects, businessmen dealing in Hawai'i found ways to bring their business's dealings back home through their letters and papers. What emerges in tracing these narratives of Hawai'i and its people is the development of a complex Hawaiian economy that underscores the rapid adaptation of local practices to new trading relations with foreigners, as well as the not-so-skilled efforts of merchants to obtain raw materials for trade and to stoke Hawaiian consumerism through the introduction of credit.

And There Remaineth Yet Much Land to Be Possessed

Many of the missionaries to Hawai'i and other foreign mission fields had been inspired to change the course of their lives and dedicate themselves to a life of foreign mission service after reading 'Ōpūkaha'ia's *Memoir*. On September 28, 1819, before a "much crowded house" in Goshen, Connecticut, the Reverend Heman Humphrey of the Congregational Church at Pittsfield, Massachusetts, stood to deliver the ordination sermon over the bowed heads of Hiram Bingham and Asa Thurston, leaders of the new Sandwich Islands Mission. The first company was composed of fifteen other Americans: five men, their wives, and five children belonging to one family. The missionaries included the taproots of a portable, plantable, yet foreign civilization: two ministers, two teachers, one doctor, a printer, and a

farmer. All church members except the doctor were expected to instruct
Hawaiians in some facet of this civilization while also spreading the gospel.
Four Hawaiian men from the Cornwall Foreign Mission School in Con-
necticut also made the journey home as members of this church: Thomas
Hopu, John Honoli'i, and William Kanui, and George Kaumuali'i, who was
not officially a part of the mission, rounded out the company.

The sermon significantly entitled "The Promised Land" analogized the
new church's journey to those who followed Moses and Joshua. Instead of
peering from the safety of mountains, these Americans were looking out
across the Atlantic toward the promised land of Hawai'i. The sermon
played upon the multiple meanings of a passage from Joshua 13:1: "And
there remaineth yet very much land to be possessed." It expressed convictions frequently espoused within nineteenth-century Euro-American foreign mission circles—that the world belonged to Christians, and it was their
duty to claim it through evangelization.[81]

The passage from Joshua 13:1 is repeated eleven times in thirty-two
pages. The word "possession" appears more than twenty times. This kind
of oral repetition worked the message into the thoughts of its listeners, its
rhythm a prayer, an utterance of sacred scripture calculated to bring about
the achievement of prophetic ends. God had given as inheritance not only
the lands that Protestants had already settled, but also all the lands in the
world inhabited by heathens, by non-Protestants. This was an assumption
American Congregationalists shared with their colleagues in the London
Missionary Society (LMS), and one that helped to fuel the explosive expansion of the foreign mission movement over the next century. Christians
were to be inspired by the phrase, and yet the realization that "much land
remaineth to be possessed" was also a "cutting reproof of their inactivity
and unbelief" as yet.[82]

When written and spoken, these convictions supplied material justifications for the importance and continuation of missionary work. "It was
simply a fact," intoned Rev. Humphrey over the congregation, that large
regions of the earth remained "unsubdued," and that the "ultimate conquest and possession of all the heathen lands is certain."[83] Promised land
operated as a motivating force in scripture, an unknown but hoped-for
place of fruition—a place to strive for, but also a labor that required faith
and demonstrations of faith to achieve. And although "God had promised
to drive out the nations," he did not use his own power, but "he thought
fit to employ his people to effect it."[84]

While the "inheritance" of heathens and their lands was assured, Rev. Humphrey drew upon the church's compendious "knowledge" to describe the degeneracy of heathens across the globe that also warranted the taking of "heathen" lands. Indians living on the American continent were in a "deplorable state of moral degradation. Even within our own limits, the savage still lights his death fires, to apease [sic] the wrath of an idol." Through the work of missionaries, "the effeminate Hindoo and the degraded African will be raised to the dignity of men and of Christians." In the United States, "the wild men of the American forests will be tamed, and all the wilderness will become the heritage of Zion." Hawaiians, "not people within our own limits," would be added to the ever-expanding catalog of heathens targeted by missions.[85] What knowledge the ABCFM had of the Hawaiian variety of "heathen" came from the students in their midst, those trained at the Cornwall Foreign Mission School. The comparison was made by the mission itself, since 'Ōpūkahaʻiaʻs stories of merciless warfare and rigorous training for a "heathen" priesthood reminded New Englanders of nearby Indians.[86] Though knowledge of Hawaiʻi also circulated in journals and sketches from explorations of discovery and exhibits of Hawaiian material objects in newly erected American museums of curiosity and wonder, it is not clear to what extent missionaries drew their ideas about the islands from these other sources of information. It is unlikely that Congregationalists like Bingham had ever seen the popular pantomime the *Death of Captain Cook* as many Americans had in the years between 1796 and 1816, since theaters would not be located in their small hometowns, and their religious discipline required that they abstain from, and even condemn such frivolity.

Rev. Humphrey's "promised land" guaranteed to Christians by God was also the land "waiting to be possessed." The missionaries were re-enacting the actions of Joshua, the inheritor of the law and the conqueror of heathen lands for his wandering people. The redemption of the heathen would deliver *the land promised* through the labor of Christian hands, instruction, and prayers, transforming it into a "promised land," one which would provide sustenance, the metaphoric "milk and honey," ensuring economic prosperity and health for the natives and the settlers, Christian missionaries. Lands like Hawaiʻi were therefore doubly *promised*, doubly spoken into being. The vision of converting heathen nations one at a time also fulfilled the Christian goal of converting the world, extending the reach of Christendom to prepare the Earth for the second coming. The missions' spoken and published sermons, letters, and correspondence would connect the activity of saving the heathen abroad to that of saving the church and its people at home.[87]

While the land was "promised" and "waiting to be possessed" on God's behalf, missionary ideology did not directly sanction dispossession of the soil nor the wresting away of control over Hawaiian lands and power away from Hawaiian leaders. Hawai'i was not the United States, where settlers had been in a long contest with Indians for control of their lands. The instructions to both the first and second companies of missionaries to Hawai'i made a clear distinction between that which was of the world (politics and commerce) and that which was of God. "As for the kingdom, to which it is your felicity to belong, and the interests of which only you are to seek, is not of this world: like Him you will withhold yourselves entirely from all interference and intermeddling with the political affairs and party concerns of the nation of people among whom you reside."[88] It is difficult, however, to apprehend the words that strikingly punctuate Rev. Humphrey's sermon without hearing a colonial intent. The sermon was filled with images of conquest—missionaries were to put on "armor" to be a "soldier of the cross, in the holy war."[89] The work of evangelization included subduing, taming, possessing, and driving out, all sanctioned by God's word. Rev. Humphrey delivered a martial message that also sought to raise American churches from a complacent slumber: "As the nation of Israel was then militant," he preached, "so is the church now."[90] For the Congregational churches at home, the exertions of missionaries in far-off fields assisted with the spread of God's earthly kingdom, a project that would help to prepare their souls and those of heathens for the coming Christian millennium.

For twenty years, missionary labors had progressed only slightly, according to Humphrey, during which time Charity, "robed in light and peace," persuaded the Society isles to "cast their idols to the moles and the bats."[91] An outcome in Hawai'i, he hoped, would involve those assembled before him. Humphrey saw in the sign of the times and in the LMS mission God's hand at work, but he argued that the Sandwich Islands Mission was especially singled out, for he saw "not where the hand of God has been more distinctly visible, even in this age of wonders, than in the events connected with the present enterprise."[92] What was astonishing about this mission was that it had sprung unanticipated from "a savage massacre in a far distant isle. Yet, but for that heart-rending tragedy, Obookiah might never have been heard of by the American Church; might now have been a pagan priest, bowing before an idol, instead of a 'king and a priest unto God,' in his heavenly temple."[93] Humphrey related the story of Obookiah to an audience fully familiar with the tale. The now-mythic origins of the mission were being spoken over the heads of those who would take up the responsibility for leading it. "Led by an unseen hand," Obookiah sought instruction in a "strange land," where he was "awakened, convicted, hopefully converted." And though "all eyes" were "turned upon Obookiah as eminently qualified to carry back the news of a Savior to his benighted countrymen," this was not to pass, as death prevented him fulfilling his great commission. It was because of this that, Humphrey argued, Obookiah "speaks from the grave to the American church in just such a voice as was needed to rouse her energies."

For Humphrey, it helped that Owhyheeans and their islands were accommodating. Hawaiians were reputedly "friendly" as opposed to warlike or bloodthirsty, and the openness of the natives would only facilitate the work of the mission: "the friendly character of the Sandwich Islanders; the progress which they have begun to make in civilization, their ardent desire for further instruction; their high regard for European settlers; the mildness of their climate, the fertility of their soil." And yet, because the church had been negligent in its work, some of the "benighted islanders," themselves impatient for the coming of the gospel, had to "come over to America and earnestly invite her to take immediate possession." In this manner yet again were the actions of Hawaiians interpreted to fulfill the prophecy that "there remaineth much land to be possessed," and that it should be the "American Israel" that could, a generation after independence, afford to "bear her full proportion of the necessary expense of converting the world."[94]

CHAPTER 3

The Isles Shall Wait for His Law:

Planting the American Congregational Mission

Aole ia e pio, aole hoi ia e uhaiia a hookumu
oia i ka pono ma ka honua nei *a e kakali*
no na aina i kona kanawai.

—Isaia 42:4

God has indeed led me in a way that I knew not. He gave me
a rich inheritance of Christian privileges, and made parental
faithfulness and piety the guardians of my childhood and
youth. During the first 21 years of my life while I kept my
father's little flock and tilled his ground, and repaired his
buildings and utensils, etc., I was employed in the delightful
and important business of instructing the rising generation
to which I was occasionally called. I indulged but little hope
that the privileges of a public instruction would ever be
conferred on me. My situation seemed to forbid it, and the
impulse of indefinite motive was not sufficient to surmount
the obstacles. The hope of obtaining a liberal education had
expired and I had concluded to pursue the business of
agriculture in which I then expected soon to be established
in some of the settlements of the west.

—Hiram Bingham, letter of candidacy to the American
Board of Commissioners for Foreign Missions (ABCFM)
to become a missionary to the Sandwich Islands

Hiram Bingham, born on October 30, 1789, was one of thirteen siblings
growing up in the rocky farm country of Bennington, Vermont. Like many

young men in his twenties, Bingham was anxious about making his way in the new American republic. As he was the fifth son in a large farming family, it was hardly possible that he would inherit the family farm, and even more improbable that his family could afford to send him to college. In this application, as in many of the writings he would produce in his lifetime, Hiram wrote himself into being: the narrow escape from a conventional life on the farm he detailed, of "little hope" forbidding of another future, one in which he could scarce "surmount obstacles," his hopes "expired." These scrapes made his application and hope for election all the more liberatory, capable of raising the young man from a dull life and into the important service of spreading the word of God to heathens abroad. For Bingham, the prospect of settlement in the west did not deliver to his mind satisfaction, adventure, or opportunity; rather his life and his education before his application to the mission afford a rare view into the social and religious impulses that impelled a generation of Americans to offer themselves for foreign mission service.

Hiram's application to the mission, like most in this genre, is aspirational—reflecting on the past in relation to a hoped-for future: a mode of consideration and a positionality of being, familiar to Christians working expectantly in preparation for the end time. His heart and cast of mind were conditioned by the suspension of hope and fulfillment as an act of faith. This made him well suited for life as a missionary in the Pacific, a place where even communication by letter over the long sea journey between Hawai'i and New England took six to eight months in one direction, if all went well.

The practice of writing prepared the individual soul for conversion and for mission work. Writing communicated interior processes of transformation of the self and at the same time externalized them in material form, allowing for easy connection and comparison with the community of Christians both present and past. The habit of writing also proved crucial to strengthening the institution of the mission church both at home in America and abroad. Just as the China trade incorporated Hawai'i into a global economy, the mission's rhetorical work produced Hawai'i as part of an emerging Anglo-American cultural, spiritual, and political network abroad. These narrative and discursive ties would strengthen over the course of the century, fixing Hawai'i and Hawaiian people firmly within the sphere of American power, largely as a product of the work of the mission and its writings.

When the *palapala* (reading and writing) was introduced in Hawai'i, it did not supplant the central authoritativeness of speech in Hawaiian social life. Speech, writing, and print were forms that circulated information simultaneously, but during the first two decades of permanent foreign settlement that opened up in the wake of the planting of the American mission (1820–1840), speech held an authoritative place in social interactions among Hawaiians and intracultural and historical engagements. Because of this, we must adopt different methods for close-hearing the archive to supplement our techniques for close-reading it.

In hindsight, the overwhelming success of the Sandwich Islands Mission made it an exemplar of the American foreign mission project. It was paradigm-setting in the achievements that it claimed: a high literacy rate among Hawaiians by 1840, numerous churches and schools established, and most, if not all, of the ali'i of the nation converted. The voluminous records of the mission sent around the world provided proof of God's intervention in the present—while also crafting ready guides that young male and female missionaries turned to for news, validation, and comfort. And yet, the world that the missionaries made was enlivened by the spoken and performed word.

This chapter argues that the Sandwich Island Mission and its encounter with Hawaiians must be read on its own terms, in its own historical context, instead of as the origin of a well-organized colonial settlement that operated as a first wave of American political occupation. We must pay close attention to the mission's theology and the humble beginnings of its leaders. Investigating missionary and Hawaiian constructions of history and cultural interactions, this chapter takes a microhistorical approach to seeing the preparations for and planting of the mission and the activities of its first year. In doing so, I illustrate the disjunctures between Hawaiian and missionary modes of meaning-making. By focusing on Hiram Bingham as a young man preparing for this life of service, I highlight the importance of education, speech, and print to the missionary project. At a historiographic level, this microhistorical approach to the first year of settlement intervenes in the dominant trope of "missionary influence" that has supplanted deeper and historically specific investigations into processes of settler colonialism and native governance. This work on the intersection of New England and Hawai'i in the 1820s is not possible without reading and hearing archives crafted in multiple languages, worlds of words with different epistemes.

Speech fixed in writing and print was experienced simultaneously by missionaries and Hawaiians as material read *and* heard aloud. Given the power placed upon the spoken word in Hawaiian society—in chant, in prayer (words spoken aloud and purposefully brought together in particular phrases generated power), as a mode of keeping history and tradition, in the proclamation of kapu—it is no wonder that Hawaiians sought after the palapala. Palapala was a new technology that could provide Hawaiian ali'i and maka'āinana with another mode of transmission and preservation of that which was prized and powerful *already*: "traditions" fixed through learned (received) speech and performance. For Hawaiians, the message was nothing without the original medium—speech—that imparted power through words.

I Sleep but My Heart Awaketh (Song of Sol. 5:2)

At the close of his Middlebury years in the spring of 1816, twenty-six-year-old Hiram Bingham was still uncertain about his life's course. Rather than take charge of a school and assist in "training up and preparing for usefulness as missionaries some of the youths from the Sandwich Islands," as suggested by his elder brother, the ReverendAmos Bingham, and the Reverend Joseph Harvey of Goshen, Connecticut, Hiram decided in favor of continuing his education at Andover Theological Seminary.

At Andover, Bingham continued his long journey from farm to mission field, employing the language of Congregationalist conversion, the spirit of his age, of awakening.

> I sleep: but my heart awaketh—Just returned from a religious conference of the students in college. Christians were called upon to awaken out of sleep. To cast off the works of darkness, and to put on the armor of light; to arise from the dead. . . . Sinners were spoken of as being dead, in trespass and sin, dead as to any out of holiness, dead as to any exercises of a divine life with which God could be pleased. But by no means as to moral action were they considered dead. But as to their indifference to things eternal, their inattention to the calls of the Gospel, their unconcern with the regard to moral interest, their stupidity respecting their awful danger.[1]

In remembering Bingham as the seasoned missionary writer of what is the most oft-quoted authoritative work on early Hawai'i, *A Residence of*

Twenty-One Years in the Sandwich Islands, scholars have forgotten the young man who was raised on the farm. On Bingham's first visit to Boston in November 1816, he visited the Boston state house and wrote of the view from its heights:

> From this elevation I had a full view of the whole town: of Roxbury, Cambridge, Charlestown and a vast extent of the surrounding country, together with the bay and cape, a more distant view of the harbor, vessels, frigates, and several very important forts . . . the broad ocean rolling its tremendous waves beyond the cape whitened with numerous sails wafting in every direction. This was a scene which I had never before witnessed but which I had long desired to enjoy— this scene was worth a journey from Bennington to Boston on foot. And you may well suppose that I spent an hour diligently in gazing with admiration and delight on the vast variety of interesting objects which on every side presented themselves to my ravished view.[2]

Bingham may have been a provincial citizen of the empire of liberty—a man who waited twenty-six years to set eyes upon the treasured sacred historical places in which the nation was born—yet his mode of expressing his experience marked him as having been schooled well beyond the Bennington farm.

For Bingham, literary exposure would come from reading, writing, and the spoken word in the school, in the church, and among family and friends. Reading the newspaper was encouraged among Bennington's resident farmers, as evinced by an essay that appeared almost simultaneous to Bingham's epiphany at the top of Boston's venerable state house.

> The charms of newspaper reading to the intelligent farmer, who values the instruction of himself and his family . . . furnish abundance for profitable reflection and conversation. Though distant from the metropolis—though secluded from society, he can know all that is necessary to be known of the pomp and bustle of city life. . . . The man who "can't find time" to read one newspaper during the week, must be truly a slave to ignorance or poverty. . . . Our political welfare too essentially depends on a general diffusion of knowledge, and we have so many examples in the old world of an ignorant people being the slaves of superstition and tyranny, that

our young republick should lose no opportunity to establish itself on the only permanent foundation.[3]

That "permanent foundation" would be the diffusion of knowledge concerning current affairs garnered through devoted newspaper reading. Literacy was an important way for a free and young republic to be preserved. While lauding the cultivated practice of reading the news to family, the article notes the importance of preserving newspapers for future generations, especially newspaper articles relating to the revolution, whose pages would provide readers with "the best account" of the political and military struggles of those years. Yesterday's news was tomorrow's history. Bingham's views of the war had been shaped by the vivid stories consumed perhaps from this very newspaper, and his imagination while standing at the statehouse aerie was loosed by the view. "I was in the very cradle of the American Revolution," he scrawled breathlessly, "the immortalized Bunker Hill in view on the north, the strong and extensive fortifications on the east, almost an American Gibraltar, in the movements of the distant sails I could imagine I almost saw the hostile British fleet, which at the commencement of the revolution filled Boston with alarming apprehensions of immediate danger and distress."[4] Bingham was from a large rural farming family, not part of New England's wealthy or divine elites—a first-time tourist in the city on the hill.

Bingham took in the sights of Boston as a new suitor both excited and enamored of the city. The celebrated mall appeared remarkable in its immensity: "6 rods wide and 40 long, having three rows of stately elms the whole length." Harvard University was glimpsed from afar, a "venerable seat of science and literature" but "forbidding and dangerous as one of the strongholds of Unitarianism." The loss of the Harvard Divinity Chair in 1805 by the Congregationalists was one of the reasons that Andover Theological Society was founded. Just to the east of where Bingham stood was Park Street Church, where "Dr. Griffen preaches his celebrated 'Park Street Lectures,' in opposition to some of the Unitarian errors."[5] Although for Bingham the very geography of Boston was stamped by religious division, the façade that struck him as the source of innumerable evils was the theater located east of the church, in the center of town. For Bingham the theater was a "prolific source of idleness, dissipation, profanity, immodesty debauchery and everything that can blacken the character, gratify the corrupt desires and destroy the soul of a carnal minded, thoughtless immortal."[6]

After recounting several shocking details about violence that had recently occurred at theaters in Boston, Richmond, and New Orleans, "the headquarters of American dissipation and public amusement," Bingham went on to describe in calculated detail the threat which the theater posed to people's lives and the lives of unsuspecting youth: "Many lives we know have been destroyed by theater living. Many more, probably by the views which they have propagated, and many souls we have reason to fear have been ruined by frequenting the theater. . . . And are not the other public amusements of the same pernicious character? I fear, I greatly fear for the youth of Bennington."[7]

Vigorous Congregationalists like Bingham were critical of public frivolity in their own homeland and hometowns. The theater, drinking, dancing, gambling, and card playing were all vices that devout Christians were told to avoid, as they detracted from the service of Christ and led to behaviors that destroyed the soul. Given these cultural views, Bingham was unlikely to have been exposed to life in the Sandwich Islands through performances of the pantomime of Captain Cook, which, though rarely played in these years, still graced stages in New York, London, and Boston.[8] These views were the context that shaped Bingham's later approach to reforming the manners and morals of Hawaiians he encountered in the Sandwich Islands.

Bingham saw the world as a contested place. His strident criticism was shaped by his disciplined Congregational upbringing and furthered by his poetic tongue. Hearing aloud while writing clearly shaped Bingham's construction of the world. That world was made up of those who were awakened, those who slumbered, and the living and the dead who must be saved dwelling in America and in heathen lands.

Attention to the daily writings of Bingham's life and preparation for mission undercut the caricature of him as the missionary Abner Hale, made legendary by James Michener's *Hawai'i*. This intervention suggests—along with Hawaiian and missionary writings, including publications that were highlighted in Chapter 1—that we renarrativize what have become the "sacred" origins of the Sandwich Islands mission.[9] Bingham was an outsider to the cosmopolitan port city of Boston, home of the ABCFM's headquarters; he was a provincial citizen of New England who had to be molded by historians of America in Hawai'i into a harbinger of American empire, bearing bitter gifts of civilization and Christianization. Shifting our focus from mythic "origins," from the "discovery" of land and the planting of mission, to the unfolding rhetorical encounter between settler missionaries and Hawaiians, as well as merchants and sailors, reattunes us to the plurality of epistemes that were engaged when people from different places, backgrounds, and histories met and lived in proximity with one another for the first time. Missionaries and merchants, sailors and whalers, while sharing some things in common, also held divergent knowledge systems and modes of perceiving based upon their own experiences and backgrounds. Hawaiians, too, were not all the same in their studied and not-so-studied perceptions of the world.

The Post-Colony, Colony

In the view from New England, Hawaiians lived in the midst of an emergent maritime frontier, connecting New England to the Pacific. But the rhetoric used by the starters of the Sandwich Islands Mission came from colonial seventeenth-century projects to convert New England's Indians. This is not to say that the 1820 mission was an organized attempt at colonizing the islands as new American territory; rather, the phrases and tropes used to entice missionaries and financial supporters to bring the mission to life drew upon references to the long Christian history of evangelizing. ABCFM missionaries looked to early Christian history for models of successful evangelization, "analogizing" their present day project in the North Pacific to those of the first apostles.[10] And they added to those biblical models examples from more proximate sources, taken from a long history of Protestant British evangelizing North American Indians, whose homelands they had settled in the seventeenth century. The rhetorical tropes still worked in the early nineteenth century, only the difference between 1629 and 1819 was that it was now Hawaiians, not Indians, who were making the imagined request to "come over and help us."

Even as the American missionaries looked back to the Bible and their colonial New England histories of evangelizing Indians to construct a meaningful and recognizable present for themselves, Hawaiians in the 1820s looked through their own rich, past histories in order to make sense of their political, social, and spiritual experiences, especially as they entered into global interactions. The Hawaiian proverb "I ka wā ma mua, ka wā ma hope" (the past is made possible by the future) not only provides an oral trace-holder of Hawaiian ideas about the past; it also reveals something about historical practice.[11] The translation only hints at the significance of

knowing the past, which is my interpretation, since "ka wā ma mua" literally means "that which came before." For our purposes, it is important to
emphasize the pedagogies that trained the retentive memories of aural/oral
intellects in each successive generation to retain oral "traditions." This
emphasis on "that which came before" (history) was structured in the form
of multiple oral genres of chants, prayers, genealogies, histories, proverbs,
songs, and also practices which were "ho'opa'a na'au" (made fast in the
guts). These practices were clearly communal and social, family- and place-
based, and undertaken to make a way through crisis or for the sheer pleasure of thinking historically. The proverb also suggests something about the
way Hawaiians perceived time—the possibility of working through the past
and future simultaneously in the present, of the possibilities for prediction
or prophecy, but also the certitude that was provided by these aurally "texted" traditions cannot be underestimated.[12]

It is relatively simple to consider that Hawaiians, too, engaged in forms
of meaning-making and obtained structure for their lives through interpreting their presents through their pasts. Until now, this knowledge has
been theorized through fuzzy structural, "traditional," or cultural categories
without the aid of Hawaiian-language source materials to assist the scholar
in building these layers of context. Understanding the sociopolitical and
historical antecedents to settlement will empower a more finely calibrated
understanding of Hawaiian actions and choices. Familiarity with the oral
literature of Hawaiians—the words spoken, the words remembered in disciplined fashion, and the words written and published—is a requirement
for better histories.[13] If scholars are invested in finding out "what natives
think," they might consider studying "what natives said and wrote."[14]

The Sandwich Islands were a six-month voyage from New England,
whereas the seventeenth-century British colonies were a mere fifty days
away from their mother country of England, the former center that directed
past missionary labors. Writing was important to sustaining the mission
both then and now. The first box of written materials from the Sandwich
Islands Mission arrived in New York on April 10, 1821, and included "more
than 100 letters from the missionaries with a copious journal."[15] The sheer
volume of materials illustrated the importance of the written word to sustaining the project and providing the missionaries in the field with a connection to family and friends at home, and it was also the way that the
mission communicated with the wider Christian public that stretched from
the Pacific to the Atlantic, from the Sandwich Islands to New England and

England. The voyage took five to six months, the letters and journals carried by ships in the sandalwood, fur, and ship trade and on ships in the burgeoning Pacific whaling fleet.

Through the reproduction of daily and weekly written letters and journal entries and monthly reports, along with publications of translations and books about Hawaiians and the Sandwich Islands, the foreign mission would gradually secure its place as the arbiter of knowledge and truth on Hawai'i and Hawaiians in the Anglo-American world. This authority, however, was not assured, and in the early years of settlement, missionaries labored to solidify their position in the islands through relations of service to the ali'i, upon whom their lives and livelihood depended.

The Isles Shall Wait for His Law (Isaiah 42:4)

> Of the company of pilgrims who attend you, it is expected
> a church will be organized. You will carry with you this little
> Vine. You are to plant it in a heathen land. Labor to guard
> it against the blast that witherith, the worm that consumeth,
> and the foxes that spoil the vine.
>   —Perry, "The Charge," 34

On a Friday afternoon, October 15, 1819, in the vestry at Park Street Church in Boston, a little more than two weeks after the ordination, the seven couples and three Hawaiian men were "formed into a church" in a ceremony performed by Rev. Jedidiah Morse and Rev. Samuel Worcester.[16] Later that evening, Rev. Asa Thurston opened the service with prayer before a large congregation, followed by a sermon by Rev. Hiram Bingham. This would be the first time both men would officiate as heads of their own church. The Reverend Doctor Samuel Worcester, corresponding secretary of the ABCFM and Congregational minister of the Tabernacle Church at Salem, Massachusetts, then rose to the pulpit to deliver the formal instructions of the Prudential Committee of the ABCFM to the departing missionaries.[17]

The Congregational mission's view of the Sandwich Islands was communicated in the instructions, though none of its members had ever before sailed to the Pacific. "Your mission is to a *land of darkness, as darkness itself*, and of the shadow of death, without order, and where the light is as darkness."[18] The passages from Job 10:22 compared the missionaries' present surroundings with a harrowing vision of the Sandwich Islands, where they would soon be laborers, toiling there until death, "to be surrounded with idols, and morals, and altars of abomination; and exposed to the impurities, the corruptions, the nameless baleful influences of an untutored nation, walking after their own lusts, and fulfilling the desires of the flesh and of the mind."[19] These words of instruction were published and circulated to congregations in the United States and Europe in order to increase interest and support in missions worldwide. Worcester's words reflected the views of the ABCFM on the state of heathen nations, views that could be generalized from previous missionary experiences among Indians in the United States, and in India, Ceylon, China, and Tahiti, and projected upon the Sandwich Islands. These views were commonly shared between the United States and England. When the men and women of the Sandwich Islands mission imagined Sandwich Island idolaters, they could reach back to the pamphlets and missionary magazines that related sensational tales of wife-burning in India, human sacrifice and lurid sexual practices in Tahiti, and the horrors of the Catholic mass.[20]

In August, a few months before this auspicious day, the Reverend Worcester had published an essay in the newspaper and as a pamphlet calling upon the public to supply material and monetary support for the mission.[21] *Mission to the Sandwich Islands, the Isles Shall Wait for His Law* traded upon the still tender grief of the benevolent public over the premature death of Henry Obookiah on February 17, 1818. The public was asked to give generously in heed to God's call "from the grave, from the celestial mansions of Obookiah."[22] For Worcester and his missionary brethren, Obookiah's voice was strikingly like those of the Indians whom Euro-Americans' forebears, English settlers in Massachusetts, had encountered almost two hundred years before. Enshrined in memory and as part of the seal of the Massachusetts Bay Colony in 1629, the call held special inspiration in the hearts and minds of Worcester's fellow Massachusetts citizens. Then, as in Worcester's time, the English imagined that the Indians, *every one*, had implored them to "come over and help us."[23] Conversion of the Indians of Massachusetts was a mission that the Puritans earnestly undertook. Saving the Indians from themselves was also a way to ensure that Indians would be good neighbors for the new colonists, the Puritan architects of the City on the Hill.

While missionary access to this new mission field was made possible by merchant ships, the US government was not interested in making colonies in the wake of its newfound independence. US treaty acquisitions through 1820 were sizable, and people living within its ever-shifting borders were daily encroaching upon Indian lands. The United States did not need the sparse land base of the Hawaiian Islands to govern, especially without a standing navy in the Pacific Ocean. Hawai'i's main contribution to the United States was as a rest and reprovisioning station for American merchant ships. In 1819, merchant ships that transported missionary correspondence, allied with the power of print in the new republic, made it possible for knowledge of remote peoples and places like the Sandwich Islands to be generated in the Pacific and shared with a domestic US audience six months later. The exploits of missionaries at home and in multiple mission fields abroad that appeared side by side on the pages of the monthly *Missionary Herald* told a compelling story about the wide-ranging spiritual and financial undertakings of a newly freed people—Americans.

"The voice of providence announces the accomplishment of prophecy. Hear the word of the Lord, O ye nations, and declare it in the islands far off. . . . The period has arrived. 'The isles wait for his law.'"[24] In this way, Rev. David L. Perry delivered the missionary charge, using the message of Rev. Worcester's popular essay as inspiration. "The Charge" was a verbal directive and commission delivered by one minister but with the weight of the Congregational clergy in support. The Isles Shall Wait for His Law became a rallying theme for the Sandwich Islands that day in Park Street Church, a motto focusing the mission's thoughts, purpose, and action and one to which the missionaries and their supporters would consistently return to for justification—as though it were a guiding prophecy of things to come.

In "The Charge," Hawaiians were cast as savages of yet another new world, this time a "mission field." Hawaiians fit neatly into this schema of prophetic reality, whose repetition in 1819 reinscribed the important call of Indians in 1629 to "come over and help us." Missionaries thought of themselves as being called to convert Hawaiians in the same way that John Eliot and Thomas Mayhew sought to convert the Wampanoag Indians.[25] This reiteration of historical and spiritual connection held deeply meaningful connotations inciting the Sandwich Islands missionaries to righteous action—a life devoted to missions. By going over to help Hawaiians, the missionaries were re-engaging the spirit of their esteemed predecessors. This was a form of ancestor worship, as if by re-enacting the now traditional actions of previous generations, they, too, would save their embattled churches, gain new lands, and, of course, convert heathens in the bargain.

The Reverend Perry's commission supplied a plan of action directed at Hawaiian people. The missionaries' main object was to first "promote the instruction, the conversion, and the edification of the Heathen," by focusing a sufficient portion of their labors devoted to the "instruction of the young." Missionaries were to "gather and organize churches," "administer baptism to proper subjects," admitting to the Lord's Supper "only such as give evidence of faith in Christ."[26]

Along with the Congregational view of the Hawaiian subject of missions, the charge and instructions were the most formal statement of the duties, expectations, and aims given to the missionaries to the Sandwich Islands before embarkation. As Worcester explained in the instructions, the objects of the mission were ambitious, and stated in visionary terms:

> Your views are not to be limited to a low, or a narrow scale; but you are to open your hearts wide, and set your mark high. You are to aim at nothing short of covering those islands with fruitful fields and pleasant dwellings, and schools and churches; of raising up the whole people to an elevated state of Christian civilization; of bringing, or preparing the means of bringing, thousands and millions of the present and succeeding generations to the mansions of eternal blessedness. Why should less be done, or is now in fair prospect, in the Society Islands?[27]

The far-off islands of Hawai'i were to be transformed into the familiar landscape of New England. New Hawaiian institutions would be raised to provide the necessary structures for nurturing the progress of Hawaiian people toward civilization, fields would be planted, and American style homes, schools, and churches would be built. The Americans were interested in their own progress in relation to the work of the English in the London Missionary Society (LMS). Implicit in the vision of raising buildings and institutions was the destruction of Hawaiian beliefs and cultural practice. Worcester's instructions suggested that the missionaries busy themselves in obtaining

> an adequate knowledge of the language of the people; to make them acquainted with letters; to give them the Bible with skill to read it; to turn them from their barbarous courses and habits; to introduce and get into extended operation and influence among them, the arts

and institutions and usages of civilized life and society; above all, to convert them from their idolatries and superstitions and vices, to the living and redeeming God, his truth, his laws, his ways of life, of virtue, and of glory; to effect all this must be the work of an invincible and indefectible spirit of benevolence.[28]

All fourteen missionaries, men and women, Anglo-Americans and Hawaiian assistants, would be dedicated to making this vision a reality. For examples of conduct and practice, they could look to the biographies of martyred missionaries both contemporary and ancient. They could pore over the reports and correspondence of other ABCFM missionaries in Indian country, among Choctaw and Cherokee people, as well as in India, Ceylon, and Palestine for models of how to run the mission. But Hawai'i was singular because it was to be the place that the American Congregational churches claimed in the Pacific. The London Missionary Society, having toiled in Tahiti for almost twenty years, had produced only meager results; it was hoped by the Prudential Committee that not only could the Sandwich Islands church benefit from the LMS example, but also that the efforts of the Americans among Hawaiians would outshine the results of their English brethren among the Tahitians.

Aside from the helping grace of God, missionaries would largely be on their own in the islands.[29] Any kind of request for advice or assistance from the Prudential Committee would take six months to travel via ship to New England, and at least another six months would pass before an answer or material assistance would be received in the islands. Except for the generous assistance of American merchants and agents and transient ship captains, the mission would have to depend exclusively upon the ali'i for their support.

On the morning of October 16, Thomas Hopu addressed the somber audience that crowded Boston's Park Street Church. It would be Hopu who would stand in as the replacement for 'Ōpūkaha'ia. Anyone familiar with the story of 'Ōpūkaha'ia's and Hopu's journey to New England would recall that here stood the young man who fell overboard and promised his new peacoat to Akooah (God), if only his life would be spared.[30] The congregation could see for themselves that day just how far an education and exposure to Christianity could carry a heathen: from Hawaiian shores to the pulpit of their venerable Boston church. There before the crowd at Park Street was proof that the mission's aim to raise a nation to civilization and Christianity could be successful, even before it had really begun.

For the readers of the *Boston Recorder*, a Hawaiian man in the pulpit provided "the most affecting spectacle to see, a native of 'Owhyhee' preaching the Gospel to the citizens of Boston." Hopu's extemporaneous address, in which he called upon the assembled crowd to "repent and believe in Jesus Christ," was, according to the newspaper, "striking and solemn." As an example of the progress Hopu had made at the Cornwall Foreign Mission School, his demeanor was reportedly "calm and self-possessed," his delivery marked as "manly and impressive."[31]

However, when Hopu turned to address five of his fellow Hawaiians in their mother tongue, his manner of speech became charged and his body language, visibly animated. The address in Hawaiian lasted from ten to twelve minutes and was "delivered with much freedom and energy."[32] What communications and emotions passed between Thomas Hopu and the five Hawaiians who had recently arrived in the country on two ships from the Northwest Coast, remains with them and the other Hawaiians of the mission church, William Kanui, John Honoli'i, and George Kaumuali'i, who were also present that morning. While the many utterances, instructions, and sermons of the American missionaries have been recorded exhaustively and preserved painstakingly for future generations, the words of the Hawaiian men about to embark on a journey home after many years of long absence have largely been forgotten. Inarticulate natives, however, are born of the illiteracy of their listeners and interlocutors—in this case, the congregation assembled at Park Street Church, the ministers and representatives of the ABCFM, and the missionaries of the newly formed Sandwich Islands Church, who had yet to learn to speak ma ka 'ōlelo Hawai'i.

The next day, after the close of the Sabbath service, the crowd reassembled at Park Street Church at 4 p.m., joining with the Sandwich Islands Mission church to share in the last sacrament of the Lord's Supper the missionaries were to enjoy in their homeland. The communicants came from venerable congregations all over the state, and the estimated number of persons assembled was between five and six hundred.[33] If the Hawaiians were looking from Park Street Church toward home, the missionaries about to embark on a six-month voyage sought within themselves and their newly formed church the strength to say goodbye to families, friends, country, and the comforts of home and church fellowship, quite likely forever.

The missionaries and their families, friends, and colleagues assembled at the end of Boston's Long Wharf on October 23, 1819, for their final farewell. The Reverend Doctor Worcester offered a prayer, after which Thomas

Hopu gave a short address. The missionaries then lifted their voices together and sang the hymn "When shall we all meet again," after which they took leave of their friends for one final time. At 11 a.m., they stepped into the boats that would convey them to the awaiting *Thaddeus*, commanded by Captain Andrew Blanchard and owned by the merchant company Bryant and Sturgis.[34]

This would be the longest journey any of the missionaries had ever taken. London was a mere fifty days away by sail, while it would take 163 days to arrive in Hawai'i. The only seasoned travelers accompanying them would be the young Hawaiian men, who each had sailed at least one leg of the journey from Hawai'i to New England.

Days aboard ship were structured by morning and evening prayer. Weekly Sabbath observances, when the weather was accommodating, were held on deck with Capt. Blanchard, his officers, and the crew invited to participate. On their sea voyage, the missionaries met with many opportunities to consider the distance that they were daily putting between themselves and their home. Several important days of thanksgiving and prayer were observed on the voyage in imagined fellowship with the families, friends, and brethren they left behind in their "native" land. Though far removed from New England churches, the missionaries observed the monthly concert of prayer that was held the first Monday of every month.

On December 2, 1819, when the *Thaddeus* passed the Tropic of Cancer, the missionaries shared a public day of thanksgiving with their friends in New England. On January 3, they joined "with the rest of the Christian world" in prayer for the "prosperity of Zion and the salvation of the heathen."[35] On that day, the missionaries gathered in their cabin and read letters aloud written and given to them by supporters before their departure. In February, the parting counsel of Brothers Fisk and Parsons was shared. The farewells and letters renewed the energy and commitment of missionaries to their cause, reminding them of their duty to the Christian public whose support made their mission possible. These shared days of observance bound the missionaries closer to their distant home, an imagined community forged through prayer, spoken word, and ritual action.[36]

Each time a ship was sighted on the horizon, or if the *Thaddeus* had the luck to be near enough to "speak" to another ship, the missionaries thought of opportunities for sending letters home. When the *Mary*, ninety days out from Calcutta and bound to Boston, approached the *Thaddeus* on December 15, the members of the mission took up their pens in haste to "finish communications already begun."[37] To everyone's delight, Capt. Smith agreed to carry back to friends and colleagues in New England some thirty letters that included official reports to the Reverend Doctor Worcester, the mission's corresponding secretary. Though life at sea carried them far from New England and their former lives, the missionaries created many opportunities for bridging the temporal, spatial, spiritual, and emotional distances between themselves and home.

The first sighting of land on January 25, 1820, also inspired comparisons between what the missionaries saw before them and what they had left behind. While overjoyed at the sight of the northeastern part of Tierra del Fuego, they lamented that it appeared nothing like home. "How unlike our beloved New England. Here no temples of the living God tilt their lofty spires to heaven, in honor of him who of old laid the foundation of these snow capt mountains, and weighed these rugged hills in his balance. No joyful sound of the church going bell invites the wretched inhabitants of these inhospitable climes to the feast of the gospel. . . . When we think of our highly favored country we are ready to exclaim, 'We shall never look upon its like again!' "[38] These words of loss would be repeated again and again by different members of the mission during its first few years, as it worked to become established in the Sandwich Islands. Distance heightened the members' attachment to home and spurred the missionaries to articulate idealized visions of their native New England, which would be used as a framework to shape the civil and religious church society of Hawaiians they discovered wanting in the Sandwich Islands.

In preparation for their teaching duties among Hawaiians, the missionaries organized their days with classes. Women and children were taught by their husbands in subjects thought to assist them in conducting native schools: a rudimentary knowledge of theology, rhetoric and grammar, geography, and arithmetic. Hawaiian-language instruction was also a top priority, though progress was admittedly slow. In all, the missionaries agreed to devote seven hours out of their day at sea to study.[39]

In the meantime, the missionaries worked to create a community within their church upon the sea. The captain, officers, and crew of the *Thaddeus* were invited to participate in church services, and a singing class was convened for the "improvement of ourselves and the officers" in sacred music.[40] Although several of the crew showed promising signs of introspection that would lead to conversion, other sailors actively opposed the missionaries' efforts to convert one of their number.[41] Farmer Daniel

Chamberlain, who kept a journal on the voyage, wrote about the Sabbath observance of March 26, and the enmity incurred by the mission from First Mate Spears.

> In the afternoon, Mr. Thurston preached on deck text, "Fools make a mock at sin." The discourse was excellently calculated for some of the hearers. The first mate, Mr. Spear is a violent opposer of religion, ridicules sacred things, and treats the name of Jesus with contempt. Mr. Cooper, the second mate, has been more thoughtful for some time past than usual—this circumstance has seemed to excite the enmity of Mr. Spear, who calls Mr. Cooper crazy. We enjoy pleasant Sabbaths here, and good society, we see enough however, to convince us that Satan is not yet bound.[42]

The mission's work would also arouse in future the passionate sentiments of some sailors against the work of evangelism that the missionaries set out to accomplish among the Hawaiian people. Aboard the *Thaddeus*, the Sandwich Islands church was getting a foretaste of the opposition they would face from their fellow Americans and Britons working in the merchant and whaling trades. On the other hand, there were Christian captains and sailors ripe for conversion, who would look with favor upon the mission's efforts in the islands, supplying money, material, and labor to the mission happily and, at times, free of charge.

Making First Contact

"Let us thank God and Take Courage," wrote the American missionaries reflecting upon their first sight of Mouna-Keah's heights swathed in cloud, a blanket of snow spread across its summit in the early morning light of March 30, 1820. After a voyage of 163 days, the mission had its first glimpse of the island of Hawai'i.

As afternoon began to settle into early evening, the temperature on that momentous day dropped, cooled by the soft yet persistent trade winds that propelled ocean swells, gently pushing the ship on unimpeded and in relative silence. The ship's captain and crew began to surmise that some *taboo* (kapu) was in place keeping people and canoes away from the *Thaddeus*. At 4 p.m., a boat was dispatched with two of the Hawaiian missionaries,

Thomas Hopu and John Honoliʻi, and Mr. James Hunnewell, one of the ship's officers, to ascertain the current state of political affairs and to seek out the king's location. When the group returned to the boat three hours later, early darkness had descended, and the shadowy figures emerging onto the ship's deck bore the first intelligence from the island, obtained of near shore fishermen: *Tamahamaha Is Dead;—The Taboos Are Broken;—The Idols Are Burnt;—The Moreeahs Are Destroyed; and the Priesthood Abolished.*[43]

The verbal exclamatory energy of the news was captured in the first wave of newspaper accounts to appear in New England. Various newspapers recapitulated this received speech in all capital or italicized letters, lending a sense of both the startling nature of the information received as well as the intense concentration demanded of listeners/readers by the startling claim. The mission's report continued: "The images of his (*Tamahamaha*) [Kamehameha] are burned; that the men are all *Inoahs* [ʻAi noa] that is, they eat with the women, in all the islands; that one of the chiefs only was killed, in settling the affairs of government; and he for refusing to destroy his gods."[44] On that first day, coasting up the southern extremity of the island, the missionaries spied "the walls of an ancient Moreeah [*Marae*] or heathen temple . . . where the sacrifices of abomination have long been offered to demons."[45] A female missionary expanded on the mission's journal in a letter she wrote home: "To tell you what wonderful tidings saluted **our ears** as we touched upon these pagan shores—how these tidings were confirmed when **our eyes** beheld the fallen Moreahs, and the broken altars and the ashes of the idol gods lying by the bones of human victims who had been offered to them in sacrifice . . . we are witnesses to its [idolatrous priesthood's] total abolition."[46] This account brings to our attention both the affective manner in which news was received through listening and the way in which sight was mobilized to confirm "tidings" that had already been heard. The earliest encounters between foreigners and Hawaiians were marked by these culturally constructed divisions, modes of meaning-making and interpretation, the priorities unequally distributed by different groups upon speech and listening, and the privileging of sight and therefore technologies of literacy—reading and writing—as more authoritative conveyors of information, truth, and knowledge.

Writing was important to the mission as a way to record daily reflections, experiences with the people they interacted with, and their work. These writings would be sent back to the missionary rooms in Boston, where letters, journals, and reports were edited, excerpted, or simply republished in various missionary newspapers and journals like the *Missionary Herald*. Whether these articles were republished in whole or in parts, American newspapers widened the circulation of news on the Sandwich Islands throughout the United States. Although the speech and writings of missionaries come down to us today only in written form, we should not forget the high degree to which daily missionary work in the foreign field strongly depended upon the dissemination of the gospel through the spoken word.

Speech was just as important to the everyday lives of Christians as writing, and foreign missionaries were no exception.[47] The gospel message of the missionaries was dependent upon the performance of the spoken word in sermons delivered in church or outdoors before hundreds, if not thousands, of assembled Hawaiians. Imparting sacred passages to pupils in intimate teaching situations seeded this speech with new resonances for Hawaiians, who still resided in a society where words "could mean life or death."[48] The first Hawaiians to receive this teaching were the aliʻi and their trained advisers, including men from priestly lineages—those whose ears and tongues were trained to ʻaʻapo, or grasp quickly, oral traditions that were taught to them.[49] These men, who were "ready scholars," were the first offered by the aliʻi to serve as Hawaiian-language teachers to the missionaries, and they also produced the first translations of the Gospel that were undertaken by the mid-1820s.[50]

Speech was still the medium that provided the gospel with its cultural authority, weight, and resonance. It is important for the purposes of this history that we attend to our own practices of reading so that the words on the page that were animated through speech can be interpreted through our ears. Historians need to *listen* to published and written sources and attune themselves to the meaning-making systems of not just Hawaiians, but also Euro-Americans, so that we do not miss in which words and whose speech mana (spiritual force) inhered in a culturally diverse world of encounter—where speech *and* writing worked simultaneously to craft or dissemble power and authority.[51]

The missionaries arrived at multiple interpretations of these unforeseen developments, the destruction of "temples of abomination," the death of "Tamahamaha," the "Inoahs" of men. A *day after* the news had time to settle in, the missionaries wrote, "Who ever heard of such a thing as a nation renouncing idolatry before the gospel was sent to them!" and in the very next sentence was the statement that has been codified in mission writings and carried forth by historians and scholars since that moment: "The Lord hath done it and we will praise him."[52]

For the briefest moment in time, the initial impression that Hawaiians might have had their own political motivations for getting rid of the heiau and the ʻai kapu crossed both the missionary mind and the page. In these first moments of *rhetorical* encounter, the missionaries seeking to settle permanently in the islands rejected to some extent what they saw and heard, the evidence of both eye and ear, turning instead to the fortifying words of ordination, instruction, and charge—words that facilitated their movement from their own world to Hawaiʻi. They did this in order to make sense out of what had transpired before their arrival, of an end that had occurred among Hawaiians before they were allowed to enter into their beginning.

Missionary thought progressed along familiarly plowed pathways of knowledge and interpretation. Knowledge filtered through and imbricated within layers of context: the religion that gave their lives structure and meaning, the Early Republic post-colony political status of the States, the merchant fleet that made the connections between New England and the Sandwich Islands possible, the farms that missionaries left behind, and the educations many of them struggled to obtain. "Christ was overturning the ancient state of things, in order to take possession; and that these isles are waiting for his law, while the old and decaying pillars of idolatry are falling to the ground."[53] This interpretation rendered the unfamiliar terrain of Hawaiian political action into words resonant in their own evangelical tradition, placing the responsibility for the myriad transformations in Hawaiian society within the limits of their own God's power. Before the missionaries arrived, Hawaiians and their history had been changed through the prayers of devout Christians at home—a transformation made material by the publication of this claim in American newspapers. So resonant was the claim that it has been taken up and repeated down the centuries since 1819.[54]

This sudden change in their situation forced the missionaries to creatively and actively reformulate their self-image as the deposers of idolatry to . . . what, exactly? Now that their work would no longer be defined by opposition to kapu, human sacrifice, and idolatry, now that they were in no real danger and had no real opportunity of martyrdom while saving potential sacrificial victims of the temples, what roles did the missionaries envision for themselves in the absence of their great, already accomplished commission? Even the news of the death of Kamehameha stirred the missionaries to reminiscences of an older, deeper calling belonging to their ancestors who had been left alone in America.[55] "Our hearts do rejoice. Though we are disappointed in not being allowed to preach Christ to that venerable chief, who has so long and so ably governed this people; . . . yet in view of this wonderful revolution our hearts do rejoice, to hear the voice of one crying, *In the wilderness to prepare ye the way of the Lord, make straight in the desert a highway for our God.*"[56] The late revolutionary casting down of the "idols" and the burning of "moreahs" convinced the missionaries that "the people are without any form of religion, waiting as it were, for the law of Christ."[57] Although the mission would eventually compose hundreds of pages on the significance of overturning idolatry and the coincident arrival of God's law, they would be wrong about the significance of its loss to Hawaiian people. The lifting of kapu did not eradicate religious belief or practice, especially among the makaʻāinana, or common people, and it also did not alter the wide range of kapu that existed to regulate most facets of Hawaiian social life and the resources of the land and sea.[58] Neither did it create a religious vacuum or leave Hawaiian people without gods. In short, while the isles may have been waiting for *God's* law, Hawaiians living upon them continued to persist under the rule and kapu pre-existing the arrival of missionaries to Hawaiʻi's shores.

The End of ʻAi Kapu

When the missionaries arrived in March 1820, Hawaiians were living in a society that was undergoing rapid and far-reaching change. It is important to understand the different processes of transformation that Hawaiians were already experiencing and actively initiating when the missionaries arrived. Several important events occurred in the ten-month period before the arrival of the missionaries, the death of Kamehameha, and the casting down of the ʻai kapu.[59] Investigating the activities of the aliʻi after the death of Kamehameha on May 8, 1819, uncovers the deliberate action of the chiefs in choosing to reorganize political and religious institutions and social relations of power. Far more than simply supplying "native agency," this narrative illustrates that Hawaiians had their own sense of history in relation to which their present lives and activities were conditioned and made sense.[60]

The death of Kamehameha created upheaval in chiefly governance and authority that had enjoyed stability for nearly a decade. Kamehameha, foreseeing perhaps that his heir Liholiho lacked his mana (spiritual power) and hold on authority, expressly forbade the high-ranking chiefs of his circle from sacrificing their lives when he died, saying only that the "lives of men were sacred to the chief [Liholiho]."[61] Kamehameha's campaigns to bring the archipelago under his rule both built and were built upon the strong support of ali'i, both male and female, and with the aid of kāhuna (priests). Liholiho would inherit these powerful networks of support as Kamehameha's successor. If he was to have a chance at ruling and maintaining the cohesion of the newly unified island group, Liholiho would need to depend on the combined skill and intelligence of the seasoned veterans who served Kamehameha in diplomacy, in battle, and in dealings with haole (foreigners).

Before death, Kamehameha also laid plans for contingency: in the event Liholiho proved incapable of upholding his rule, Kamehameha saw to it that another chief, Kekuaokalani, would have a legitimate path to pressing an alternate claim to rule. Kamehameha gave this potential rival care of the war god Kūkā'ilimoku, while Liholiho was given rule over the land and the ability to reallocate these lands (kālai'āina) to those ali'i he saw fit to raise or lower in status.[62] This ability to dispose of the administration of lands, resources, and people gave Liholiho power and the loyalty of the chiefs he appointed as governors of lands and people. The significance of this arrangement lay in the powers with which each position was imbued and the deliberate separation of these roles by Kamehameha. The chief who inherited the god also held within his power the ability to pursue a proper path to war, a means of legitimated usurpation through the restoration of heiau dedicated to the god Kūkā'ilimoku, whose very name, "land-snatching Kū," gives insight into his power to undermine the rule of an opposing enemy. The chief who possessed the god could also sacrifice chiefly captives in preparation for war. These practices would legitimate his challenge of a rival chief's rule, allowing him to correct any misdeeds in governance and administration through the favor of the god.[63] These were the pathways to just war. By shaping succession and alternative leadership to rule in this fashion, Kamehameha was also enacting what had occurred within recent memory, making recourse to precedent. In the late 1790s, as a young upstart warrior Kamehameha had been given Kūkā'ilimoku, while his cousin Keōuakū'ahu'ula was given rule over the lands by the chief Kalani'ōpu'u.[64]

While the death of Kamehameha created a significant reordering of the web of chiefly relations, the casting down of the 'ai kapu also radically transformed the fabric of daily life for both ali'i and maka'āinana. At the forefront of this movement for 'ai noa (noa "free of kapu" eating) were Kālaimoku, Kamehameha's chief counselor and general in war, and Ka'ahumanu, one of Kamehameha's widows, who became kuhina nui, coruler of the islands along with Liholiho after Kamehameha's death.[65] In this decision, Kālaimoku and Ka'ahumanu enjoyed the support of their extended chiefly families. Ka'ahumanu's brothers, in particular, were high-ranking chiefs and priests. A most important validation of 'ai noa came from the highest-ranking chiefess Keōpūiolani, who was Liholiho's mother and the widow of Kamehameha. This chiefess's decision to eat publicly with her son, Kauikeaouli, set off a series of public eating events in which men and women ate together, a practice that had formerly been forbidden, leading to the eventual end of the 'ai kapu. On several occasions, Liholiho was invited to dine with the chiefesses, an invitation which he initially resisted at the behest of Kekuaokalani, but to which he eventually succumbed. The longstanding tradition of 'ai kapu, sacred eating, was cast down in a public feast that Liholiho shared with the chiefesses of his extended family.

Although the removal of the 'ai kapu led to the destruction of temples and the casting down of ki'i akua (god images), the effects were not strictly religious but religio-political. The chiefs supporting Liholiho eliminated the ceremonial path to regime change and rule that Kekuaokalani had been granted by Kamehameha when he was given the god, Kūkā'ilimoku. Kekuaokalani was dependent upon the sanction of gods and ceremony in the heiau to legitimate his attempt to rule. What Ka'ahumanu, Kālaimoku, and the other ruling chiefs removed with the casting down of the 'ai kapu was the religious and political path toward legitimate usurpation available to any rivals of Liholiho. They quite literally placed the battlefield beyond reach, since the prosecution of war required sacrifices to gods in the heiau, which had been razed, officiated by kahuna whose genealogies had been cut off and disenfranchised. The destruction of heiau and dismantling of the lineages of priesthoods removed all obstructions, all challenges to rule—in effect, all comers could be seen approaching for miles, without the malu (shelter) of the akua to protect them.[66]

The 'ai kapu, to eat under restriction, was not just a set of rules governing eating, but was part of a broader institution that also structured relations between Hawaiian men and women.[67] This kapu also demarcated the

Figure 2. "Queen Kaʻahumanu with her servant on rug." Lithograph by Jean-Pierre Norblin de la Gourdaine after painting by Louis Choris, Hawaiʻi State Archives.

spaces men and women inhabited during food preparation and consumption and the labor of men and women in cultivating, fishing, and gathering and preparing foods. Under ʻai kapu, women and men adhered to different rules for eating. Women were prohibited from eating particular foods and entering the heiau where men prayed and conducted ceremony. This kapu akua regulated the sacred calendar dictating which days and evenings men were to be separated from women and ritual observances were to be marked. From its very origin, the kapu communicated something about the potential political and sacred power of women and the need to keep women separate from men during ritual observance.

The ʻai kapu structured relations not only between men and women, but also between men and gods, since the kapu had its origin in the actions of the male akua Wākea and was derived from a discussion with his kahuna (priests).[68] When the ʻai kapu was toppled, heiau formerly consecrated to akua (gods) of politics and governance were destroyed, while kahuna who could claim ancestral lineages that reached back for centuries were rendered ineffective without the familiar institutional structure of heiau ceremonies to oversee. The life's work, experience, and expertise of the kahuna in guiding the chiefs and people were rendered irrelevant at the casting down of the 'ai kapu. The religious observances, both *mo'okū* (belonging to the god Kū) and *mo'olono* (belonging to the god Lono), along with the carved material manifestation of the gods (akua ki'i) were destroyed, too, upon the oral pronouncement of ali'i.[69] Just eight months before the arrival of the missionaries and their premature pronouncements of thanksgiving to their God, Hawaiian ali'i were deliberately reconfiguring the structures and institutions of their rule, transforming Hawaiian society and inaugurating a new, unprecedented phase of chiefly governance, authority, kapu, and kānāwai (law). These changes were sparked not by matters of religion, but in order to maintain the rule of the ali'i genealogies that were intertwined with Kamehameha through service, which included the women who birthed and fostered children, supplied their kapu and mana to further legitimate Kamehameha's rule, along with their strong familial alliances.

The toppling of 'ai kapu was not, however, the end of all kapu. Indeed, the personal kapu of the ali'i continued to be observed, while kapu continued to be pronounced by the ali'i and would be mobilized to regulate new questions concerning tense relations between haole and Hawaiians. Kapu was instrumental in interceding in the fraught relations between Hawaiian women and sailors just as the mission's civilizing project arrived, alongside the expansion of the Pacific whaling fleet, which brought more and more ships into Hawaiian ports each year.

Kapu: Ordering of Time and Space

The material and temporal impact upon the populace of the casting down of kapu have also been little considered by scholars. The end of 'ai kapu took along with it the schedule of rituals regulating the pace of people's agricultural lives over and against battles for territory initiated by the ali'i.[70] People's time was marked by seasons of labor, of planting *kalo* and *'uala* and a host of other vegetable and fruit crops. The rhythms of island life were still punctuated by the movement of stars, seasons of rain, wind, and the swelling and ebbing of tides. The life cycles of plants, sea creatures, and human birth continued to provide structure people could count on.[71] But in one afternoon's meal between male and female ali'i, centuries-old practices regulating communal social behavior on a scale larger than extended family and village had been altered and destroyed. A new regime of time had not yet taken hold when the missionaries arrived in March 1820, and there was no political avenue available to reinstate the kapu of temples and the lineages of priestly knowledge.

The absence of temple and ritual practice meant that the lives of Hawaiian men and women were no longer structured by the ritual calendar. Lives were marked to a different time and new activities inflected people's lives. One of these was the twice-a-year arrival of merchant and whaling ships in port, along with their demands for provisions and for women. Market and trading days became new social events. The newest arrivals, missionaries, began to build and introduce their philosophies of time into Hawaiian society. The weekly Sabbath, biweekly prayer meetings, classes, and school examinations were new places to gather, providing a different regimen of time and sociability—one that was shared with and at times supported by the pronouncements of chiefs, and which began to slowly redistribute power in the islands. Along with these changes came a new law pronounced through speech: the 'ōlelo a ke Akua (the words of the Christian God).[72]

It seems necessary to point out that resetting the chronology of events is purposeful; by highlighting discrete moments of rhetorical production, I seek to place "Hawaiian time," in relation to "missionary time." While the former was conditioned by the rhythms of kapu and by processes in the natural and spiritual world that were interconnected, missionaries interpreted events of national significance and those connected to the mission in terms of chronological and biblical time. The past, present, and future were interpreted through the unfolding of God's plan and the journey of their souls, in which time was marked by that which was eternal or occurring outside of time.[73]

Planting the Sandwich Islands Mission

Although enjoined by their instructions not to interfere "with the political affairs and party concerns of the nation,"[74] the missionaries' first recorded concerns after hearing about the casting down of the 'ai kapu regarded the state of the Sandwich Islands government. "There is some reason to fear, that the government is not settled on the firmest basis," they mused, "and that there is less stability and sobriety in the present king, than in his father."[75] Like their fellow Americans in the islands, transient merchants and sailors, the missionaries assumed that their work depended upon security in governance.

For the first three years of its residence in the islands, the first permanent settlement of Americans on Hawaiian shores consisted of fourteen men and women and five children divided between three mission stations on the islands of Hawai'i, O'ahu, and Kaua'i. The gendered nature of "settlement" and transience in the islands has been little before considered in the history of relation between Hawaiians and foreigners.[76] Since 1778, transient male sailors and ship captains from merchant and exploratory vessels made up the total number of visitors to the islands. Thus, the females of the mission were the first foreign women to settle in the islands.

In the first few weeks after their arrival, the missionaries had to adjust to the news that "the venerable chief" Kamehameha was dead. In his absence, the missionaries made the acquaintance of many ali'i, since as a matter of course they needed to figure out to whose authority they should appeal in order to gain permission to begin their work in the islands. The first meeting of the company with several chiefs took place aboard the *Thaddeus* on April 1, 1820. Kālaimoku had arrived on ship with his wife, two former wives of Kamehameha, and a retinue of male and female ali'i. Kālaimoku had been Kamehameha's close adviser, one of his leading war councilors, and, like Kamehameha, had received training in priestly arts. Kālaimoku's name was also a formal title, meaning "carver-of-land."[77] As the kālaimoku, he had been responsible for the management and distribution of lands under Kamehameha. He was also one of the ali'i charged with superintending the laborers, Hawaiians and foreign, and the business of cutting sandalwood. Kālaimoku had also been a general in battle, and since Kamehameha's death had led warriors against the chiefs who sought to preserve the 'ai kapu—a battle he led to victory when the chief Kekuaokalani, his wife, and followers were slain on the battlefield of Kuamo'o, Hawai'i, less than six months before the missionaries arrived.

The chiefly party greeted the missionaries individually, shaking hands, murmuring the "usual compliment, *aloha*." The missionaries may have expected to meet high chiefs garbed in stunning long feathered capes made famous in Cook's journals, and which even then graced the halls of Charles Wilson Peale's Philadelphia Museum.[78] Or perhaps they anticipated some character from the theatrical production of the *Death of Captain Cook.*[79] Farmer Daniel Chamberlain was impressed by the appearance of the war- rior chief Kālaimoku, who arrived dressed instead in a "white dimity jacket, black silk vest, nankeen pantaloons, white cotton stockings, shoes, plaid cravat, and neat English hat."[80] Such finery may have taken the missionaries aback, these young American men and women who were garbed in gifts from family and donations of Christian benevolence, and who had renounced individual possessions and monies in exchange for a common stock existence.[81] It must have registered among the missionaries, these dif- ferences in station and rank between themselves and the targets of their evangelism made manifest in the clothing worn by the aliʻi and their means to purchase luxury goods unavailable to those of common American farm family background.

Kālaimoku's clothing was indicative of the chief's station and pointed to the rich cosmopolitan mix of goods that were lavished upon the aliʻi and that arrived in Hawaiian ports daily—goods transported to the islands on ships from Europe and America. To Chamberlain, the chief appeared to be "dressed like an American gentleman, [and] his manners were considerably refined."[82] After sharing a meal, one of the ministers stepped forward to communicate the "design of the mission" to the chiefs. While the mission- aries report that the female aliʻi "appeared to express much joy," Kālaimoku provided "no opinion on the subject," saying only that he "must see the King first, and consult with him."[83] These reports that provide us with a view of first encounter need to be read in terms of their one-sided nature, of their failure to provide readers with a robust accounting of what is hap- pening in Hawaiian society at the moment of arrival. These sources cannot relate to readers information on the distribution of power among the aliʻi and what Hawaiians discussed among themselves about their first meeting with American missionaries because of the obvious limitation of their knowledge.

The next day, Rev. Bingham went ashore with Capt. Blanchard to meet again with Kālaimoku. The chief took Bingham on a tour of Puʻukoholā heiau, which Bingham called, "the most celebrated moreeah of the islands." The visit inspired a lengthy description from Bingham regarding the appearance of the heiau and the activities he imagined had once taken place there. "Within this inclosure [*sic*] are the ruins of several houses, burnt to the ground, the ashes of various wooden gods, the remains of cocoanuts and other like offerings, and the ashes and burnt bones of many *human*

Figure 3. "Karaimoku Regent of the Sandwich Islands." Pencil drawing of Kālaimoku. Drawing by Robert Dampier, Bishop Museum Archives.

victims sacrificed to demons. . . . The walls and areas of these open buildings, once tabooed and sacred, are now free to every foot, useless, and tumbling into ruins."[84] Bingham's impressions are still crafted from the fabric of his own imagination, as they were when he imagined British ships in Boston harbor. Did he see ashes and burnt bones? And why were Hawaiian gods necessarily demons, if not that Christians needed to invent their competition? Perhaps his most important observation was that the heiau was now open and "free to every foot," including his own. As a pedestrian, an American missionary strolling through the formerly sacred enclosure, Bingham may have been the most unlikely of visitors to the heiau. He was also making a religious and political statement, albeit unwittingly. After 'ai noa, the kapu enclosure was transformed into a space of social leveling—men, women, chiefs, and commoners could enter into its embankments without fear of death or punishment—but this act of treading upon ground freed from kapu, when exercised by those who recalled its previous state, was one which may have still smacked of loss and transgression for Hawaiians, even while it stood for Bingham as the quintessential example of a fortress of savagery that had been toppled, a culture fast going down to ruin.[85]

It was through this kind of statement, and others that soon followed, that the tradition of marking and manufacturing the disappearance of natives from their lands was inaugurated in Hawai'i, on the third day after the missionaries arrived in the islands. The priestly houses on the heiau were ruined, the gods they tended, ashes. Even the bones of "sacrificed Hawaiians" were barely recognizable, uncared for, and exposed amid the destruction.

It is ironic that here at the awesome heiau of Pu'ukohola, built by Kamehameha to fulfill a prophecy that he would unite the islands, Bingham began to pen a narrative of native displacement. The destruction of the heiau and 'ai kapu may have made "ruins" of this particular place, but for the newly arrived missionaries, this moment in Hawaiian history offered Bingham and his fellows an opportunity to craft roles for themselves in a continuing evangelical history their forefathers had inaugurated. This *mentalité*, connecting native displacement and foreign settlement, became a dominant feature of the writing and printed materials generated by the Hawaiian mission; Hawaiians from the nineteenth century were compared to heathens in the Bible and to Indians in the British Atlantic colonies of the seventeenth and eighteenth centuries. Before the first printing press was set up in Honolulu in January 1822, the missionaries kept journals, wrote letters, and sent off handwritten official reports to Boston framed as part of a familiar narrative record of native displacement. Printed in newspapers, religious magazines, and books, the missionary record would make a perceived disappearance of Hawaiian civilization into fact and history, in turn validating the members of the mission as witnesses, historians, and (eventually) the deserving inheritors of Hawaiian lands.

Later that afternoon of April 2, the New England missionaries and Hawaiian ali'i shared the first Sabbath observance in the islands, aboard ship. Kālaimoku, his wife, and the widows of Kamehameha, along with fifteen male attendants dressed in *malo* (loincloth) were present. As the ship left Kawaihae, Rev. Bingham, inspired no doubt by his visit to Pu'ukohola, preached from the familiar words of injunction from Isaiah 42:4 *The Isles shall wait for his law.* With Pu'ukohola receding in the distance, an icon to the religio-political ambitions of Kamehameha and his people, the missionaries preached that morning about the nature of the law of their Christian God and the character of the lawgiver as they stood in the searing heat upon sovereign American ground, the exposed deck of the ship *Thaddeus*. The entire company of chiefs and missionaries were sailing south to meet Liholiho Kamehameha II to acquaint him with the designs of the mission and receive permission for the missionaries to stay in the islands. On April 4 at 10 a.m., the missionaries recorded the auspicious moment of their official arrival: "This morning 163 days from Boston, we came to anchor in Kirooah [Kailua] Bay about one mile from the king's dwellings." Liholiho, his first wife, and his mother were pointed out "bathing in the surf." A large crowd of five or six hundred people gathered near the shore—"Natives of different ages and sexes swarmed around us."[86] The high chief Kuakini, who had an excellent command of English gained from trading, greeted ministers Bingham and Thurston and Thomas Hopu at the shore and took them to his residence and then to the nearby home of John Young, Liholiho's acting secretary.[87]

When Liholiho arrived, the formal ceremony of introduction began. Rev. Bingham read aloud an official letter from Rev. Samuel Worcester, the Secretary of the ABCFM, which had been addressed to the King's father, Kamehameha. The minister also read from other official correspondence, letters from American ship captains granting the missionaries permission to dwell in their vacant houses. These communications, although heard in English, were translated into Hawaiian by Thomas Hopu and John Young for better understanding. Through these interpreters, the missionaries made known "the views of the American Board of Missions" and of the "mission family" to settle in the islands. Although the mission considered its news "perhaps the most important message that could be sent to any earthly potentate," Liholiho seemed "far from being in haste to weigh the subject deliberately," no doubt to the disappointment of the missionaries.[88] As had taken place at every initial meeting of foreigners with heathen chiefs since the arrival of Captain Cook in the islands, a gift was offered. The board had sent a spyglass to the king, which he "accepted very thankfully."[89]

If the missionaries could spy themselves enacting this scene through a glass from far-off New England, what might their words and images seem to resemble? Here they were presenting themselves before a heathen ruler, 163 days out from home, country, and civilization. Were they like Captain Cook, intrepid discoverers on the brink of some new revelation? Or were they like the London missionaries in Tahiti who, two decades before, had inaugurated what would soon be a long-promised harvest of souls? Were they like John Eliot meeting the Wampanoag for the first time? Would they be remembered by succeeding generations of Americans as extending the light of God's word to the darkest reaches of the Earth? Or would they be swallowed up like the settlers at Roanoke, never to be heard from again? For now the missionaries could only wait on the shore, and as the chief Liholiho reposed with the other male chiefs after a full meal of fish and *poi*, the missionaries endeavored to "interest the royal family in the great object" of their mission. This, while his four wives (one his father's former wife, and another his sister) played a leisurely and scandalous game of cards in the corner![90]

But the question of missionary settlement reignited fears of Hawaiians and haole (foreigners), Americans and British alike, in the islands. While Hawaiians worried about the hidden designs of haole, the topic of American missionary settlement brought simmering national rivalries among foreigners to the surface. Due to Capt. Blanchard's haste to leave Kailua, the missionaries were forced to pursue the question of settlement with increased urgency. On April 8, Rev. Bingham met with the king, asking that missionaries be allowed to settle on Oʻahu and in Kailua, the place of Liholiho's chiefly residence. Liholiho replied, "You wish to go to Woahoo [*sic*] because provisions are so plenty there—all white men wish to live in Woahoo." It is unclear at this point what the significations were for "haole," which the missionaries translated as "whiteness," but it was not discriminating when it came to vocation or country of origin.

According to the missionary journal, Liholiho had also alluded to the idea that perhaps Americans intended to get possession of the island. The missionaries had heard this kind of talk before, noting on April 5 that "Great Britain might not be pleased with our settling here"—though, unsure of the source of this conjecture, they had come to the conclusion that "some inconsiderate American seamen, perhaps in the independent spirit of patriotism, which often breathes itself out in high sounding words, have told this too credulous people that America would take these islands; and it is believed that some English residents have insinuated or maintained the same thing."[91] Thus, while the Sandwich Islands church was poised to raise the banner of Christ in the islands, their fellow Americans would seem to prefer raising an American flag. Missionaries worried that these kinds of statements would provide "no inconsiderable impediment" to their settlement. After days of anxious waiting, Liholiho gave his word, allowing them to settle in Kailua, contrary to the mission's wish that some of them be allowed to live on Oʻahu as well.

On April 11, all the brethren went ashore to make "one more united effort" to persuade Liholiho to allow a settlement at Honolulu. The journal's record reveals the fraught process by which missionaries learned about Hawaiian social relations of power. "We unexpectedly found that Crymakoo [Kālaimoku] who had left Kirooah [Kailua] before the final decision was given had now returned. He has considerable control over Woahoo [Oʻahu]. To him, John Adams [Kuakini], to Nihe [Naihe] another native chief, to the King and to Mr. J. Young, individually we made known our wishes that a part of our number should have liberty to proceed to Woahoo and to settle there."[92] Petitioning anyone with authority who would listen, the ministers, in disbelief and worried that Capt. Blanchard would sail away on the *Thaddeus* with all their belongings, wrote critically that Liholiho "pretended to be waiting" for the advice of Kaʻahumanu, who had sailed off in a double canoe "on a fishing expedition." Though the ministers were reluctant to believe that the will of the king depended upon this woman's opinion, Kaʻahumanu was observed nonetheless as "having been the favorite wife of Tamahamaha," possessing "more property and power than any other woman in the islands."[93] The ministers had also sought the assistance of Gov. Cox [Keʻeaumoku],[94] who they were told had been "lost in a gale." Later that afternoon, when the chiefess who had "gone fishing" returned at the same time her brother "lost in a gale" resurfaced, the missionaries, instead of hearing the humorous verbal deflections of Hawaiians, who preferred not to discuss the matter, instead considered the coincident return of the chiefs as "a smile of providence peculiarly auspicious."[95]

Preparing for an event of historic proportions, the ministers went in haste to meet with the assembly of chiefs. But their plans were cut off when "two youths presented themselves on the common near the King's dwelling, prepared for a public dance."[96] For the first time, missionaries like Rev. Bingham, who had so disapproved of the theater as a "prolific source of idleness, dissipation, profanity, and immodesty,"[97] were to witness Hawaiians dancing, along with some two thousand natives who had swiftly "collected to see the childish amusement."[98] Straitened by impatience at this "idle, time-killing employment," the missionaries were forced to wait until evening to see the chiefs. Ka'ahumanu, Liholiho, and the chiefs in council ('aha)[99] listened to the petition of the ministers and, after asking many questions about the mission's design and the number of arts church members were equipped to teach, the journal notes that the chiefs were most satisfied with the idea that missionaries "might be of service to them." After some conversation, the ministers departed, leaving "the king and his advisers" to "consult among themselves."[100]

The next morning, Rev. Thurston and Dr. Holman went ashore to hear the decision of the chiefs. Permission had been given for a settlement at O'ahu, but the chiefs had also decided a division of the little group was in order. Two of the brethren with their wives and two of the Hawaiian men should remain in Kailua, while the rest were allowed to settle on O'ahu.[101]

On April 12, scarcely two weeks after the missionaries first sighted land, the mission to the Sandwich Islands was being planted in Kailua, Hawai'i. On that day, the missionaries recorded the long-awaited event: "Thus in the name of our God have we set up our banner on the benighted shores of Owhyhee; and have stationed a little band to support it there . . . make their house a Bethel, their instructions a light to those who sit in darkness, and their influence a perennial stream whose gentle flow shall fertilize the barren waste, and make glad the city of our God."[102] The City of God was Boston, the acknowledged city on the hill, and the missionaries wasted no time in relaying the important news of this first settlement in the islands to their superiors in Boston. On the first Monday of every month, a prayer meeting was held at Park Street Church. On April 2, 1821, excerpts from the journal of the Sandwich Islands Mission, beginning with the arrival of the missionaries in March 1820, a year before, were shared with the assembled congregants. The stated purpose of the public reading of the journal was so that the "natives of the Sandwich Islands and the missionaries" might be "placed before the eyes of the audience," who would "fix their contemplations on the interesting moment, when a Christian mission was, for the first time, approaching a long neglected heathen people."[103]

That evening, after the journal was read aloud in Park Street Church, the remarks of those assembled were collected and selectively republished on the front page of the May 1821 issue of the *Missionary Herald*, amplifying both the Hawaiian mission and the impact it was already having upon Christians in America. The circuits across which information traveled radiated out from the islands to the ocean, and from the page into the ears of attentive listeners in churches, whose words of discussion were taken up again on the printed page and reflected back to a home audience. Though the information made its journey across land and sea, it also reached back temporally from the present to the past, ruminations over this new American mission inspired a genealogical incantation calling up the names of dead and gloriously martyred missionary divines.

> With what holy exultation would the sanctified and glorified minds of Dwight, and Spring, and Huntington, the father and son, and Mills, and Warren and Harriet Newell, and Obookiah again visiting his birth-place, witness these overtures of mercy: and how would Elliot and Swartz, Brainerd and Martyn, Vanderkemp and Thomas, with multitudes of others, possessing the same character, and having devoted their lives to the same ennobling employments, join in mutual congratulations, and in the ascribing the most exalted praise to God and the Lamb.[104]

Clearly, the work of the Sandwich Islands Mission was important to the progress of American Congregational efforts to Christianize the heathen. Those at home had a venerable genealogy and history to live up to, and now that genealogy included the names of Hawaiians like ʻŌpūkahaʻia. Soon, many more names of important chiefs and foreign dignitaries with which the mission came into contact in the islands would be made known to the reading public back in America through the written and published correspondence of this new, interesting mission field in the Sandwich Islands.

Missionaries, Merchants, and *Aliʻi*

Rev. Bingham, Daniel Chamberlain, Elisha Loomis, Samuel Ruggles, and Samuel Whitney, together with their wives and the children, sailed from Kailua, past the islands of Maui, Molokaʻi, and Lānaʻi, and anchored in Honolulu Harbor after four days' sail. At Honolulu, the missionaries interjected themselves into the existing relationships between aliʻi and people, merchant, sailor, and ship captain. It was the issue of providing houses for the mission on Oʻahu that spurred the first formal meeting of merchants, missionaries, and chiefs in the Sandwich Islands. The missionaries had planned to build a mission station in Honolulu, Oʻahu, one of two popular harbors and a place of trade and home to New England stores and storage houses. The missionaries bound for the island of Hawaiʻi had already been given a letter in Boston by Capt. Nathaniel Winship, who kept a house at Honolulu. The letter gave them permission to use his home until accommodations could be built for their use. At Honolulu, Mr. Scovill, Capt. Adams, and Mr. Navarro graciously offered up the use of some of their houses while Capt. Babcock, Mr. Beckley, and Mr. Marin provided space to store the supplies and other materials belonging to the mission.[105] When houses were not provided by Boki, the chiefly governor of Oʻahu who was also Kālaimoku's brother, Capt. Pigot and Capt. Starbuck offered to "make a vigorous effort" to help get the houses built.

In order perhaps to pressure the aliʻi into giving more assistance to the mission, the missionaries convened a meeting on May 10, 1820, "inviting cooperation of the friends of humanity and truth." A circular was issued in the morning requesting that "European and American residents, both temporary and permanent, masters and officers of vessels of different flags, together with the chiefs of the islands" assemble to "hear a statement of our views, and of the views of the government"[106] with respect to the missionary enterprise. At five o'clock that afternoon, a meeting was assembled at Rev. Bingham's, with Capt. Adams appointed as moderator and Mr. Loomis as scribe. The missionaries then explained through an interpreter to Boki the purpose of the meeting. With regard to the houses, Boki replied that he intended to oversee the building personally, as this was what Liholiho wished. The missionaries demurred, saying that they understood that the aliʻi were "embarrassed with other claims" and that they did not wish to be burdensome nor "detrimental to the claims of foreign traders,"[107] who the aliʻi owed. The missionaries suggested that there were men on hand to assist with the building of houses, which they wished to take advantage of. Boki's answer to this proposal was "no." He would build the houses himself according to the word (command) of Liholiho. At this point in the conversation, Capt. Pigot spoke up and asked Boki if he intended to build comfortable homes for the mission soon and free of expense, to which Boki replied plainly that he did.[108]

It seems by this account that the eight missionaries in Honolulu smartly engineered this meeting to secure what they desired—namely, a promise from Boki that the houses would be built soon.[109] Certainly they had a sense of their authority as messengers of God. But what gave them the confidence to convene a meeting in a foreign place and call forth all resident chiefs and foreigners? Public performances such as this would feed their sense of importance and become the germ of their authority in the islands. The missionaries also used the presence of merchants and ship captains to their advantage, publicly denying that their object to have houses built would in any way deter the chiefs from fulfilling their obligations to repay debt by reallocating Hawaiian laborers away from cutting sandalwood to house building. This statement may have ingratiated them with the merchants, allaying any fears the merchants might have had about the impact of the mission on trade.

Boki held fast to the authority of the ali'i. By denying the ability of the haole newcomers to erect buildings, he reserved for himself the power to choose when the homes would be built.[110] This was because foreigners in Hawai'i were not allowed to own or purchase land, and neither were they able to erect buildings without the verbal assent of the ali'i. What is the calculus for assessing what transpired during cross-cultural negotiation in Hawai'i during this time? Missionaries and merchants, though haole, did not have the same reasons for being in the islands. Ship captains, officers, and foreign residents had years of experience in the islands, while the fourteen missionaries, of whom only two were ministers, were recent arrivals, outnumbered by other foreigners and Hawaiians. Merchants and the ship captains employed by merchant houses wrote letters back to the home offices in New England. But little or none of their business correspondence and activities was shared with Americans back at home. That the missionaries recorded these events—which were then published in newspapers, journals, official reports, and books—accounts for the overwhelming prevalence of their interpretations of their interactions with Hawaiians which reverberate through the historiography.

Missionaries depended upon home-bound merchants and whaling ships to carry reports, journals, and letters back to the American Board.[111] Ships brought letters and gifts to family and friends left behind in New England and also between mission stations located on different islands. Ships also carried letters and gifts to the Sandwich Islands. Mr. Alfred White of Brookfield, Massachusetts, learned how much former neighbor Daniel Chamberlain and his wife missed home since their departure from Massachusetts almost a year before. The letter, dated October 2, 1820, probably would not have come to Mr. White's hand until April 1821 at the earliest.

> Probably you and your neighbours are now gathering in your crops and preparing for a cold winter—O how rejoicing would it be to meet with you and your neighbors and assist in husking corn, and hear of what was passing among you. Probably all is life and activity among you—all conducting wisely for this world—laying in stores for winter of such provisions as will keep. . . . When I sit down to write, so many subjects come into my mind, that I do not know which to write upon. It would occupy a fortnight's time, to write all I should be glad to write. O how sweet it would be to sit down (as we often have) in some lonely place, under cover of the night, and talk of those past scenes, and pray with and for each other. O dear friend, I cannot express to you in words how I long to see you—Mrs. C. observed the other day that we should be almost too happy if Mr. White, with his wife and family should come out here. I long to see you and some of my beloved friends at Bd [Brookfield] and sit down and talk of what God has done for us—But hush my feelings, I will be patient.[112]

Farmer Chamberlain longed for the rhythms of communal labor that kept time in New England with the changing of seasons. The act of writing letters to the board or to family and friends in New England would draw the missionaries back to the memory of their former selves and lives. The distance between home and Hawai'i would be overcome through these bursts of emotion, introspection, and reportage, through the stroke of a pen on paper. Considering the audience at home would encourage the missionaries to reflect upon their own labors and weigh and measure their aspirations against the support of those at home. The act of writing reinforced their reality, while all around them in the islands, Hawaiian lands, people, and lifestyle pointed to different rhythms and ways of living, which shaped different modes of relation.

The perennial "summer" of Hawai'i wreaked havoc with Chamberlain's Protestant sense of labor. He reported that Hawai'i had "perhaps the most beautiful delightful climate in the world," the temperature being "scarce over 82 and seldom below 78 in the shade."[113] "It is astonishing how vines and fruit will grow here." Chamberlain wrote in his journal regarding the things he saw on his first trip into the uplands of Kailua, Hawai'i: "We saw plenty of cocoanut trees, Bread fruit, bananas, sugar cane, some orange trees . . . the soil is the richest by far that I ever saw, with good springs of water—I should suppose that a man might live here by working only one day in a week."[114] Missionaries like Mr. Chamberlain and Rev. Bingham brought with them regimes of time that were tied to the rhythms of the New England farm. But this concept of time, like the mission's crusade to obliterate "altars of abomination," was rendered ironically anachronistic on lands that did not demand the constant attention of farmers to be productive.[115] Relieved of the immediate necessity to turn land into farms, the missionaries focused their attentions upon conducting schools for the chiefs and the children of foreigners and spreading the word of God.

Although the missionaries had been enjoined to cover the islands with "fruitful fields and pleasant dwellings," they had found that the land was already fruitful and the chiefs were the only ones who could grant permission to build houses. The aim of building "schools and churches" was daunting, as the missionaries were spread thinly across different island mission stations (Kailua, Hawai'i, and Honolulu, O'ahu). The thinned-out group had their hands full providing individual instruction to chiefly households. At Kailua, Hawai'i, several "schools" were in operation. Rev. Asa Thurston taught Liholiho, his wives, and the king's eight-year-old brother, Kauikeaouli, and two of his young male attendants. Dr. Holman, the mission's doctor, also taught reading and writing to high chief Kuakini, Ka'ahumanu's brother, a son of John Young, and several other chiefly children. While the king made excellent progress, "read[ing] intelligibly in the New Testament," others were taught to read plainly, using exercises from Noah Webster's spelling book. Kauikeaouli was proficient enough to spell "words of four syllables." The king objected to the mission's design of teaching the common people to read "before he has himself become master of the art."[116] For Liholiho, the palapala (reading and writing) were skills that conferred mana (power) upon the individual through specialized knowledge, and it was also true that in Hawaiian society, to be trained to the traditions of the ali'i was a process not all people in society had access to. The purpose of certain kinds of learned vocations was to maintain and pass on history and chiefly traditions.

Reading and writing would be useful to the chiefs, who sought to keep track of the sandalwood "debt" they owed to American merchants in payment for the goods that the chiefs purchased. Instruction would be another area that would solidify relations between the missionaries and ali'i, granting them unprecedented access to chiefs and chiefly households. Missionary ascendance in society was made possible through the very utilitarian roles they played in providing skills the ali'i wanted for themselves and for their people.

While instruction in the palapala would forge lasting ties between missionaries and ali'i, the dining table would cement relationships between the "missionary family," the common settled foreigner, and those who commanded visiting ships. Members of the missionary family were often invited to dine aboard visiting ships, a floating microcosm of the civilized world. Within the confines of foreign ships, hierarchies of civilization maintained people in the proper place. Ships brought missionaries letters from lost family and friends, newspapers and goods from home, and also doctors with medicine. One evening, soon after the missionaries first arrived in the islands, they were pleased to "set an American table, in humble but decent order," as Bingham reported.[117] The "American table" was spread for a cosmopolitan circle of visitors hailing from different countries separated by vast seas. Sharing in the festivities that evening were Capt. Starbuck of London, originally of Nantucket; Capt. Pigot of New York, originally from England; Capt. Best of London, formerly from Ireland; Dr. Williams of London, the surgeon of the British ship *L'Aigle*; Mr. Clark of the Russian ship *Kamschatka*, formerly from New England and a temporary resident in the islands; and Mr. Green, an American trader from Boston. The missionaries were pleased to "quietly sit down on heathen shores, in such a circle of ladies and gentlemen." Visits with these foreigners from "different countries and different pursuits"[118] afforded opportunities for genteel discourse; intellectual conversation over tea helped missionaries maintain the frail tether of connection to home weathered by distance and time, while new faces brought the missionaries welcome relief from their daily drudgery of ministering and teaching among "savages."[119] These gatherings strengthened the bonds between itinerant foreigners and missionary settlers in heathen lands while helping to reinforce the divide between savage and civilized.

Invitations to dine among visiting dignitaries added to the perception of the missionaries, many from rural farming backgrounds, that they held important status in the islands. On December 24, 1821, Rev. Bingham attended a Russian Orthodox prayer service aboard the Russian imperial ship of war *Otkritic*. The ship was visiting the islands as part of a larger voyage of discovery in the Pacific. After enjoying refreshments, Commodore Michael Vassilieff presented Bingham with an elegant silver medal "containing a good profile of the Emperor, and the names of the two ships under his command." The Russian captain and several of his officers were invited to tour the orphan school set up by the missionaries. There, they met a young Hawaiian boy who lived with the family and had been renamed "William Beals." Beals provided a living example of the progress of the school. The Russian contingent was moved to donate the hefty sum of "seven gold ducats and eighty six Spanish dollars."[120]

Encounters with important foreign personages elevated missionaries' estimations of their work. Who could have guessed that Hiram Bingham, the farmer's son from Bennington, Vermont, would be enjoying the attentions of the commodore and officers of a Russian national royal discovery vessel? As foreign mission fields compared, the Sandwich Islands afforded the ministers, teachers, and assistants, exposure to international personages of importance—exposure that missionaries laboring among Indians in America lacked.[121] As the first permanent American settlers in the islands, missionaries were frequently accorded notice, and therefore status, by visiting foreigners from Russia and England. At religious services, parties, and public meetings, missionary encounters with important foreigners elevated their status, marking them as the semiofficial representatives of the young American republic in the islands, though the mission enjoyed slight notice from the United States government and received absolutely no government support.

The Sandwich Islands Mission developed relationships of obligation and service to the ali'i in the islands. Teaching the palapala gave them intimate access to the high chiefs, their families, and their extended households. Other foreigners in the islands gave much assistance to the mission; using their familiarity with chiefs like Boki, they made sure that missionaries would have homes to live in and food supplied for their tables. In the first few years of the mission, ship captains offered to take missionary correspondence back home to the United States, while conveying presents, supplies, and the latest news from home directly to the hands and eyes of thankful missionaries. Perhaps it was the distance from home and civilization that made the missionaries of the Sandwich Islands such prolific writers. The construction of missionary authority has been overlooked in the historiography of the Sandwich Islands. As actors in American history, foreign missionaries take their final curtain call as they exit the wharf. As figures in an island, oceanic, and colonial history of the islands, missionaries like Bingham are captured all out of proportion, Bingham encountered mostly in hindsight as the man who dwelt "21 years in the Sandwich Islands."[122] While many of his colleagues, who never penned a biography or history, lived and were buried in the islands, he left the mission to return to the United States in 1840. The missionaries in this historiography are the bringers of law to a lawless nation, the bearers of the cross to a people bereft of religion. That story is tempered by Hawaiian historical and linguistic interpretation into moments of miscommunication and encounter between Hawaiian chiefs and missionaries.

When ships brought news of their homeland to the Sandwich Islands, the missionaries saw for the first time their own written production reflected back at them on the pages of the published missionary journals, no doubt emboldening them further to continue their work. Receipt of the published works in the islands both magnified and transcended distance from family, home, and nation. The auspicious news of the successful planting of the Sandwich Islands Mission had been published in the April 1821 *Missionary Herald*, and if the *Herald* had been mailed on a Pacific-bound ship that very month, it quite possibly reached the islands by December 1821. Perhaps as Hiram Bingham conversed with Commodore Vassilieff in Honolulu, he already had a different view of the boy from the Bennington farm.

As self-satisfying as this reflection of success might have been, the planting of the ABCFM mission in Hawai'i came at a moment of political tension between different chiefly factions and economic stagnation. Various merchants somewhat ineptly pursued resource acquisition and the development of a consumer market in the islands, while ship captains and sailors continued to move raw materials and goods through the Pacific, stopping in Honolulu for respite from their long oceanic crossings. This confluence of missionary, maritime, and merchant parties and interests began, in the unfolding of the 1820s, to intensify in volume and character of interactions. For with success came more and more sailors, merchants, and missionaries to the Hawaiian Islands, and the chiefs, as we shall see, were discovering just how difficult it might be to attend to the various poor behaviors that inevitably came with these foreigners and their desires.

Candidacy of William Richards

As a young prospective candidate to the ABCFM, William Richards set his sights on the Sandwich Islands. Richards was no stranger to thinking about missions; while other young men were moved to act on behalf of the perishing heathen, or were inspired by the tragic end of ʻŌpūkahaʻia's aspiration to evangelize his own people, William Richards was bound by familial connection to the missionary effort. His own brother James was one of the five Williams College men that helped to ignite the foreign missionary movement in America in the haystack prayer meeting. Of the five, only Samuel Mills and James Richards chose for themselves a missionary's life. James had been sent as a missionary to India seven years before William made his own formal application to the board in 1822.

William and his brother James were raised in Plainfield, Massachusetts, on their family farm, one of the first American settlements in the area. Their father James had been a soldier in Washington's army during the revolution. In Plainfield, James Richards had helped to establish their church and open the school in their area. He taught the common school in winter months for thirty years and also conducted a singing school in his and neighboring towns. Mr. Richards had held various public offices, some of which he was elected to: town clerk, selectman, assessor, and justice of the peace. He served as representative of the general court for eight terms, and in 1820 he was a delegate to the convention for amending the state constitution. Although Richards, like Bingham, was raised in a farming family, his father also held prominent roles in public service, both locally and on behalf of the Commonwealth. Perhaps it was this exposure to politics that shaped Richards' service in the islands.

William, the seventh of ten children, had been named after his ancestor who was one of the settlers at Plymouth Colony. It would seem that both William and James would continue the tradition in their family of moving from their place of birth to plant roots, colonizing a foreign land.

Like James, William also attended Williams College, graduating in 1819 at the age of twenty-six. He began his ministerial training at Andover Theological Seminary, then a dynamic place of awakening and revival, and also a place where many missionaries received their professional religious education.[123] Richards barely completed his course of studies when he was accepted as a member of the second company to the Sandwich Islands mission.

Young men and their wives who felt the call to minister to "heathens" were required to submit a letter of candidacy to the Prudential Committee of the ABCFM. Along with the letter, a candidate needed to solicit letters of support from ministers to testify to their membership in good standing in church, as well as letters from professors who could attest to their eloquence in preaching or adequacy as teachers. Prospective missionaries were the subject of close scrutiny—their behavior, deportment, and commitment, as well as their intellectual and spiritual achievements, were commented upon. Character and reputation were everything.

In these letters a candidate provided a self-evaluation of his suitability for this vocation, which included a brief biography of their education and details about when they had professed religion. William Richards' profession of faith occurred in 1811, when he was seventeen, and his brother's change of heart came at the age of nineteen.

Richards' letter of candidacy illustrates, as it was designed to, the serious cast of his mind, his dedication and desire to "preach Christ where he has not been named." It was well publicized that his brother James was sick unto death in Ceylon, and William conducted his own exercises in self-discipline that were designed to test his resolve. "I have some time, changed situations with my brother, and thus found myself with a sickly body in a heathen land, at one moment hanging in suspense on the borders of the grave,—at the next . . . life prolonged only to suffer the spiritual deprivations of a moral desert." Projections such as these were commonplace activities for prospective missionaries; the conditioning and preparation of the mind and body for hardship in heathen lands required that one project one's expectations onto the unknown—of one's own fate, and the unknown peoples and places one was devoting a life and one's energies toward.

Though the sensation of switching places with his dying brother may have been disturbing, it was not sickness or death that made William fearful; instead, it was life away from "Christian society and those Christian privileges which are now so indispensible [sic] to spiritual enjoyment, my heart does almost faint." Nonetheless, Richards made very clear that he had settled upon becoming a missionary to the Sandwich Islands. If he were not chosen, he asked that the board defer his application until such time as he could be accepted as a missionary to that field.

Departure of the Second Company

During a week's worth of festivities, the first reinforcement of missionaries to the Sandwich Islands, the community, their families, and members of the ABCFM were preparing for the imminent departure of this long-awaited second company. The *Missionary Intelligencer* may have highlighted the reason for the solemn and interesting occasion that drew a large crowd in the early evening to church in New Haven, Connecticut, on Monday, November 18, 1822, to join "these heralds of the Cross for the last time in a Christian land, united in the solemn worship of the God of their fathers."[124] On that occasion, the corresponding secretary of the ABCFM, Jeremiah Evarts, delivered the Instructions of the Prudential Committee to the ministers and the fledgling missionary band. Evarts provoked much thought with the idea that the missionaries, "upon whom every eye rested, were to go to those far distant isles, there to live, there to labour, there to die; and that there their bones must rest till the archangel's trump shall summon them to the Judgement [sic]." This would be the last time they expected to share in the sanctity of ceremony among their fellow Christians in a Christian land. Evarts' message was clear: missionaries were consecrated to their work for life. The anointed company might have just as well stepped off the wharf into a grave as onto the ship *Thames*—such was the way in which their undertaking was cast in the many pamphlets, newspapers, and sermons that rang out before New England congregations, as it had that evening in New Haven before the assembled, now introspective throng.[125]

That evening, the congregation heard the voice of Rev. William Richards preaching from Isaiah 60:9 "Surely the Isles shall wait for me." Richards helped his listeners connect themselves with the receptive audience of Hawaiians he imagined awaited their Christian message in the Sandwich Islands. Richards' sermon hearkened back to Rev. Samuel Worcester's call for support for the maiden company that departed some two years earlier, entitled "Surely the Islands Shall Wait for His Law." The isles in the missionary imaginary both waited for the law of God and the missionary laborer. Rhetorical significance through the re-evocation of words spoken in honor of such events connected Richards and his audience with the biblical past, the American present, and the Hawaiians he hoped to convert from their savage past into a shining Christian future, which these Americans projected that all would share.

Evarts' message also delineated the scope of the American mission for his fellow citizens, as surely as the eyes of those assembled were upon these missionaries, so, too, the eyes of the world would be fixed upon them if they should prove to be unfaithful in their work. "The Scottish peasant as he read the account by his evening fireside would mourn over their delinquency," while in Switzerland perhaps, "some pious widow in her rock-sheltered cottage would weep."[126] The Sandwich Islands Mission would draw with it the material and monetary support and prayers of Christians in Europe and New England. It would ensnare the people's interest from the familiar chill of their Atlantic to the unplumbed depths of the warm Pacific.

At the close of the moving service, some six to seven hundred devoted members of the congregation separated themselves from the rest of the audience to take communion. A collection of $334 was taken on this occasion, which would be added to the $1,000 already collected from throughout the city from inhabitants "of all classes" for the support and comfort of the missionaries to sustain them on their long voyage and after their arrival. The missionary effort was an egalitarian/democratic endeavor in which both the wealthy merchant and the young widow could donate their support to the cause. Monetary and material donations made to the cause of American missions would not only register in heaven, but would also be published in the monthly *Missionary Herald* magazine for all to see.

On Tuesday afternoon, a large group of well-wishers came to Tomlinson's wharf to say their farewells; the band of fifteen missionaries stood in a group as their relations and close friends encircled them, backed by the larger crowd. "Wake, Isles of the South!" rang out, the hymn composed by William B. Tappan, which was followed by a final prayer. Notice arrived from the ship that the missionaries had only a few minutes to say their final goodbyes. As the image of those whom they loved diminished on the far-off shore, the words of Christ's promise were remembered: "I will be with you even to the end of the world."

Missionaries knew explicitly that they were expected to live out the rest of their lives as laborers on behalf of the Kingdom of Christ. This sure knowledge of being dead to the world, their world—of never expecting to see family, friends, and homeland again in this life—made their project that much more definite and real. The missionaries were very clear that there was only one way now to go: toward an unseen place, people, and future, and they put all their energies into converting Hawaiian souls to Christ.

CHAPTER 4

Hawaiian Women, *Kapu*, and the Emergence of *Kānāwai*

Ua olelo kakou aole e holo ka wahine hookamakama i ka moku.

We have said, female prostitutes would not be allowed to go on ships.

Outrages, or attacks on missionaries, began in the islands in 1825. The assailants were not the descendants of the Hawaiian warriors, who almost a half century before slew Captain Cook, an event which etched Hawai'i indelibly into the history and memory of both Europe and America. Nor were they the fearsome savages sensationalized in European and American literature and travel writing. Attacks on the mission in Hawai'i were not perpetrated by the ubiquitous heathens spawned by missionary pens, those million souls crying out for the gospel, who were at risk of perishing in the fires of everlasting torment. Even the missionaries found it ironic that outrages against them and their families were carried out by men from civilized and Christianized nations. From 1825 to 1827, English and American ship captains and their crews launched verbal, physical, and military assaults upon the mission for its perceived role in "influencing" the ali'i to proclaim a kapu against prostitution, effectively preventing women from visiting the ships. When the missionaries wrote home about the attacks, they referred to them as "outrages," since these actions of sailors provoked "indignation, shock, anger," and constituted a "gross or malicious wrong or injury" to the feelings and principles of the missionaries.

The ali'i proclaimed this kapu sometime between April and October 1825 under circumstances that are poorly understood in histories of

Hawai'i. Because the 1825 kapu restricting Hawaiian women from visiting ships was proclaimed orally, locating the actual date of its issuance and its wording proves difficult. It is not until 1827 that a source, a letter written by the chief Hoapili, the governor of Maui to Ka'ahumanu, the kuhina nui, reveals the wording of the kapu: "Ua olelo kakou aole e holo ka wahine hookamakama i ka moku" (We have all said, female prostitutes would not be allowed to go to ships).[1] While written in this 1827 letter, we know that such a kapu was issued by the ali'i in 1825 because attacks by foreign ship captains and sailors began in 1825; Hawaiian women observed the oral pronouncement of the ali'i, enraging foreign sailors who expected access to these women aboard ship, as had been the case before this kapu. Complaints against the kapu that were raised by ship captains, foreign residents, and transient sailors before the chiefs, in personal correspondence, and journals, range widely on a continuum: from those who believed that missionaries were responsible for writing new religious laws for the Hawaiian nation to those who viewed the mission as simply wielding "influence," a troublesome but only mildly irritating passing development.

Despite such suspicions of the foreign source of this kapu, instead, we find in it evidence of the continuation of Hawaiian governance and rule and the centrality of speech to that governance. We find this authority in the manner that Hoapili references the 1825 kapu in his 1827 letter to Ka'ahumanu. He supplies us with a written citation of the oral text of the kapu. Words of speech and consensus mark the phrase as an authoritative utterance—"Ua 'ōlelo kākou" (We have spoken, we have authorized) is a phrase that signals that what comes subsequent to it carries the force of chiefly law—what the missionaries were calling "tabu" or kapu.[2] The use of "'ōlelo kākou" expresses strong unanimity among the ali'i, a unanimity that depended upon the forming of political and legal consensus. And, I argue, we find here proof that kapu continued to have a life as oral law to which Hawaiian people were subject, even after the 1819 casting down of the 'ai kapu.

This phrase "'ōlelo kākou" was spoken before the repetition of words of importance, like a kapu or the words of a chief. By using the phrase "we have said," Hoapili signaled that he was about to repeat the kapu. The use of the phrase also emphasized the official formulaic of preserved speech and emphasized the binding nature of an oral "text" as a sign that nothing has been altered or changed significantly in the process of respeaking. The veracity of such statements can be counted upon especially when the phrase

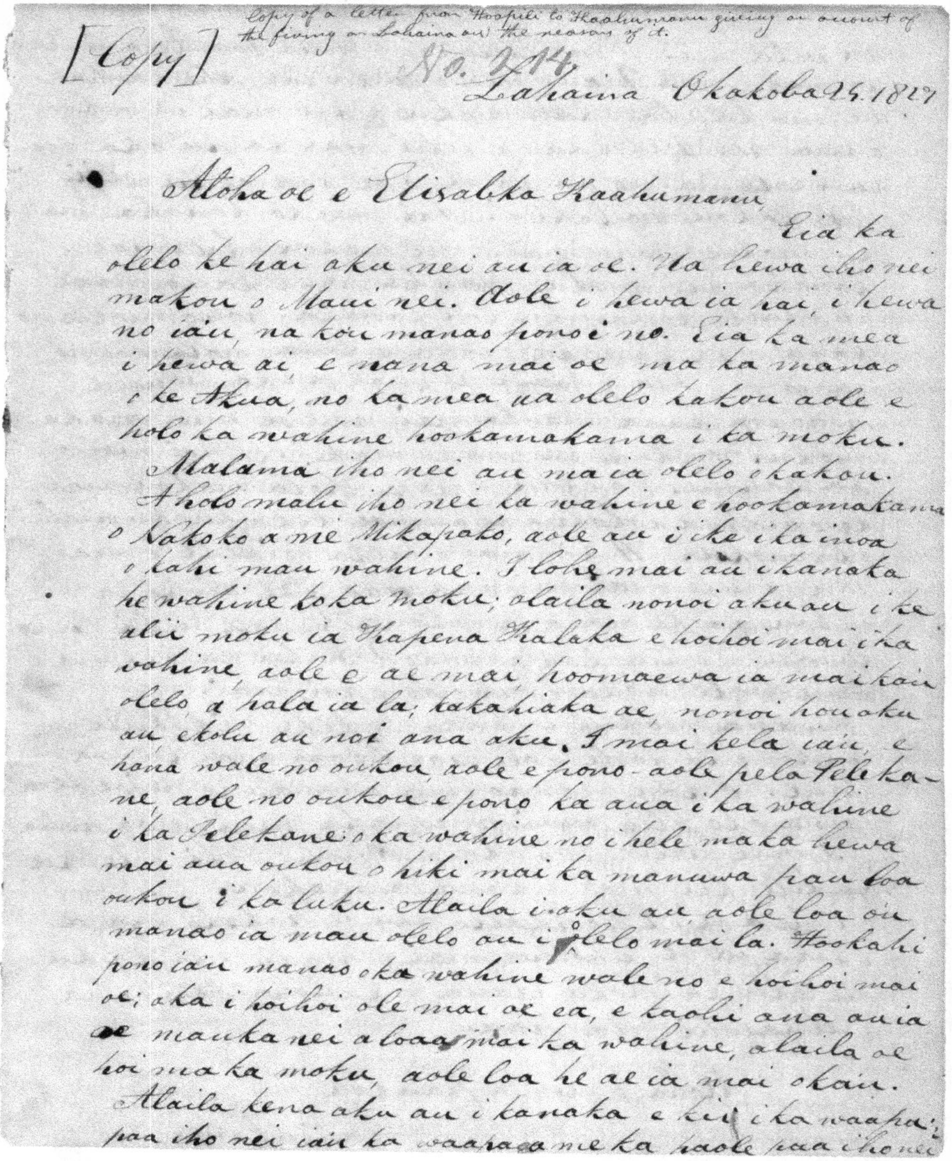

Copy of a letter from Hoapili to Kaahumanu giving an account of the firing on Lahaina and the reason of it.

No. 714

Lahaina Okakoba 24, 1827

Aloha oe e Elizabeta Kaahumanu

Eia ka olelo ke hai aku nei au ia oe. Ua hewa iho nei makou o Maui nei. Aole i hewa ia hai, i hewa no iau, na kou manao pono i no. Eia ka mea i hewa ai, e nana mai oe ma ka manao o ke Akua, no ka mea ua olelo lakou aole e holo ka wahine hookamakama i ka moku. Malama iho nei au ma ia olelo i kakou. A holo malu iho nei la wahine e hookamakama o Kakoko a me Nikapako, aole au i ike i ka inoa o kahi mau wahine. I lohe mai au i kanaka he wahine loka moku; olaila nonoi aku au i ke alii moku ia Kapena Kalaka e hoihoi mai i ka wahine, aole e ae mai hoomaewa ia mai kou olelo a hala ia la; kakahiaka ae, nonoi hou aku au e hele au noi ana aku. I mai kela iau, e hana wale no oukou, aole e pono - aole pela Pelekane, aole no oukou e pono ka aua i ka wahine i ka Pelekane o ka wahine no i hele ma ka hewa mai aua oukou o hiki mai ka manawa pau loa oukou i ka luku. Alaila i oku au aole loa ou manao ia mau olelo au i olelo mai la. Hookahi pono iau manao o ka wahine wale no e hoihoi mai oe; aka i hoihoi ole mai oe ea, e kaoli ana au ia mauka nei a loaa mai ka wahine, alaila ae hoi ma ka moku, aole loa he ae ia mai o kau. Alaila kena aku au i kanaka e kii i ka waapa; paa iho nei iau ka waapa a me ka haole paa iho nei

Figure 4. Letter from Hoapili to Kaʻahumanu, October 24, 1827. American Board of Commissioners for Foreign Missions Pacific Islands Missions Records, 1819–1960 (ABC 19.1–19.7). Houghton Library, Harvard University. Used by permission of Wider Church Ministries.

iau iuka nei. I mai kela iau, piha loa keia aina
i ka moku, noa maui nei o wela loa, aohe kauhale.
ua makaukau kuu moku e kii mai ia oukou
i keia po. I aku au, a i kii mai ka pu o ka moku malama no au ia oe, o oe o au okuu alii
hele kakou ma kahi e. I ki mai ko kanaka maka moku, noho malie no makou, oka i pae
kanaka o ka moku mauka nei e kaua mai
ai alaila kaua aku kou kanaka. noho malie no
kaua, o na kanaka o kaua e kaua, malama no
au ia oe. Ina i haawi ole mai oe i ka wahine
noho loa kaua mauka nei, aole oe e hoi ma ka
moku. Hookahi au makemake o ka hoi mai o
ka wahine. Pau kau   noho iho la makou mai
ke ahiahi a kokoke i ke aumoe kika pu kuniahi
o ka moku. Hiki mai o mika Rikeke i mai
iau, i hele mai nei au iwao, i ke aloha ia
oukou a i ke aloha ia lakou". Ninau mika Rikeke iau, "Pehea kou manao"? I aku au, o ka wahine wale no kau manao, e hoi mai.
    Uwaoia makou e mika Rikeke, oia kuu
hoihoi i ka haole, aole nae i loaa mai ka wahine. O kou manao keia i hana iho nei i keia
aina o ko alii, mai poro paha, mai hewa paha.
    I mai nei e holo aku a Oahu, o Pohi o ke Ka-
nikele kii mai e kaua ia makou.
Akahea oe, E hooikaika aku oe Nakoko ma a
i loaa ia oe, e hoihoi mai i maui nei a i ku
ole aku ka moku ilaila, e kauoha aku oe ia
Pelekaluhi. Ua pau.

        Aloha oukou a pau loa,
            Hoapilikane.

is uttered by a chief, or chiefly counselor like David Malo, whose faculties were trained to retain the past official utterances of aliʻi. These words, "ua ʻōlelo ʻia," usually precede the telling of a story passed down *mai loko mai o ka waha*, a history or a genealogy, and signals and calls upon the authorizing power of the original speaker or source.[3]

Locating kapu in writing and print is daunting, since the primary medium for kapu was speech. Kapu carried the force of law as chiefly proclamations performed before assembled groups of people. They were dependent for wider dissemination upon trained "messengers," whose auditory faculties and memories were trained to recall faithfully that which was imparted to their care.[4] Prominent aliʻi had their own messengers, who would travel far distances to deliver important words of the aliʻi to assembled people or represent the aliʻi at events which they could not be present for, in order to listen, recall important words and speeches, and relay information back to chiefly circles.[5]

The writing of early Hawaiian legal and political history is dependent upon cultural fluency in language. Identifying and interpreting legal pronuncement in Hawaiian source material requires a method of listening for its imprint in a wide range of sources, including missionary letters and journals, English-language "translated" or abridged retellings of interactions, chiefly statements, and events. Linguistic and cultural fluency in the Hawaiian language is necessary for us to be able to find oral kapu in textual sources as well as to begin to piece together how and why changes in Hawaiian law came about in the 1820s. Without this fluency, without this kind of listening for the workings of oral modes of chiefly deliberation, citation of legal precedent, and references to older models of pono governance in Hawaiian- and English-language sources, the stories of this transformation in Hawaiian law and politics will be missed or misapprehended.[6]

Speech began to be scripted in the 1820s as chiefly writers and their counselors learned how to write letters to one another. Scripting speech in writing and print thrived over the course of the nineteenth century with the proliferation of print culture in Hawaiʻi.[7] Even as Hawaiian men and women observed the 1825 prohibition, foreign sailors on visiting ships from Britain and America did not. Their status as subjects of foreign nations made their problematic behavior in the Hawaiian Islands a real issue for the aliʻi as they sought to maintain a lawful society. As a case study, the kapu on Hawaiian women and its fallout illuminate a moment of transition in the legal landscape of Hawaiʻi. While previous histories of

this moment reproduce the erroneous perceptions of the captains and sailors who blamed the New England missionaries for giving this law to the
aliʻi to declare, this chapter demands a fundamental revision to this view
that law was introduced in Hawaiʻi to civilize a "savage" people. The aliʻi
themselves recognized the need to adopt kānāwai, or written and published
law in the islands as the best way to control and discipline foreigners behaving badly on Hawaiian soil.

A key question to raise is "Why did the aliʻi proclaim the kapu in 1825?"
Is it possible to historicize legal change in this context when it has been
assumed that the kānaka maoli populace was operating in the absence of
kapu or law? This intervention into early nineteenth-century Hawaiian legal
history makes clear that "orality" as praxis should not be conflated with
unequal colonial measures of native "tradition" or "story" that have been
reified as modes of authentic native knowledge, but should be seen as the
first and primary medium that conveyed kapu, law, and political speech
through the early nineteenth century. In excavating the textual terrain to
reveal Hawaiian modes of deliberation and consensus, the persistence of
authoritative speech, and how Hawaiian precedent was employed by chiefly
advisers, this chapter and the next contribute evidence of Hawaiian governance in transition. In doing so, these chapters argue that this exercise of
"native" self-governance operated beyond restrictive scholarly models of
"agency" and "resistance." This work sets aside an assumption of haole
dominance and power at the planting of the mission and argues instead
that strife within the foreign community resulted in benefits for the mission
and new moral laws to be promulgated by the ruling Hawaiian aliʻi to
discipline an increasingly complex society of makaʻāinana, missionaries and
sailors, ship captains and merchants: natives, settlers, and transients.

Chiefly conversion to Christianity was an important factor in giving the
declaration of this kapu the new moral foundation it needed to garner
support by aliʻi on different islands, a process that required broad consensus. Additionally, Hawaiian modes of deliberation, forums for discussions,
and conventions for the dissemination of knowledge predated the arrival
of foreigners and the mission.[8] Rather than simply a product of tyrannical
and unenlightened chiefly rule—or proof of "missionary influence," as the
merchants and sailors claimed—the kapu on women was proclaimed as a
result of several factors.

The public discussion regarding the prohibition of prostitution developed over time. An initial kapu from 1823 barred Hawaiian women from

going on board vessels and was tied to a requirement of ships to "pay one dollar at the fort for every female going on board." Levi Chamberlain wrote that "some of the captains are enraged on account of the tabu & some fears are entertained that they will make disturbance."⁹ The "kapu" was set up to respond to a change in context, once sailors and ship captains paid money, its restrictive nature was lifted, and as a result, no "disturbances," or "outrages" were reported in the next two years over the kapu on women going to ships.

Discussion also took place in relation to newly introduced ideas about marriage and adultery that were slowly being embraced by the aliʻi. On November 10, 1824, the aliʻi Opiʻia, a former wahine of Kamehameha and sister of the kuhina Kaʻahumanu, was faced with a husband whose wife wanted to leave him for another man. Opiʻia "censured" the woman, threatening a punishment of being placed "in irons" were she to disregard Opiʻia's word. Soon after, the woman's lover offered Opiʻia money, which the aliʻi refused, remarking to Rev. Bingham, "He thought he could buy the woman." Bingham, for his part, found the behavior of the aliʻi commendable, noting that her decision would have "done credit to a Christian magistrate."¹⁰

The peace of Hawaiian society was challenged by a transient population of sailors who believed that sexual access to Hawaiian women was a right, albeit one that they were willing to pay for. The aliʻi were the authority in maintaining order among the Hawaiian populace. They navigated between the needs of their people, the unruly behavior of transient sailors, the demands of merchants, and the new teachings of missionaries. For this reason, the importance of deliberation and consensus among the aliʻi increased during this period. The kapu on Hawaiian women going to ships was a continued expression of chiefly governance years in the making. According to the missionaries, Opiʻia was "very desirous that the great irregularities in relation to marriage may be corrected. She *says*, when the chiefs generally agree to it, prostitution of females on board ships shall be prohibited." Though the kapu on prostitution had been a topic of discussion among the aliʻi, and also between the aliʻi and the mission, it would take more than mere "influence" on the part of the mission to effect its pronouncement and enforcement.

The shifting morality of the people and the tensions among ship captains, commercial agents, and missionaries over the subject of sexual access to Hawaiian women was also a problem the kuhina Kaʻahumanu and Kālaimoku had to contend with while considering the best way to control both a complex and highly interacting native and foreign population. Innovations in Hawaiian governance and law were required, and while kapu continued to be placed upon Hawaiian subjects, foreigners not bound to the pronouncements and jurisdiction of the chiefs required different instruments of understanding, especially when their conduct was involved. The 1820s is a period in which Hawaiian kapu and law are expanded to deal with this problematic conduct of foreigners; the introduction of writing and printing gave Hawaiian law new forms. The publication of laws in Hawaiian and English—the kānāwai—in 1822 regulated the comings and goings of foreigners in Hawai'i and required captains to submit accurate crew lists to the Hawaiian government, provide for Hawaiian enforcement of order through punishment and levying of fines for sailor desertions.[11]

With the growing influx of foreigners to the Hawaiian Islands, the chiefs needed to address domestic political issues that arose from the continuing consequences of unification and those brought through interactions with foreigners. These problems included the public drunkenness and violence that sailors—many of whom were deserting their ships—brought to land. While at sea, captains exerted firm control over their crews, but once on land, these men often seemed to have no masters.

Attempting to rein in these men, some of the ship captains and the missionaries put forth publications urging quasi-contractual agreements to enforce restraint on intemperate seamen. Other ship captains, however, directly caused trouble, especially when it came to the pursuit of Hawaiian women for themselves and their men. Faced with ship captains behaving badly as well as the *hewa* behavior of a particular high chiefess on Maui, the chiefs of the islands proclaimed the 1825 kapu forbidding Hawaiian women from going out to ships for the purpose of prostitution.

This chapter traces the events leading up to and causing the pronouncement of this kapu, as well as the development of a new form of law, published kānāwai, as an evolution in Hawaiian governance. I argue that the 1825 kapu and subsequent new law was spurred on by an increasing need for the ali'i to deal with the "outrage-ous" behavior of foreign sailors and some of their captains. Past historical narratives of this moment have not sufficiently investigated reasons for why the ali'i might have declared the 1825 kapu, preferring instead to simply repeat foreign seamen's complaints that it was a missionary law parroted by the chiefs. To correct this one-sided view of the 1825 prohibition and the decade's changes in law and governance, this chapter uses a broader range of source materials in Hawaiian and English, reconstructing possible ways to hear and see Hawaiian statements and performances that held weight and were resonant in governance, law, and authority.[12] When a second company of New England missionaries arrived in 1823, they brought further support to mission school-building and education of the Hawaiian ali'i and their people. Their subsequent interactions with the ali'i in whose jurisdictions they lived and worked reveal much about the complex political and familial confluences and tensions between various ruling ali'i. I argue that one chiefess in particular, Wahinepi'o, played a central role in events that led to the pronouncement of the 1825 kapu prohibiting women from going to foreign ships to be with sailors. Restoring a larger source-base of this moment rebalances the measure of how and why the 1825 kapu was proclaimed.

The Progress of the Mission

Soon after his arrival with the second company of missionaries on April 24, 1823, Rev. William Richards and his colleague Rev. Charles Stewart assumed their post at Lahaina, Maui. They were two of five ministers now spread across four islands—Kaua'i, O'ahu, Maui, and Hawai'i—a largely ocean-spanning distance of some 370 miles. The post these two men held was one of importance, since they would be attached to the chiefly alo ali'i of Keōpūolani, the most sacred widow of Kamehameha I, the mother of his three chiefly children Liholiho (Kamehameha II), Kauikeaouli, and Nāhi'ena'ena.

The second company of missionaries differed in composition from the first company. Rather than sending a farmer to promulgate foreign agricultural practices among Hawaiians, they sent Levi Chamberlain as secular agent to handle the mission's business transactions and keep track of its stores. The depository that Chamberlain had charge of was located in Honolulu, O'ahu's major port, where all the supplies for the mission were received, divided, and distributed: ink and paper for the press, school supplies and books, and clothing and foodstuffs. It was Chamberlain's job to purchase and keep track of all transactions with incoming ships for necessities that had not been adequately provided by the Boston-based mission. Chamberlain had given up his former life as a merchant and accountant in his family firm. His new vocation required him to sail regularly between the islands to deliver supplies to the different stations. These engagements positioned him as a liaison between the mission and merchants and ship captains whose social circles he entered when negotiating for and purchasing items and delivering packages and letters to ships for conveyance. Chamberlain would prove to be an important and exhaustive recorder of daily occurences as he moved fluidly between these groups.

His was a more tactile view of missionary, Hawaiian, merchant, and maritime relations, since he frequently circulated in and between these discrete spaces; he also interacted a lot with the ali'i and wrote down his personal reflections of each day's transactions: social, commercial, and religious. Chamberlain and Richards produced letters, journals, and accounts that provide detailed insight into relations between foreigners and Hawaiians. Although all missionaries wrote and kept journals as part of their daily labors, each individual produced knowledge and information in different ways and for diverse imagined audiences.

Far from being a cohesive force of colonists settling in Hawai'i, missionaries were isolated from one another, settling in six different stations spread out across four islands in order to maintain proximity to the local alo ali'i (chiefly households). Hawai'i Island, located at the eastern end of the archipelago, was home to three stations because of its large size, at Kailua, Hilo, and Ka'awaloa. Rev. Hiram Bingham, printer Elisha Loomis, Dr. Abraham Blatchely, their wives, and Levi Chamberlain were all stationed on O'ahu at Honolulu. Working at the Maui mission were Rev. Richards and his wife Clarissa, Stewart and his wife Harriet, and Betsey Stockton, a "negro" assistant, who accompanied the Stewart family from Boston. Keōpūolani had chosen the Richards and Stewarts to accompany her and her alo ali'i to take up residence in Lahaina, Maui, in May 1824. Keōpūolani was the highest-ranking chief in the islands; she and Ka'ahumanu were "widows" of Kamehameha I. Keōpūolani was the mother of the mō'ī, Liholiho Kamehameha II, his *kaikaina* (younger male sibling), Kauikeaouli, and their *kaikuahine* (female sibling of males) Nāhi'ena'ena. The ministers served as instructors to the ali'i and those in her extended household. Mr. Richards held the important task of serving as the personal instructor of the eight-year-old Nāhi'ena'ena and Kauikeaouli, in a new position that would make him eventually the *kahu* haole to these ali'i. It would be in this capacity of servant to the ali'i that individual missionaries like William Richards would find themselves taken in and deeply entwined (*hihia*) in the concerns and interests of the chiefs.

By 1825, eight churches had been built and numerous schools inaugurated throughout the islands. On every island, chiefly governors (*kiaʻāina*)
approached the missionaries in their locale to instruct members of their alo
aliʻi. At Kaʻawaloa, the chief kuakini (Governor John Adams) desired to
have "all the new chiefs about him instructed," going so far as to propose
that a new schoolhouse be built and that he would "become himself a
teacher."[13] At the western end of the archipelago on Kauaʻi, the chief Kaikioʻewa approached Mr. Whitney, "expressing a determination to establish
schools in all the districts of that island."[14] On Maui, Rev. Richards reported
on August 9, 1825, that there were "nineteen schools in Lahaina, containing
about three hundred and eighty scholars." Under the patronage of the aliʻi,
Richards "sent seventeen teachers to different parts of the islands," providing some idea of the spread of education on Maui alone.[15] Education had
to be carried forward by Hawaiians trained by missionaries, as there were
not enough missionaries to fulfill the command of the aliʻi.[16] At Honolulu,
on the neighboring island of Oʻahu, the number of students in attendance
at various schools was said to be seven hundred. These included aliʻi, their
households, and makaʻāinana children and adults.[17]

The progress of the schools was hastened along by the successful dissemination of printed materials. In the year that elapsed between June 1825 and
October 1826, the mission's presses had been exceedingly productive: 22,000
revised copies of a spelling book had been printed, bringing the number of
spelling books available to schools to 63,000 copies. Additionally, 11,500 copies were printed of a small catechism, 7,000 of an unspecified tract, while
10,000 copies of the Decalogue and Lord's Prayer had been printed and disseminated among the chiefs and people. Added to this output were 3,000
copies of original compositions by the chiefs, 500 copies of the Good Samari-
tan, and 10,000 copies of a new edition of hymns, bringing the total number
of materials published by the mission press to a staggering 74,000 copies.[18]

Hawaiian intellectuals and chiefly advisers were now engaged in another
new project of education, the progress of the palapala, reading and
writing—one that was grafted onto their already established skills, memories, and faculties trained to memorize and recall knowledge through
speech. The "new education" of the missionaries would take root in soil
already well nurtured for its reception; it would grow out of an already
established Hawaiian education.

By March 1824, Lahaina had become a major center of Hawaiian political and mission life, as many of the chiefs moved there to live near the

chiefess Keōpūolani. Rev. Charles Stewart and Rev. Richards described Lahaina in their letter to Jeremiah Evarts: "Of the twenty-four highest chiefs of the islands, twelve have resided almost constantly at this place, and it has been the occasional residence of nearly all the rest."[19] Because of the large number of chiefs who lived in Lahaina, the population of makaʻāinana in the area also increased. Lahaina, the ministers marveled, was transforming due to the chiefly presence: "Since we arrived at Lahaina, only nine months ago, one hundred and fifty houses have been erected on the beach and many more have been rebuilt back from the sea. The population then estimated at 2,500, is now probably 4,000."[20]

Keōpūolani became the first chief to be baptized by the missionaries, as she passed from this world on September 16, 1824. Soon after her death, the population of Lahaina changed again, with many of the aliʻi relocating to Oʻahu, while the governess Wahinepiʻo, the chief Hoapili, and his wife, who were the guardians of Nāhiʻenaʻena, remained in residence. In November of 1824, the number of pupils in Lahaina were "not less than six hundred," whereas "in the school of Nāhiʻenaʻena were 270 scholars." But success was dependent upon the interest of the chief, and some six months later, when Nāhiʻenaʻena seemingly "grew inattentive" to instruction, the number of scholars in Lahaina was reduced to about four hundred.[21]

Rev. Richards and Rev. Stewart began to have difficulty with the chiefess Wahinepiʻo as early as March of 1824. She was the sister of Kālaimoku and the governess of the island; thus the ministers recognized "the necessity of treating her with particular attention." The chiefess had offered to supply the missionaries on numerous occasions with food, telling them, "If you want pork or fish, come to me." When they finally approached her for meat, she "expressed her sympathy in very strong terms" and promised to send them a hog. The missionaries were shocked by the gift of the governess—an old hog that "had been so affected by disease that it had lost nearly all its bristles, and its flesh so wasted away, and it was so covered with sores" that the ministers concluded that "even with the best care, it could probably have lived but a short time." They resolved thenceforth to be more "cautious about asking favors, than we have heretofore supposed necessary."[22] Perhaps the sickly pig was a not-so-veiled symbol of Wahinepiʻo's regard for the ministers and their work. It could also have been a critique of their lack of manners in failing to reciprocate in like fashion, by fulfilling the desires of the chief on different occasions when she asked for instruction, trade goods, or other materials or books. The missionaries were receiving an education in Hawaiian decorum; hospitality clearly had its limits.

The missionaries were concerned both with raising the nation from "idolatry" to Christianity and civilization and about the bad example that immorality among foreigners gave to Hawaiians. Missionaries were also introducing new structures of morality as part of their Christianizing and civilization project by introducing the institution of marriage and discouraging sexual liaisons outside of marriage as well as relations between multiple partners.

The missionaries were making headway with the aliʻi. On June 28, 1825, Kālaimoku was married to ʻAkahi. Five months later, on November 23, Opiʻia, along with Deborah Kapule, the first chiefly "wife" of Kaumualiʻi, high chief of Kauaʻi, were married to Hawaiian men of lesser chiefly rank, the former to Laʻanui, the latter to Kaʻiu.[23] These aliʻi marriages publicly formalized and legitimized these practices, providing new paradigmatic behaviors for the makaʻāinana to emulate. Following the lead of the aliʻi was perhaps a more powerful enticement to Christianity than theology. These new standards of relation, especially when adopted by the chiefs, would have a significant and long-reaching impact on the future of Hawaiian governance that was not quite imaginable among the aliʻi themselves at this time.

While Hoapili, Kaʻahumanu, and Wahinepiʻo's brother Kālaimoku were turning to the Lord, Wahinepiʻo herself continued to encourage the teaching and performance of hula dancing and chanting as both an effective way to assert her opposition to the mission's teachings and as part of maintaining everyday practice.[24] Writing a year later, on February 2, 1825, Rev. Richards noted that although several of the chiefs of Maui had written to Kālaimoku to "silence the *hurahura* (hula) which now occupy the attention of most of the people of Lahaina," the chiefess Wahinepiʻo "has done much to encourage this heathenish practice."[25] A month and a half later, the competition between chiefs patronizing the mission and those who opposed it escalated, highlighting the political and familial rifts that were already present among the aliʻi in the postunification period after the death of Kamehameha I.

The divisions over Christianity exacerbated rather than engendered disagreement among the chiefs regarding everything from access to trade to everyday jostling for power. When on March 23 Nāhiʻenaʻena had "forbidden all who could not read the hymns to go into her house," resulting in a small, select number of attendants remaining with her, Wahinepiʻo, in retaliation, forbade "any to enter her house who are not skillful in the *hurahura*."[26] Such retaliatory acts need to be seen in terms of the continued elevation of Hawaiian female power and the prerogatives of older generations of aliʻi leading by example, teaching and chastising the younger. Upon closer examination, it appears that a more sophisticated politic operated among younger native female leaders than has usually been imagined by scholars writing about this period in Hawaiian political history.

Leoiki (Little Voice)

> Kekauonohi: Wahine Pio—Wahine Pio!
> Wahinepio: What is it?
> Kekauonohi: I am the daughter, and you are the mother, I
> am a child, and you are an old chief—it is mine to listen:
> But I am wise and you are dark hearted—you do not fear
> God nor regard his word, therefore hear me—have no hula
> in Lahaina—the hula is not good.[27]

Wahinepiʻo, like all other high-ranking chiefs, was attended by a number of people who made up her alo aliʻi, those who lived in the presence of the chief. Members of the alo aliʻi included chiefs of lesser rank and people of high standing in the community. Knowledgeable counselors, teachers, and genealogists, as well as those who cared for the extended community attached to a particular aliʻi, would be part of her alo aliʻi. Kahu—attendants of the aliʻi—enjoyed an elevated status in society; a kahu's proximity to the chief's person was still structured by kapu. Living and working in the presence of the chief was a recognized honor but was freighted with much responsibility and attention to detail, as Marie Alohalani Brown illustrates quite vividly in her biography on chiefly kahu, John Papa ʻĪʻī.[28] The role of kahu was passed down, with younger members of the family trained by fathers, mothers, or grandparents. One of Wahinepiʻo's kahu was a chief of middle to lower rank named Leoiki. As kahu, Leoiki might do such things as handle and care for the personal effects of the chief, items that were imbued with Wahinepiʻo's spiritual and political power (mana).

In March 1825, Leoiki spent several days and nights aboard the British whaleship *Daniel IV*, one of several ships recruiting sailors in the sheltered waters off Lahaina, Maui. After a few days aboard ship as the "companion" of Captain William Buckle, Leoiki returned to shore to deliver a request from Buckle to Wahinepi'o asking if he could take Leoiki on a seven-month whaling cruise.[29] Coming to Wahinepi'o's home, entering into her presence, and addressing her words to her chiefess, Leoiki placed eight dollars (doubloons) into Wahinepi'o's palm, saying, "Here is the money of the foreigner, he wishes you to give me to him for his—the money is yours, but if you take it I am to go with him to a foreign country. So the foreigner said to me."[30] In delivering Buckle's words, Leoiki may have hinted at her own desire to remain on Maui and not accompany her lover on his whaling voyage.

Captain Buckle, pursuing another avenue to achieve his desire, approached Wahinepi'o's husband Kaukuna Kahekili in Lahaina. He intended to give the money to Kaukuna in exchange for Leoiki. David Malo, adviser to many of the highest-ranking ali'i from Hawai'i Island, was also present for Buckle's conversation with Kaukuna. Malo noted that Buckle "insisted on having Leoiki." Buckle tried to pay the money to Kaukuna, saying, "The woman shall be mine and the money yours." Buckle may have thought that taking his bargain to Kahekili would produce superior results, as he worked from the structural norms of coverture and patriarchal status that applied in England. Perhaps Buckle surmised that Kahekili would be able to command his chiefly wife to bend to his demands. But Kaukuna could not agree simply because, as he said, "The woman is not mine, but Wahinepi'o's," to which he also added, "She is a woman that has turned to the Lord."[31] Kaukuna's foremost reason for not accepting Buckle's proposition was that Leoiki was not subject to his will (his word); he could not order her to do anything. Kaukuna then returned to shore and told Wahinepi'o of Buckle's offer.

Buckle took Kaukuna's advice and approached Wahinepi'o, after which he sent eight doubloons, which were again refused.[32] Just a few days before the *Daniel IV* was to sail out of Hawaiian waters, Captain Buckle, in a final attempt, invited Wahinepi'o and Kaukuna to his ship for dinner. Although Wahinepi'o had assured Leoiki that she would not give her consent, at this dinner, the chief agreed to let Leoiki go with Buckle for more money.[33] Overhearing the verbal agreement, Malo attempted to intervene, remarking to Wahinepi'o, "I am very sorry for the woman." Wahinepi'o replied, "So am I." Elated, Buckle agreed to one condition stipulated by the chief: that he bring Leoiki back to Maui at the end of the *Daniel IV*'s voyage to the

"Japanese whaling grounds," that stretch of ocean between Japan and Hawai'i that was just beginning to be mapped out as a place abundant with whales.

Leoiki "wept bitterly" when told that Wahinepi'o had agreed to Buckle's terms and that she must now go with him. Her response was witnessed by several of the ali'i and their attendants. Hoapiliwahine noted it, as did her husband: Hoapilikāne remarked that "her very weeping made it plain to us that she was sold."[34] Malo also commented on Leoiki's emotional reaction to Wahinepi'o's reversal, noting that Leoiki "could not see on account of her excessive weeping."[35]

Seeking advice, Leoiki visited Taua, a Tahitian missionary and a protégé of Rev. William Ellis of the London Missionary Society, who had arrived in the islands in 1823 and now worked with the Sandwich Islands Mission, translating the Bible with Rev. Richards and David Malo. Taua served as a living and relatable example for Hawaiians of a nonwhite Christian who shared their island, oceanic world.[36] Leoiki asked Taua, "What indeed can I do for my part to set this to rights?"[37]

A brief conversation between the two ensued. "My patroness Wahinepi'o tells me to go as a woman for the foreigner," Leoiki said to Taua, who replied, "Perhaps you will not be able to say no to the thought of the chief."[38] Taua perhaps understood the relations of obligation between Leoiki and Wahinepi'o from his own experiences in Tahiti, or perhaps it was an observation he had made while in the islands. Whatever the case, Taua, too, acknowledged that once Wahinepi'o had come to a decision and spoken to Leoiki, she had little recourse but to consent.

At this point in the conversation, Leoiki introduced another concern: "I do not wish to go on board the ship, for I greatly love God. If it were the old time that would be right." Leoiki may indeed have become a convert to Christianity by 1825, as she made a distinction between behavior appropriate to the old time—*ka wā kahiko*, the time when Hawaiians worshipped "idols,"—and a new time of Christianity, associated by the missionaries with the phrase *ka wā hou* (the new time). One other point of significance arises in this exchange between Leoiki and Taua in Leoiki's use of the word "pono" to mean "right or correct." Leoiki's use of the word illuminates the different layers of pono she had to consider as a woman living between ethical and moral systems in the making, between the introduced pono of the Christian Akua and the way in which social relations between ali'i and their people were transforming in the wake of daily encounters with merchants, sailors, and missionaries. "Pono," or proper behavior between chief and attendant, was framed by relations of regard and care, by the way the chiefly malu of protection was extended over all within the residence of the aliʻi.

Leoiki asked Taua how to come to a decision that was both "right" for her, yet would not slight the will of Wahinepiʻo, her chief. But Leoiki had also been a pupil of the mission, probably against the wishes of Wahinepiʻo. Notwithstanding her chief's *manaʻo*, she had recently turned to the Lord. In Hawaiian and missionary parlance, the way of Jehovah was called "ka pono a ke akua," the correct or right way of God. Leoiki was therefore faced with competing, significant demands upon her service: how can she serve her chief or the will of the God of the newly introduced "religion"? If Leoiki cared to preserve her own position and social standing as Wahinepiʻo's kahu, she had to fulfill the word of the chief or risk losing her ties and social place.[39]

In the end, Leoiki unhappily upheld the pronouncement of her chief, boarding *Daniel IV* to go with Buckle on the seven-month voyage. Aboard the ship readying for departure, Leoiki sent three messengers to her teacher, Rev. Richards, "earnestly entreating that [he] would use [his] influence to procure her release."[40] According to a letter Richards wrote to the corresponding secretary of the American Board of Commissioners for Foreign Missions (ABCFM), Jeremiah Evarts, on November 30, 1825, some eight months after Leoiki had been taken, "the 'law' [*kapu*] on the subject was not then passed and, there was no chief or sufficient authority in Lahaina to whom I could apply. She was therefore compelled to go notwithstanding all her entreaties."[41] Richards could not locate a chief in Lahaina at the time who could, by superior rank, overturn the oral pronouncement of Governess Wahinepiʻo. He therefore had no choice but to put aside Leoiki's pleas and watch as she and Buckle sailed away.

As news spread from Lahaina to the other islands, other high-ranking chiefs began to form an opinion of the significance and possible repercussions of Wahinepiʻo's actions. Wahinepiʻo sailed to Oʻahu soon after Leoiki's sale where she was confronted by her brother, Kālaimoku, the prime minister, who, having been informed of the exchange, demanded, "Was Leoiki sold by you for gold dollars?" Wahinepiʻo replied, "It is indeed true, I have acted wrongly [*hewa*]. The woman has gone to the foreigner, and the money has passed over to me." Incensed at her words, Kālaimoku railed, "You are exceedingly bad, I too perhaps shall be implicated in this horrible wrong and perhaps my soul along with yours shall die because of your misdeed."[42] Perhaps Wahinepi'o's hewa was doubly magnified, a violation of the relationship between ali'i and kahu, and the flouting of the Christian pono regarding sex outside the bonds of marriage. What is clear is that Kālaimoku understood the hewa of his sister as a collective burden he too shouldered due to their relationship.

Kālaimoku, too, was feeling the pressure of his observance of the pono of the new God. But as a close familial relation of Wahinepi'o, he had other cause for concern. Her actions not only reflected upon him, but as a member of the 'aha ali'i, he had to live with the political and social consequences of her decision as well. As kuhina nui, coregent with Ka'ahumanu during the rule of Kamehameha III, Kālaimoku was charged with the responsibility of making sure that each island was governed in proper fashion. Wahinepi'o's actions as governor of the island of Maui provided a particular challenge to the larger functioning of the ali'i governing structure. Authority was distributed across the archipelago and vested in the ruling capacity of closely intertwined families of chiefs. While Wahinepi'o exercised control over Lahaina, her husband Kaukuna and the chief Hoapili and his wife were also chiefly presences on the island during this time. However, even they could not claim Leoiki as a subject of theirs, as she particularly answered to the chief Wahinepi'o as her kahu and member of her extended "household." Thus, while these chiefs carefully observed their political rights and limits with each other, Wahinepi'o's actions, condemned by many of Kālaimoku's closest chiefs and Hawaiian and Christian advisers, pointed out how one chief's justifiable actions could have serious personal and political consequences. More importantly, the discussion over Leoiki's sale allows us to see relationships between ali'i, their particular alliances, and the way that the chiefly governing structure operated or responded to address *internal* crises.

Condemnation of Wahinepi'o's actions spread among the high chiefs. Reacting perhaps to their negative comments, Wahinepi'o tried to rid herself of the money by giving it to Nāhi'ena'ena, the young sister of Kauikeaouli. When Nāhi'ena'ena asked, "From whom is the money?" Wahinepi'o replied, "from my *kahu*, from Leoiki who was insisted upon by the foreigner, captain Buckle to sail with him as a woman for him. I assented and the thing which I received was the money."[43] Nāhi'ena'ena suspiciously regarded the doubloons that Wahinepi'o offered, but did not take them. That no chief accepted the money is an indication of the seriousness of the matter among the chiefs.[44]

Kālaimoku angrily accused his sister of "bringing death upon his soul because of her *hewa*." Wahinepiʻo's judgment in the affair was questioned and pointedly criticized. If Wahinepiʻo's profession of guilt was not damning enough, her action in trying to rid herself of the money by handing it off to Nāhiʻenaʻena was proof that Wahinepiʻo was feeling the weight of chiefly disapproval. As Leoiki sailed toward the Japanese whaling grounds on Buckle's ship, the ʻaha ʻōlelo met and pronounced a kapu forbidding women to go out to ships for the purpose of prostitution. It is certain that Kaʻahumanu and Kālaimoku, the two highest-ranking aliʻi in the islands after the young Kauikeaouli, were the main supporters of the kapu. The proclamation of this kapu by the ʻaha ʻōlelo is revelatory of kānaka maoli structures of deliberation, the continued practice of oral pronouncement in the islands at this particular moment, and the dynamics of governance between aliʻi and makaʻāinana alike.

Though Wahinepiʻo was not a subject of Kaʻahumanu or Kālaimoku, the pronouncement of this kapu against women going to ships was a very public, material manifestation of chiefly disapproval of Wahinepiʻo's "sale" of Leoiki to Captain Buckle. Thus the kapu became a kind of censure of Wahinepiʻo's actions, even as it reinforced aliʻi jurisdiction over Hawaiian women's conduct as members of Hawaiian society. The kapu could not directly address the behavior of foreign men; nor could they violate the kapu because they were not subjects of the kapu and aliʻi authority. But by proclaiming this kapu, the aliʻi created a way to protect Hawaiian women from the depredations of foreigners and chiefs alike, even as it forcefully compelled women who were trading sex to cease their activities, and its legal precedent in Hawaiian kapu and governance came from close to home for the kuhina nui Kaʻahumanu.[45]

The 1825 *Kapu* on Women in Hawaiian Legal History

Five months before the kapu on women was uttered, on November 10, 1824, Opiʻia, Kaʻahumanu's sister, perhaps presciently noted in conversation with Rev. Bingham that "when the chiefs generally agree to it, prostitution of females on board ships shall be prohibited."[46] The sale of Leoiki was the event which may have catalyzed chiefly opinion in favor of the kapu.

While the mission had an interest in bringing an end to prostitution in the islands as part of their instruction in Christian behavior in keeping with

God's word, they had no authority or power to proclaim kapu or institute law in the islands. Rev. William Richards wrote this detailed observation of how kapu operated in a letter to Corresponding Secretary Jeremiah Evarts of the ABCFM:

> The power of laying tabus is vested in the chiefs. Any chief has power to lay a tabu, and this tabu extends to all the people of that chief, who are more or less numerous according to the rank and popularity of the chief. The tabu of the highest class of chiefs extend in a great degree to all the people of the islands. I have known frequent instances of punishment, where the tabus of one chief of one island have been broken by the people of a chief belonging to another island. The tabus of the king, and also the tabus of the Regent or Regents are according to my observation alike binding on all the people of all the islands.[47]

According to Richards' account, kapu could be a local district or island phenomenon; it could apply to the persons and subjects of a particular chief, or, when proclaimed by one of the *kuhina* (regents) or the king, to all the people in the archipelago. The kapu on prostitution proclaimed by the king and his kuhina, therefore, applied to all women on all the islands. While the ABCFM's guideline cautioned against missionary intervention into local politics, it did not prevent Rev. Richards from being a keen observer of political structures of chiefly governance and the ways that kapu was pronounced and observed.

The kapu that was ordered by the chiefs upon Hawaiian women sometime between April and October 1825 prohibited women from journeying out to ships for the purpose of prostitution. In order for us to think about this kapu, it may be useful to consider how past kapu were applied to the body of one of the most powerful *ali'i wahine* of this time, Ka'ahumanu, by her *kāne*, Kamehameha, during the late 1790s. Placing this 1825 kapu in this broader Hawaiian historical context allows us to read mo'olelo (Hawaiian histories) as offering evidence of legal precedents.

Ka'ahumanu was the daughter of a high chief of Hawai'i Island, Ke'eaumoku, who was one of Kamehameha's four chiefly advisers.[48] At some point in the 1790s, Ke'eaumoku was sick unto death. An epidemic was making its way through the ranks of Kamehameha's warriors, felling ali'i and maka'āinana alike. The epidemic carried off many of Kamehameha's important

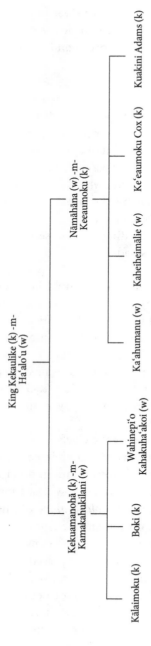

Figure 5. Genealogy of Kaʻahumanu.

chiefly advisers (*nā kuhina*). Kamehameha, hearing of Keʻeaumoku's feeble state, went to his side to obtain the aged chief's final counsel. "If perhaps you die," Kamehameha asked, "will my rule be conspired against?" Keʻeaumoku replied, "There is no chief who will rebel against your dominion; there is only one great threat within your government, your *wahine*[,] and if you take great pains, your rule will not be conspired against."[49] Heeding Keʻeaumoku's final counsel, Kamehameha placed a kapu on the body of his wife Kaʻahumanu, decreeing that any chief or common person having sexual relations with her would be killed.

The regulation placed upon Kaʻahumanu's body was not simply about sex or gender oppression. If anything, the kapu on her person was Kamehameha's acknowledgment of Kaʻahumanu's mana, mana which both Keʻeaumoku and Kamehameha recognized as stemming from her similar, central position within a web of chiefly liaisons that could rival Kamehameha's. Kaʻahumanu, like Kamehameha, could count on the power of family connection in the event she sought to secure her rule over her kāne and chief. The kapu on her person sought to block the possibility that she would seek alliances with other, younger male aliʻi, allies who could tip the balance of power away from Kamehameha to Kaʻahumanu. Since she had no children, it cannot be assumed that the kapu was placed upon her body to simply prevent her from having offspring with other chiefs. Additionally, multiple sexual liaisons resulting in expansive, intertwined genealogies were the norm among aliʻi.[50] The kapu was not about restricting the transferring of inherited mana to the next generation of children. It was about Kaʻahumanu's ability to be the maker of the next aliʻi nui (high chief) in her generation through a partnership created by sexual union.

While such an act of sexual alliance between younger male chiefs and older chiefly women was commonplace, Kaʻahumanu's qualities made her potential relationships different. Because of her refined political intelligence, rank, and family ties, she was a powerful threat to Kamehameha's rule, especially because she came from very high-ranking aliʻi in her lineage. The kapu that Kamehameha placed on Kaʻahumanu's body prevented rebellion and usurpation of his rule by placing restrictions on the sexual behavior of the most politically powerful woman of the times. This was his act to check her political ambition and the ambitions of any other chiefs seeking rule through alliance with her.[51] Repercussions for any men violating this kapu would be extremely serious if not deadly.

Keʻeaumoku's words were not, as we might be tempted to read them, simply warning that rival male aliʻi sought the kingdom of Kamehameha. Rather, Keʻeaumoku clearly identified Kaʻahumanu as the root of future political struggles and intrigue.[52] For sex was not the only exchange transacted on the *moena* (mat) of the chief. Political machinations and discussions would, of course, be part of intimate liaisons with a chiefess so powerfully placed as Kaʻahumanu.

We have another example of Kaʻahumanu's importance and power, found in a chant of criticism attributed to Pele, the akua wahine (goddess) of fire and the destructive force of the volcano: "Lilo kā mākou kāne i ka hāʻawe ʻoloʻolo, Haʻalele ʻia ka hāʻawe leilei e leilei e" (Our husband has been subdued by the unwieldy burden, while the lighter load / adornment has been cast aside). The words suggest that a dangerous flow of lava was a consequence of Pele's rage at Kamehameha; the goddess was angry because he was devoting himself to another female chief instead of Kaʻahumanu. Kamehameha went to provide an offering to appease Pele, who was devouring the productive lands and residences of North Kona, Hawaiʻi. It was said that Pele appeared to him, leading a procession of goddesses chanting those lines. This chant acts as a register of Kaʻahumanu's mana, this time through a chant attributed to an akua (god). In it, the chiefess' potentially superior claims to rule were enshrined, available in this discursive form to be memorized and cited during political discussions and deliberations during the lifetime of these chiefs and in the generations that followed.

It is important to consider at this point the kinds of evidence that might be mobilized to illuminate legal and political precedent in Hawaiian sources. While it appears logical to focus on 1825 by privileging "eyewitness" accounts to establish the reason for this kapu, Hawaiian standards of "evidence" are open to different kinds of source materials, like chants, for example, which were forms of political ideology or discourse. The confusion here lies with the way sources like chants are routinely miscategorized and reified by scholars as ethnographic, mythological, or folkloric texts revelatory of facets of Hawaiian religion, Hawaiian "traditions," and Hawaiian identity.[53]

Kamehameha's 1790s kapu limiting access to Kaʻahumanu gives us a particular example of how chiefly authority and law might work, especially when important political and governance issues were at stake. And while a kapu prohibiting high-ranking aliʻi from forming sexual alliances with one of the king's wives looks rather different from a kapu proclaimed by the ali'i in 1825 prohibiting Hawaiian women from going to ships to sleep with foreign sailors, it is in the nature of legal deliberation to construct a history of precedent from the similarities between situations, contexts, and authoritative utterances. Not only does this guide an ali'i to make political and legal decisions consonant with past decisions, so as not to appear arbitrary. But also, this kind of historical construction of kapu declared by present ali'i in relation to kapu declared by past ali'i adds to the authoritativeness of the current chiefs' pronouncements. Kapu and law in Hawai'i resound, gaining mana from this echoing invocation.[54]

Another version of kapu that was placed upon the body of an ali'i wahine—which ensured the preservation of a carefully engineered system of mana and rank—was still in force as late as 1822, when a man named Ha'alo'u was put to death for "adultery" with one of the Hawaiian ali'i named Pauahi.[55] Ha'alo'u was not punished for "adultery" in Christian terms. Instead, he was punished for his audacity at interfering in politics and for treasonous behavior, violating a kapu upon another important ali'i wahine. This kapu on Pauahi and its consequences for Ha'alo'u show us that this kind of rule and restriction were still being observed and enforced two years after the mission was planted and the 'ai kapu was overturned.

For both the sailors and missionaries, missionary interference in politics was in itself a taboo. While certain missionaries were attempting to cultivate good relations with ali'i, the missionaries were not in fact the arbiters of kapu or law in the islands. They had no power, personnel, or authority to promulgate or enforce such kapu, nor did they have the power to exact punishment against those who transgressed it—namely, Hawaiian women. Those women who disregarded the kapu were punished for their transgression, while the foreign men who purchased their services were not. Rather than simply a religious law promulgated through a reductive view of "missionary influence" over chiefs, the kapu should be considered as a measure of control meted out by the ali'i over their own subjects.[56]

The heated clashes soon to come between sailors, missionaries, and ali'i over the kapu on Hawaiian women were precipitated by the frustrated desires of sailors, who had been accustomed to having access to Hawaiian women for almost two and a half decades, since the beginning of the sandalwood trade brought increasing numbers of sailors to the islands. The kapu on women must, therefore, also be seen as a reaction to the increased presence of transient sailors in the islands and as a measure of control over

Hawaiian social interaction with foreigners deployed by the aliʻi in their governance of the islands.

The Problem of Unruly Sailors

The first whaleship in Hawaiian waters came in 1820, the same year that the first company of missionaries arrived in the islands. By the time the second company of missionaries came ashore on April 28, 1823, newcomer Rev. Charles Stewart reported that a crowd of about one hundred attended the morning service, sixty of whom were ship captains, officers, and seamen then in port. By 1825, Honolulu, Oʻahu, and Lahaina, Maui, were visited by at least fifty-seven whaleships; these ports had fast become two of the favored stopping places for ships engaged in the whaling trade. The numbers of transient sailors visiting the islands grew yearly. Unlike the apparently finite resource of the Hawaiian sandalwood forest, or the whaling grounds of the Atlantic, the Pacific Ocean in the early nineteenth century provided the opening of a new commercial maritime frontier—the ocean with whales in it—spurring further exploration as ships from England and the United States competed to locate new and populous whale hunting grounds, from Hawaiʻi in the north to Aotearoa in the south.

Many whaling voyages ran from three to five years. For sailors, the Sandwich Islands were places of recreation and respite from the discipline of shipboard life. The new commerce in whales, which was on the rise more than sandalwood or furs, would pull Hawaiʻi deeper into commercial and political relations with the United States and England at a crucial time when America's economic development overseas served to facilitate American expansion on the continent.[57]

With the increase of foreign ships in Hawaiian ports, disturbances by sailors due to public drunkenness and desertions of duty occurred with increasing frequency. During the eight-month period from April to November of 1822, the journal of Don Francisco de Paula Marin recorded six disturbances, a drunken brawl, a few quarrels, a row, and a riot. Some of these disturbances were between individuals, some involved altercations between different ship crews, and some incidents took place between individual ship captains. Amid the public disturbances to the peace, Marin also made note of days when sailors deserted their vessels, sometimes in large numbers.[58] In order to lessen the effects of unruly foreigners among kānaka maoli, Liholiho Kamehameha II had published a Notice by the missionary press on March 8, 1822, to masters of vessels informing them that any seamen found "riotous or disturbing the peace in any manner" would immediately be "secured in the fort," where they would be detained until "thirty dollars is paid for the release of each offender."[59] The Notice was the first of its kind published to assert the right of ali'i to restrict the movements of foreigners visiting the islands.

Adding to the numbers of foreign sailors deserting ships were those crews cut loose by their masters after the successful sale of an incoming vessel to ali'i. In 1822, the merchant house of Bryant and Sturgis instructed Captain Charles Preble of the ship *Champion* that if Supercargo Charles Hammatt was able to secure a sale of the ship to the ali'i, "the crew must be discharged, and passage found for the officers."[60] Given the number of ships that were purchased by the ali'i in the period between 1819 and 1825, it is certain that many sailors were left behind in the islands until another opportunity to sail back home presented itself. One can only imagine how these sailors passed the time while waiting for another ship assignment. It is possible that some never made the passage home, remaining in the islands to raise families with one or several Hawaiian women.

Good Devised and the Suppression of Vice

The chiefs were not the only ones worried about the activities of unruly sailors visiting the islands. In 1824, a committee of whaleship captains came to the mission to request its assistance in printing a paper on the importance of protecting their sailors from the corrosive effects of intemperance and vice.[61] Clearly not all the ship captains felt it their right to insist on access to Hawaiian women. The publication of two broadside texts in 1824 marks a moment of agreement and collaboration between missionaries and ship captains about the problem of vice and intemperance.

On March 29, 1824, a paper was drawn up by Capt. F. Arthur addressing his concerns with sailors' behavior; this document was then signed by a number of "respectable masters of whale ships" then in port, "with a view to suppress intemperance and encourage exemplary deportment among those engaged in the whale fishery." This paper was then presented to the Honolulu mission by a committee of the captains—Capt. J. Allen, Capt. G. W. Gardner, and Capt. S. Chase—who requested that it be printed for distribution. The captains intended to take the printed paper and "furnish the different ships in the fleet each with a copy."[62]

The mission gladly published the sea captains' document, and then the mission also supplied, wrote, and published its own meditation on the problem of vice entitled "Good Devised." This broadside, published on March 31, 1824, "intended to second the first [captains' paper], explaining more clearly its design, and more fully recommending its object."[63] "Good Devised" was composed by a character named "Spectator," whose appellation suggested the scrutiny of God upon the actions of Christian sailors, even in the faraway Hawaiian Islands. The piece opened by lauding the recent efforts of "the union of a respectable number of the masters of whale ships in this port, for the suppression of intemperance."[64] The object of this broadside was to give support to the joint efforts of masters and officers of vessels to suppress intemperance and vice among sailors.

While missionaries were concerned for the souls of visiting sailors and ship captains, they also worried about the effect that foreigners behaving badly, in an unchristian and immoral manner, would have on their Hawaiian charges. In "Good Devised," the author argued that all Euro-Americans from Christian nations claimed the "privileges of civilized society," making their lives and behaviors exemplary to heathens. Also, because of their ethnicity, the broadside continued, ship captains and sailors wielded superior influence over Hawaiian heathens, which could have a salutary influence on the "various tribes of men whom they visit and who need to be purified as well as enlightened."[65] The missionaries sought to prevent these sailors from squandering their influence on Hawaiians by providing poor Christian examples.

Spectator suggested that the greatest difficulty facing sailors during their time in the Hawaiian Islands was the lack of social and familial support of sailors' self-control and moral judgment: "the danger to which men are exposed when far from the restraints of well regulated society, from the direct and salutary influence of affectionate wives and sisters, and out of reach of the monitory voice of parental and filial affection, and liable to be carried down the current with those who would fain think that even distance, removes the most reasonable restraints which the good order of society and the laws of heaven invariably require."[66] The problem of foreign sailors in the islands was that they belonged to no other society that could mediate or judge their actions other than that of the ship. "Distance" from homeland and social institutions left the sailor vulnerable to the excesses of

THE suppression of vice is at once a duty and

a privilege. However secret in its character, however local and limited in its effects, its existence, wherever it is known, calls for the exercise of any influence that can control or check it. This is true of all vice; but it is most emphatically so of every grosser excess affecting the morals not of a few individuals only, but of a whole class of men, and threatening them with consequences of the most unhappy character. To such an excess it is believed the seamen navigating the waters of the Pacific are peculiarly exposed, from the general licentiousness of the islanders of this ocean, and from the facilities to debauchery which that licentiousness affords. The evil is already too glaring to be concealed—has already been too often felt to be denied; and most imperiously demands the decisive and spirited exertions of every friend of morality and virtue for its limitation and suppression. This to a certain degree is practicable, and as far as it is so, it rests with the masters and officers of the vessels which traverse these seas. Fully persuaded of this fact, we whose names are undersigned, in whatever light we view the evil, whether in its too frequent detrimental consequences to our voyages, in the disease it disseminates, and in the sufferings it too often imposes on its unhappy victims; or whether we view it in the poisonous influence it must ever have on the morals of the young and inexperienced who are placed under our guardianship, and to whom we are bound to act the part of fathers and of brothers, of parents and of friends; or whether we view it in consequences not less lamentable —the broken peace of the fireside and the imbittered joy of all we hold most dear at home; or whether we view it in that which is still more remote, in the effect it must have on the various relations of society, and even on the morals of a succeeding generation—on those who will virtually be our sons, and on those who will in reality be our grand-sons and our grand-daughters;—in whichever of these various lights we view it, we feel bound in duty to ourselves, in duty to our employers, in duty to our crews, their parents and their friends, and in duty to society at large, without a moment's delay, to exercise every authority we possess, in the correction of an evil so pregnant with great and far-spread misery. From these considerations we have determined to attempt a reform on this point; and while we pledge ourselves by a mutual and solemn promise to remain firm to our purpose, we most earnestly call on our compeers in the whaling service to aid us by their prompt and energetic support.

With these views and feelings, we by this article, deliberately and seriously resolve, that from the period of placing our signatures to this instrument, in whatever part of the world we may be, we will never permit any female to come on board our respective ships for the purpose of prostitution; that we will immediately make this resolution known to our present crews, and in every future shipment will propose it to all submitting themselves to our authority, as an inviolable order on board the vessels committed to our charge.

Lahaina, Maui, (Sandwich Islands,)
Nov. 5, 1824.

Ship Hydaspe
PETER PADDACK, *Master.*
LUTHER FULLER,
STEPHEN PARR,
CHARLES PENDLETON,

Ship Thames
REUBEN CLASBY, *Master.*
JOHN H. PEASE,
MARCUS LANE,
GRANVILLE MANTOR,

Ship Enterprise
REUBEN WEEKS, *Master.*
BENJAMIN F. HUSSEY,
GEORGE G. CHASE,
EDWARD J. FOLGER,
JARED WORTH,
CHARLES C. RUSSELL,

Ship Aurora
SETH COFFIN, Jr. *Master.*
GARDNER SWAIN,
JOHN HUSSEY, Jr.
WILLIAM PERKINS,
BENJAMIN F. RIDDELL,

Figure 6. "The Suppression of Vice." Mission Houses Museum Library.

GOOD DEVISED.

THE union of a respectable number of the masters of whale ships in this port, for the suppression of intemperance, as appears from a printed document of the 29th inst. drawn up among themselves and subscribed with their own hands, is a fact of no small importance, and cannot fail to have a favorable inffluence upon the interests of those concerned in the whale fishery.

The design is noble, and commends itself at once to the approbation of every man who is a friend to the order and peace of society, and to the prosperity of his fellow men.

In a tender and impressive manner they touch a subject which is worthy of the serious attention of all who visit the North Pacific, that is, the danger to which men are exposed when far from the restraints of well regulated society, from the direct and salutary influence of affectionate wives and sisters, and out of the reach of the monitory voice of parental and filial affection, and liable to be carried down the current with those who would fain think that even *distance*, removes the most reasonable restraints which the good order of society and the laws of heaven invariably require.

Looking with regret upon the downward course of " some heretofore promising young men," and deeply deploring the fatal consequences to which they see them exposed by the " liberal use of ardent spirits," especially in a place of such iminent danger as this, these gentlemen unitedly propose to do what is in their power to discountenance this growing evil, and by their own exemplary deportment and by using their influence with others "to *suppress* the intemperate use of this *deadly poison.*"

It is indeed the dictate of sober reason and interest, as well as of virtue and benevolence, to check the progress of this sweeping and desolating contagion which not only breeds mutiny among crews, and ruins many an expensive voyage, but destroys the peace of once happy families, wrings tears of bitterest anguish from the eyes of amiable wives and disappointed parents, and clothes neglected children with poverty and wretchedness, blasts the reputation of many a rising young man, overspreads with disastrous gloom the fairest prospects of early life, lays in the grave the fond hope of many a doating parent, and drives multitudes to shipwreck and hopeless ruin both for this world and that which is to come.

To guard suitably and seasonably against consequences like these, to shun or resist every temptation, to oppose the torrent of iniquity which if unrestrained would sweep away every thing that is lovely in the order, purity and peace of society, and by kind and well directed efforts to withdraw the unwary from the whirlpools and quicksands of folly and wickedness, must be regarded as the indispensable duty of every man who has the slightest claim to the privileges of civilized society, or the least power to promote his own or his neighbors welfare.

Should there be a general union or co-operation among masters and officers of vessels and others immediately interested in their success, to accomplish so desirable an object, how great would be the result—how happy the effect, not only on the sons of commerce themselves "who go down to the sea in ships and do business in great waters" and who are called upon by a voice from heaven, to " praise the name of tne Lord," but how salutary might their influence be on the various tribes of men whom they visit and who need to be purified as well as enlightened; but more especially how vast and incalculable would be the advantage of such united efforts, to that part of the rising generation who are greatly exposed to the corrupt example of those who are far gone in the way to ruin—who, tossed by unpropitious gales, without the "anchor of hope," but fearless of consequences, are under a press of sail, driving with terrible rapidity upon an iron bound shore just under their lee, lined with countless wrecks, where inevitable destruction awaits them.

The men who with decision undertake, and with energy and consistency carry through this good work of discountenancing vice, and encouraging purity of morals, must be regarded as the benefactors of man, though the more extensive and salutary their influence, the more likely will they be to become the " song of the drunkard."

Let him then who approves of this design; let him who wishes well to the rising generation; let him who would value the satisfaction which arises from the consciousness of having done his duty; let him who above all things desires the final approbation of his Maker—" *go and do likewise.*"

SPECTATOR.

Oahu, (S. I.) March 31, 1824.

Figure 7. "Good Devised." Mission Houses Museum Library.

sailing in the North Pacific among heathen peoples. Furthermore, the use of the name "Spectator" suggested to sailors and ship captains that their behavior far from home was being scrutinized. Reminding these men of their surveillance by civilized colleagues—people with ties and communication lines "back home" to cities along the Atlantic—was a tool used to build a sense of accountability for their actions among sailors and other foreigners, though they were far from home and family.

The authors of "Good Devised" sought to curry favor with ship captains and merchant agents by pointing out the commercial benefits of temperance and correct moral behavior: "It is indeed the dictate of sober reason and interest, as well as of virtue and benevolence, to check the progress of this sweeping and desolating contagion which not only breeds mutiny among crews, and ruins many an expensive voyage, but destroys the peace of once happy families."[67] Spectator couched the problem in the language of disease, epidemic, and plague, raising for the first time in published public discussion the subject of sexually transmitted disease, which was one of the immediate visible results of engaging in vice. Illness among crew members had the potential to ruin a business venture, injuring not only the sailors and ship captain but also merchant houses in New England and England. On a more serious note, Spectator suggested that an unhealthy and immoral crew was one that could also turn mutinous. Engaging in vice and intemperance had repercussions both in the Pacific and at home. Men's behavior in the islands had the potential to destroy reputation and sever tenuous family bonds that spanned across the long years of a voyage and across vast distances.

A few months later, on November 5, 1824, a new broadside, "The Suppression of Vice," was published. This broadside signed by the captains and officers of four ships, the *Hydaspe*, the *Thames*, *Enterprise*, and *Aurora*, resolved that: "from the period of placing our signatures to this instrument, in whatever part of the world we may be, we will never permit any female to come on board our respective ships for the purpose of prostitution; that we will immediately make this resolution known to our present crews, and in every future shipment will propose it to all submitting themselves to our authority, as an inviolable order on board the vessels committed to our charge."[68] Ship captains pledged their commitment to completely bar women and prostitution within the immediate jurisdiction of their ships. For captains, the ship and her people were the site of regulation, whereas the kapu proclaimed less than a year later sought to enact the same result by regulating the bodies of Hawaiian women. The contractual and quasi-legal language the officers and captains employed is evident. Together they signed their names to "this instrument," transforming the document from a casual statement of opinion into a contract of sorts. In naming the vice they were targeting "prostitution," they were bringing notice to an infamous practice that, though condoned in many places, inhabited a grey area between morality and law. The captains' "resolution" to keep prostitutes from boarding their ships extended to every crew member "submitting themselves" to their authority and in every port of call visited, not just the Sandwich Islands. Finally, as a show of their determination to uphold this practice, these ship captains pledged that keeping females from their ships was an "inviolable order on board the vessels committed to our charge."[69]

"The Suppression of Vice" made ship captains responsible for protecting and fostering the healthy moral development of their crews. Captains overseeing crews oceans away from home claimed the part of "fathers and of brothers, of parents, and of friends," evoking the claim of kinship to inflect shipboard life with the bonds and responsibilities associated with family. The men's vulnerability to prostitution was highlighted in the "spirited exertions" which must be taken on their behalf by "every friend of morality and virtue."[70]

Ship captains framed the "evil" of vice in several ways, hoping to appeal to every sensibility in order to garner more support in the fleet for its suppression. Vice had an immediate negative impact on voyages as a vector for sexual disease and the "sufferings it too often imposes on its unhappy victims." Similar to the "Good Devised" metaphorical representation of sinful behavior as a plague or contagion, "The Suppression of Vice" also raised fears about the "poisonous influence" prostitution had upon the "morals of the young and inexperienced" men who were "placed under" the guardianship of the captains.[71]

The captains also projected the role that prostitution and intemperance in the islands would play in "the broken peace of the fireside and the imbittered [sic] joy of all we hold most dear at home." "The Suppression of Vice" made it clear that the temptations affecting sailors came from "the general licentiousness of the islanders of this ocean," or the unnatural sexual advances and predilections of island women.[72] Here the captains reiterated their central message to sailors and other captains in the fleet: their actions in the Pacific would yield terrible results at home. Rather than saying pointedly that infidelity in the islands amounted to adultery, the captains coyly evoked the image of the "broken peace of the fireside" to evoke feelings of loyalty and fidelity to home, hearth, and, by extension, wives who had been left behind.[73]

In perhaps their most far-reaching argument, the captains framed vice in the present as having an impact on future generations: "Whether we view it [vice] in that which is still more remote, in the effect it must have on the various relations of society, and even on the morals of the succeeding generation—on those who will virtually be our sons, and on those who will in reality be our grand-sons and our grand-daughters."[74] If the current generation of sailors were corrupted by vice and intemperance, the captains worried, who would serve as role models for succeeding generations? The persistent strain of family connection raised by the captains belied another fear of the offspring of vice: children of mixed parentage. One can't help but think about the children of the sailors and Hawaiian women, the next generation, who would always be linked by paternity to their siblings and cousins in New England and England. The captains projected their anxiety about the immediate and long-term effects that sexual intercourse with "heathens" outside of marriage would have on traditional families back home in America and England. The ship captains felt obligated to act, as they were "bound in duty to ourselves, in duty to our employers, in duty to our crews, their parents and their friends, and in duty to society at large, without a moment's delay, to exercise every authority we possess, in the correction of an evil so pregnant with great and far-spreading misery."[75] What emerges, then, from this call to "their compeers in the whaling service" to give their "prompt and energetic support" to this effort is not simply their present environment in the Sandwich Islands of 1824, its women, or the concerns of the mission, but the threat which they imagined Pacific Island women's sexuality would have in undoing the orderliness of their societies back home. Sex with Hawaiian women, they argued, would affect the stability of family in this generation, as it was held together through normative relations between men and women in monogamous marriages and through the acceptable reproduction of nonmixed parentage.[76]

While "The Suppression of Vice" of November 5, 1824, was a foreign response to retarding prostitution aboard whaling ships, that placed agency and blame upon sailors and ship captains, it also targeted Hawaiian women as vectors of immorality and licentiousness. But as much as some captains saw the problem this way, there were many others who refused to temper their desires—those like Captain Buckle, who, a scant four months after the publication of the broadside, would buy Leoiki from her chief, Wahine-piʻo. This moment of cooperation between ship captains and missionaries would remain brief and yield few lasting results. Difficulties between the mission, merchant agents, and ship captains would worsen in the coming year, as the business of the mission was increasingly perceived as getting in the way of the business of making profits.

The progress of Christianity among Hawaiian chiefs began to produce a shift in people's moral attitudes. Women like Leoiki began to question the practice of going out to ships. It seems that while some Hawaiian women and many of the chiefs began to incorporate Christian moral ideas and practices into their lives, this shift was not universal, as is evidenced by Wahinepiʻo's sale of Leoiki. While some ship captains attempted to institute a moral discipline over the sailors on their ships, they were unable to discipline other ship captains and sailors who saw prostitution not as a problem but as a necessary release valve that supported shipboard discipline.

Even after Leoiki was "sold" by Wahinepiʻo, ship captains sought to purchase Hawaiian women. On April 28, 1825, printer Elisha Loomis noted in his journal that a "Capt. B.," commander of an English whaleship, had "for some time been making strenuous efforts to induce a certain female to accompany him on a cruise, promising to return her again, and furnish her well with clothing &c."[77] The woman in question was Polly Holmes, daughter of Oliver Holmes, a Massachusetts sailor who had lived with a Hawaiian woman for over a decade. Holmes had a house full of daughters who were all sought after by merchant agents and ship captains for companionship, and it was alleged by missionaries that the women were prostituted by their father.[78] Polly had refused the captain's advances and "fearing she would be taken on board by force . . . fled to Karaimoku for protection."[79] Though the captain, who was not named by the missionaries, offered Kālaimoku money to compel the woman, the chief refused, saying, "She shall not go without her own consent."[80] The captain also tried to offer large sums of money to the other chiefs, who also refused to send her on board. When all these attempts failed, the captain, in desperation, approached Rev. Bingham twice that day to ask for his assistance. When he had failed in his remonstrances, he then reproached the minister, saying that "if it had been any other person than a clergyman" who had frustrated his wishes, "he would have kicked him down the street."[81]

Failing utterly to "persuade" Polly Holmes to accompany him on his voyage, the elusive Capt. B. visited the home of a "Mr. J. (An American resident who has several children by a native wife)" and "endeavored to get possession of H. his eldest daughter." He offered the family eight hundred dollars to take the girl, but the family refused, her mother exclaiming, "Do you think we will sell our daughter like a hog?"[82]

In writing about this exchange, Elisha Loomis did not comment on the attempt of the ship captain to obtain a Hawaiian woman, and there were no extended reflections on sex between Hawaiian women and foreign sailors. The more serious crime was adultery, since the ship captain had "a wife and several children in England." Loomis was worried that Hawaiian people would not see "the iniquity of such conduct" in time to save their immortal souls.[83]

Port Law: "He Mau Kanawai no ke Awa Honolulu, Oahu"

On June 2, 1825, Kālaimoku, the prime minister or kuhina nui, published "He Mau kānāwai no ke ava Honoruru, Oahu" (Regulations for the Port of Honolulu, Oʻahu). Published in Hawaiian and English, the rules highlight an important shift in the production of law in the islands. Out of necessity, the aliʻi were beginning to direct their laws and prohibitions at different publics, Hawaiian and foreign. Hawaiian harbor pilots needed to be apprised of the charges that were owed to them when bringing foreign ships into port. However, Hawaiian subjects did not need to have laws or prohibitions published for them to be obeyed; words proclaimed in public by the aliʻi as kapu were still firmly adhered to and observed in 1825.

At this time, all the chiefs were searching for ways to make revenue in order to repay "debt" owed to New England merchant houses. Instituting port charges was one of several means the chiefs used to raise revenue for the emerging Hawaiian kingdom. The regulations also elaborated on the first published government notice of 1822, which informed captains that "no seaman shall be left on shore without permission from the King."[84] The 1825 regulation laid stricter rules for regulating the movement of foreign sailors on shore: "All commanders of vessels arriving at this island are to produce . . . a list of their crew: and no seaman is to be left on the island without the consent of the Governor, in writing, under a penalty of $30 for

HE MAU KANAWAI,

NO KE AWA HONOLULU, OAHU.

1.

Na alii moku a pau ke ku mai i keia aina, e hoike lakou i ka palapala a ka moku, a me ka inoa o na kanaka o ka moku o lakou, i ike ka Pailota ka me nana e malama ke awa: aole hoi e waihoia iuka ko ka moku kanaka, ke ole ae aku ma ka palapala, ke alii malama i ka aina. I na waiho waleia ke kanaka iuka, e uku mai hoi ke alii moku i ko uka alii kanakolu Dola.

2.

Aole loa e holo wale aku ka moku no loko aku o ke awa, ke ole loaa aku ka palapala a ka me nana e malama ke awa: ke hoike aku a ua pau ke kanawai o ke awa i ka malamaia; he pono hoi e loaa mai ia ia hookahi Dola no ua palapala la.

3.

O kanaka o ka moku ke holo malu mai lakou iuka, e hopuia lakou a paa a (i ole hoihoiia i ko lakou moku) e hoohanaia lakou i ka hana ikaika eono malama.

4.

I na haalele ke kanaka i ka moku, he mea pono e hai mai ke alii nona ka moku i ke alii malama i ka aina, e hopuia ka poe e holo mai; e hoihoiia aku i ko lakou alii moku, no laila hoi no ke kanaka i hopuia e loaa mai ai ka uku i ka mea nana e malama ka aina no ke kahi kanaka eono Dola.

5.

Na moku ke komo i ke awa i ka ai hou a i ke kapili wale hoi, e uku mai lakou penei :
No ke awa mawaho, - - akahi tona, 6 Kenata,
No ke awa maloko, - - akahi tona, 10 Kenata.

6.

Na moku ke komo i ka awa i ka kuai maoli, e uku mai lakou penei :
No ke awa mawaho, - - akahi tona, 50 Keneta,
No ke awa maloko, - - akahi tona, 60 Kenata.

7.

Eia hoi ka uku no ke alakai ana :
I ka hookomo mai, - - - - akahi futa, 1 Dola,
I ka hoopuka i waho, - - - - akahi futa, 1 Dola.

KALAIMOKU. [L. S.]

Oahu, ka pae aina o Hawaii,}
June 2, 1825. }

REGULATIONS,

FOR THE PORT OF HONOLULU, OAHU.

1.

All commanders of vessels arriving at this Island are to produce their certificates of registry to the pilot or port captain; also a list of their crew: and no seaman is to be left on the Island without the consent of the Governor, in writing, under a penalty of $30 for each person so left.

2.

No vessel shall leave the harbor until a certificate from the harbor-master is granted, certifying that the port regulations have been complied with; for which he is entitled to demand one dollar.

3.

Seamen deserting will be taken up, and (unless returned to their respective ships) be kept at hard labor for six months.

4.

Commanders of vessels are to give immediate notice to the Governor of the Island, in case of any of their crew deserting, that they may be apprehended and returned; and on delivery to their respective commanders, the Governor is to receive six dollars for each person so apprehended.

5.

Ships entering the harbor for the purpose of refreshing or refitting only, are to pay the following rates :
For the outer harbor, - - 6 cents per ton;
      inner harbor, - - 10 cents per ton.

6.

Ships entering the harbor for the purpose of trading, are to pay the following rates:
For the outer harbor, - - 50 cents per ton,
      inner harbor, - - 60 cents per ton.

7.

The Pilotage shall be at the following rate :
For taking a vessel in, - - $1. per foot,
For taking a vessel out, - $1 per foot.

KALAIMOKU. [L. S.]

Oahu, Sandwich Islands,}
June 2, 1825. }

OAHU, PRINTED BY THOMAS W. CUMMINGS. APRIL 1827.

Figure 8. "He Mau Kanawai no ke Awa Honolulu, Oahu / Regulations for the Port of Honolulu, Oahu." 1825 broadside. Mission Houses Museum Library.

each person so left."[85] While the charge for retrieving sailors apprehended on the island without permission had not changed since 1822, the sheer number of ships arriving made it necessary for captains to provide lists of their crew in writing to the ali'i.

As more ali'i studied the palapala, writing was being incorporated as part of a new way of keeping records among the chiefs. Rather than the Christian palapala, documents generated by the chiefs and their advisers were utilized for the benefit of trade. The mission press made itself available to publish other things for the use of the ali'i, like port regulations.[86] The Hawaiian government made it the responsibility of the masters of vessels to report any deserters among the crew so that the men might be apprehended by Hawaiian authorities if caught on shore. If deserters were captured, the commander of the ship was fined six dollars, payable to the governor upon the sailor's return. Finally, those deserters that were not successfully returned to their ship before it sailed away were to be kept at hard labor for a period of six months.[87]

Sailors who visited shore on leave, those who deserted, and those who were relieved of duty, their contracts paid off, posed a problem for Hawaiian chiefs. While we may never know for sure the sheer number of sailors who took up residence in the islands during the 1820s, it is clear that the ali'i began to see the necessity for additional civil measures to be put in place regulating the movements of foreigners in the islands. Kānāwai extended the jurisdiction of the ali'i beyond a Hawaiian populace to punish those foreign sailors and hold accountable foreign captains who could not control their crews. These laws were instituted to ensure that deserters would not threaten the peace and safety of Hawaiians or the government.

Hawaiian chiefs continued to shape and regulate social behavior through kapu, even as they began to publish kānāwai in Hawaiian and English.[88] Kapu were largely directed at regulating the actions and behaviors of Hawaiian subjects and rarely directed at foreigners. Simultaneous with orally pronounced kapu, the chiefs began to promulgate kānāwai, laws and regulations that were published.[89] Though the chiefs continued to pronounce kapu, none of the laws published was ever categorized as "kapu."[90] As Hawaiian oral pronouncements were targeted at Hawaiian subjects, published kānāwai were aimed at foreigners, those who expected laws to be published in order to be binding and authoritative. The highly mobile and fluctuating population of captains, sailors, and merchants would not have made orally pronounced kapu efficacious among their population.

Beginning in the 1820s, Hawaiian society was beginning the slow trans-formation of incorporating reading and writing into its strong aurality-orality-based foundation. In Honolulu, on December 21, 1823, a kapu was proclaimed by the chiefs' crier requiring the people to observe the Sabbath. Six months later, at Lahaina, Ka'ahumanu proclaimed a set of kapu forbid-ding murder, theft, boxing, and fighting and ordering an observance of the Sabbath. This set of proclamations also included the injunction that when schools were established, all the people should learn the palapala.[91] Since literacy was a new priority for the ali'i, the adoption of a general literacy program among the maka'āinana would require the training of more teach-ers and the building of schools.

These considerations made the publication of kapu superfluous, espe-cially since the strength, power, and binding nature of the oral utterances of the chiefs were still regarded as law. This power is exemplified in the saying "I ka 'ōlelo nō ke ola, I ka ' ōlelo nō ka make" (In speech there is life, in speech death). Rather than a general statement about the power of speech, this idiom is descriptive of the power of chiefly utterance to mete out life or death over an individual. Instead of literacy replacing orality as a primary mode of expression, coexistence remained the reality among Hawaiians well into the late nineteenth century.[92]

The Outrages Begin

By 1825, relations between merchants and missionaries were beginning to show signs of strain. The mission, as we have seen in previous chapters, was dependent upon the goodwill of merchant vessels to carry personnel, letters, journals, reports, and other items between islands, or back to the home office in Boston, sometimes free of charge. Things began to change as the mission became more successful in its objective to Christianize and civilize the Hawaiian people under the aegis of the chiefs, who demanded that missionaries teach them the palapala—reading and writing—and Christianity.

One of the biggest complaints of the captains was the missionary removal of a Hawaiian labor force from commercial enterprise. Captain Eliab Grimes, who worked for Marshall and Wildes, observed on June 7, 1825, that Mr. Bingham was a "religious despot," and he blamed the mission for the present state of business, which was "dull and very little prospect of getting wood at present." Instead of harvesting wood, Grimes complained, "The chiefs' attention is too much taken up, with the missionaries, with their preaching, praying, and schooling."[93] All of this labor in the service of Christianity and education took essential workers out of the service of maritime commerce. Farmers produced less food for provisions, and fewer men went to cut sandalwood. Quite literally, bodies were in the classroom and the church, and not in the forest or the sweet potato patch.

Captain Rutter, who also worked for Marshall and Wildes, wrote on August 16, 1825, about his dissatisfaction with missionary plans for a grand new church on Oʻahu. The building would be "120 feet by 48, the sides 18ft high of hewn stone." The missionaries, particularly Rev. Bingham (or "Bishop," as merchants called him, because of his "pride and ambition"), had been successful at persuading Kālaimoku and Kaʻahumanu to support this project, which Rutter feared would take laborers away from the important task of supplying sandalwood owed to merchants on the debt and would "actually be more work than to cut all the [sandal]wood now due."[94]

Ship captains and merchants also laid blame on the mission for the Christian "reforms" that it sought to introduce among Hawaiians. Nonmissionary foreigners imagined that kapu placed by the aliʻi originated with the mission, and not the aliʻi.

The observations of Rev. Richards provide important insight into the furor over the 1825 kapu: "I frequently saw and conversed with Kalaimoku and Kaahumanu who were the acknowledged and I believe regularly appointed Regents of the island during the minority of the King. During the first few weeks after my arrival [on Oʻahu] I often heard them speak of a tabu or prohibition on females visiting ships for the purpose of prostitution. They usually spake of it as ke tabu, or the tabu. I frequently heard them speak of the anger of the foreign residents and visitants on account of this tabu."[95] Richards' comment shows that the two highest chiefs in the islands, Kaʻahumanu and Kālaimoku, deliberated frequently about the kapu on women. The chiefs were increasingly concerned about the anger of foreign residents and visitors over the kapu. The success of the kapu in preventing women from going out to ships would soon turn anger among ship captains and sailors into outrage.

Seven months after being "sold," Leoiki was cheered by the sight of the islands as they hove into view. On October 3, 1825, the English whaleship *Daniel IV* returned to Lahaina, but something had changed since they last visited the islands in March. A kapu on Hawaiian women visiting ships for the purpose of prostitution had been proclaimed by the chiefs. As Leoiki stepped onto the shore, men from the *Daniel IV* went in search of Hawaiian women and were disappointed to find that none could be persuaded to accompany them to their ship. The anger of the men over the kapu soon turned them to disorderly and violent behavior, which they directed at the Lahaina mission station of Rev. William Richards.

By October 1825, when the first outrage was launched against the Lahaina mission station, the mission was still being managed by only two reinforcements of missionaries, consisting of twenty-eight souls in all. The Sandwich Islands Mission consisted of five ministers, two licensed preachers, two teachers, a doctor, a commercial agent, a printer, their wives and children, one female "negro" assistant, and three Hawaiian teachers.

The sailors of the English whaleship the *Daniel IV* returned expectantly to Lahaina, Maui, on October 3, 1825. After seven months at sea in the Japanese whaling grounds, the men looked forward to the rum they could purchase in the makeshift towns growing up around Hawaiian harbors. These towns were expanding to accommodate the growing commercial infrastructure. Drinking in several of the town's grog shops, they swapped and savored tales of their adventures with other sailors, all passing the time while passing through. In 1825, Lahaina was a preferable port to Honolulu, being deeper and easier of approach.

The men of the *Daniel* were looking forward to returning to the women of their dreams. Hawaiian women were exotic for many reasons—because of the way they looked, the color of their skin and their dress, and because many lacked the inhibitions of "civilized" women. Whether they came out to ships as willing partners or as women compelled by relatives or chiefs, the opportunities these women provided for transgressing the bonds of civilized society only added to their allure.

Fueled by their frustrations, a mob of disgruntled sailors paid a visit to Rev. William Richards, whom they held responsible for the promulgation of the new kapu. Richards and family were alone for the first time since they settled into the Lahaina mission station (one short month after their arrival in the islands in April 1823). The other couple stationed there, Rev. Charles Stewart and his wife Harriet, had been forced by her illness to remove to Honolulu, where the only mission physician could attend to her.

At sunset on October 5, 1825, after two days of trying unsuccessfully to persuade women to defy the kapu and come aboard ship, two sailors from the *Daniel* paid a visit to Richards' home. Calling the new "law" improper, they charged that Richards was the cause of its adoption. Richards "entirely disclaimed having anything to do in enacting this or any other law of the nation" and only admitted to providing religious instruction to the chiefs, by "inculcating the principles of the scriptures."[96]

The dispute between sailors and missionaries highlights the deep miscommunication that occurred between sailors and missionaries. By emphasizing his duty as a missionary to reform the morals of the Hawaiian nation, Richards echoed the policy mandated by the American mission. His statements were in keeping with the verbal instructions delivered to the second missionary company at the Middle Church in New Haven, Connecticut, on November 18, 1822, two days before the company's departure for the islands. The missionaries were advised to "abstain from all interference with the local and political interests of the people. The Kingdom of Christ is not of this world, and it especially behooves a missionary to stand aloof from the private and transient interests of chiefs and rulers."[97] What sounded so simple in a Connecticut church proved much harder to accomplish in the far-off mission field. Often, the dual missionary project of Christianizing and civilizing "heathens" blurred the line between religion and politics.

Richards personally had little to do with the adoption of the kapu, since it was initially proclaimed by Kauikeaouli Kamehameha III, in concert with the kuhina nui, Ka'ahumanu, on the island of O'ahu, where many of the paramount ali'i were in residence at the time. Honolulu was also the home of Rev. Hiram Bingham, head minister of the first company, who was also a close adviser to both Kālaimoku and Ka'ahumanu. From O'ahu, the news would have been carried by canoe to the different islands and spread via oral proclamation.[98] In addition to denying any involvement with the kapu, Richards also explained to the sailors that the only way that he could recommend the removal of the kapu as a missionary would be to tell the chiefs that it was "inconsistent with the word of God." He asked the sailors if in speaking thus to the chiefs, would he "be speaking the truth?" After a half hour of persuasive conversation, the men abandoned their importunities and departed. Just as they left, a mob of sailors who were not inclined to discussion came to the door. One of the angry sailors entered the house and threatened Richards' property, his life, and the lives of his family if the "law" were not rescinded.[99]

Richards responded to these dire threats by reiterating his life's purpose: "We left our country to devote our lives whether longer or shorter to the salvation of the heathen, that we hoped ourselves equally prepared for life or death, and should therefore throw our breasts open to their knives, rather than retrace a single step we had taken."[100] While prepared to forfeit their lives to the habitual violence of heathens, missionaries in Hawai'i were surprised, though no less willing, to die at the hands of foreigners like themselves.

Fearful that the mob would make good on their taunts and wreck their house and beat them, Richards' wife threw herself upon the mercy of her "fellow Christians": "I am feeble and have none to look to for protection but my husband and my god, I might hope that in my helpless situation I should have the compassion of all who are from a Christian country, but if you are without compassion or if it can not be exercised but in the way you propose, then I wish you all to understand that I am ready to share the fate of my husband and will by no means consent to live upon the terms you offer."[101] The Richards' seeming readiness to martyr themselves for the mission's cause may have struck a chord with one of the sailors, who said that he would play no part in such abuse, but warned that Richards should "look out for others." As the man turned to leave, the minister and his wife took the opportunity to preach to the sailors and made one last plea to them to have compassion for themselves and to control their behavior in order to ensure they could justify themselves on Judgment Day. Throughout the injunction, the restless company uttered "the most horrid threats," but after the man they were addressing directly left the house, all the sailors departed.[102]

While Rev. Richards emphasized his role as a Christian missionary, spreading the word of God, Mrs. Richards appealed to the sailors' sense of compassion for a female in her situation, helpless in a foreign land, relying solely upon the protection of her husband and God. By seizing upon their common Christian backgrounds, Mrs. Richards sought to leverage the righteousness of herself and her husband against the riotous actions of the sailors in order to persuade the sailors to sit in judgment of their own deeds. Her statement also challenged the rioters to consider whether or not they were heathens or Christians.

During the fretful night of October 5, Richards employed several Hawaiian men to watch over his yard. The next day, two intoxicated sailors attempted to enter the yard and were repelled by the Hawaiian guard. Richards sought protection from the American ships in port, but found the captains "felt no interest" in the subject.[103] Finally he appealed to the *Daniel*'s Captain Buckle in writing, recounting the occurrences of past days and requesting that the captain come to see him. Buckle replied that his men had left the ship "with a full determination not to return on board again unless they obtain[ed] women."[104] Claiming he had no control over the men while they were ashore, Buckle recommended that Richards use his "influence with the chiefs" to have the kapu removed, "after which all will be peace and quietness."[105]

Contrary to Buckle's pronouncement, all was peace and quiet until six days after the first attack, when Richards encountered a company of sixteen sailors. Walking single file on the narrow path near his home, the sailors uttered threats, accompanied by "awful oaths and gestures." Their behavior suggested to Richards that they were "ripe for the blackest crime."[106] That evening at about nine o'clock, a group of fifteen to twenty men, some armed with knives and one or more with pistols, approached the gate of Richards' yard. The small unarmed guard of four Hawaiians attempted to close the gate, which the sailors ordered be opened, one of them striking out at the guards with a knife. A scuffle ensued, and the knife-wielding sailor made another jab at one of the guards, the blade sinking deep into the gate, as the Hawaiians made a hasty retreat.[107]

One of the chiefs overseeing the guard observed the scene and called out, "The play is over, we must be serious now," and he gave orders to the people to arm themselves.[108] Richards watched the scene from the safety of his home. When the mob reached his windows, they called out, "Where is the _____ missionary?"[109] By this time, Hawaiians armed with clubs, swords, stones, and guns were emerging from every direction—thirty of them entering the Richards' home by the back door to offer the family protection. Recognizing that they were outnumbered, the sailors abandoned the attack and, scattering, returned to their ships.[110] As soon as the threat passed, the ali'i increased the number of men guarding Richards and his family, supplying them with guns, something they had previously declined to do. Over the next few days, rumors flew that the entire crew of the *Daniel IV* were planning to assault the missionaries; however, no other attack materialized.[111]

In what seemed like coordinated attacks, the outrage in Lahaina coincided with a similar though less dangerous outbreak in Honolulu. On the morning of October 4, approximately twenty sailors from "the English ships in port came in a body . . . to the house of Mr. B. [Bingham] and demanded the reason why females were not allowed as formerly to go on board the ships."[112] The sailors were told to go and consult with the chiefs, although it was their understanding that Mr. B. had "made the prohibition." When the sailors met with Ka'ahumanu, she replied through a translator that "females were strictly forbidden going on board ships," and that the rule that guided them in this respect was the word of God. The chief began to lecture the men, but they replied that they did not "come to talk about religion, but came after women." If the sailors could not get women "by fair means," they "would catch them where they could find them and drag them on board ship."[113] The sailors also claimed that "this measure would be borne out by their captains and officers." Kālaimoku, having been informed of the sailors' purpose in speaking with Ka'ahumanu, sent word that "if they did not speedily depart," he would have them secured.[114]

The authority of these chiefs was recognized by the sailors, who feared the possible repercussions that would occur if they did not heed the directive of Kālaimoku and disperse quickly.[115] Two weeks later, on October 19, after news of the Lahaina outrage reached Honolulu, Ka'ahumanu ordered Don Francisco de Paula Marin (a Spanish sailor who had settled in the islands twenty years before and served as translator to the ali'i) to accompany Boki, the governor of O'ahu, to the port at Honolulu and let all captains of vessels know not to allow women to go on board their ships.[116]

When the *Daniel IV* arrived in Honolulu around October 23, the chiefs took precautionary measures to protect the Honolulu mission station. The ali'i ordered a guard of men to patrol the streets and "suffer no suspicious foreigners to come to the mission house." On the evening of October 24, three boat crews from the *Daniel IV* landed and "took up their march to the mission house." The guard clashed with the *Daniel's* crew, taking five of the men in custody; the rest returned hastily to their boats. The men were taken in irons to the fort, where printer Elisha Loomis surmised they were "likely to remain awhile," since Captain B. had "tried in vain" to obtain their release. Loomis believed that the sailors would only be sent on board when the vessel was ready to sail.[117]

The outrage of the English whaleship *Daniel IV* marked the first time a Hawaiian kapu was met with violent opposition by foreigners.[118] This turn of events compelled the ali'i to consider the consequences of the kapu they placed on Hawaiian subjects now that there were more foreigners in the islands to contend with. In the coming years, the rage and violence directed at the kapu on women would escalate, necessitating a response on the part of the ali'i that would change the course of how Hawaiians governed over both native and foreign subjects.

CHAPTER 5

Libel, Law, and Justice Before the *'Aha 'ōlelo*

The outrage loosed by sailors of the *Daniel* upon the Lahaina missionaries in October 1825 was not the last time sailors rioted in opposition of the kapu on prostitution. Attacks by sailors upon ali'i, missionaries, and other mission stations occurred twice more in as many years. Non-missionary foreigners resisted the changes that the work of the American Board of Commissioners for Foreign Missions (ABCFM) encouraged in Hawai'i, since new moral regulations enjoined Hawaiian women not to engage in a sex trade with foreign sailors and worked upon Hawaiians to resist purchasing goods in excess from the merchants. Material possessions and trade, too, were eschewed by the austerity the Congregational ministers preached to converts and congregants.

Even as Hawaiians engaged with this new Akua, a new religion's preachers and practices, the governing choices that the ali'i made in the face of foreigners' outrageous behaviors arose from a long history of native governance and law. Closely examining the outrages reveals Hawaiian legal formations transforming. The kapu of the ali'i continued to be disseminated orally, even as kānāwai (published law) were being produced and circulated through a print medium. The breaking of kapu in 1825 was absolutely freighted for Hawaiian transgressors with the breaking of unwritten, always spoken, conventions of behavior, which before 1819 were attached to punishments as severe as death, sacrifice, or exile from home place and family.

Kapu has little been studied as law, as existing simultaneously with kānāwai, or as necessary to the maintenance of particular social relations among chiefs and between the ali'i and maka'āinana. While kapu were proclaimed to control the activities and behavior of Hawaiian subjects, kapu during the period 1820 to 1827 was further modified to govern the social interaction between Hawaiians and foreigners.[1] But as this period progresses and into the 1830s and 1840s, kānāwai would become a binding legal instrument for transient, settler, and native populations alike if only because orally pronounced precept would be difficult to convey, as sailors' arrivals and departures varied.[2]

Additionally the promulgation of kānāwai introduced challenges to traditional constructions of "jurisdiction," since kapu only applied to Hawaiian bodies, marking out a maoli body politic that did not have—or need, before this period—mechanisms in place to address the behavior of a large influx of foreigners or regulate their actions. The binding nature of kānāwai in contradistinction to the exercise of kapu meant that published law was not as reactive to immediate conditions of context—a difference that was obscured when new ideas about the superiority of published law as the only medium that conveyed permanency were introduced. The instantiation of kānāwai may have resulted (though not purposefully) in a diminished role for chiefly deliberation in the 'aha 'ōlelo, necessitating further evolutions in governing mechanisms and instruments beyond the 1820s and into the 1840s.

Published law inaugurated unforeseen and unsought-for transformations in social relations between the ali'i and maka'āinana, since punishments over violations of kapu were adjudicated on a case-by-case basis, rather than being arbitrarily fixed. Also, the venue for the pronouncement of punishment was more communal than personal, occurring before the ali'i and assembled people. Punishments for violation of the kapu on prostitution varied, but for repeat offenders, a form of exile from community *as* imprisonment was typical. In contrast, by 1828, or just after this period of outrage, the punishment for adultery or *moe kolohe* was hard labor or the payment of a fine as mediated by the newly produced *letter* of the law and not the 'aha 'ōlelo, which involved deliberation through speech and oral pronouncement, or recourse to the decision of the kuhina nui, on a case-by-case basis.

The production of a hybrid oral and written promulgation of laws was mirrored in similar evolutions in governing practices. 'Aha 'ōlelo deliberations and decision-making now included business that foreign merchants, seamen, and missionaries considered their own, which brought written documentation of ali'i proceedings and decisions into being alongside their memorialization in (oral) mo'olelo or *mele*. Furthermore, Hawaiian governance in the 1820s is also notable for its expansion of Hawaiian political deliberation and opportunities for foreigners to engage in political speech

NO KA

MOE KOLOHE.

I MOE ke kane i ka wahine, e huhu ae la ka wahine kahiko, i manao ua wahine kahiko la, e hemo, e hai aku i ke alii kia aina a na ke alii kia aina e haawi aku i palapaala no ka hemo ana, alaila hemo laua. I manao ua wahine la, e haalele ia ia, mare i kane hou nana, ua pono; aka o ua kane moe kolohe la, aole loa ia e moe i ka wahine hou, a make ka wahine ana i haalele ai, alaila mare ia i ka wahine, aka i hoopaa ua kanaka la, i ka moe kolohe, eia kona uku, i ekolu puaa, na ka mea nana ka wahine ana i moe ai, i ekolu hoi a ke alii kia aina puaa, na ke kia aina e manao ka ke alii nui; i hana a i ole na puaa ekolu, i waiwai e ae, e hoolike ka waiwai, me ke kuai ana o na puaa ekolu.

I moe ka wahine i ke kane e huhu ae la ke kane kahiko, ua like pu ke ano, o kona olelo ana, me ko ke kane, o ka wahine i moeia'ku ai, elima ana a dola e uku mai na ke alii nui, Elima hoi a ke alii kia aina, Elima hoi i ka wahine nana ke kane ana i moe ai, i ole ke dola, i waiwai e ae, e hoolike me ke kuai ana o na dola elima, pela no hoi ke kane i moeia'ku ai. O ke kane hewa, o ka wahine hewa, ina eha hewa ana, aia no i ko ke alii manao ka hemo o ka aina.

Ina he alii ka i hewa, Elua haneri dola, e uku mai, na ke alii nui, i na eha hewa ana aia no i ko ke alii manao ka hemo o ka aina.

Aole loa e pono elua wahine i ke kane hookahi, Aole e pono elua kane i ka wahine hookahi; o ke kane, me ka wahine, i manao e hana pela, ua hewa no ia, no ka mea, aole ia e like, me keia kanawai.

O ke kane, me ka wahine, i hoao pono mamua, ua paa no laua, i keia wa hou, aka i moe kekahi i ka mea e, ua hewa no ia.

O ke kane me ka wahine, ina e hoao malu, i keia wa hou, ua hewa no ia, O keia mau mea a pau, e ukuia lakou, ua like ke ano o ka uku me ka olelo maloko o na lalani maluna.

O ke kane hookamakama, o ka wahine hookamakama, akahi po, e hookamakama ai, elima dola e uku mai na ke alii, alua po, umi ke dola e uku mai, akolu po, iwakalua dola e uku mai, aha po, akahi kanaha dola e uku mai na ke alii ia, ina e malama ole lakou i keia uku, ua hewa, eia ka uku he umi kumamawalu malama e paa ai i ka hao.

No ke kane mare ia, no ka wahine mare ia.

Eia ka pono, o ka mare ana e mau loa ai, o ke kane me ka wahine, i makemake laua e mare, ina i kapu ko laua mare ana i ka olelo a ke Akua, aole e pono ke mare, aka i kapu ole, ko laua mare ana i ka olelo a ke Akua, e hoike ko laua manao mamua i ke kumu, i pono ai, alaila e mare pono ia laua, imua i ke alo o ke Akua, a me ko ke ao nei, a e paa ko laua mau inoa iloko o ka palapala mare, pela e like ai, me ke kanawai i keia manawa.

KAUIKEAOULI.

Oahu, Sept. 21, 1829.

Figure 9. "No ka Moe Kolohe." Mission Houses Museum Library.

and rhetorical performance in front of the 'aha 'ōlelo. As we will see, the more foreigners appeared with conflicts or issues before the 'aha 'ōlelo, the more the political and legal authority of the ali'i can be seen within a global context of jurisdiction and governance.

In order to see how this authority functioned, we need to be able to hear how chiefly speech and oral pronouncement are marked as authoritative through certain verbal formations or hallmarks. These hallmarks often precede or follow important formal speech acts, such as a decree, an order, or a judgment or finding. When encountered in an English translation, such a phrase can appear as innocuous as "here is my opinion, or thought." Translations lack the salience of the Hawaiian-language original. "Eia ko'u mana'o," is a standard phrase marker that suggests that what follows is the thought or considered opinion of the ali'i, which was important to heed. As these moments arise in importance over the course of the chapter, I will highlight and unpack their significance where needed.[3]

In letters passed between the ali'i on different islands and in their verbal and written correspondence with the mission, important hallmarks draw our attention to speech that is authoritative. In the form of kapu, orally pronounced public decree, and in kānāwai, these formal oral formations illustrate that the authority of newly published kānāwai rests in their association to chiefly speech. Rather than a wholly foreign imposition, early kānāwai were syncretic texts that when studied can emphasize the ways in which oral legal pronouncement gave *legitimacy* and authority to written expression, rather than the other way around.

In the aftermath of the outrages, a series of 'aha 'ōlelo, or chiefly councils, met to address the problem of foreigners behaving badly on Hawaiian shores. The kapu on Hawaiian women gave rise to the first chiefly discussions about the importance of adopting Hawaiian laws in a global context. Conflicts that arose between foreign sailors and missionaries over the kapu were addressed by the ruling ali'i in their formal deliberations within the 'aha 'ōlelo. Histories of this period overlook the significant role of the 'aha 'ōlelo in creating laws and administering justice, an absence that took its cues from the mission's insistence that Hawai'i became both a legal and religious vacuum when the 'ai kapu was "overthrown."[4]

This chapter focuses on the continuing consequences of the 1825 kapu, specifically two new "outrages" in which an American naval captain and a British whaling captain and their men expanded their attacks on the American mission stations to include maka'āinana and ali'i on multiple islands. This threat of military and civilian violence pushed the aliʻi to declare kapu upon makaʻāinana, food, and drink in order to restrict the foreigners' access to what they desired. Yet violent threats continued, and the aliʻi were faced with more complex decisions about how to deal with them. This chapter carefully traces these deliberations and decisions in order to give a robust account of how Hawaiian governance was changing and adapting.

The chapter continues with Rev. William Richards' legal problem as he faced a potential charge of libel, levelled at him by Captain Buckle—who took Leoiki from Wahinepiʻo—and the British consul Richard Charlton. The British men insisted that the American missionary should face charges for his written and published statement that Buckle had "purchased a woman" in Hawaiʻi. The aliʻi then found themselves with an issue: should they surrender the American to the British to have him face justice thousands of miles away in either America or England? The chiefs convened several ʻaha ʻōlelo to deliberate this problem, and I argue that Richards' advocacy on his own behalf in one of these ʻaha is critical to how Hawaiian governance changed in this period. Richards defended himself in the ʻaha aliʻi against removal to an American or British jurisdiction. But *how* Richards defended himself, how he used Hawaiian political language and rhetorical performance before the chiefs, marks this moment as a turning point in Hawaiian political history and Richards' role in it. Unlike most of the foreigners in the islands, Richards exhibited a remarkable level of cultural and linguistic fluency at this ʻaha ʻōlelo, especially with respect to religiopolitical matters. In this moment, I argue, we find Richards placing himself under the malu of the chiefs, beginning a process that will culminate in his later work with the aliʻi to write the first Hawaiian Constitution in 1840, and to future naturalizations in its wake.

The idea of the breaking of kānāwai, written and published laws promulgated by the aliʻi, belonged to another legal tradition, one lacking historical precedent in the islands. While breaking the kapu transgressed the will of the chief and placed the kapu breaker at odds with the social fabric of a specific community, the breaking of new published kānāwai portended a different social ordering, lacked history or precedent in a Hawaiian social context, and did not necessarily require the input of chiefly advisers knowledgeable in Hawaiian tradition and precedent for mediation. Most importantly, kānāwai, or published laws, lacked the salient power of speech as its mode of deployment.

The Outrage of the USS *Dolphin*

The need for new instruments of law was demonstrated again in the second outrage and sailor attack on American missionaries that occurred in Honolulu and was initiated by the crew of the USS *Dolphin*. The *Dolphin*, the first American warship to visit Hawaiian waters, was dispatched to the Pacific to round up the murderous mutineers of the whaleship *Globe*. It had stopped in Hawai'i to pressure the ali'i to pay the sandalwood debt supposedly owed to New England merchants. Lt. John Percival, the commander, however, had his own ideas about what to impress upon the chiefs—namely, his dissatisfaction with the kapu against prostitution. The *Dolphin* arrived in the islands on January 13, 1826, and several rounds of official dinners ensued among the resident American merchant agents, occasions at which Boki, the governor of O'ahu, and Francisco de Paula Marin, a Spanish chiefly adviser, were often in attendance.[5]

Percival's inquiry into the chiefs' debt proceeded in Honolulu, and on January 24, he sent a letter to Eliab Grimes, Stephen Reynolds, Alpheus B. Thompson, and John W. Spurr, merchant agents in the Sandwich Islands. Percival's letter was addressed to the "citizens of the United States requesting information relative to the debts owed by the government, and other, of the Sandwich Islands," which, according to Stephen Reynolds, would be acted upon "by and by."[6] But while he was in Honolulu, Percival and the men of the *Dolphin* found their stay in port to be less than accommodating to their desires. On January 27, 1826, missionary printer Elisha Loomis wrote in his journal that Percival, upon returning to Honolulu harbor from a quick visit with some Americans in the Pu'uloa (Pearl River) area of the island, complained that he had received less than adequate treatment. He and his party could obtain no fish, though the area had large fishponds, and they found no Hawaiian willing to allow them to light a fire. All labor had been expressly forbidden by chiefly pronouncement in observance of the Sabbath. Furthermore, Ka'ahumanu, having previously gotten wind of Percival's plans to go to Pearl River, had sent orders ahead of time that "none of the females of that place should visit them for the purpose of criminal intercourse." Being unable to catch a fish, start a fire, or bed a woman sent Percival into a rage, with the froth of his anger directed at Ka'ahumanu, whom he accused of dispatching a "spy to watch over him."[7]

The regulation of sexual intercourse with foreigners by chiefly decree became more pronounced over the coming months. On February 1, 1826,

Elisha Loomis, who had set about his work at the Honolulu mission printing press for the day, was suddenly distracted by a "great crowd of natives coming from the village." According to Loomis, it "appeared that a female who had been on board one of the ships, venturing on shore was seized," and the crowd was now "carrying her to Ka'ahumanu." In the crowd's wake came her foreign paramour, who "entreated earnestly" of Ka'ahumanu that the woman be permitted to live with him. Ka'ahumanu replied, "If you marry her you may, but otherwise you cannot have her." The man argued that the woman did "not know what marriage [was]." He said, "I know, but as she does not it would not be proper to marry," to which Ka'ahumanu replied, "If you know what marriage is, take her, be married and treat her accordingly." According to Loomis, as the foreigner could not do this, he was "forced to return without his dear."[8]

On February 20, several "girls [who] were taken from white men" were set to "getting stones for the church," a very public punishment for prostitution. That day, Percival paid a visit to Governor Boki, the chief Kaikio'ewa, and others to tell them that this punishment was "not right," that it "ought not to be."[9] Elisha Loomis noted in his journal that during this meeting Percival also inquired as to who gave orders to prevent females from visiting ships. He was told, "The King [Kauikeaouli Kamehameha III] and his guardian [Ka'ahumanu]." According to Loomis, Percival "declaimed with great violence against the missionaries," saying that they "trade upon Ka'ahumanu," but that "he would come and tear down their houses."[10]

Percival did not believe that the ali'i were capable of exercising their own judgment when they pronounced the kapu prohibiting women from going to ships. Rather, he preferred to argue that the missionaries were exploiting chiefly rule to further spread the gospel. He railed that such laws were "unknown in England and America; and that if any chief or minister should attempt to stop prostitution in either of those countries, they would lose their heads immediately."[11] According to Rev. Richards, when Percival realized that "Boki had not the power of repealing the law, a general Council of Chiefs was appointed at his request." For the word of one ali'i was insufficient to lift the kapu. Recognizing this, Percival sought a hearing before the 'aha 'ōlelo.[12]

A formal council procedure was required to deliberate the kapu. But this convening of the 'aha 'ōlelo was marked by an important requirement. Before the 'aha, Boki had been ordered by Kālaimoku and Ka'ahumanu to relay the message to Percival that "it was the desire of the chiefs to have their public business transacted in writing." Percival swore in response that he would not comply, that he would come and talk with the chiefs, and that if they did not accede to his demands and remove the prevailing restrictions on women going to ships, he would open fire upon them.[13]

The ali'i had met other dignitaries such as Captain George Anson Byron, who visited the islands the previous year bearing the bodies of Liholiho, Kamehameha II, and Kamāmalu, who perished in London. They were accustomed to requesting written communications in preparation for council meetings that were held between themselves and prominent foreign visitors. In all likelihood, the written communications would be translated by a haole chiefly counselor or one of the missionaries into the Hawaiian language. It is interesting to note here that Percival's response to this request was anger, insisting that all communications be verbal without the presence of members of the mission who might write about what was said. Certainly, pressuring the ali'i to lift a kapu on prostitution fell far from Percival's official mandate to persuade the ali'i to pay the debts they purportedly owed to New England merchants.

According to several missionary accounts, Percival's language and threats became increasingly incendiary leading up to the 'aha 'ōlelo. Percival remarked at one point that though "his vessel was small, it was like fire," a threat that touted the military might of his vessel. His rage seemed focused on particular American missionaries, especially Rev. Bingham, whom he threatened to shoot should he come to the 'aha. Percival also threatened that if a native should attempt to "take a native [woman] from one of his men, he would 'shoot him.'"[14] Boki suggested that Percival go to speak directly with Ka'ahumanu. But in the midst of his passion, Percival accidentally struck another foreigner, Captain Brooks, with his walking stick, whereupon Brooks poured a decanter of brandy into Percival's hat. This, according to Stephen Reynolds, put Percival into a "great rage."[15] It seems that Percival's arrogant demeanor could set more than just the chiefs on edge.

Percival's verbal threats placed the chiefs in a protective stance. Two ali'i were dispatched to the Honolulu mission house, as the ali'i were "very much alarmed" for the safety of the missionaries. They inquired what they should do in case Percival attacked the mission, whereupon they were told to "let them alone." The missionaries assured the chiefs that they were "not afraid of Capt. P.—he would not dare molest us. If he should commence an unprovoked attack upon us or upon them the American Government would disapprove it and bring him to justice."[16] In making this statement, missionaries made clear that this was an issue that should be handled between Americans. The missionaries' reaction seemed to rest in their belief that should calmer heads not prevail, back in the United States, American justice would hold Percival accountable for his actions in Hawaiʻi.

The next day, Percival did as Boki suggested, meeting with Kaʻahumanu and speaking with both Kālaimoku and Boki about Hawaiian "girls." According to merchant agent Stephen Reynolds, Prime Minister Kālaimoku told Percival, "It was good to burn the white men's houses and let them begin to fight, for he was tired of seeing them come in sight!"[17] Kālaimoku's statement illustrates that aliʻi found certain foreigners arrogant and burdensome. His words also demonstrated that the aliʻi were responding to a shared field of discourse, the aliʻi drew on Percival's threats to make "fire," with a promise to burn the houses of those who provoked chiefly ire. While it is not clear if Percival was inclined to engage in two-way communication with the aliʻi, the aliʻi certainly were listening to him and responding in like fashion: fire for fire, word for word.

On February 22, 1826, the peace of Honolulu was ruptured at sunrise, noon, and sunset by the ominous sound of the twelve guns of the *Dolphin* presenting salutes in honor of George Washington's birthday, in a show of both honor and force.[18] That same day, Percival met the aliʻi at an ʻaha ʻōlelo at which no missionaries were present. Elisha Loomis noted in his journal that the proceedings were, however, circumstantially related to the mission.[19] To the disappointment of the missionaries, Percival appeared that day to be "unusually pleasant, giving many suggestions to the chiefs with the course they should take with their own people." Both Elisha Loomis and Levi Chamberlain related in their diaries a laundry list of Percival's suggestions: "he advise[d] them [the aliʻi] not to proceed to [sic] fast in reforming their people. The children should be instructed, but no others. . . . It was not right to take away any females that might go on ships, it was not right to put them into irones, or to shave their heads or make them do any work, it would be proper . . . to advise them."[20]

In the mission's early years, merchants and ship captains, much more so than missionaries, traveled with the belief that the government of the islands should bend to their will. Percival also opined to the chiefs, saying, "for himself he did not want a mistress, he was old, but his boys, [crew] did want them, it was no concern of his. If it was wrong they alone were to blame. It was proper that those who became pious should keep themselves free from these things, but those who wished to live in prostitution should be let alone."[21]

According to Chamberlain, Percival had "much to say in favor of their [the ali'i] tolerating such practices," arguing that "England and America do the same" and, according to him, "it would not be safe for government to interfere to put a stop to it."[22] Percival had made clear why it would not be safe for the chiefs to disregard his "advice." When told by Percival that they should draw a line between "such as were pious and such as were not," the chiefs replied that they wished to "draw no such line" and that "they wished all the people under their care to turn from such wickedness." One of the chiefs added,"if prostitution is allowed in America, then let Americans get their prostitutes there, and not seek them from here."[23]

This unnamed chief's statement makes clear the ali'i's understanding of the different categories of people and place that shaped domestic and foreign subjects' behaviors and morals. Instead of a simplistic retort to Percival's demands, this chief set forth an argument about jurisdiction and governing authority. Unswayed by claims that what was good for Britain and America should be good for Hawai'i, the chief's distinction between the women over there (America) and the women over here (Hawai'i) is one constructed by the kapu's application to Hawaiian women, subjects of Hawaiian governance. The subtle dig at the power of Christian morality in America—such that prostitution was allowed in a Christian country—also stands as a marker of ali'i understanding of their own capacity to determine the "pono" of their islands, even as foreigners attempted to challenge their decisions or insist that the missionaries were the real origin of this kapu.[24]

Making no headway with his line of argument, Percival changed tactics, arguing that when the English captain Lord Byron had visited the islands from May through July, 1825, women were allowed to go on board his vessel, the *Blonde*, and the "chiefs had made him [Byron] their favorite." He continued to complain that when he, Lt. Percival, an agent of the American government, visited, the chiefs did not "treat him as a favorite."[25] Couched in this rhetoric of fairness and equal diplomatic treatment, Percival thus claimed sexual access to Hawaiian women as a diplomatic courtesy, one that he and his crew had been denied. In evoking the comparison between himself and Lord Byron, and between the civility shown to the British Byron rather than his American self, Percival also complained that he was not a *punahele,* or favorite of the chiefs, chiding the chiefs for his ill treatment using a Hawaiian social category of relation. Percival's use of the term revealed some of his own familiarity with Hawaiian language and his negotiational savvy in speaking with the aliʻi, since punahele were given special treatment and gifts by the aliʻi. Percival grew increasingly incensed, however, ranting that he would rather "have his arms and legs cut off, than to be thus insulted."[26]

In diplomatic discussions, "translating" the self and one's needs into unfamiliar terms was an important skill. Percival finally attempted to appeal to, if not outright flatter, what he imagined was their sense of importance, telling the aliʻi that "your" missionaries, "tell you so and so but they are only *Kanakas* [common low men]—I know nothing about them—I am a *Chief* from the United States, and you must listen to me."[27] In trying to persuade the aliʻi that the American missionaries were no better than common kānaka, Percival made the assumption that relations between aliʻi and makaʻāinana were like those between the monarchy and the people in England—class based and monolithic. Many transient haole passing through the islands were insistent that their modes of governance, relation, and commerce were civilized and normative. These haole persisted in seeing all people they encountered in relation to their own social structures and behaviors, often insisting that these people should adopt haole ways to make the interactions more comfortable to the foreigner. Percival's attempt to draw on Hawaiian categories of punahele and chief on the one hand, and the treatment of prostitution in America on the other, was not put forth to find common ground or understanding between himself and Hawaiians. He employed these Hawaiian words—poorly understood, it would seem—in an attempt to insist on his equality of rank and the inferiority of the missionaries, in service of achieving the removal of the kapu, making ports of Hawaiʻi *noa,* free of kapu, and enabling prostitution to continue.

The aliʻi restriction of Hawaiian women's sexual intercourse with foreigners, which Percival mocked, was a simple exercise of chiefly rule consonant with political and legal relationships between aliʻi and the makaʻāinana as they had existed continuously since days before ʻai kapu removal in 1819. Kapu differentiated maoli bodies from haole, structuring maoli belonging and political relationships. The continuation of this legal and governing mechanism had nothing to do with Percival, or his entreaties, or observations of the word of God. As subjects of their aliʻi, Hawaiian women and their sexual acts with foreigners, like the actions of subjects in any country, were subject precisely to an exercise of governmental power. Simply put, Hawaiian subjects were under Hawaiian chiefs' legal jurisdiction, and the kapu restricting women from prostitution confirmed these women as chiefly subjects.

Two days later, Percival demanded that Ka'ahumanu release Hawaiian women who had been imprisoned for violating the kapu. She replied, "We have turned to the Lord, and we wish all our people to do the same;—for this reason we have laid the law. We make no law for you, nor for your men, nor for your women—it is for our own females we have made the law."[28] Ka'ahumanu's response to Percival should be heard in relation to the way kapu operated in a Hawaiian legal context. Rather than a coy game between "influenced" missionized Hawaiians and a ship captain from a "civilized" nation, let us try to imagine that kapu is sensical when deployed in the way Ka'ahumanu described it. Because kapu was proclaimed, pub-licly, via professional "criers," ma ka 'ōlelo Hawai'i, it was applicable only to the Hawaiian populace.

Despite evidence to the contrary, one of the most persistent myths about the 1820s is that all kapu had been "overthrown" with the 1819 strik-ing down of the 'ai kapu. The 'ai kapu (as we have seen in prior chapters) had been a very important set of rules and restrictions that set social norms for and governed men and women's relations with one another, demarcat-ing separate spheres of labor and diet and participation in religious activi-ties and spaces. The 'ai kapu was one pillar of governance that structured the relations between ali'i and maka'āinana. But as we can see in this exami-nation of the foreign sailors' and captain's "outrages" over the 1825 kapu, the 'ai kapu was not all kapu, nor was it the sum total of the form of authority that ali'i exercised over Hawaiian lands, waterways, seas, and its people. After 1819, kapu continued to function in relation to orally pre-served precedent familiar to the ali'i and kākā'ōlelo who were their counselors.[29]

It is precisely at this moment of the "outrages" over the 1825 kapu that we see the proliferation of an intersecting myth: that the missionaries were the cause of foreign sailors' inability to have easy access to Hawaiian wom-en's bodies. If there was no kapu, no Hawaiian law after 1819, then of course the missionaries were to be blamed for the 1825 prohibition. But the "out-rages" are evidence instead of the functioning vitality of kapu on Hawaiian terms; for Hawaiian women's adherence to the rule of their chiefs elicited rage among the foreigners. Although ship captains railed fiercely against the kapu, it was so clearly conformed to and well enforced that three ships in the space of three years had "outraged" against the law. Each captain had threatened to burn down the homes of the people and ali'i. Giving substance to these threats was the fact that one was captain of an American warship, while one other threatened to send for British warships to intervene on their behalf.

As if anticipating Percival's next move, Kālaimoku ordered that "some [women] who persisted in violating the tabu were [to be] taken into custody, and either sent inland under keepers, or more closely confined nearer the chiefs."[30] Mission printer Elisha Loomis notes that it was the prostitutes that had been confined at Waikīkī who were ordered transferred, "presumably to a location where they could be better guarded from foreigners."[31] The next day, Percival sent a messenger to the ali'i "demanding the liberation of five noted prostitutes, and threatened that he would blow the town down if they did not listen to him."[32]

Afternoon services on the Sabbath, February 26, were to be held indoors due to the rain. Rev. Bingham and a "considerable number" of the ali'i gathered at the new two-story stone house of the ailing chief, Kālaimoku. "A company of seamen from the *Dolphin*, accompanied by two or three others from among the whaleships," entered the enclosure of the royal establishment, a space that could accommodate "the congregation of the village, consisting of nearly three thousand people." Four of them went upstairs into the hall where the ali'i were gathered "attending on the sick languishing couch of their venerated chief." The men, clubs in hand, had arrayed themselves in a line, and they were ordered by the ali'i attending Kalaimoku to leave, a request they refused. Instead, the men demanded that prostitutes be made available or they would demolish the houses if their request was ignored. They began to shatter the valuable window glass, breaking sixty-seven panes in all as people from the area began to arrive for Sabbath service.[33]

One of the kānaka present ran to the mission house to report the attack on Kālaimoku's home. Secular agent Levi Chamberlain and printer Elisha Loomis rushed over to find a melee of eight to ten sailors attempting to fight off an ever-growing group of Hawaiians. To Mrs. Sybil Bingham, the conflict appeared intense: "The people now rushed forward with spirit, and fell upon the rioters with such fury, that their lives must surely have been the forfeit."[34] Over the sound of tumult and riot, the ali'i called out, "Don't

Palace of Karaimoku. — Native Chapel. — Cottage of Mr Ellis.

Figure 10. "Kalaimoku's house." Hawai'i State Archives.

kill them," to which kānaka replied, "Shall we stand and be killed?" The chiefs then gave the order, "Seize the men but do not hurt them," to which was heard in response, "How can we seize them when they are armed with knives?"[35]

A sailor about to have his skull smashed in with a stone was spared when Chamberlain and Loomis intervened. If not for the "vigorous exertions on the part of both chiefs and missionaries, to save them," the sailors would have been killed. Percival arrived on scene with two or three midshipmen and began to beat his men with cane and cudgel, calling out to any kānaka within shouting distance to bring ropes to restrain any sailors who still resisted.[36]

Leaving the riot, Mr. Bingham hastened to his nearby home to check on his wife and daughter. Two Hawaiian women were also with Mrs. Bingham at the time. A sailor swung at the minister with his club, which Bingham deflected with his umbrella. Two sailors had entered Bingham's yard and attempted to force open the doors and windows. "One struck with all his might against the door, but made no impression. The other demolished a window, breaking sash and all, and in attempting to get in received a blow (from his comrade) which laid him prostrated."[37] Bingham tried to gain entry into his home, but his wife had bolted the door in fear against the attackers. A sailor cornered him, drew his knife, and tried to stab Bingham, but he avoided the thrust. According to Loomis, when the people saw the sailor's assault on Bingham, they all launched themselves in his direction. During the whole contest, Loomis noted, "no weapon except clubs and stones" were used by the Hawaiians.[38]

The sailors—only two of whom were crew members of Percival's ship— were taken back to the *Dolphin*. As punishment meted out by their captain, the men of the *Dolphin* involved in the riot received two or three dozen lashes for their conduct. Perhaps this was a bit of public theater, since according to Elisha Loomis, the attack that had been made on the chiefs and the mission was a "preconcerted plan," intimating that Percival himself was involved; the family of "a Mr. J" had been told beforehand to stay away from the meeting, as a "disturbance would take place."[39]

In order to address the attack, the ali'i called a meeting on February 26 with Bingham and an irritable Lt. Percival at one of the chiefly residences. Percival confronted Bingham, arguing that the missionaries "exceeded the limits of their charter in the communication of instruction to the people."[40] On February 28, two days after Percival's meeting with Bingham and the chiefs, Levi Chamberlain wrote with alarm that he had heard that the kapu on women had been lifted. He wrote hurriedly: "Learn that the tabu put on the *hookamakama* [prostitution] business has been taken off and that all who wish to go on board ships for the purpose of prostitution have full liberty to do so. Capt. P. it is said is now *maha* [at ease] and it is also said that it is in his intention to visit Maui and Hawaii for the important purpose of effecting the removal of the tabu on prostitutes!!"[41] Chamberlain suggests here that the kapu was lifted in response to Percival's anger, as a means to stay the possible threat of his visiting other islands with violence in order to force the chiefs to rescind the kapu. Elisha Loomis stated as much when he wrote that the suspension of kapu was "no doubt in consequence of the repeated threats and persevering efforts of Lieutenant Percival and many others now in port."[42]

During March, an even darker side of Lieutenant Percival began to emerge. Coarse in his dealings with the missionaries and ali'i, he also took his still seething rage out on the merchant agents, ship captains, and Hawaiian women that he felt had crossed him in some way. Stephen Reynolds' journal marks the extreme fluctuations of Percival's temper, illustrating a pattern of rage that cannot be easily ignored. At times, Reynolds writes of Percival attending dinners that end cordially and politely, while on other occasions he notes Percival's violent behavior. On March 6, Percival got into a heated verbal altercation with Captain Alfred P. Edwards of the *London*, which escalated into a fistfight. A week later, on March 13, Percival attacked Edwards again, striking a severe blow to his head that resulted in a lump "raised on the crown of his head, nearly three inches in length as large as a man's finger."[43] In retaliation, Edwards went for an axe and then took up a rammer and went after Percival. Three days later, an enraged Percival threatened another person in order to gain access to some houses belonging to Capt. Ebbetts.[44]

Given his disposition, which in the coming years would earn him the nickname "Mad Jack," Percival's treatment of Hawaiian women tended to be horrific. Stephen Reynolds noted that on March 19, Percival visited Governor Boki to demand that a young girl "who thro' fear [had] ran away from him" be returned to him. Reynolds, in disbelief, noted that "Boki gave the word and she was sent to him."[45] The next day Reynolds reported in disgust: "After dinner several went to his [Percival's] house, to whom he related his treatment to a young girl—too disgraceful to be related."[46] This naval officer, an agent of the American government, had decided to pursue his vendetta against the kapu on prostitution in both official and personal ways. His hectoring of the aliʻi and missionaries, the planned riot of his crew, and his very individual victimization of a young Hawaiian woman gave a particularly vicious face to 1826–1827 American diplomacy in the islands. The few stories of the sexual abuse of Hawaiian children and women that come to us from these textual sources suggest larger patterns of violence that scholars may never be able to establish clearly or empirically.[47]

For the duration of the USS *Dolphin*'s stay in Hawaiʻi, from February through April, the kapu remained suspended, and women began to visit ships again. On the evening of March 31, the evening before the day given by Percival for his departure, two gunshots were fired at nine o'clock, signaling the beginning of a new curfew. Sailors were to return to their ships, and women on ships were to return to shore. Any drunken sailors or others found outside after hours were imprisoned in the Honolulu fort, to be liberated only if their captain came to pay the six-dollar fine for their release. That evening a crier was sent out to notify all of the will of the aliʻi: that the practice of females going aboard ships for prostitution would cease.[48] The kapu on Hawaiian women had been reinstated.

Percival's threats and the attack of his crew differed from the first outrage of the *Daniel IV* because the *Dolphin* was a US ship of war and Percival
an official representative of the US government. Hawai'i had been visited
by naval ships from Russia and Great Britain, and the ali'i had come to
expect respect and decorum from the men of such vessels. But Lieutenant
Percival's outbursts in the 'aha and the riot of his men against the mission
and the ali'i Kālaimoku made the chiefs question the intentions of American representatives. Printer Elisha Loomis worried that Percival's behavior
would affect relations between the Hawaiian government and the United
States: "Nothing that I know of has ever happened here, which will have
such a tendency to degrade the American name in the eyes of this government."[49] For Loomis and the rest of the missionaries, Captain Percival's
conduct before the ali'i also spurred "feelings of shame and regret" at such
treatment from a fellow American who often exhibited un-Christian-like
behavior.[50]

For Percival and his men, the lifting of the kapu supplied immediate
satisfaction for their demands, a return to the good old days when ships
visiting the islands could obtain women without obstacle. Percival, along
with other ship captains, sought to bend the kapu of the Hawaiian Islands
to suit their own personal needs and that of their crews. Percival had clearly
exceeded his authority, as he would discover when he was forced to stand
before a naval court of inquiry on May 1, 1828, in Charlestown, Massachusetts, to answer to charges brought against him by the ABCFM. For the
missionaries, the temporary lifting of the kapu meant that the "enemies of
purity and good order have gained a victory," and they worried that the
loss of this kapu would provoke the downward slide of the people toward
their former sinful practices.[51] The ali'i response to Percival, however, preserved the peace and safeguarded the lives of their missionary teachers and
the people.

The suspension of kapu and its reinstatement was the normal way that
kapu functioned. Kapu on diverse natural resources, like fish and birds, or
on activities like fishing, planting, going to war, or sexual intercourse were
proclaimed for different reasons. At times, kapu were instituted on a cyclical basis that responded to different periods of the year, changes in climate
and environment. Some kapu were highly responsive to context, modifiable
to respond directly to changing situations. The removal of kapu this time
was also responsive to context, as the ali'i were acting to protect the population and to avoid a larger, perhaps international incident. Rev. Bingham's

wife Sybil noted in a letter later that year, "as the present season for the return of foreign shipping drew near, the tabu or prohibition forbidding lewd women visiting the ships was renewed." This observation illustrates that the kapu on Hawaiian women was cyclical, "renewed" or removed depending on the seasons of arrival and departure of ships and sailors.[52]

Hawaiian law and governance had entered into a new age because the islands' populace now included settled and transient haole. Laws that aided in social cohesion were disrupted to some extent by the cyclical appearance and departure of transient foreigners whose conflicts necessitated the creation of law that addressed the new relations forming between visitors and the native government. As legal transformation slowly unfolded, this outrage was not about the difference between multiple legalities—American and Hawaiian—but about how Hawaiian ali'i were going to maintain their rule and governance as the number of foreigners visiting the islands grew, especially foreigners who behaved badly. Chiefly reorientation of kapu in the face of Percival's pressure pointed out the difficulties in applying kapu to foreigners, raising the question as to whether the malu of the ali'i would apply to foreigners as it did to native subjects, or whether a new instrument of law would need to be adopted in order to make foreigners heed the word of the ali'i. Kapu continued to knit together a Hawaiian polity, reinforcing long-standing relations between ali'i and maka'āinana. In the midst of this consideration, the kapu on prostitution was renewed when the *Dolphin* departed the islands on May 11, 1826, although preliminary measures had been adopted to reinstate the kapu as early as April 1.[53]

A month after the *Dolphin* departed from Hawaiian waters, Ka'ahumanu made a public show of pronouncing judgment over two individuals who had broken kapu. On the evening of June 12, an 'aha 'ōlelo was convened in Lahaina to deliberate on the punishment to be meted out for a thief and a "notorious" prostitute. The thief had been sentenced by Kālaimoku and Ka'ahumanu several months previously to be "transported in irons" to the sparsely populated island of Kaho'olawe. When the ship had touched at Lahaina en route to Kaho'olawe, one of the chiefs, probably Wahinepi'o, had set the convict to liberty. He had been recaptured and brought to the 'aha 'ōlelo to answer once more for his crimes. The woman prostitute's transgression seemed more serious, however, since she had "not only broken a law of the chiefs," but had also "both publickly and privately expressed her contempt of the law," and she had on too many occasions been "counselled by Ka'ahumanu and as frequently promised reform."[54]

Early on the morning following the 'aha, an 'āha'ilono or professional crier was sent out inviting all the people of Lahaina to be present. They assembled on the beach, and the two prisoners were brought before the council. According to the Lahaina mission journal kept by Rev. Richards, "the chiefs then unanimously expressed their approbation of the sentence that had been passed upon them [the prisoners] by the chiefs at Oahu and expressed their determination to punish all who should be guilty of like crimes."[55] The public pronouncement of punishment before the assembled residents of Lahaina by the chiefs was performed as a deterrent to warn people about what they risked if they broke the kapu: separation from homeland and family, and exile to the inhospitable island of Kaho'olawe.

The chiefs then turned the prisoners over to the governor of Kaho'o-lawe, charging him to "keep them [the prisoners] safe," while at the same time warning him that "if they escaped from the island, he would be called to account for it."[56] The chiefs then addressed the people, admonishing them to be "witnesses of their determination to stop the former iniquitous practices of the islands" and assuring them that "they [the chiefs] shall persevere in the new course which they had adopted."[57] The thief and the prostitute were then ordered to canoes in front of the people, after which the crowd was released.

Percival's threats of more violence and the riots themselves forced the chiefs to reevaluate their judgments and the pronouncement of kapu within an international sphere of political action rather than simply a domestic sphere. The 1825 kapu had been deployed by the ali'i to censure Wahinepi'o for selling Leoiki and to protect Hawaiian women, shaping their conduct. It had also been pronounced as part of the ushering in of new moral laws that were being fashioned to uphold ka 'ōlelo a ke Akua (the word of God). This process of the promulgation of kapu was one which we have seen took several years for the ali'i to deliberate. And the ali'i continued to rule with long-standing Hawaiian governing and legal practices through the 1820s as a response to changing conditions and the social disruptions caused by unruly foreigners. No history of this moment can be told without investigating Hawaiian law and governance, especially the historicizing of kapu and transgressions past that took place during deliberations of Hawaiian legal precedent.[58]

Missionaries easily elided kapu into "law" in their writings, yet the nature of "breaking" kapu (hehi, 'a'e) needs to be interpreted within a

broader Hawaiian historical framework that precedes the arrival of foreigners to the islands. To tread (hehi, ʻaʻe) upon kapu was to flout social convention, an abuse of and repudiation of the social relations between aliʻi
and makaʻāinana. This treading metaphor for violating kapu points us to
the importance of physicality and action—and so too the necessary presence of aliʻi, messenger, makaʻāinana—in the conception of kapu, which
we also see in kapu's medium of oral pronouncement. The metaphors used
to describe aliʻi and makaʻāinana relationships, like the term *malu* or
"shade" naming the manner in which a chief's care for and physical and
spiritual protection extended canopy-like over a person or group, are indicative of this manifest basis of social interrelationship.

But the development of published written law in kānāwai introduced
another dynamic into Hawaiian legal and social relations. Whereas kapu
functioned in a manner that brought transgressors to account in social
performances before chiefly authorities (recall Kaʻahumanu's public punishment of the two kapu breakers), kānāwai's printed medium worked outside the legal performances of verbal proclamation, crier dissemination, and
social accountability. Printed law did not require the interactive presence
of aliʻi and people, moving hewa (morally corrupt) behavior away from
contextually specific punishment by chiefs, instead manufacturing recom-
pense in individual terms of fines, hard labor, and imprisonment. Even as
kānāwai at its start made it possible for the aliʻi to extend Hawaiian law
over unruly foreign subjects, it also made this side of Hawaiian law an
instrument capable of alienating aliʻi from makaʻāinana. As Hawaiian law
evolved, its changes introduced new dynamics that sometimes strained
orderly social relationships.

The Final Outrage

On October 23, 1827, a year and eight months after Percival threatened to
force the lifting of the kapu in every Hawaiian port, an English whaleship,
the *John Palmer*, fired its cannons on Lahaina in retaliation for the detention of Captain Elisha Clark by the aliʻi governor Hoapili. According to
David Malo's account of the cannonading, "females were the ground of the
difficulty."[59] Reporting to Kaʻahumanu the next day, Hoapili wrote that he
had heard that two women, Nākoko and Mikabako, along with a few
others, had gone surreptitiously to the *John Palmer* for the purpose of

prostitution, or hoʻokamakama.[60] Hoapili patiently asked Clark to return the women, but his request was met with ridicule.[61]

The next morning, Hoapili approached Captain Clark. "I urged him again, three times I insisted." Clark replied: "You [the chiefs] are just making this up, it is not right, it is not thus in Great Britain, it is not right for you [the chiefs] to withhold women from the British, don't restrain the women who go in the bad way [hewa] lest a Man of War come to put an end to you all by slaughter."[62] Clark excused his behavior through a claim that Hawaiian law was not authoritative, that the kapu and the accusation that the women aboard his ship were violating the prohibition against sex with foreign sailors aboard ship were "made up" fictions. His insistence that he could assert British rules and order—or license, in this case—over Hawaiian women was backed by an overt threat of violent annihilation of the aliʻi ("you all").

Hoapili replied to Captain Clark's scornful words: "I do not give thought in the least to the words you have said to me, I have only one resolve in my thoughts, the women, that you must return them to me. However if you do not return them, you know, I will detain you here on shore until I obtain the women, then you may return to the ship."[63] According to Hoapili, Captain Clark "in no way complied" with his demands, so he ordered several men to bring him Clark's boat, detaining the captain ashore.

Clark, in his anger, began to sputter off more threats: "This land will be full of ships, Maui will be noa [free], or entirely burnt, no kauhale left. My ship is ready to fire upon you this night."[64] Hoapili met Captain Clark's threats by saying that noncompliance with his demands would result in his detention ashore. Maui, Captain Clark argued—albeit in broken Hawaiian, as indicated by the short pokepoke (cut off) phrases Clark spoke in succession, rather than a thoroughly composed sentence—"noa Maui nei, o wela loa, aohe kauhale."

Attention to language in these moments of diplomatic exchange is important, because though the civilization narrative that was peddled by missionaries is uncritically echoed in histories of Hawaiʻi, we are not often helped to see and hear how haole ignorance and incivility appeared or sounded to Hawaiians. To assert that kānaka maoli of this time had finely articulated senses of decorum in speech and behavior, which transient haole like Clark were wholly unfamiliar with, seems obvious. But that point bears reiteration. Indeed, we might ask how behavior like Captain Clark's drove

Hawaiian sympathy for and interest in the Christian mission, while spurring innovations in governance and law to control the behavior of foreigners on Hawaiian soil. These foreign outrages against Hawaiian law (kapu),
these threats to burn Hawaiian towns to the ground, were becoming alarm-
ingly commonplace.

In the face of Clark's threats, Hoapili gave this simple, measured reply:

> A i kii mai ka pu o ka moku **malama no au ia oe**, o oe o au o kuu
> alii hele kakou ma kahi e. I ki mai ko kanaka ma ka moku, **noho
> malie** no makou, aka i pae kanaka o ka moku mauka nei e kaua mai
> ai, alaila kaua aku ko'u kanaka. **Noho malie** no kaua, o na kanaka
> o kaua e kaua, **malama no au ia oe**. Ina i haawi ole mai oe i ka
> wahine **noho loa** kaua mauka nei, aole oe i hoi ma ka moku. Hoo-
> kahi au makemake o ka hoi mai o ka wahine.

> If the cannons of the ship fire, **I will take care** [mālama] **of you**.
> You and I and my chief shall go to another place. If your men fire
> from the ship, we, the people of the island, will **remain calm** [noho
> mālie]. But if the people of the ship land here on shore to fight us
> [kaua], then my people will fight them. You and I will **sit still** [noho
> mālie], let your people and mine do the **fighting** [kaua]. **I will take
> care** [mālama] **of you**. If you do not give me back the women, you
> and I will **dwell here for a long time** [noho loa] on shore, and you
> shall not return to your vessel. I have only one wish, the return of
> the women.[65]

Hoapili's lengthy reply to Captain Clark was an example of Hawaiian diplomatic speech and threat. Hoapili's calm and steady resolve is illustrated by
his use of *mālama* (care for) which was also a veiled threat, as if saying,
"I'm going to take care of you—by controlling you physically, even messing
you up." The reiteration of the phrase *noho mālie*—the people will remain
calm, you and I shall remain still—culminates with the very serious threat
to Captain Clark of *noho loa*—dwelling permanently, perhaps suggesting a
very long detention and even making a veiled reference to Clark's potential
long rest in death.[66] Interspersed between these ambiguous phrases of
"care" and remaining quiet are statements about fighting and violence,
making the "speech" of Hoapili an artful retort to Clark's many threats.
Hoapili was *confident in his power* to bring consequences to bear upon
Captain Clark and his crew, expressing the might behind ali'i authority. He

was prepared to react in defense of the people of Lahaina and physically control unruly foreigners.

Clark was allowed to leave Hoapili's immediate presence, but he did not attempt to return to his ship. Instead, incensed, he traveled to Rev. William Richards' house. Just a little before sunset, Richards and his family were enjoying the company of the Binghams, who were visiting from Oʻahu, when they heard "an unusual cry." Looking from the house, they saw a "great collection of people" outside their home. Captain Clark eventually appeared out of this crowd, accompanied by "two gentlemen and followed by a great concourse of natives." The Hawaiians shouted, "Shut the gate and do not let him go into the yard of the missionary!" Richards disregarded the shouts, opening the gate himself, and ushered the three men into his home. Clark explained what had transpired and what he considered "so base and unjustifiable conduct in the Governor," and that he had no doubt "but that in one hour from the time the news should reach his ship, the town would come down."[67]

Soon a messenger from Hoapili arrived requesting that Captain Clark go to the governor's house. Clark departed, and after tea, Richards began to write a letter to ask the captain what he could do to effect "a settlement of the difficulty and procur[e] his release." Richards also was planning to invite the captain to stay the night at the mission house.[68] But before he could finish writing the letter, one of the foreign residents came to say that the second mate of the *John Palmer* had arrived from the ship to "demand the release of his Captain," and also that "the ship was in readiness to commence firing on the town if the Captain was not released in one hour."[69]

When he heard the alarming news, Richards "hastened to the beach," hoping to catch the mate and beg for a delay so that a settlement could be effected, but the boat had already returned, "discharging one or two pistols as evidence of their determination to carry their threats into execution." Richards then went to Hoapili's residence, where he found Captain Clark and most of the aliʻi.[70] Richards interceded between the two contentious parties (*uwao ia makou*), and in the end, Hoapili decided that the best course of action was to allow Captain Clark to return to his ship.[71]

Just as the messenger returned to announce that the boat to carry Captain Clark back to his ship was ready, "a light appeared aboard ship and the firing commenced." Rev. Richards hurried home as cannonballs whizzed overhead. After the first three shots, Richards and the rest of the missionary family took refuge in the cellar where they felt safer from the cannonballs and flying debris. No one was hurt at the station.

The *John Palmer* sailed away from Lahaina the following morning, October 24. In a show of his defiance of chiefly rule, Captain Clark landed the women he said he did not have aboard his ship on Oʻahu. Messengers on canoe were quickly dispatched from Lahaina to Oʻahu carrying Hoapili's letter of explanation to Kaʻahumanu regarding the conversations that had just transpired on Maui. As discussed at the start of Chapter 4, his address in this letter to the kuhina illuminates the integral role that speech played in Hawaiian governance and how it operated as the authority that sanctioned the written word. Taking a closer look at the way Hoapili speaks of his conversations with Captain Clark, we can see how his phrase choices illuminate the relation between kapu and an aliʻi conceptualization of jurisdiction. Words resonant and measured in one tradition, when translated, require much explication.

Hoapili's letter opens with a phrase that indicates that what follows in the letter is a formal statement: "Eia ka olelo ke hai aku nei au ia oe" (These are the words I have to declare to you). Hoapili then takes sole responsibility for how he dealt with Captain Clark and the situation with the women. In the next sentence, Hoapili cites the kapu on prostitution: "**Ua olelo kakou** aole e holo ka wahine hookamakama i ka moku" (**We have declared** that female prostitutes will not be allowed to go on ships). Hoapili went on to exclaim, "Malama iho nei au ma ia **olelo o kakou**" (I have myself taken care to uphold this **decree** [kapu] **of ours**), which is to say that he worked to ensure its enforcement, though he was one aliʻi and the kapu represented the decree of all (*kākou*) the aliʻi in the ʻaha ʻōlelo. While merchants and ship captains believed and railed exhaustively that the mission was responsible for the kapu, and while sailors attacked chiefly homes as well as missionary stations, all of the chiefs' discussions and correspondence address how the aliʻi would enforce and uphold the words decreed by the ʻaha. In these discussions, allusions to Christianity emphasize "ka ʻōlelo a ke Akua" (the word of God) and the "ka ʻōlelo a ke aliʻi" (the decrees of the chiefs), the confluence of words and worlds in motion.

Continuing his account for Kaʻahumanu, he wrote that when Clark threatened that a man-of-war would come and destroy everyone, Hoapili replied in a strongly derisive fashion, "I aku au, **aole loa oʻu manao ia mau olelo au i olelo** mai," that he gave no thought to what Clark had said. Rather, he was solely focused on one determination, even to the exclusion of Clarks' words: "Hookahi pono ia'u manao o ka wahine wale no e hoihoi mai" (I had room only for one thought, that the women should be returned). This *mana'o* of Hoapili is reiterated to Clark, Richards, and Ka'a-humanu, an indication of its importance. The letter's conclusion ends as it had begun: "O ko'u manao keia i hana iho nei i keia aina o ko alii, mai pono paha mai hewa paha" (This is the thought which I have exercised in this land of your chief, perhaps it is sufficient, perhaps it is lacking). Measuring his actions and statements for the kuhina nui, Hoapili maintained that he exercised the legal jurisdiction of the ali'i, attempting to enforce the 1825 kapu to retrieve the Hawaiian women on Clark's ship.

Although the sale of Leoiki to Captain Buckle had occurred two years earlier, in March 1825, the story published in an American newspaper had been circulating in the Hawaiian Islands a month before the *John Palmer* outrage. Levi Chamberlain, a secular agent of the ABCFM, had warned Rev. Richards by letter that Captain Buckle had returned to Honolulu, furious after seeing the publication of Richards' letter in the newspaper. The discussion surrounding the letter was that any intimation of Buckle's purchasing Leoiki constituted slavery, even when the word "slavery" was not used in the original letter. The mission's new policy to expose publicly the outrages of ships' captains and their crews was beginning to have an effect. Exposures of the names of those connected with such acts, the mission hoped, would work to suppress more outrages only if captains like Buckle understood that their reputations would be ruined back home if they condoned or supported attacks and if they continued to engage in the sex trade.

Criticism was a tactic that merchants also deployed in an attempt to dissuade missionaries from publishing more exposures. Levi Chamberlain clearly felt the pressure of merchant disapproval in Honolulu, where most of the agents were based. In his letters to Richards, Chamberlain raised the specter of a British public inquiry into the veracity of Richard's published account. In his September 18, 1827, response, Richards denied having any knowledge of the publication. He insisted that he never made himself "as an individual responsible" for anything that could have caused injury to Captain Buckle, and that he "never authorized the publication of any thing" he had written back to the ABCFM home office.[72]

Having more thoughts on the subject, Richards penned another letter to Chamberlain later that day. "As to the slave trade carried on at Lahaina, it is for the consuls to get evidence as they can." He would "tell all I know" only when "summoned by a lawful authority."[73] As for troubling himself further about the business, Richards proclaimed, "I shall not do it until there are some judges beside cane judges and some law besides club law."[74]

Richards questioned the authority of both Captain Buckle and the English consul, Richard Charlton. Juxtaposing the image of riotous sailors with law and its enforcement, Richards ridiculed the possibility that any inquiry into his guilt or innocence could be conducted by foreigners in Hawai'i who were promoters of both vice *and* violence. That orderly government was absent in Buckle's and Charlton's actions was evident in their previous dealings with the ali'i. As the affair of the sale of Leoiki persisted in the coming months, the excessive passion and overreaching of the English consul would become clear and foreshadow excesses in his behavior for years to come.

Although regretting the personal repercussions that the publication of the letter was causing him, Richards stood by the board's decision, since he knew from "four years experience that nothing is to be hoped from the most guarded silence."[75] Revealing his anger for the first time, to his good friend Chamberlain, Richards proclaimed adamantly, "It will take more than one lace jacket to Buckle my lips, that is to say, when a man stabs at my breast or in any way endangers the life of my family, I shall not ask him whether or not I may tell of it."[76] The anxiety of being held individually responsible for the publication clearly began to wear on Richards' nerves. To Richards, being coerced through violence to "buckle his lips" resembled the mission's situation during its first four years in the islands. The policies of silence and exposure were a joint missionary decision, involving input at all levels of the organization, stretching from Hawai'i to New England.[77]

The arrival of the *John Palmer* in Honolulu coincided with the arrival on O'ahu of news of Captain Clark's men's late outrage on Maui. Perhaps in reaction to this news, the next day, October 26, 1827, Chamberlain wrote to Richards describing matters in Honolulu as if "the dust was literally agitated by the wind, that frequently the ships in the harbour and the roads could not be seen. Apply the circumstance figuratively and you may form some idea of what is passing."[78] Adding wind to this dust storm was a more recent newspaper account of the 1825 outrage involving the *Daniel*, which reached Honolulu on October 23—the same day as the Lahaina outrage—aboard the ship *Becket*. In his metaphor, Chamberlain spoke of the agitation of the foreigners and the inability of missionaries like himself to predict what actions would be taken against the mission in response to the publication of Buckle's deeds.

The day the *Becket* arrived in port carrying another printed account based on Richards' report of the October 1825 outrage of the *Daniel IV*, Chamberlain had stopped in to see Mr. Hunnewell, an American merchant. Chamberlain's job as secular agent meant that he, perhaps more than any of the other missionaries, had to sustain cordial relations with the merchant agents and ship captains if he was to secure provisions for the mission, carry them between islands for dispersal, and obtain space for letters and publications on American ships bound for home. He was handed the American newspaper containing Richards' account of the outrage and the purchase of Leoiki. As Chamberlain stood reading, one of the men present remarked that publishing the account had been a "very improper thing."[79] Chamberlain attempted to "exculpate the mission from blame in the publicity given the affair," and another gentleman appeared to take his part.[80] In conclusion, however, the sympathetic gentleman said that "if he should while at the islands live with a female contrary to our views of religious propriety and we should expose him in America, he should be enraged at that."[81]

As to the reaction of the foreigners on Oʻahu, Chamberlain reported to Richards that the furor over his published letter produced "a greater excitement in the fleet and among the foreigners at the Honolulu Exchange, than even the seizing of a Captain's boat and the detention of his person."[82] The publishing of the account was "condemned in the most unqualified manner."[83]

Richards had more to worry about than the angry opinion of foreigners, since Chamberlain also wrote that he had heard that afternoon "from good authority" that "Captain Buckle is going to Lahaina with his ship to ʻobtain satisfaction.'" Chamberlain had also heard that the captains of English whaleships have declared "their determination to go to Lahaina and cause a removal of the *kapu*."[84] Hawaiians had informed Chamberlain that a ship would bear a letter to Maui the next day, October 27: "carrying official directions to Nahienaena and a few others to remove from Lahaina to a place of safety, as a fleet of whaling ships under the command of Captain Richard Charlton, the English Consul is to sail for that place to punish the Governor of Maui, Hoapili for what he was now calling the ʻoutrage' on Captain Clark."[85] Richard Charlton was becoming skilled at capitalizing on the discourse of outrage for his own benefit. Charlton clearly believed that the chiefs had no authority to detain British ship captains. In his assertion that ship captains need not recognize Hawaiian kapu, not being bound by its domestic jurisdiction, Charlton was attempting to extend and introduce a new form of extraterritorial English governance to the islands by seeking control over Hawaiian political subjects, the women. Yet his position as consul did not empower him to dictate to the aliʻi the will of the British government. He was responsible for keeping track of the arrivals and departures of British ships in the islands and logging the amount of whale oil or goods they carried. He would have been responsible for the return of deserters to ships as well as setting up care for those too sickly to travel. The consular position in the islands was essentially a commercial one, without vested political authority in the islands. "In response to this news, Chamberlain poured out his concern to Richards. If I were a native and a chief I should give my advice that every female of Lahaina should on the notice of Capt. Buckle's ships arrival in the roads with a view to cause a removal of the kapu, leave for a place of safety, and if the houses of Lahaina must be destroyed, let them be destroyed."[86] On September 12, 1826, almost a year and a half after Charlton's arrival in Hawaiʻi, the aliʻi convened a public ʻaha ʻōlelo to address the people on the subject of the interference of foreigners in their government. It seems that Richard Charlton and other foreigners had prevented the young king Kauikeaouli, Kamehameha III, from traveling to the island of Hawaiʻi from Oʻahu. In attendance at the ʻaha were Mr. Samuel Ruggles, Levi Chamberlain, and missionary printer Elisha Loomis, who recorded what transpired. The number of people in attendance to hear the words of the aliʻi was estimated at between twelve and fifteen hundred. Kālaimoku addressed the crowd, saying,

> Hitherto we [the chiefs] have had but one mind but now the foreigners are laboring to excite dissensions among us . . . before he [Liholiho] left us he told Kaahumanu and I to take charge of the government till his return, but in case he should die abroad, his brother Kauikeaouli was to succeed him, and we were to take care of Kauikeaouli till he should become of age to govern. This it is our desire to do. We acknowledge him to be our king, but we wish him to listen to the counsels of experience. He is, however, in danger of being led away by wicked foreigners.[87]

At that point, Charlton was at the heart of the difficulties. Now, a year later, in October 1827, Charlton was still actively interfering in the government of the islands, having threatened to cut off the head of the governor of Kaua'i, Kaikio'ewa, and to tear down the Kaua'i fort. His statements about the chiefs would have been seditious had they been uttered in a European context. According to Levi Chamberlain, Charlton had railed against Kaikio'ewa, saying that "Kuakini was King of Hawai'i, Ulumaheihei [Hoapili] of Maui, Naihe of O'ahu, and Kaikio'ewa of Kaua'i and that the King and Boki are make iā lākou [going to be killed by them]."[88] According to another account by David Malo, Charlton then told Kaikio'ewa that he was "not afraid to make war with the chiefs of the Sandwich Islands for he had the power to put them all to death, that he had five hundred men, that he was guarding the king, Kauikeaouli and Boki lest Kaahumanu should put them to death . . . that he [the king] and Boki would have been put to death by Kaahumanu if he had not guarded and saved them."[89] Malo also described the plotting of American and British residents, along with both consuls, in order to wrest control of the islands from the chiefs Ka'ahumanu, Opi'ia, Hoapili, Kuakini, and Kaikio'ewa which involved the abduction of Kauikeaouli.[90]

After Charlton threatened Kaikio'ewa, the rumors flew that Charlton was on his way to "put to death all the chiefs of Maui except two, Nahi'ena'ena and Kekauonohi."[91] In the wake of these alarming stories of threats to the chiefs and the loss of Hawaiian control of the government, Hawaiians also began to circulate stories that it was Captain Buckle's intention to "punish by death" Mr. Richards.[92]

In response to these tensions, the chiefs on O'ahu held an 'aha 'ōlelo on November 1, at Ka'ahumanu's chiefly residence in Mānoa. Ka'ahumanu, Opi'ia her sister, Kaikio'ewa, Boki, and others were present to hear the claims of the British consul against Rev. Richards for writing the accusatory letter against Captain Buckle that had been published in American newspapers. Charlton claimed that the government was also to blame for Richards' misstep. Ka'ahumanu and Opi'ia were worried for the safety of Mr. Richards, believing that it was the intention of the British to put him to death.

While Charlton formerly accused the ali'i of not recogizing the authority of "King" Kauikeaouli, by calling the chiefly governors of each island a "King," he now tried a different tactic before the 'aha 'ōlelo, baiting them with the assertion that "Mr. Whitney was the King of Kaua'i, Mr. Bingham of O'ahu, Mr. Richards of Maui, etc."[93] Charlton's words supply another clear example of how disagreements between ship captains, sailors, merchants, and missionaries gave birth to the idea of "missionary influence" over the ali'i. His insult to the chiefs' authority fed the myth of the haole civilizers. If he hoped to stir the chiefs to be wary of the mission taking over the government, he was sadly disappointed, for most of the chiefs, with the exception of Boki, were more concerned that Mr. Richards would be harmed by Charlton or Captain Buckle, or that Charlton would continue to spread incendiary speech that required a stronger chiefly response.

On November 3, Levi Chamberlain was sent for by Ka'ahumanu, who asked him to write letters to the missionaries on Maui and Hawai'i and "give an account of what is going on at this place." Ka'ahumanu wanted Mr. Chamberlain to write to Rev. Richards and Rev. Bingham and ask them to come to O'ahu. Ka'ahumanu informed Chamberlain that the chiefs had already dispatched letters to "Nahi'ena'ena ma, Hoapili ma, Kuakini ma, Naihe ma,"[94] summoning them to O'ahu. The high chiefs and chiefly governors of each island were asked to come to O'ahu to "discuss business of state" and to investigate the "affair of the *haole*."[95] The division of labor in letter writing—Hawaiians directing missionaries to write to their fellow brethren, and missionaries discovering that the ali'i had dispatched letters to other ali'i without their assistance—suggested that intra-ali'i communication and matters of Hawaiian governance often proceeded without missionary or merchant involvement.

On November 3, before Richards' departure for Honolulu, Chamberlain wrote him that "the woman [Leoiki] has been questioned respecting her having been sold, and she denies it and probably denies having accompanied him reluctantly."[96] Because Leoiki could not be compelled to say that she was purchased by Captain Buckle, Chamberlain advised Richards to collect certificates from eyewitnesses to the sale of Leoiki, as much "evidence . . . of the unwillingness of the woman to go with Captain Buckle."[97]

On November 13, Rev. Richards, Rev. Bingham, and their families arrived from Lahaina and received a warm welcome from the kuhina nui Ka'ahumanu, who accompanied them to the safety of the mission house. The next day, Richards received a letter from the British consul, Charlton, regarding the publication of the statement that "Mr. William Buckle, master of the ship *Daniel the Fourth* of London had purchased a female slave at the island of Maui for the sum of one hundred and sixty dollars."[98] Charlton elaborated on the seriousness of the charge and asked that Richards swear an oath to the truth of his statement: "As the purchasing of a slave is by the laws of Great Britain declared to be piracy, and my instructions regarding slaves are very explicit, I have to request that you will confirm your statement upon oath; that the offender, (captain Buckle,) may be brought to justice."[99] The letter supplies Charlton's basis for inserting himself legally into the situation, albeit one that dealt with the crime of piracy and not prostitution.

Richards responded with his own letter the next day that although he had not "seen the printed communication," he had "never authorised any thing of the import which you [Charlton] mention, against Mr. William Buckle."[100] In the end, Richards declined swearing an oath in the most official terms: "I have never said that the above named Gent. [Buckle] has been guilty of engaging in the slave trade, which is pronounced piracy by the British laws; nor have I ever written any thing which I think by a fair construction can bear this interpretation. Of course I cannot make oath to any new paper declaration implying that Capt. Buckle has made a purchase for the purpose of slavery."[101]

Charlton sought to extend his own "judgeship," but it was the prerogative of the Hawaiian government to preserve general order and punish those who broke the law in Hawaiian waters and on Hawaiian soil. Charlton appended an ominous postscript to his letter: "I beg leave to add that the purchasing of any person, male or female by any British subject serving on board any ship even for the purpose of liberating them from slavery, is an act of piracy and punishable with death without benefit of clergy."[102] Perhaps Charlton was hoping to scare Richards into retracting his statements by raising the specter of Captain Buckle's death "without benefit of clergy." Richards noted that the paper that Charlton had forwarded was the February 1827 *Missionary Herald*, which the mission itself had not yet received. After reading the account in the *Herald*, Richards responded by letter to Charlton that the account was "very nearly a faithful transcript from my journal." Richards demurred, however, that while he was an eyewitness to the "riotous conduct" of the sailors in the outrage, he could not make on oath "as to the principal facts mentioned in [his] journal respecting the mistress," as he was "not an eyewitness to them."[103]

On Monday, November 19, Charlton sent a note to Richards requesting a meeting with the minister. Richards was under the impression that they would be discussing the role of Captain Clark in the latest assault on Lahaina, since Charlton mentioned that Clark would be present at their interview. Later that day, Richards and Levi Chamberlain visited Charlton, who immediately introduced the subject of Clark's detention and threatened to make another official complaint to the US secretary of state. Soon, however, the discussion turned toward the published letter about Buckle, and Charlton impressed Richards on this occasion with his impassioned and bitter speech.

Richards noted Charlton's "ridiculous ranting at the tabu and his infamous slander of Hoapili and the other chiefs, and his insinuations, and angry unfounded charges against the mission and those who support the mission."[104] Justice, like kapu, was dependent upon context and jurisdiction. But for Charlton, justice could only be had in a "civilized" setting: in London perhaps, but not on Hawaiian shores before the aliʻi.

The disagreement between Charlton and Richards illustrates that foreigners in the islands were trying to negotiate among themselves their own ideas of fairness, according to the legal systems of their own nations. Insisting on adjudication in London in order to gain authority to punish Richards for the injury to Buckle's character, Charlton would have to persuade the ʻaha ʻōlelo of the correctness and legitimacy of his claims. Barring this development, Charlton would be forced to quell his own anger long enough to wait for official answers from England and the United States on whether or not to proceed to build a case against Rev. Richards for libel and pursue an avenue of punishment or redress. Bringing closure to international and transoceanic disputes like this was going to be difficult, as there was no British or American administration in the islands to serve as an arbiter of such claims. Those involved could either wait six months for an answer to every letter or take their grievances before the chiefs.

Charlton's many outbursts before the chiefs and missionaries illustrate nonmissionary foreigners' desire to imagine the extension of their courts' jurisdiction to the islands. Charlton's prosecution of the case against Richards and his carrying forward of claims against Hoapili by Captain Clark illustrate his contempt for Hawaiian chiefly rule and the threat he posed to the stability of Hawaiian society. And yet there were some foreigners, like merchant agent Stephen Reynolds, who thought it improper to extend American jurisdiction into Hawaiian territory. Upon hearing a rather premature report that Rev. Richards was to be tried by a "jury of his peers," Reynolds noted in his journal of November 6, 1827, "Pray who gave us the power?"[105]

While dissension between foreigners simmered on the sidelines, the chiefs in the ʻaha ʻōlelo were also dealing with already pronounced factions within their ranks. Different groups of chiefs stepped forward to present their views about the "affair of the haole," providing an important glimpse into Hawaiian modes of political decision-making and the process by which legal precedent was raised and deliberated.

Deliberations Within the *'Aha 'Ōlelo*: The Affair of the *Haole*

In attendance at the meeting were two rival factions among the ali'i who were vying for control over the young king Kauikeaouli. Boki, high chief and governor of the island of O'ahu, had been given the honor by the ali'i to serve as guardian of the underage king. Boki had visited England with the late king Liholiho in 1826, a visit that included an audience with King George. Boki was interested in continued economic, legal, and political relations between England and Hawai'i and, as such, was close to British consul Richard Charlton. Boki also had little love for the American missionaries because he had seen firsthand that the strict rules they promoted in Hawai'i over "entertainments" such as gambling, horse racing, card playing, singing, dancing, and prostitution were all things practiced, tolerated, and even encouraged among the English.

As kuhina nui, Ka'ahumanu had the sole power to recognize the next king and vest him with power over his lands, his people, and his military. As kuhina nui, she was the most powerful woman in the islands and ruled the nation with Boki's elder brother Kālaimoku throughout most of the king's minority. The high-ranking chiefs, however, were reeling from Kālaimoku's death on February 8, 1827. With the loss of the great chief, who had been called Kekaulahaoonāmoku (the iron cable that held fast all the islands), the chiefs had to be more vigilant in their dealings with foreigners and with one another. Both ali'i were converts to Christianity and had been baptized and accepted as members of the church. Ka'ahumanu and many of the powerful chiefs who supported her had been the closest allies of Kamehameha I, part of his extended family and his counselors in matters concerning the nation.

The 'aha 'ōlelo was convened to address the unrest among the resident foreigners and to deal with the furor over the publication of Richards' letter. Before meeting with any of the foreigners on November 26, however, the ali'i held a private meeting of the 'aha 'ōlelo at Pohukaina, the home of the chiefess Kekauluohi. The 'aha deliberated over Richards' fate for two days without reaching a resolution.[106]

Evidence exists of the contending arguments in those private deliberations. Boki sent a letter to the Maui ali'i subsequent to the 'aha 'ōlelo that had been held on November 2, at around the same time that Ka'ahumanu had sent letters ordering the ali'i to come to O'ahu. Boki's letter to the Maui ali'i argued that it was best to hand Richards over to the English consul and let the haole take care of their own matters: "To the Maui chiefs, greetings to you all. If Captain Buckle, Captain Clark, and the English consul come for your teacher, look to yourselves, and don't withhold your teacher, release him, they are *haole*, and it is a *haole* complaint, it is for them to settle, your mistake is that you try to intercede among them."[107] Boki here reminds the Maui chiefs that there is an important difference between Hawaiian and haole interests and between native-born and foreign settlers' legal and political status. Ka'ahumanu and her supporters, however, were not so sure of the wisdom of relinquishing either their teacher or their authority over this matter. After much argument, the 'aha had reached an impasse.

When David Malo, a trusted adviser to the high chiefs, entered the building, a tearful Ka'ahumanu called the counselor over to discuss the issue. Malo began by framing the problem for the chiefess with an analogy. If a pig were stolen and someone saw the thief in the act and told you who stole it, Malo reasoned, who would be considered wrong, the one who stole the pig, or the one who reported it stolen? Richards, he implied, was not wrong because he had simply written a report about Buckle's purchase of Leoiki. In his second example, Malo interpolated Ka'ahumanu's personal history more directly into weighing the situation: "You were Kamehameha's wife, and Kanihonui sought to sleep with you, Luheluhe told Kamehameha about the two of you sleeping together. I ask you, which of the two did Kamehameha execute? Was it Luheluhe?"[108] Ka'ahumanu replied, "Kanihonui." Malo then provocatively summarized this line of questioning by asking: "In which country on this earth is the wrongdoer commended and the informant against him pronounced guilty?"[109] Ka'ahumanu responded, "A'ole," or nowhere. Malo then asked a final question regarding Richards himself: "Why should Mr. Richards be convicted, the one who spoke, and Captain Buckle, the one who committed wrong against Mr. Richards commended?"[110]

Through his careful reference to a common example, past kapu, and comparative justice, Malo cleverly connected the 1825 kapu rendering women's bodies off-limits to foreigners with the kapu Kamehameha had placed upon Ka'ahumanu specifically prohibiting men from engaging in sexual intercourse with her. But the connection Malo made did not just highlight the kapu placed on Ka'ahumanu, but also the manner in which Kamehameha was notified of the flouting of the kapu. Malo thus showed the skill of kākā'ōlelo and their role in chiefly deliberation and decision-making.

Malo's counsel is an example of a chiefly adviser applying historical precedent to a contemporary dispute, a practice that had secured the rule of the ali'i over the course of Hawaiian history. He constructed historical precedent and a framework consistent with past Hawaiian governance supplying a view of justice and law for the ali'i to use in these proceedings.

More significantly, Malo's solution reserved control of the situation for his ali'i Ka'ahumanu in a way that also supported a Hawaiian approach to governance. By framing the entire Buckle affair and Richards' place in its reporting as something the ali'i could and should rule on, Malo settled the question in her mind as to whether or not Richards was the subject of British law or was under the malu of the ali'i. This response was distinctly different from Boki's solution, which was to refuse to interfere with foreigners and their law in ways consonant with the way kapu was applied only to Hawaiian bodies. His assertion was that haole should resolve their own disputes because their laws applied to them alone. This approach also allowed Boki to excise the missionaries from his circle of protection and favor. Perhaps he and his ali'i considered it advantageous to gain status with the English by staying out of their affairs. Perhaps they were afraid of the repercussions of being implicated in matters they felt they did not understand.

Malo's solution showed Ka'ahumanu that the chiefs commanded their own powerful understanding of law and the politics involved in settling such questions and disputes, even when applied to foreigners in their islands. More importantly, his solution demystified the conflict for his ali'i, convincing her that the apparent differences between what the English claimed was the ground of difficulty and Hawaiian approaches to such situations were not that great and that she, like the ali'i before her, could exercise authority and apply the kapu to all subjects—both foreign *and* native.

A week after his interview with Charlton, Richards, still on O'ahu, was notified that the ali'i were convening another 'aha 'ōlelo on November 26 to meet with the foreigners concerning the publication of his letter. Hoapili called on Richards, and in the course of their conversation, he said that he had heard that "all the foreigners in the village were coming up to have a general council with the chiefs respecting [Richards'] letter about Captain Buckle."[111] Richards asked Hoapili if a definite charge had been brought against him. Hoapili replied that the charge was that Richards had "stated a falsehood in saying" that Buckle had purchased the woman.[112] Placing his fate in the will of the ali'i, Richards replied, "you chiefs know respecting that:—if I have been guilty of that crime, it is right you should punish me."[113] Hoapili responded that all the chiefs knew that Buckle purchased the woman; "it cannot be denied."[114] Balking at the prospect of the English "justice" he feared would be exacted by Buckle or Charlton, Richards cleverly placed the ali'i between himself and his accusers. Most significantly, however, his statements show that he willingly submitted himself to Hawaiian justice, a process of adjudication before the 'aha 'ōlelo.

Hoapili asked if Richards planned to attend the council, and Richards replied that he "should by no means go to your [chiefly] councils, unless you send for me, but if your chiefs send for me then I shall surely go."[115] Richards also requested that the accusations leveled against him be written down so that he could see plainly what the charge was. He also pointed out that though the chiefs did not understand English, "if the business is done in writing, then the writing can be translated and there can be a fair understanding."[116] Richards' request that the charges be recorded as they would be in a court of law was made to ensure that there was a record of the charges against him and that the charges were reasonable. Richards probably counted on the muddled and frequently angry speech of the British consul to show the opposition in its weakest light. Shortly before noon, Richards received word that "a large company of foreigners, and all the chiefs were together."[117]

Buckle's threats raised concerns among the chiefs, and later that evening, they convened a separate private council.[118] After an hour of deliberation, they sent for Mr. Richards to discuss the possibility of setting up another meeting at a later date, with all parties involved. Richards was accompanied to the 'aha by Rev. Hiram Bingham and his wife Sybil, Mrs. Clarissa Richards, and Levi Chamberlain. By the time the group departed from the mission house, members of the king's guard informed them that the "foreigners had gone and the council had broken up." Upon their arrival at the 'aha 'ōlelo, the missionaries found that "a large proportion of the chiefs were still in the hall." The chiefs told the missionaries that "as soon as the foreigners heard that the chiefs had sent for [them], they jumped like persons taken with the cholic." Ka'ahumanu asked them to stop until Mr. Richards and company arrived, but they refused, saying that "they had been waiting a long time and it was now late dinner time." The chief then asked them to appoint a time the next day to reconvene, but they refused again. Captain Buckle then "declared his intention of taking personal revenge and warned the chiefs against defending [Richards]."[119]

Appearing before the ali'i, Richards reiterated that he would act according to the desire of the chiefs; if they wished him to be present at another council, he would come.[120] He went further this time in expressing his relationship to them: "When I receive your orders it is mine to obey, for it is to your laws that I am now subject, and if I have broken them, it is by you alone that I am to be tried and punished."[121] Richards suggests an intimate relationship between himself and the ali'i in his use of the parallel constructions of "it is mine" (*na'u*) and "it is for you/your" (*nāu*). Also, it is important that Richards uses the word "order" in English, which would be rendered "kauoha" in Hawaiian, to indicate a verbal command. Again, Richards evokes the power of chiefly speech as integral to the force of "law" and the rule of the ali'i, thereby drawing attention to this fluency in language and identifying himself as a haole who understood the intricacies of deferential speech and the role that such verbal performances played in Hawaiian political actions.

The chiefs were silent for a while, until one asked, "We have heard the simple question of Mr. Richards, shall we not answer it?" Hoapili responded, "I think the foreigners will read to Mr. Richards, the printed letter and inquire of him whether he wrote it, to which it will be his duty to make answer."[122] All the chiefs agreed. Then Richards affirmed that he had indeed written the published letter and asked, "What farther?"[123] According to Richards, "all [the chiefs] were again silent for a long time," until finally Hoapili spoke: "That must be the end of it, for we all know that Leoiki was sold, and if it is a crime to say it then we are all in fault for we have all said it. That must be the end of it."[124] Hoapili's statement points up again that though Richards' "crime," according to the British consul, was writing about the sale of Leoiki, the ali'i were more concerned with what was "said." Hoapili was, of course, also referring to the oral depositions that many of the chiefs, councilors, and teachers gave to Richards with respect to Leoiki. The truth, uttered by so many ali'i themselves, was in Hoapili's estimation a fair defense against libel. All the chiefs knew that Leoiki had been sold. Another chief spoke up, asking, "What is the object of the (proposed) council? We have heard the charge against Mr. Richards, we have heard his confession that he wrote the letter but we have already pronounced it no crime. Why then shall we assemble again for another council?"[125] When no one responded, the chiefs all agreed to "proceed no farther," but to "tell the foreigners to desist and do nothing more."[126] Boki gave his opinion that "the foreigners would not be satisfied with this," insisting that "it would be improper for them to interfere on his behalf," and that Richards should "suffer whatever should come."[127]

At this point Richards skillfully intervened on his own behalf:

> **It is for you** to deliver us over to such hands as you see proper, **for you are our chiefs.** We have left our own country and can not now receive the protection of its laws. . . . We have now resided among you four years and a half during which time you have watched our conduct and have become acquainted with our private as well as our publick character. If I am a bad man or have broken the laws of your country, **it is for you** to try, and acquit or condemn me—you alone are my judges—**it is for you** to send me from your shores, or protect me here. **With you** is my life, and with you my death. **The whole is with you.**[128]

In this striking speech, Richards raised questions of jurisdiction, arguing that the missionaries were dependent upon an existing Hawaiian legal and governing structure, that of kapu, and the strength of the ali'i and their councils for protection and justice. This submission to Hawaiian law would deprive Charlton of his asserted position as judge over the "case." And Richards does this in an emphatically Hawaiian rhetorical fashion. The reiteration of "it is for you" and "for you are," balanced against Richards' use of "we have," suggests an intimacy of connection, since the construction for these phrases designated responsibility for a particular action, a kind of claim of connection that could only be made between those who were in close relation to one another. The final two sentences, however, build in emphasis beginning with the phrases "If I am/It is for you." "You alone are my judges," he says, that it is "for the ali'i alone," gracefully using this Hawaiian rhetoric of submission, Richards invokes the intimacy of the chiefly malu and the ali'i's responsibilities to care for and protect those under their authority.

The chiefs provided more than just armed protection to the missionaries, offering in some cases to forfeit their own lives to protect their teachers. By convening the 'aha 'ōlelo frequently over these matters, the ali'i continued to engage various important Hawaiian modes of deliberation, mediation, and advocacy in questions of jurisdiction and justice.

Richards thus showed his skill at deploying the language of deference, marked by familiar Hawaiian rhetorical devices, to construct himself as a subject of the ali'i, obedient to both the laws of the nation and their chiefly will. By submitting to the authority of the chiefs, Richards cleverly suggested that as rulers in their own nation, they could not defer their authority over his case to another nation. He concluded his plea by evoking the words *I ka ʻōlelo nō ke ola, I ka ʻōlelo nō ka make* (in speech there is life, in speech there is death) in the rendering of his own statement, "with you is my life, with you my death." The idiom was a statement descriptive of the power of chiefly utterance to decree life or death over persons who transgressed kapu. Richards' *proper* interpolation of the phrase transformed his continental American self into a subject of the jurisdiction and polity of the Hawaiian Islands. His statement as a speech act, constructed in Hawaiian terms, recognized Hawaiian chiefly power over his body. In doing so, he skillfully reflected some of the phrase's idiomatic power back upon himself. By wielding the phrase in this context, Richards had also illustrated that words spoken at the right time could give life and authority (mana) to the speaker. In calling upon the chiefs' understanding of authority and justice—namely, their ability to pronounce life or death over a subject—he deftly made his words speak with the voice of their mana.

Richards' speech had the desired effect, for no additional ʻaha ʻōlelo was called to discuss the matter, and Buckle and the British consul's attempts to further pursue the charge of libel were forever frustrated. Without the supportive power of the aliʻi behind their claim, Buckle and Charlton lacked any authority in the islands to act against Rev. Richards. In this competition for power—or rather, in the scramble between foreign groups for greater proximity and access to the chiefs—Richards and the mission triumphed.

The day after the ʻaha ʻōlelo, Richards observed that the *Daniel IV* had moved from its moorings to a place near the mouth of the harbor, a "signal of being nearly ready to sail." Richards was concerned that Captain Buckle should sail away still enraged at the proceedings of the previous weeks. "Feeling it desireable to do all [he] could consistent with truth and propriety to calm the angry feelings of Capt. Buckle," Rev. Richards wrote Buckle a conciliatory letter. Richards disavowed ever authorizing the publication of his letter and claimed that he was "accountable for it in no other way, than as a man of truth." Richards was also regretful that the letter should have been "interpreted as asserting that you [Buckle] had made a purchase for the purpose of slavery," since he did not think a reading of the letter would "bear such an interpretation."[129] Finally Richards described the routine nature of correspondence as a way to deflect responsibility from himself onto the ABCFM: "The reasons of my writing were these. I am distinctly directed to give a private account to the Board from time to time of my circumstances and prospects, and also of the state of the mission, and the Board publish at their own responsibility whatever they please, I being accountable only for the truth of what I write."[130]

Two days later, Richards received a letter from Captain Buckle in response. Buckle's letter reveals a man who is well spoken and thoughtful in his reasoning, illustrating that the brutish "whoremonger" Richards imagined was also well educated and refined. Buckle took issue with Richards' claims and communicated that he wanted to inform Richards of his opinion of the minister and his "publick attempt to injure my [Buckle's] reputation." Buckle reported that he was not "a little surprised at the tenor of this [Richards'] publication," for he did not expect that a minister of the gospel would so far forget himself and descend so low as to become the author of a piece so scandalous and so totally void of truth.[131]

In Buckle's view, Rev. Richards had "forgotten himself" by overstepping the bounds of propriety and the authority given someone in his humble station. Buckle also dismissed Richards' excuse that he did not authorize the publication of his letter and as such was not responsible for the harm it was causing. Buckle wrote: "It [the letter] appears in the publick prints, as a production of yours, and how you could have dared to have had the presumption to have penned so false an accusation against a person who had never injured you, I can not conceive. It is well for you indeed that you are not in a civilized country, where the laws of justise would inflict on you such punishment as the baseness of your crime deserved."[132] It seems ironic that the captain who was unable to prevent his crew from rioting could complain that there was no "justice" to be had in an "uncivilized" place like Hawai'i. During this period, foreigners seeking redress against one another took their claims before the ali'i. In the absence of a British or American colonial administration to settle their claims in the islands, foreigners like Charlton and Buckle indignantly evoked the rhetoric of "civilization" in order to cover over their vulnerability, lack of fluency, and their irritation at having to be subject to chiefly justice before the 'aha 'ōlelo.

Buckle accused Richards of writing an account filled with "gross misrepresentations and without a shadow of truth." Buckle suggested that it was only a matter of time before missionaries were exposed for their manipulations: "The spirit of inquiry is abroad in the world, and the enlightened community begin to perceive how much they have been duped and how much their credulity has been imposed on, by the flattering accounts of missionary labours and the exaggerated descriptions of missionary suffer-ings and missionary privations."[133] Sailors, whalers, and merchant agents threw doubt upon missionary narratives, their textual version of life in the islands covering over miscommunication and a lack of prestige with the ali'i with tales of "missionary influence." Buckle then accused Richards of capitalizing on the publication of the outrage, crafting it for the purpose of raising funds for the mission and his own personal comfort:

> The affair with the people of the *Daniel*, you no doubt thought afforded a good opportunity to get up the tragical story which you have published to impose on the feelings of a credulous community and wring from the hard earnings of industry another contribution to add to your own comfort and ease . . . such a narration is well calculated to call forth the charities of the fanatical community and no doubt has been the cause of taking bread from the mouth of many a half starved child, to enable the deluded parent to contribute his proportions for the relief of the poor persecuted missionary.[134]

Richards carefully copied all the communications and reports of what transpired from September through December 1827. The sprawling hand-written letter took up over forty pages, and it was included with Hoapili's account of the outrage of the *John Palmer* and the certificates of witnesses to the sale of Leoiki. If Richards had learned anything from the exchanges between himself, Richard Charlton, and Captain Buckle, it was that the mission would need to be cautious about future exposures. "Since reading the above to some of the other members of the mission, they have expressed their opinion that great caution should be used in presenting the above mentioned facts before the publick in case it should be thought but to give them to the publick at all."[135]

While the 'aha 'ōlelo might have brought closure to Rev. Richards and the members of the mission, the chiefs were now sobered by the reality of having to deal with the claims foreigners brought in conflict against one another. The outrages had also demonstrated that the chiefs must now consider the effects of their kapu on others beyond their native subjects. The issue over women and prostitution was the catalyst that had brought foreign conflict in Hawai'i to the surface, forcing the chiefs to re-evaluate the way in which kapu and kānāwai would be proclaimed and promulgated in the years to come.

On December 1, 1827, the chiefs called an 'aha 'ōlelo about the "establishment of some general laws for preventing crimes."[136] Although the chiefs spent a "considerable time" discussing the matter, they did not agree on anything definite. According to Levi Chamberlain, several days later, on December 7, the chiefs agreed to the establishment of laws relating to "murder, theft, adultery or whoredom, selling spirituous liquors and gambling."[137] That day, the king, Kauikeaouli Kamehameha III, signed his name to the laws and sent them to the mission for publication.[138]

The following day, an 'aha 'ōlelo was called by Ka'ahumanu in order to consult the chiefs about sending Kuakini, the governor of Hawai'i Island, to England with "a code of laws to present to King George for ratification."[139] Ka'ahumanu was considering this diplomatic journey only because the chief Boki objected to the establishment of laws until the "consent of the British Government" could be obtained. Richard Charlton had also been a vocal opponent of the adoption of laws (beyond kapu) by the ali'i and had threatened that if the king attempted to establish laws "independent of King George, England would at once send an army and take possession of the islands."[140]

A "sharp conversation" took place between Ka'ahumanu and Boki on the subject of sending Kuakini to England. The kuhina nui concluded by adamantly stating that Kuakini would go to England and that "they [the chiefs] will frame a full code of laws, writ[ten] plainly and translate them into English . . . and submit them to King George and let him strike out such as he pleases and such as he approves let him send back."[141] Boki objected to Kuakini being sent, and another chief suggested that Boki should make the journey in his place. Boki refused, saying that Kuakini would not be seen by the king. Ka'ahumanu countered that if Kauikeaouli sent him a "letter of introduction," this "should secure him [Kuakini] an interview." Boki fired back, saying that "Liholiho did not see King George," and therefore Kuakini would not be seen either.

Given Boki's resistance on this matter, Ka'ahumanu then demanded, "What shall we do? Why did you say to me this morning 'send to England before establishing a law?'" Boki answered that he thought the consul should write to England. Ka'ahumanu responded angrily, "Do you not know what the Consul is? That no dependence can be placed upon him, he calls good, evil, and evil, good and turns and whirls in every way."[142] She then demanded of Boki, "What did the King of England tell you, did he say 'send your laws to me before you establish them?' "[143] To this Boki replied "No, he left it with us."[144]

At this point, Governor Kuakini got the attention of the chiefs and requested that they attend to his words:

> I can read a little English and I can understand some, and I know perhaps some things which you do not. I know when the chiefs of any nation send to England to establish laws for them they make them fixed and firm. If they give laws they send men to cause them to be obeyed—if England gives us laws she will send men to see that they are executed. Our harbors will be filled with ships of war and our vessels can not go out or come in without their permission. We shall not be visited with American ships without leave from Great Britain, and we shall forever be their servants. We shall no more be able to do as we please.[145]

Kuakini was being humble when he said that he understood a little English. By most accounts, Kuakini was perhaps the most fluent speaker of English among the older chiefs still living. He was known for his interest in foreigners and reputedly spent much time in the company of visiting ship captains asking for information and gleaning from them information about the world beyond Hawai'i's shores. But the sagacious chief had also lived through the campaigns of Kamehameha I and had risen to a high position in governance among his fellow chiefs. Therefore, he was also an excellent judge of the political terrain and knew that no good could come from requesting another powerful nation, an empire like Great Britain, to "approve" laws for the Hawaiian people.

In response to Kuakini's eloquent speech, Ka'ahumanu simply concurred, saying, "This has long been my opinion." Hoapili also expressed his agreement with Kuakini and Ka'ahumanu, while the chief Naihe suggested that all the chiefs "look thoroughly at this subject." Boki, angered by this decision, commanded "Uoki" (Enough already!), and the 'aha 'ōlelo came to an end.

On December 8, the same day the 'aha 'ōlelo met, the first "code of laws" was published in Hawaiian under the title "He Olelo No Ke Kanawai." The title suggests the hybrid and transforming nature of the state of law in the islands. The first two words, *He 'ōlelo* (A word), point to the common practice of orally proclaiming "law" through kapu. The rest of the title, *no ke kānāwai* (on the law), distinguishes these rules from kapu and indicates also their published form. Another striking feature of these laws is that they were expressly directed at haole, those belonging to that land (*ko kēlā ʻāina*), as well as maoli, those belonging to this land (*ko kēia ʻāina*), marking yet again an important distinction between groups—not just of "racial" difference but demarcating ʻāina (homeplace) as definitional of group belonging, a Hawaiian way of contextualizing the inclusion of haole as subjects of the law in Hawaiian waters and on land.

This 1827 kānāwai marked a transformation in Hawaiian governance and law, but interpreting this law as source requires language and cultural fluency, whether the text being analyzed is in Hawaiian or English.

> Ke hai aku nei makou i ka olelo, e hoolohe mai, *e ko kela aina*, a me ko keia aina, e malama no hoi ko keia aina, a me ko kela aina: o ka mea i lohe i keia mau olelo, e malama ia; aka i malama ole e hewa ia.

> We proclaim the word, take heed [listen!], those from foreign lands, and those of this land [Hawaiians], take notice those of this land, and those from foreign lands. He who hears these words must observe them, however, if he does not observe them, that is a crime.[146]

The hybrid nature of the new kānāwai between oral pronouncement and publishing is evident in the emphasis upon speech and listening in the above passage. The code of laws prohibited murder, theft, adultery, selling liquor, prostitution, and gambling. The punishments ranged from death by hanging (murder), imprisonment (theft, adultery, selling liquor, and gambling), and fines (prostitution).[147]

On December 14, the people were assembled in the coconut grove located on the ocean side of Kālaimoku's old house. The people were there to hear the laws read and listen to the opinions of the chiefs respecting these new laws. The king rose and told the people that the first three laws against murder, theft, and adultery were to be established and that he wished them to be observed. Kaʻahumanu rose and addressed the foreigners and natives from other islands to "hear and regard the laws about to be established." Boki addressed the crowd last and reportedly "harranged [sic] the assembly," telling them that in three months the laws would go into

HE OLELO NO KE KANAWAI.

—◦◦◦—

KE hai aku nei makou i ka olelo, e hoolohe mai, e ko kela aina, a me ko keia aina, e malama no hoi ko keia aina, a me ko kela aina: o ka mea i lohe i keia mau olelo, e malama ia; aka i malama ole e hewa ia.

I

Ke papa aku nei makou i ka pepehi kanaka; mai pepehi kela aina maenei, mai pepehi keia aina maenei; o ka mea e pepehi maenei e make ia, i ke kaawe ia.

II

Eia ka lua; ke papa aku nei makou i ka aihue; o ka mea e aihue, e paa ia i ka hao.

III

Eia ke kolu: ke papa aku nei makou i ke kuai rama maenei: o ka mea e kuai rama, e paa ia i ka hao.

IV

Eia ka ha; ke papa aku nei makou i ka hookamakama: o ka mea i hookamakama, e uku ia oia i ke kala.

V

Eia ka lima: ke papa aku nei makou i ka pili waiwai; o ka mea e pili waiwai e uku ia oia i ka hao.

KING KAUIKEAOULI.

Oahu Honolulu, Dekemaba 8, 1827.

Figure 11. "He Olelo No Ke Kanawai." 1827 proclamation. Mission Houses Museum Library.

effect. He then invited them to come on the first day of March 1828 to see the law against murder take effect "against the man now in confinement for a murder."[148]

Although the laws had been printed as a body, the chiefs still had not come to agreement over whether or not to approve the last three laws prohibiting the sale of liquor, prostitution, and gambling. While the law on prostitution was being debated, it is not clear, although highly probable, that the kapu on women visiting ships had finally been rescinded.

A transformation was occurring in the islands. The aliʻi in the ʻaha ʻōlelo now had to consider crafting laws to bring order to unruly foreigners in the islands as well as for their own native subjects. The way that the chiefs addressed the problem of prostitution—by placing local political concerns (the censure of Wahinepiʻo) and exercising power over native women— gave way during this transition under the pressure of unruly sailors and foreigners behaving badly. Prostitution eventually became the crime of an individual woman, punishable under new laws in a nascent Hawaiian Kingdom. Law in Hawaiʻi was a remedy that needed to be adopted, not to bring civilization to a savage people, but to make sure that men from civilized nations understood that the law of the aliʻi, in its published and proclaimed form, was to be observed by foreigner and native alike. "Here also is another great thing, the anger of the foreigners at the chiefs, which . . . for its greatness is unexampled. . . . This is the cause of the anger. The chiefs are assembled at this place, Honolulu, the chiefs of Hawaii, the chiefs of Maui, the chiefs of Oahu and the chiefs of Tauwai [Kauaʻi], are assembled to consult about establishing laws for the country. All the foreigners are angry at the chiefs of this country—they exceedingly desire to make war upon the chiefs of the Sandwich Islands."[149]

David Malo supplies a view of the anger of the foreign community in the wake of the chiefly ʻaha ʻōlelo. In Hawaiʻi, kānāwai, published law emerged as an extension of the continued exercise of chiefly governance and was not simply a colonial imposition. New instruments for social control were necessary in order to apply the rule of the aliʻi to foreign bodies and to manage emerging relations that were not structured by genealogy, but by new forms of sexual engagement and commercial exchange. Surprisingly, the issue of Hawaiian women and the kapu was the major event that catalyzed change, accelerating the pace of the transformation of Hawaiian governance and law.

AFTERWORD

On May 8, 1845, William Richards stood again before an ʻaha ʻōlelo of the aliʻi, a place of distinction that he had grown accustomed to over the years. Today was unlike others in the legislature, just after votes were taken to finalize decisions regarding the previous day's discussion, Richards stood and declared his intention to swear allegiance to Kauikeaouli, Kamehameha III, and Ke Aupuni Hawaiʻi, the Hawaiian Nation.

Years earlier, on July 3, 1838, Richards "accepted the invitation of the chiefs to become their teacher." By signing a contract with the king he had assumed, but did not desire, that his relationship to the mission would be dissolved. Materially this meant that the government would be paying for his living rather than the American Board of Commissioners for Foreign Missions (ABCFM). In practice, Richards saw his service in the government as an extension of the work of the board, and the will of God.[1]

Richards was asked by the king and aliʻi to be their teacher only after he returned from his recent trip to the United States, where he was unsuccessful at locating a person interested in taking the job. The mission responded to the news of Richards' new position with a resolution adopted at the 1838 annual meeting, "1st. Resolved, 'That we consider the business of instructing the chiefs of sufficient importance to claim the immediate and entire services of a person qualified for the office,'" and they declared that they left it to Richards to decide whether or not he wished to "accept or reject the appointment."[2] As to whether Richards' American ministerial education qualified him to "instruct the chiefs" in running a government was a question that was not entertained at the time.

When Richards arrived in the islands in 1823, a minister of the American Board, Liholiho, Kamehameha II was the aliʻi nui, and his younger brother was a boy of ten. Now, nearly twenty-eight years after he elegantly argued, "with you is my life, with you, my death," claiming the malu of the aliʻi in the ʻaha ʻōlelo over his person, Richards stood before a new generation of

chiefs to formally affirm that he had indeed become a subject of the kingdom. Gone, however, were the high chiefs of that former *wā* (era), witnesses
to his first speech: Keōpūolani, and Kaʻahumanu; Wahinepiʻo, Kālaimoku,
and Boki.

Richards' performance in the ʻaha ʻōlelo of the words that exemplified
the power of chiefly speech, his show of comprehension and fluency in
1827, most certainly recommended him for the many important positions
which he later held in the Hawaiian Kingdom.

As soon as he accepted the position, as "interpreter and translator"
Richards "commenced [on] the compilation and translation of a work on
political economy following the general plan of Wayland." He prepared
materials and read them aloud to the king and aliʻi, "in the form of lectures," which he "endeavored to make" as "familiar as possible, by repeat-
ing them, and drawing the chiefs into free conversation on the subject of
the lectures." In response, he noted that the aliʻi "uniformly manifested a
becoming interest in the school thus conducted, and took an active part in
the discussions of the various topics introduced in the lectures."[3]

Richards' *reinterpretation* of Francis Wayland's 1837 text *The Elements of
Political Economy* into Hawaiian was not a translation of the original book;
rather his textual adaptation inspired his method of teaching: "The lectures
themselves were mere outlines of general principles of political economy
which of course could not have been understood except by full illustrations
drawn from Hawaiian custom and Hawaiian circumstances."[4]

Only a person fluent in language and somewhat knowledgeable about
custom could have imagined adapting and approaching the text in this
manner. Richards produced these "illustrations" as *hoʻohālike*, compara-
tives, utilizing a mode of deliberative thought to which those like himself
were accustomed, comfortable in the act of translation, a movement
between words and worlds. Hoʻohālike was a way of considering and com-
paring precedent earlier employed by Davida Malo in his counsel to the
kuhina nui Kaʻahumanu, an activity that helped her to process her thoughts
and deliver a decision in the charge of libel brought against Richards in
1827. Richards wrote about how he adapted the text to include these examples, "In these illustrations I endeavored as much as possible to draw their
[the king's and chiefs'] minds to the defects in the Hawaiian government,
and Hawaiian practices and often contrasted them with the government
and practices of enlightened nations . . . .But when the faults of the present

system were pointed out & the chiefs felt them & then pressed me with questions, *'Pehea la e pono ai?'* [How shall this be set to rights?]"[5]

In working through his own impressions Richards arrived at this insight, "I have often felt that it is much easier to point out the defects of an *old system* than it is to devise *a new one,* suitable to take its place."[6]

How many people of the time, haole or maoli, imagined Hawaiian governance in the way that Richards did? From where did such concepts of an "old system," and a "new one" arise? A *wā kahiko,* an ancient time, and a *wā hou,* a new time, Hawaiian time newly organized by the introduction of the word of God in the islands, historical experience reinterpreted through the filter of another oral-tradition-made-textual. As missionary writings reiterate: the imagined idea that the native future will come forth from a system that is "new," a new government, a new world, the children of the American Revolution planting a new mission in Hawaiian soil.

In 1837, the year before Richards became the king's instructor and translator, the kuhina nui, Kʻinaʻu II, and her husband, the chiefly governor of Honolulu, Mataio Kekūanāoʻa, requested that Davida Malo come to Honolulu to supply counsel in a serious matter involving the French. Malo was detained on Maui by one of the missionary teachers, because Lahainaluna was short of teachers. Instead of going in person, Malo sent his counsel via letter, recommending a particular course of action to address this and other situations that might arise between the aliʻi and people from other nations.

> Auhea olua? Ua manao nui au e kuka pinepine oukou me na lii a pau me ka molowa ole, no ka imi i *na mea e pono ai keia aupuni,* mai manao oukou, **ua like *keia wa me ka wa kahiko*** o oukou wale no na alii e hiki ai ia oukou ke waiho wale, e nana oukou.[7]

> Where are you two? I have thought much that you two should frequently deliberate with all of the chiefs without laziness to seek for **the things that will benefit this kingdom,** do not think that **this time is like the ancient time** that you all are the only aliʻi and that you can simply leave aside these matters, you must be watchful.

The remedy for Malo came not only from the word of God, but from the word of the aliʻi, from past good practice, from precedent that would arise through discussion. All of the aliʻi should frequently meet and discuss matters as an ʻaha ʻōlelo without laziness to seek for the benefit of this nation.

Eia ke kumu, ina i pii mai ke kai nui, e hoea mai no na ia nui; no
loko mai o ka maona [moana] eleele, kahi au i ike ole ai, a ike lakou
i na ia liilii o ka papau, e ai no lakou i ka ia liilii, pela no, na holoho-
lona nui, e ai no i na mea liilii, pela no, ua pii mai na moku haole,
a ua hoea mai na kanaka naauao, no na aina nui mai au i ike ole ai,
ua ike lakou ia kakou, he lahui kanaka uuku, e noho ana ma keia
aupuni uuku, ua makemake lakou e ai ia kakou, pela wale no na
aupuni nui, ua lawe wale ia na aupuni liilii ma ka honua nei a pau.[8]

This is the reason. If a big wave comes in, large fishes will come from
the dark ocean from a place unseen, and when they see the small
fishes of the shallows, they will devour them; such is also the case with
large animals; they will prey on the smaller ones. Likewise, the ships
of the white man have come, and knowledgeable people have arrived
from powerful countries which you have never seen before. They
know our people are few in number and living in a small country;
they will eat us up. Such has always been the case with large countries;
the small ones have been taken over throughout the world.[9]

It is difficult to discern, to interpret the subtle differences and nuances
between the similar turns of phrase that appear in the writing of William
Richards and his former Hawaiian-language teacher, Davida Malo. While
trained scholars may hear the trace of the Hawaiian in the English wording
of Richards' report, there are differences in the way Richards and Malo
formulated their divergent concepts and application of ka wā kahiko and
ka wā hou / kēia wā. For Richards, ka wā kahiko was associated with former, faulty Hawaiian practices; the "old system," was not associated with
the present practice of enlightened nations. Malo had a shallower field for
comparison regarding "the present practice of enlightened nations"; rather
than seeing the Hawaiian past as bereft of guidance, he was being sought
after as an expert, conversant with the past practices, decisions, and precedents that had been pronounced and executed by the ali'i of ka wā kahiko.
    Both Malo and Richards considered the question of how the leaders of
the nation should "'imi i nā mea e pono ai ke aupuni" (seek for the things
that would benefit the kingdom). And yet they suggested different
approaches to the project of reform because each man had a different
understanding of a concept fundamental to Hawaiian governance: pono.
    While some portions of Malo's letter framed his advice to the ali'i
according to the new "pono" of God's word, the counsel given above arose

out of his training in traditional schools of Hawaiian knowledge, the period
when he was taught under kapu by his grandfather who was a kahuna,
when he accompanied the ali'i Kuakini to care for the heiau in Kona,
Hawai'i, as a man who engaged in ceremonies among the alo ali'i of
Kamehameha.[10]

William Richards lacked the knowledge Malo obtained over many years
of learning; Richards also did not know how to organize Hawaiian knowledge like Malo. Customary "texts" illuminating past practice, words uttered
in the 'aha 'ōlelo by prior generations of ali'i; mo'olelo, mele and pule
were unknown to him. While Richards capably illustrated his fluency in the
Hawaiian language to the degree that he was hired as the king's translator,
it is Malo's advice, couched in the form of a wānana or prophecy employing
imagery and language, which marked Malo's words as a particular form of
Hawaiian counsel contiguous with Hawaiian narrativizations of the past.
And though missionaries were abundant in Honolulu, the kuhina and governor still called upon Malo to supply counsel in the interest of the continuation of good (pono) chiefly governance.

More difficult to apprehend than the intrinsic or ideological differences
that scholars have attributed to "the missionaries," "merchants," or "the
Hawaiians," between maoli and haole, are the educational and historical
contexts from which counselors supplied precedent, example, and advice.
Large-scale reformation of the Hawaiian government and law that began
with the period of Kamehameha's campaign for unification and continued
well into this period occurred through multiple vectors; the ali'i continued
to rely upon chiefly advisers to facilitate decision-making, especially during
the crisis-ridden 1830s and 1840s.

Counselors from this period forward that served the ali'i in the 'aha
'ōlelo were maoli and haole, and they drew upon their various literacies
rooted in multiple historical pasts and conceptualizations of time. Malo and
Richards were examples of this new kind of counselor, neither absolutely
knowledgeable or comfortable in the others' knowledge traditions, but both
trained and fluent to a broad extent in multiple forms of literacy: oral and
written, maoli and haole, Christian and for Malo non-Christian precedents
and practices that still operated in relation to kapu.

In the years that followed Richards' leaving the mission he, Malo, and
others would work alongside the ali'i and the 'aha 'ōlelo to draft a code of
laws, a declaration of rights and the first Hawaiian constitution of 1840.[11]
In 1842 Richards was appointed along with the ali'i Timoteo Ha'alilio as an

envoy to go on a diplomatic mission to America, England, and France to secure the recognition of the Hawaiian nation in an international context, an assignment that necessitated the pair traveling abroad for nearly three years.

When Richards stood that day in the 'aha 'ōlelo in 1845 he had already served for eight years in various important government capacities. Declaring his intention to swear allegiance to Kamehameha III "a lilo loa i kanaka nona" (completely become a subject of his), his verbal performance augmented the words printed on the oath of allegiance he signed to become a naturalized citizen. "Ua lilo mua au i kanaka no ka Moi Kamehameha III mamua o ko'u hele ana aku e imi i ka pono o ka Lahuikanaka Hawaii"[12] (I first became a man of King Kamehameha III because of my going to seek for the benefit [pono] of the nation of Hawai'i).

In this book I have suggested that transformations in Hawaiian governance and law were a continuation of Hawaiian customary practice. I have shown that the orally pronounced kapu of the ali'i persisted well after the casting down of the 'ai kapu in 1819 and that published law, kānāwai, were initially adopted not simply to bring law to an uncivilized people, but were introduced by the ali'i as a means to control the behavior of foreigners behaving badly on Hawaiian shores. The malu of the ali'i would extend to foreigners like Mr. Richards forever transforming the rule of the ali'i in ways that have yet to be illuminated through the work of future scholars.

Kānaka maoli have long maintained a historical consciousness in the form of orally maintained texts which were passed on through particular pedagogies ensuring the veracity of the text for hundreds of generations. Counterintuitively, as processes of settler colonialism became more entrenched over time, the Hawaiian-language textual source-base grew enriched by a flood of these oral texts, those which had been passed down for generations and many which were newly composed.

As I have shown repeatedly over the course of this history, language is not the most difficult challenge facing scholars trying to write Hawaiian history, or histories of encounter. What historians need to work toward is acquiring both linguistic and cultural fluency, in order to engage the nuance and complexity of these highly mediated sources. The often binary categories of maoli and haole and the reified subject positions that have attained to them over time communicate less as we delve deeper into the sources themselves.

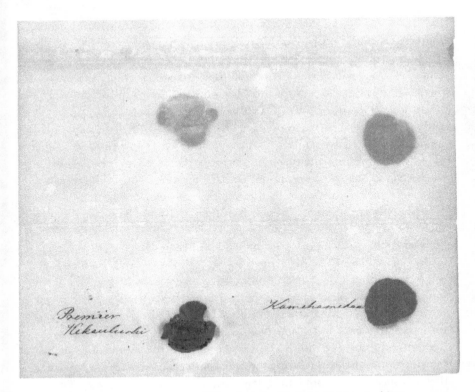

Figure 12. Seal and signature of Kamehameha III. Hawaiʻi State Archives.

This project has centered Hawaiian ways of learning, passing on knowledge, speaking, hearing, writing, and interpreting history as its *iwikuamoʻo* (backbone). This book has illustrated a way of writing history that is appropriate and relevant because the methodology structuring my work arose from the sources themselves. I treated the oral-made-textual sources that kānaka maoli of the period and just before contact composed, as my *kumu*—my sources, my teachers; and I studied intently the way intellectuals and chiefly counselors thought historically and preserved and passed on history during this period of important transformations from and between orature and literature, speech and text.

In a file folder at the Hawaiʻi State Archives containing Richards' journals during his time as envoy for the Kingdom of Hawaiʻi, I found among other pages a sheet of fine paper, weathered and yellowed with age. The length of the paper was empty save for two signatures at the bottom: Kauikeaouli, Kamehameha III, and his kuhina nui, Kekauluohi. Both were followed by congealed red wax impressions, the recently adopted Hawaiian seals of government. Along with this rather official page, were other empty sheets, these lined, with the same signatures at the bottom, but lacking the official seals.

In 1845, there was no way Haʻalilio or Richards could write to Hawaiʻi and receive ready answers to pressing questions facing them on their diplomatic mission. In recognition of this situation, the king and his kuhina placed in their hands the power to compose the necessary words between themselves as envoys of Ke Aupuni Hawaiʻi and those authorities to whom they were seeking audience in the highest offices of government in the United States and Europe. The words of the mōʻī would be dictated not by the king or his counselors, but by necessity, composed of deliberations between William Richards and Timoteo Haʻalilio.

When William Richards arrived in the Hawaiian Islands he had come as an emissary of God, a bearer of ka ʻōlelo a ke Akua; as an envoy of the king, bearing ka ʻōlelo a ke aliʻi, he had become a trusted wielder of the power of chiefly word and name. Richards gained this trust from his performance of fluency in an ʻaha ʻōlelo, a fluency which then extended to the written and published word. He was one of the many emissaries of that mana sent into the world during the nineteenth century, words in Hawaiian that still speak to us from letters, journals, newspapers, and books.

I ka ʻōlelo nō ke ola.

In speech there is life.

Textual Sources and Research Methods

It is because of Hawai'i's late "discovery" in the late eighteenth century that the textual legacies of encounter in the islands between natives and Euro-Americans are markedly different from those of other native peoples of North and South America, Africa, and the Pacific. Indeed, due to innovations in print in the early nineteenth century, and due in large part to the printing presses of the missionaries and educational imperatives of the chiefs, Hawaiians began to write and publish Hawaiian histories, genealogies, and "traditions" less than a decade after the death of Kamehameha I and the arrival of the missionaries in 1820. As a result, continuity in the passing on of Hawaiian oral, historical, and cultural "traditions" into writing and print may be unparalleled in the history of native peoples. Hawai'i may arguably have the largest historical and literature base in any native language in the Pacific, and perhaps all of native North America, exceeding 1,000,000 pages of printed text, a staggering 125,000 of which were Hawaiian-language newspapers published between 1834 and 1948.[1]

The "rediscovery" of Hawaiian-language textual materials comes at a time when researchers interested in writing US-Hawai'i history are able to remotely access Hawaiian-language materials never before available to scholars outside the reading room. To those researchers and writers who do not live in Hawai'i, or who have not visited its archives, the huge quantity of Hawaiian-language newspapers available online appear to be born-digital, even as digitization continues at a headlong pace.

Nogelmeier has written about the magnitude of the newspaper "archive," while independent scholar David Forbes has compiled and annotated an impressive four-volume by-year bibliography on Hawai'i spanning 1790–1900, which encompasses a huge number of Hawaiian-language publications, including broadsides, school primers, books, and official government documents. Forbes' bibliography provides a chronology of nineteenth-century Hawaiian-language print culture, and the print history of each publication where available, supplying in synthesis and snapshot the sizable production and volume of materials made available to a Hawaiian-language speaking and reading public. Handwritten source materials in the Hawaiian language housed in archives and libraries across the archipelago, New England, and England appear yet unaccounted for.

Even a cursory look into the breadth of Hawaiian-language textual materials brings particular clarity. The textual production of Hawaiians of all stations and backgrounds is voluminous and quite diverse: letters, journals, family genealogies, stories, songs, and chants are all records of "traditional" knowledge and new contemporary compositions in ʻōlelo Hawaiʻi. The Hawaiian government promulgated laws, published broadsides, conducted the business of government, education, religion, and commerce in Hawaiian language from the early nineteenth century through the beginning decades of the twentieth century.

Hawaiian-language newspapers (1834–1948) are an important source medium that historians can engage to fortify their ability to place texts in context, especially with so many now available online. It is within the newspapers that scholars can begin to see the significant interpolation of Hawaiian oral texts in numerous genres appear in print—traditions once passed down orally, newly composed pieces for a Hawaiian-reading public of diverse ethnic background. These materials present innumerable opportunities to study and construct "text as context," as Pocock has suggested.

American missionaries produced a high volume of textual materials on the "Sandwich Islands." Another hidden portion of the Hawaiian-language textual source-base is the materials published by the mission in the Hawaiian language for the purpose of converting and educating the Hawaiian public. Materials also aimed at Hawaiian Christians include works in Hawaiian history, world geography, biblical studies, mapping, music, and moral and political economy. Hawaiians became familiar with the wider world through the medium of Hawaiian language, and initially through the production of the mission's presses, whose work they too aided through writing, printing, and dissemination of printed texts which they also taught in schools. By the midcentury, when an independent native Hawaiian newspaper press mightily rose, kānaka maoli were responsible for producing the work of news of the world and news from home for a Hawaiian-language-reading public.

While sifting through the journals and letters of missionaries, it is possible to hear and locate segments of Hawaiian language embedded in the text. In the first decade after their various arrivals, missionaries were usually working toward a level of fluency in Hawaiian language as part of their labors. Because they needed to interact with congregations, write sermons and educational pamphlets in the native language, and translate the Bible into the vernacular language of the people, this was necessary work. Some, like Richards and his comissionary Levi Chamberlain, tended to reproduce formulaic turns of phrase from Hawaiian into English and provide Hawaiian terms in their writings as a way to practice language and strengthen their fluency. By engaging in this auditory-to-writerly activity on a daily basis, they were practicing to express themselves, to speak, read, and write in Hawaiian. The process involved replaying what they had heard (since for the most part, writing in Hawaiian was also in preparatory stages), transferring some of that material to writing, and then engaging in an act of translation so that the original Hawaiian was approximated into English, their mother tongue. Their mediations between the English text and the Hawaiian that had sounded in their ears render missionaries' primary writings complex, requiring attentiveness to Hawaiian language and oral formulaic turns of phrase, its idioms, and its discourses. The texts when studied further reveal that they have not simply been written in English, but they are texts that mediate between languages and systems of knowledge production. It is this practice of translation, of mediation between, that scholars can learn from through replication of this praxis, acquire a level of fluency in a native language that uses the texts themselves as kumu, as source and teacher.

By sifting through sources, I try to historicize words, phrases, and concepts, attempting to pinpoint when they have been introduced into Hawaiian discourse. In this way, I am able to perceive a larger conversation in a way that Hawaiian intellectuals participating in an oral historical tradition would have *heard* it, for these intellectuals were responsible for maintaining oral traditions—from the deep past and *their own presents*—as a repository from which they could provide things as diverse as advice to ali'i based on past utterance and present sense or the creation of "new" traditions in the form of mele (song), oli (chant, prayer), and mo'olelo (history, story).

In order to build a framework for interpreting evidence, I am forced to read widely, culling examples or conducting searches in the online Hawaiian-language newspaper database on key terms and phrases that recur to teach me about the broadest and narrowest ways in which a particular word or phrase was used. From the different ranges of meanings that I gather, usage supplies me with contexts in which the word is embedded. From this operation, I can better interpret writings by making words and actions intelligible within the Hawaiian contexts and perceptions of the past that I have built up as a result of several searches.

How does one read texts in order to be able to constitute different fields of meaning? One way I do this is to stack the different usages I collect from multiple texts of particular words or phrases in order to apprehend the range of meanings a word or phrase has over time. This technique helps me locate the particular meanings of a word in order to understand its connotations and its connections within a related web of meanings of other words and phrases. A very easy example of this can be expressed if we consider the word *wai* and a portion of its field of meaning. On one hand, wai means fresh water, but open out its connections and web of related words and you end up considering the connotations of wai as symbolic of health and life. The Hawaiian word for wealth is a reduplication of the word, waiwai, and so if I were to consider the ways in which the word was deployed in discussions regulating access to water, or kānāwai (law), as opposed to its application in terms of monetary or property rights, I would have some kind of idea of the way that inquiry into usage can tell us something about the particular meanings of a term or concept.

This kind of stacking and building of the "meaning web" of individual key words is important if we are to apprehend the ways in which Hawaiians constructed meaning through language. This way of understanding language helps me to interpret the verbal and written exchanges between Hawaiians and between themselves and foreigners in a very new way. It also allows me to keep building cultural history over time, by tracking the change in meaning fields over time.

Another technique that I employ is studying the grammatical and rhetorical structure of the writings of missionaries, as well as others who spent a lot of time interacting with Hawaiians, to see the extent to which their own language in Hawaiian as well as in English bears the trace of rhetorical turns of phrase that have a formal life in Hawaiian oral tradition. In this way, I search for not only eyewitnesses but "ear-witnesses" to the action. For example, Richards' innovative use of the phrase "With you is my life, with you my death," before the 'aha 'ōlelo illustrates his knowledge and proper application of the *'ōlelo no'eau* (proverb). Rather than a broad statement about the power of words, Richards had learned that the idiom referred to the power of the chief to speak life or death over a subject. His use of the term before the ʻaha illustrated his respect for chiefly authority and the extent to which he was truly fluent in Hawaiian language and cultural usage. This interjection on his own behalf also illustrates that he understood the proper contexts in which to deploy the phrase, demonstrating a knowledge of language and culture that went far beyond the poor Hawaiian literacy his English and American foes could wield and revealing an adeptness that eluded most of his missionary brethren. While I have excellent sources to tell me about how Rev. Richards became fluent in Hawaiian, who his teachers were, and so forth, nothing else comes close to illustrating the extent of his knowledge, nor his own personal proximity to the Hawaiian intelligentsia and governing structure, as this kind of public display of eloquence.

Rather than using these literary techniques to talk about particular authors and how they are changing language, I am using this method to interpret documentary sources that report what people said and thought, and what others were saying. These techniques also raise to the fore the cultural power of language, since the way to know that something has historical gravitas as a source depends in large part not only upon whose mouth it comes out of, but also whether that person is able to speak in a way that is culturally and politically authoritative and ultimately persuasive.

GLOSSARY

'a'apo—Ready, quick to receive knowledge. A ready scholar. To learn or grasp meaning quickly, to memorize. Based on the word 'apo (to snatch, to grab, catch on). Indicates that the listener is quick to grasp the flow of words to repeat, memorize, understand, and utilize.

'a'e—To step over, get on top of, to tread upon a kānāwai or kapu. 'A'e seems to be an action done with more force than hehi.

'aha—Meeting.

'āha'i 'ōlelo—Messenger trained to listen and memorize faithfully the words of the ali'i to disseminate among the populace. Also, someone trained to relay messages back to the ali'i.

'aha 'ōlelo—Chiefly council; a place where ali'i were called to deliberate or discuss matters, often with their counselors (kākā'ōlelo).

ahupua'a—Land division extending from the uplands to the sea, further divided into smaller portions of 'ili and mo'o.

'ai kapu—Rules that governed eating, food gathering, and preparation. The 'ai kapu framed relationships between men and women and provided the structure between genders and their interaction within social spaces. The 'ai kapu also regulated time and ceremonial observances in the heiau (temple).

'ai noa—The state that exists when the 'ai kapu is lifted for ceremonial reasons. The state that persisted after the tumbling down (hiolo) of the 'ai kapu and the heiau in 1819. To eat without restriction, free of kapu.

'āina—Land, ancestor, that which feeds.

akua—God, ancestor.

akua ki'i—Carved temple image, ancestral image.

akua wahine—Female deity, god, ancestor.

'alihi kaua—A chief who directs the battle, commander.

ali'i—Chief. Ali'i were distinguished in rank both by genealogy and the kapu that they inherited via their matriarchal lineages.

ali'i nui—High chief who ruled over several districts, an island, or several
   islands.

alo ali'i—Those who live near and serve the chief. Someone who belongs
   to the chief's extended residence and takes care of the chief's person
   and personal effects, including the chants, genealogies, and stories of an
   ali'i's lineage. Literally, those who dwell in the presence (alo) of the
   chief and carry out his or her will.

aloha—Affection, love, pity, sympathy, regard. A greeting, also farewell.

'a'ohe—Without, to have none or nothing, lacking.

'a'ole—No, not, never, to be none, to have none, lacking.

'ano—Nature, character.

'auhau—Tax.

aupuni—A region governed by a chief or king. Several aupuni might be
   located on one island. Government, kingdom. The ruler and those who
   dwell within this region. au (place, time); puni (surrounded, around,
   encircled).

'iliahi—Sandalwood.

'imi—To seek, a Hawaiian approach to learning and acquiring knowledge,
   moving and not fixed.

'iniki—To sting, to pinch.

'iwi—Bones, repository of mana in the body. A metaphor for genealogical
   connection among those living and between those living and in spirit
   form.

Kapu—chiefly legal pronouncement, legal restrictions

'ōlelo—Word, speech. Hallmark of speech that can be discerned in written
   or published letters, as in "Eia ku'u 'ōlelo" (Here is my word, opinion,
   decision).

'ōlelo Hawai'i—Hawaiian language.

'ōlelo no'eau—Proverb, wise saying, traditional saying.

oli—A chant that was not danced to. Oli come in numerous genres, a way
   to convey mo'olelo.

ua 'ōlelo 'ia—It was said, according to, a phrase which precedes speech that
   is authoritative, memorized, previously spoken, and remembered.

ua 'ōlelo 'ia—Lit., it has been said, a "hallmark" of authoritative speech
   that signals that what is about to be related is a traditional text, something memorized, precedent, an opinion, a finding, the word of the
   ali'i.

'ulu—To grow, increase, spread. To be possessed by a god; inspired by a spirit, god, as for artistic creation; stirred, excited; to enter in and inspire. To be extensively known, as a report, as news spreading.

hālau—School.

hālau 'ike—School of knowledge.

haole—Foreigner, off-islander, outlander, Caucasian.

hāumāna—Students.

hehi—To tread, step on, trample. Conceptually, a manner of disregarding kapu.

heiau—Temple, shrine, place of worship for Hawaiian ancestors and gods.

hewa—Morality. Entering the state of having transgressed. To err, make mistake; fault, error, defect, offense, crime, wrong, incorrect. Not pono.

hihia—Entangled, interwoven, snarled, confused, obscure and difficult to understand. Entanglement as a difficulty that goes before the 'aha 'ōlelo.

hiolo—To topple, tumble down, collapse. The word is used in Hawaiian to describe what happened to the 'ai kapu.

ho'oholo—To agree upon, to decide, as chiefs in the chiefly council. The decision arrived at after deliberation.

ho'okamakama—Prostitution, lit., to cause children.

ho'omana—To revere or worship, to empower. Often translated as "religion."

hou—New.

hulihia—To overturn; a complete change, topsy-turvy, chaotic, overturned. Activity associated with Pele and the volcano, of the earth hot with fire, churning and exploding.

ka wā hou—The new time. Usually refers to the time after Christianization and the introduction of the word of God.

ka wā kahiko—Old, ancient, long ago, the past. Used in historiography, with much resonance, to describe the period before the arrival of Captain James Cook in 1778.

ka wā ma mua—The time before. A phrase with less resonance in historiography than "ka wā kahiko," but used more frequently by kānaka maoli writers of the nineteenth century to speak of what came before (the past).

kahu—Honored attendant, caretaker, servant of the ali'i.

kahu ali'i—Royal guardian in the family of a high chief.

kahuna—Priest. When qualified by another word, an expert in any profession, both male and female.

kākāʻolelo—Counselor, adviser, one who is skilled in language and history, trained in the art of oratory. Lit., to fence with words.

kālaiʻāina—Politics. Lit., land carving, division of lands.

kālaimoku—One concerned in managing the affairs, the resources of the moku (district or island). The title of one who performs such an office.

kalo—Taro, from which poi is made. The elder sibling, ancestor of the Hawaiian people, whose story provides the reciprocal paradigmatic relationship for the people to care for the ʻāina (land) and for the land to feed the people.

kanaka—Man, person, people.

kanaka maoli—Hawaiian person.

kānaka maoli—Hawaiian people.

kānāwai—Published or written law, distinguished from kapu as that which is proclaimed expressly by the aliʻi or ʻaha ʻōlelo.

kāne—Man.

kanikau—Lament, grief chant.

ka ʻōlelo a ke akua—The word of God, the Gospels.

ka ʻōlelo a ke aliʻi—The word of the aliʻi. A "hallmark" of Hawaiian performative speech that verifies, authenticates, or confirms an authoritative utterance. The hallmark phrase may precede or follow the authoritative utterance.

kaona—Polysemy, multiple meaning. Concealed or hidden reference or meaning in prayer, song, chant, or poetry.

kapu—Orally pronounced law; forbidden, prohibition; special privilege or exemption from kapu. Also, sacred, holy, consecrated. There are many different categories of kapu; some kapu proclaimed as law could also be inherited and passed on through the maternal line. There were also kapu that pertain to the person of a chief and which were inherited through the maternal line.

kapu system—Classified by settlers, nineteenth-century chroniclers and nineteenth- and twentieth-century historians as a "system," the ʻai kapu was thought by this disparate group to be a system of "religion," or sometimes religio-politics, grounded in numerous restrictions and prohibitions, which were by their definition "oppressive," especially to women. According to missionary lexicographer Lorrin Andrews, who complied a dictionary, kapu was a thing "keeping the common people in obedience to the chiefs and priests." There is no Hawaiian word of equivalence for "kapu system."

kauhale—a group of houses composing a Hawaiian home. The configuration varied but could include a men's eating house, women's eating house, sleeping house, cook house, canoe house, place of worship for the gods.

kaumaha—weighted down, heavy. A word used to characterize the burden of adhering to and observing kapu. Also, sadness, grief, a heavy load.

kauoha—Order, command, demand, decree, precept, will of the chief, command. The dying wish or will of someone that directs future action.

kinolau—Many forms taken by a god or ancestor, whether spiritual or physical.

konohiki—Land manager or administrator, head of an ahupua'a land division under an ali'i. Responsible for regulating access of maka'āinana to plants and materials from the land and to fish and limu from the seas.

kū—To rule or reign, as a land. God of war and politics, who had many different names and instantiations. To stand, upright, erect, anchor, moor, to rise, extend, perpendicular, steep, standing.

kū'auhau—Genealogy, lineage. Genealogist.

kuhina nui—Often translated as premier, but a term that bears further definition by scholars. The title of Ka'ahumanu and arguably also held by Kalaimoku at the same time. Ali'i who corules with the mō'ī; the two ali'i who were given the title after Ka'ahumanu were also women.

kuleana—Right, privilege, authority, responsibility that was dictated or assigned by skill, knowledge, expertise, or kapu rank. One's business or affairs.

kumu—Teacher, source.

kupuna—Elder, ancestor, teacher, source of knowledge and wisdom.

lā'au wahie 'ala—Sandalwood. Perfumed wood.

lāhui—The Hawaiian people.

loina—Rule, custom, code, rules governing conduct and behavior. Also, modes of observation, and scrutiny.

mā—When applied to the ali'i indicates the alo ali'i or retinue of the chief, the chief's people.

maha—Eased, or relaxed as applied to kapu.

ma ka 'ōlelo Hawai'i—In the Hawaiian language.

maka'āinana—Hawaiian people in general. The populace or citizenry. Those people not of chiefly lineage or expert training.

mālama—To care for, to attend to, to observe as a kapu.

mālama ʻāina—To care for the land, to ensure its continued beauty and productivity.

malu—Lit., shade, or shelter. The protection of the aliʻi. To be protected by kapu, set apart. The stillness and awe of kapu.

malu aliʻi—To rule over or govern as the chiefs. To keep in order the affairs of state.

maluhia—To be under kapu. To enjoy a sense of peace or stillness and calm. The calm that prevailed during ceremony. Stillness from fear or dread.

maluʻia—To be in a state of protection or safety, placed under kapu, kept separate and apart.

mana—A difficult word to define because it is often qualified by context. Power, spiritual power, charisma, strength. Official power or authority.

mānaleo—Native speaker, a term invented by Larry Kimura and William H. Wilson in the late 1970s. Lit., inherited language.

manaʻo—Thought, opinion, often found in letters written by aliʻi as part of a "hallmark" phrase, as in "Eia kuʻu wahi manaʻo" (here then is my humble opinion), to relate a finding, decision or official opinion that has been considered.

manaʻo (o nā aliʻi)—The thought or opinion of the chief was a hallmark of speech; when located in writing, denotes an official opinion, authoritative speech.

maoli—Real, native, indigenous, true.

mele—Song.

mele inoa—An honorific chant to honor the name of a person, an aliʻi. A chant to elevate or uplift someone, a mark of status.

moena—Woven mat, resting place, bed.

mōʻī—King.

moku—1. A district of land or island. 2. A boat or ship. 3. A forest.

moʻo—Succession, series, a discrete piece.

moʻokū—Kū priest.

moʻolelo—History, legend, story, myth, tale, account. Succession of fixed or memorized speech acts, texts.

moʻolono—Lono priest.

moʻokūʻauhau—Genealogy, dynamic and successive, spreading and growing lineage.

mo'o'ōlelo Hawai'i—Succession of fixed or memorized speech acts, texts. Hawaiian history. The name of several histories written in the Hawaiian language.

na'au—Intestines, guts, thought to be the seat of intuition, mood, affections. The place where memories are stored and feelings felt. Translated frequently as heart, mind, place where memories are stored.

noa—The state of being free of kapu. Without restriction.

noho ali'i—Rule of the chief, reign.

noho loa—To remain for a long time. Fig., to die.

noho mālie—To remain quiet, sit still.

palapala—Reading and writing. Document of any kind. The act of making a mark, to paint on, stamp, print.

poi—Mainstay of Hawaiian diet, baked and mashed kalo mixed with water.

pono—Correctness, righteousness, justice. A moral standard, a central value of proper governance and rule.

pono ali'i—Wise or good ali'i, whose government was marked by peace, abundance of the land and sea.

po'olua—A child who could claim the paternity of two fathers. Such relations were considered beneficial and were fostered for the purpose of proliferating genealogical connections. After the introduction of Christianity, the word and relation became associated with adultery and sin.

pule—To pray.

punahele—Favorite person or companion.

punalua—A word denoting the several companions, or lovers of an individual whether male or female.

pu'ukū—A tax collector, one entrusted with the care of resources given as tax.

wai—Water.

waihona—Repository, a place where things, like knowledge, are stored and cared for.

waiwai—Wealth.

NOTES

Introduction

1. William Richards to Jeremiah Evarts, December 6, 1827, ABCFM-Hawaii Papers, Houghton Library, Harvard University, 1820–1900, Hawaiian Mission Children's Society Library, Mission Houses Museum, Honolulu. Unless otherwise noted, all translations that appear in this book are my own.

2. Richards' own writing is well documented in English and through Hawaiian-language manuscripts, translations, and letters he wrote, and those productions in Hawaiian that were written about him. Richards went on to become an honored diplomat, translator, and adviser to Kamehameha III, one of the architects of the first Constitution of the Hawaiian Kingdom (1840).

3. There are several words used to describe the breaking of kapu in Hawaiian. In order to model a set of better practices, this work sets out to sketch the nexus between political language and social practice ma ka 'ōlelo Hawai'i; some endnotes will supply broader definitions of words important in Hawaiian legal discourse in order to help scholars engage in and add to a broader conversation. It is important in some cases to get the kinesthetic sense of the concept in order to understand the nature of law and the manner in which its violation was characterized. Endnotes will sketch connections between related concepts with which a term is resonant or intertextual. 'A'e: To step over, get on top of, tread upon, trespass; to break a kapu or violate a law; to transgress. Hehi: To stamp, tread, trample, pedal, step on; trampling. Fig., to repudiate, deny, desecrate, break.

4. Mana can be of a spiritual and genealogical kind. It can be passed down as kapu or created through the acquisition of knowledge, prestige, and pono or right action. Mana can also be evidenced in the charisma of a person's speech and or physical bearing and prowess.

5. For normative concepts that structure Hawaiian governance in American history, see the following accounts. For arguments regarding oppression and feudalism, see Ephraim Eveleth, *History of the Sandwich Islands: With an Account of the American Mission Established There in 1820* (Philadelphia: American Sunday School Union, 1829). See also Jean Hobbs, *Hawai'i : A Pageant of the Soil* (Stanford, CA: Stanford University Press, 1935). Ralph Kuykendall applies the word "feudal" liberally throughout the first volume of *The Hawaiian Kingdom*. His three-volume history is still the most comprehensive synthesis on nineteenth-century Hawai'i published, and for that reason, it is drawn upon extensively, though he, too, ignores Hawaiian-language sources: *The Hawaiian Kingdom* (Honolulu: University of Hawai'i Press, 1938). Jocelyn Linnekin offers a critique of the use of "cultural referents" in the writings of foreign observers, particularly touching on feudalism, but she does not use Hawaiian-language

244 Notes to Pages 5–7

sources in her study: *Sacred Queens and Women of Consequence: Rank, Gender, and Colonialism* (Ann Arbor: University of Michigan Press, 1990), 75–81. See also Sheldon Dibble, *History of the Sandwich Islands* (Lahainaluna, HI: Press of the Mission Seminary, 1843). On the tyranny of Hawaiian rule, see James Jackson Jarves, *Jarves' History of the Hawaiian Islands: Embracing Their Antiquities, Mythology, Legends, Discovery by Europeans in the Sixteenth Century, Rediscovery by Cook, with Their Civil, Religious and Political History, from the Earliest Traditionary Period to the Year 1846*, 2nd ed. (Boston: J. Munroe and Company, 1844). Hawaiian scholars have critiqued the practice of contemporary scholars in furthering these concepts in their scholarship. See Haunani Kay Trask, "What Do You Mean "We," White Man?" in *From a Native Daughter* (Honolulu: University of Hawaiʻi Press, 1999), 123–134; David Chang, *The World and All the Things Upon It: Native Hawaiian Geographies of Exploration* (Minneapolis: University of Minnesota Press, 2016); Kamanamaikalani Beamer, *No Mākou ka Mana: Liberating the Nation* (Honolulu: Kamehameha Press, 2014).

6. Puakea Nogelmeier, *Mai Paʻa i Ka Leo: Historical Voice in Hawaiian Primary Materials: Looking Forward and Listening Back* (Honolulu: Bishop Museum Press, 2010), 2:96.

7. Lilikalā Kameʻeleihiwa, *Native Land and Foreign Desires: How Shall We Live in Harmony?* (Honolulu: Bishop Museum Press, 1992). Jon Osorio also sought to illuminate key relationships between the aliʻi, nobles, and people necessary for understanding Hawaiian governance from a "native perspective." Tracking the "Dismembering of the Lāhui" through legal means, where language was both "creator and destroyer," Osorio's work gave nuance to the picture of Hawaiian governance well into the late nineteenth century. See Jonathan Kay Kamakawiwoʻole Osorio, *Dismembering Lāhui: A History of the Hawaiian Nation to 1887* (Honolulu: University of Hawaiʻi Press, 2002). While Osorio's work does much to insist on the rebalancing of Hawaiian historical narratives through looking at political and legal discourse in the Hawaiian language, his work does not challenge and instead bolsters the paradigm of "missionary influence" evident in settler colonial historiographies. This tendency is not unique to Osorio's intervention, a subject I will address.

8. Nogelmeier, *Mai Paʻa i ka Leo.*

9. Common major and minor synthesis histories on Hawaiʻi, which are often quoted, were written without the use of Hawaiian-language sources; see, for example, the works of Gavan Daws, A. Grove Day, Lawrence Fuchs, Arrell Morgan Gibson, Edward Joesting, Ralph Kuykendall, and more recently, Stuart Banner, Sally Engle Merry, and Gary Y. Okihiro. Popular histories and works of literature also conform to this trend; see also the work of James L. Haley, James A. Michener, Susanna Moore, Julia Flynn Siler, and Sarah Vowell. The voluminous and conceptually provocative writings of anthropologists like Sahlins, as well as Greg Dening, *History's Anthropology: The Death of William Gooch* (Melbourne: Melbourne University Publishing, 1995); Patrick Vinton Kirch, *A Shark Going Inland Is My Chief: The Island Civilization of Ancient Hawaii* (Berkeley: University of California Press, 2012) and *How Chiefs Became Kings: Divine Kingship and the Rise of Archaic States in Ancient Hawaiʻi* (Berkeley: University of California Press, 2010), provide quite recent yet fairly typical examples of scholars writing on the subject of Hawaiian governance having consulted a few "canon" texts translated from Hawaiian into English or drawing upon those which were simply written in English.

10. Noenoe Silva, *Aloha Betrayed: Native Hawaiian Resistance to American Colonialism* (Durham, NC: Duke University Press, 2004).

11. Silva's work is an important corrective in this respect. However, in taking "native resistance" as its focal paradigm, her narrative risks re-entrenching settler colonial historiographic tropes of "influence" and the irresistible hegemony of American colonial power, leaving "Hawaiian" historical understandings of this period mostly defined as a reaction to colonialism. This aspect of certain revisionist work will be addressed below.

12. Beamer, *No Mākou ka Mana*.

13. Marshall David Sahlins, *How "Natives" Think: About Captain Cook, for Example* (Chicago: University of Chicago Press, 1995), 14.

14. The creation of agential natives has constrained most of the newer accounts of nineteenth-century Hawaiian history to rehearse a narrative of "native resistance" to certain American colonization.

15. While the period I am writing about is rife with colonialism in other parts of the globe, even the Pacific, what is unfolding in Hawai'i is not yet an organized colonialism. American history of the 1820s and 1830s indicates that American efforts at solidifying political authority over territory resulted in Indian Removal of the Five Nations. However, individuals in this history who represent colonial or imperial powers in their capacities in other parts of the globe vainly aspire to bring the power of their nations to the islands. Any American or British colonial aspirations in 1820s Hawai'i did not quite catch on among kānaka maoli then.

16. For more on "negative" missionary influence, see "Naval Correspondence: The Necessity of Colonizing the Sandwich and Bonin Islands," *Metropolitan* 10 (May–August 1834): 219. As a "positive" reflection of global missionary efforts, see Heman Humphrey, *The Promised Land. A Sermon, Delivered at Goshen (Conn.), at the Ordination of the Rev. Messrs Bingham and Asa Thurston as Missionaries to the Sandwich Islands* (Boston: U. Crocker, printer, 1819), 8; Hiram Bingham, *A Residence of Twenty-One Years in the Sandwich Islands, or The Civil, religious, and political history of those islands: comprising a particular view of the missionary operations connected with the introduction and progress of Christianity and civilization among the Hawaiian people* (Rutland, VT: C. E. Tuttle, 1981). For those authors that simply take "missionary influence" as a given, see Norman Meller, "Missionaries to Hawaii: Shapers of the Islands' Government," *Western Political Quarterly* 11, no. 4 (December 1958): 788–799; Jennifer Fish Kashay, "Competing Imperialisms and Hawaiian Authority: The Cannonading of Lahaina in 1827," *Pacific Historical Review* 77, no. 3 (August 2008): 369–390. For narratives quoting negative connotations of "missionary influence" and coming to the defense of missions, see William Orme, William Ellis, and F. W. Beechey, *A Defense of the Missions in the South Sea, and Sandwich Islands, against the misrepresentation contained in a late number of the Quarterly Review, in a letter to the Editor of that Journal by William Orme* (London: S. Holdsworth, 1827), 26–31; also, this important letter of December 6, 1835, by Thomas Ap Catesby Jones, "The Sandwich Islands," *Military and Naval Magazine of the United States* 6 (December 1835): 282–288; Aarne A. Koskinen, *Missionary Influence as a Political Factor in the Pacific Islands* (Helsinki: Suomalainen Tiedeakatemia, 1953).

17. Jean M. O'Brien, *Firsting and Lasting: Writing Indians Out of Existence in New England* (Minneapolis: University of Minnesota Press, 2010).

18. O'Brien, *Firsting and Lasting*, xii, 55.

19. This statement is borne out by the ubiquity of the "missionary influence" thesis supported in mainstream Euro-American historiography on Hawai'i, but also by scholars' reliance upon manuscripts, letters, journals, diaries, and books published by the mission and

its critics in English. Footnotes for most books written on Hawai'i illustrate the preference of scholars to base their inquiry upon sources written in English. Surprisingly very few of the mission's numerous works in the Hawaiian language are in fact consulted by scholars, to the detriment of the complexity of the Sandwich Islands Mission's history. David Forbes' four-volume *Hawaiian National Bibliography* provides a view of the mission's vast publication record in the Hawaiian language: David W. Forbes, *Hawaiian National Bibliography, 1780–1900* (Honolulu: University of Hawai'i Press, 1999).

20. Many excellent scholars have produced important paradigms for cross-cultural engagement and encounter. But to reiterate again, this study emphasizes the importance of language to our work as historians. See Richard White, *The Middle Ground: Indians, Empires, and Republics in the Great Lakes Region, 1650–1815* (Cambridge: Cambridge University Press, 2010); Greg Dening, *Islands and Beaches: Discourse on a Silent Land, 1774–1880* (Honolulu: University of Hawai'i Press, 1986); Tony Ballantyne, *Entanglements of Empire: Missionaries, Māori and the Question of the Body* (Durham, NC: Duke University Press, 2014); Colin Calloway, *New Worlds for All: Indians, Europeans and the Remaking of Early America*, 2nd ed. (Baltimore: Johns Hopkins University Press, 2013); James H. Merrell, *Into the American Woods: Negotiations on the Pennsylvania Frontier* (New York: W. W. Norton, 2000).

21. For representative secondary works on missionaries, see John A. Andrew, *Rebuilding the Christian Commonwealth: New England Congregationalists and Foreign Missions, 1800–1830* (Lexington: University of Kentucky Press, 1976); Sandra Wagner-Wright, *The Structure of the Missionary Call to the Sandwich Islands 1790–1830: Sojourners Among Strangers* (San Francisco, CA: Mellen Research University Press, 1990); Sally Engle Merry, *Colonizing Hawai'i: The Cultural Power of Law* (Princeton, NJ: Princeton University Press, 2000); Clifford Putney and Paul T. Burlin, eds., *The Role of the American Board in the World: Bicentennial Reflections on the Organization's Missionary Work, 1810–2010* (Eugene, OR: Wipf & Stock, 2012); Paul William Harris, *Nothing but Christ: Rufus Anderson and the Ideology of Protestant Foreign Missions* (Oxford: Oxford University Press, 1999); Rufus Anderson, *History of the Sandwich Islands Mission* (Boston: Congregational Publishing Society, 1870); Mary Zwiep, *Pilgrim Path: The First Company of American Women Missionaries to Hawai'i* (Madison: University of Wisconsin Press, 1991); Arrell Morgan Gibson, *Yankees in Paradise: The Pacific Basin Frontier*, completed with the assistance of John S. Whitehead (Albuquerque: University of New Mexico Press, 1993).

22. J. G. A. Pocock, "The Concept of Language and the *métier d'historien*," in *The Languages of Political Theory in Early Modern Europe*, ed. Anthony Pagden (Cambridge: Cambridge University Press, 1987), 21.

23. Pocock, "The Concept of Language," 21. See also the work of Nepia Mahuika, "'Closing the Gaps': From Postcolonialism to Kaupapa Māori and Beyond," *New Zealand Journal of History* 45, no. 1 (2011); Lachlan Paterson, *Colonial Discourses: Niupepa Māori, 1855–1863* (Dunedin, New Zealand: Otago University Press, 2006); Hiapokeikikāne Kichie Perreira, "He Ki'ina Ho'okuana'ike Mauli Hawai'i ma ke Kālailai Mo'okalaleo," *Hūlili* 9 (2013); Silva, *Aloha Betrayed*.

24. Pocock, "Concept of Language," 21.

25. During a project to translate the Bible into Hawaiian, Rev. Richards noted the ability of his cotranslator and language teacher, David Malo, to supply multiple proofs of the usage of words from texts that he had been trained to retain in his memory; he supplied evidence

that kānaka maoli built contexts across texts maintained orally, without recourse to writing or print. During the same period, Sandwich Island missionary writers wrote with fascination about the ability of the blind man, who they named "Batimea" after the man whose sight was restored by Jesus. Batimea Puaaiki came to know God through his ears, they wrote, and had the ability to memorize passages of the Bible in Hawaiian faithfully and make a discourse of them when provided a topic. A series of articles was published about him years later, beginning in 1844, in various Hawaiian-language newspapers. See, for example, "Batimea Puaaiki: Mokuna IV," *Ka Nonanona* (Honolulu) 5, 4, no. 2 (May 14, 1844); "Batimea Puaaiki," *Ke Alaula* (Honolulu) 3, no 10 (January 1, 1869). See also Noelani Arista, "I ka moolelo nō ke ola," *Anglistica* 14, no. 2 (2010): 15–23, where I explain how training the memory and the performance of oral texts contributes to this method.

26. Dibble, *History of the Sandwich Islands* (Lahainaluna, HI: Press of the Mission Seminary, 1843).

27. Cherokee scholar of indigenous and English literature, Daniel Heath Justice, and Māori indigenous studies and literature scholar, Alice Te Punga Somerville, note the centrality of indigenous contexts to their inquiry into how to approach the writing of indigenous lives. "To privilege a range of Indigenous voices and perspectives is to explicitly insist upon our contexts as the central structural ethos of this project." See Alice Te Punga Somerville, Daniel Heath Justice, and Noelani Arista, eds., "Indigenous Conversations About Biography," *Biography: An Interdisciplinary Journal* 39, no. 3 (Summer 2016): 240. This important call for attention to indigenous contexts is a call to decolonize scholarly practices in literature and history, which too often employ Euro-American chronologies and textualities as the context into which "native" lives are rendered sensical.

28. Chanters use this method when they memorize entire bodies of chant works in order to then be able to improvisationally compose new chants in public rituals and procedures. In these contexts, novelty and skill are measured by a chanter's ability to produce meaningful and mana-ful intertextual rephrasings and references.

29. For example, chants of genealogy may not have been recorded until the mid-nineteenth century in a Hawaiian-language newspaper, but they were probably performed for Kauikeaouli at a much earlier period, since they referred to his birth. Of course, I am not assuming that the way a word was used in the late nineteenth century matches its range of usage earlier in the century, but we can pinpoint my selections based on who the writers are, how they are genealogically connected to the actors of whom they write, and whether they served the aliʻi in an official capacity. I can judge a lot about the veracity of a writer's production by learning more about the kinds of pedagogical training he or she received in order to become a bearer of oral-into-text sources. By paying attention to the heated debates between Hawaiians over the veracity of the "traditional" texts that they published in the newspapers—a clear sign that a disciplined discourse is underway—we can see the parameters of what experts considered as constituting *correct* knowledge and interpretation in their critiques of other writers. This is how a historian can make skilled judgments of interpretation of word usages and the significance of Hawaiian actions in the 1820s.

30. This method that I have developed assists me in writing a history that is not simply about "perspective," but instead gets to the root of how meaning is constructed a deeper way, through knowledge of how the oral textual genres were structured, how they functioned, and the ways in which people's speech acts reserved for them places of authority or marginalization. This method of slowly acquiring language and cultural literacy and using it to interpret

sources is how this book seeks to transform histories of cultural encounter and confluence. These methods are especially suited to the study of legal and political history, since laws, treaties, and constitutions were regularly composed in Hawaiian and English. Much work has been done on the study of Māori legal language and encounter over the Treaty of Waitangi. See Claudia Orange, *The Treaty of Waitangi* (Wellington: Port Nicholson Press, 1987); J. N. Matson, "The Language, the Law and the Treaty of Waitangi," *Journal of Polynesian Society* 100, no. 4 (December 1, 1991); Paul Moon, *Te ara ki te Tiriti: The Path to the Treaty of Waitangi* (Auckland: David Ling, 2002).

31. There are literally hundreds or more extant koihonua that have yet to be addressed in Hawaiian histories.

32. Scholar, genealogist, and *kupuna* (elder, teacher), Edith McKinzie collected numerous chants of this genre from various sources that remain unpublished and are housed in a private collection.

33. Abraham Fornander, *Fornander's Collection of Hawaiian Antiquities and Folk-Lore* (Honolulu: Bishop Museum Press, 1917).

34. For divisions of the ocean, see David Malo, *Hawaiian Antiquities: Moʻolelo Hawaiʻi*, trans. Kapali Lyons and Kale Langlas (Honolulu: Bishop Museum Press, forthcoming); also, *The Kumulipo: A Hawaiian Creation Chant*, trans. and ed. Martha Warren Beckwith (Honolulu: University of Hawaiʻi Press, 1981); Rubellite Kawena Johnson, *The Kumulipo: The Hawaiian Hymn of Creation*, vol. 1 (Honolulu: Topgallant Publishing 1981).

Chapter 1

Note to epigraph: "Tamaahmaah, King of the Sandwich Islands," *Boston Intelligencer and Evening Gazette*, January 1, 1820, vol. 6, p. 2.

1. "Owhyhee; Capt. Cook; Capt. Vancouver; King; Vancouver," *Newburyport (MA) Herald*, October 22, 1805; "From a British Publication," *Charleston (SC) City Gazette and Daily Advertiser*, October 2, 1806.

2. "Natural Curiosity," *Philadelphia Poulson's American Daily Advertiser*, October 8, 1805. The man-of-war was built by Vancouver's carpenters, under Kamehameha's direction. When the ship was completed he named it the *Britannia*. See also "From a British Publication," *Charleston (SC) City Gazette and Daily Advertiser*, October 2, 1806.

3. "From a British Publication"; "Chinese Intelligence from Lang's New York Gazette of the 2nd Inst.," *City of Washington Gazette*, December 5, 1817; "Natural Curiosity."

4. "Miscellany: King Tamahama," *Salem (MA) Gazette*, December 7, 1813. Some of the frequently quoted materials that appeared in American newspapers particularly about the "enterprising spirit of the Sandwich Islanders," came from John Trumbell, *A Voyage Round the World in the Years 1800, 1801, 1802, 1803, and 1804; in which the Author visited the principal Islands in the Pacific Ocean and the settlements of Port Jackson and Norfolk Sound*, vol. 2 (London: Printed for Richard Phillips by T. Gillet, 1805), 10–83.

5. The myth of Kamehameha as "great man" has also been enshrined in the history of Hawaiians, suggesting the mutually constitutive, intertwined histories of colonialism and indigeneity. The historiography constructing Kamehameha as legend, as *great man*, has its origins in the newspapers of the early nineteenth century.

6. Hawaiian historians wrote extensive histories about the life of Kamehameha that were published in Hawaiian. Samuel Mānaiakalani Kamakau wrote a series of articles that ran in *Ka Nupepa Kuokoa* from October 20, 1866, through February 15, 1868. These articles were

collected, edited, and published as Samuel Mānaiakalani Kamakau, *Ke Kumu Aupuni: Ka Moʻolelo Hawaiʻi no Kamehameha Ka Naʻi Aupuni a me kāna aupuni I hoʻokumu ai* (Honolulu: ʻAhahui ʻŌlelo Hawaiʻi, 1996). See also Stephen Desha, "He Moolelo Kaao no Kuhaupio ke Koa Kaulana o ke au o Kamehameha Ka Nui," *Ka Hoku o Hawaii* (Hilo, HI), December 16, 1920–September 11, 1924. This series was recently translated and published as well: Stephen Desha, *Kamehameha and His Warrior Kekūhaupiʻo*, trans. Francis Frazier (Honolulu: Kamehameha Schools Press, 2000). Unfortunately one must still go directly to the newspapers to read all the original articles in Hawaiian. The title of the translation emphasizes Kamehameha as the primary actor, while Desha's series title reads: "A History of Kūhaupiʻo Famed Warrior of the Time of Kamehameha the Great." Here is another, albeit local example of the privileging of the "hero" strain in framing Kamehameha's history.

7. In other words, the histories, American and Hawaiian, told still to this day, remain separate. Historians will face difficulties in attempting to mediate between Hawaiian historical narratives and those constructed by a Euro-American historical discipline. The differences between the genres in which the histories are written, and the modes in which they are expressed, are so disparate that it will be challenging to synthesize materials into a singular narrative.

8. This is a logical assessment of what happened to Kamehameha I's kapu upon his death, especially as his death allows his chosen successors to further disrupt and modify the workings of kapu in a manner that will be examined in Chapter 2. No particular sources attest to the rescinding of these earlier kapu. But documentation of the behavior of lesser chiefs and foreign traders in re-engaging in sandalwood harvest and trade after 1819 suggests a de facto end to Kamehameha I's sandalwood kapu.

9. Noel J. Kent, *Hawaii: Islands Under the Influence* (Honolulu: University of Hawaiʻi Press, 1993), 20.

10. Another name for ʻiliahi in Hawaiian is *lāʻau wahie ʻala*, or fragrant wood (of the kind suitable for burning—*wahie*).

11. Harold Whitman Bradley, *The American Frontier in Hawaii: The Pioneers 1789–1843* (Stanford, CA: Stanford University Press, 1942), 30.

12. M. D. Merlin, L. A. J. Thomson, and C. R. Elevitch, "*Santalum ellipticum, S. freycinetianum, S. haleakalae,* and *S. paniculatum* (Hawaiian Sandalwood)," ver. 4.1, in C. R. Elevitch, ed., *Species Profiles for Pacific Island Agroforestry* (Hōlualoa, HI: Permanent Agriculture Resources [PAR], 2006) accessed July 11, 2009, http://www.traditionaltree.org. The four species of Hawaiian sandalwood are *S. ellipticum, S. freycinetianum* (endemic to all islands), *S. haleakalae* (endemic to Maui), and *S. paniculatum* (endemic to Hawaiʻi Island).

13. The Hawaiian historian Samuel M. Kamakau surmised that the abundance of sandalwood on Oʻahu led to its lands being taken, providing a new perspective on the impetus behind Kamehameha's conquest of the island. Kamakau, "Ka Moolelo o Kamehameha I: Ke au o Kamehameha, mai ka A.D. 1811 a hiki i ka A.D. 1819. No ka Hoi ana o Kamehameha i ka A.D. 1811 I Hawaiʻi. Kana mau Hana a hiki i ka Make ana," *Ka Nupepa Kuokoa*, August 31, 1867. Kamakau says that Kalanimoku (Kālaimoku) and all the chiefs in 1816 went to cut wood in various places on Oʻahu. They searched, cut, and dragged the trees from the mountains to the sea. Kamakau notes that it was because of the abundance of sandalwood that all the lands of Oʻahu were taken. "A no ka nui o ka laau ala, ua lawe nā aina a puni Oahu."

14. Mark Rifkin, "Debt and the Transnationalization of Hawaiʻi," *American Quarterly* 60, no. 1 (2008): 49–53, 61. See also James R. Gibson, *Otter Skins, Boston Ships, and China Goods: The Maritime Fur Trade of the Northwest Coast* (Seattle: University of Washington Press, 1992).

15. A search of the online Hawaiian newspaper database reveals that poetic references to 'iliahi begin to be published in 1862, remaining popular throughout the decade. References to 'iliahi and its flowers appeared especially in *kanikau*, Hawaiian laments. The connection between the heady fragrance of sandalwood and the sadness of the passing of a loved one may also suggest the burdensome labor of the sandalwood trade which Hawaiians of the 1820s endured. The recollection of such hard times, would, like death, engender *waimaka*, tears, and *kaumaha*, feelings of grief. None of the references in published chants came from the period of 1820–1830 or before it, though earlier oral compositions were frequently published much later in the papers.

16. These chiefs and the political changes that ensued after Kamehameha I's death are discussed in detail in Chapter 2.

17. Charles Hammatt Journal, May 12, 1823, Bryant and Sturgis (Boston, MA) Records, vols. 14–15, C. H. Hammatt Journal 1823–1825, Baker Library Historical Collections, Harvard Business School.

18. Samuel Mānaiakalani Kamakau, "Ka Moolelo o na Kamehameha no ka Noho Alii o Kauikeaouli aluna o ke aupuni, a ua kapaia o Kamehameha III," *Ka Nupepa Kuokoa* (Honolulu), May 23, 1868.

19. John C. Jones noted in his letter of July 6, 1821, that "Pitt and Carhoomano do most of the business." John C. Jones to Josiah Marshall, Esqr., and Dixey Wildes, July 6, 1821, Josiah Marshall Letters and Accounts, 1821–1841, MS AmW 63, Houghton Library, Harvard University. Bryant and Sturgis agent Charles Hammatt also agreed that Kālaimoku and Ka'ahumanu were the most influential ali'i in the islands. See Charles Hammatt Journal, June 2, 1823, June 17, 1823, p. 105.

20. Hawaiians reckoned connection through bone ('iwi), *not* blood, as a unifying, ideological discourse.

21. This idea of "recording" is important in thinking about "taxes" and reckoning of what is owed and what has been paid, as well as "recording" in the sense that orally kept genealogies were considered reliable and material by virtue of being held fast through the exacting training of experts who were not only repositories, but active agents in the deployment of orally inculcated words. On the seriousness of training of experts and the sacred nature of genealogical "texts," see for example Mary Kawena Pukui, "How Legends Were Taught" Hawaiian Ethnographic Notes [HEN], Bernice Pauahi Bishop Museum, Honolulu, and Iosepa Keohokana, "Ka Mo'olelo o Davida Malo," *Ka Elele Hawaii* (Honolulu), May 15, 1854.

22. Lalepa Koga shared his insight in a discussion we had about the term *mo'okū'auhau*. Lalepa Koga (instructor of Hawaiian language) in conversation with author, University of Hawai'i at Mānoa, April 29, 2009.

23. "Species Profiles for Pacific Island Agroforestry," accessed August 27, 2009, http://www.agroforestry.net/tti/H.tiliaceus-beach-hibiscus.pdf.

24. This conceptualization of creeping roots as expressive of genealogical connection is also manifest in the saying *E kolo ana nō i ke ēwe i ke ēwe*, "rootlet creeps to rootlet."

25. Dixey Wildes to Josiah Marshall, March 27, 1825, Josiah Marshall Letters and Accounts, MS AmW 63, Houghton Library, Harvard University.

26. Daniel Chamberlain, farmer for the mission, described parts of the island of O'ahu that he saw on an expedition to kill cattle, "We saw plenty of coacoanut trees, bread fruit

bananas, sugar cane, some orange trees &c. The land was covered with wood near the top of the mountain, and good to transport over—the Soil is the richest by far that I ever saw, with good springs of water—I should suppose that a man might live here by working only one day in a week." The natural fertility of the land must have given pause to men who were used to the rhythm of work punctuated by the coming of winter. If a man could subsist by working one day a week, what would he do with the rest of his unstructured time? Daniel Chamberlain Journal, April 8, 1820, American Board of Commissioners for Foreign Missions Archives, 1819–1824, ABC 19.1: Hawaiian Islands Mission, Houghton Library, Harvard University.

27. Bryant and Sturgis to Charles Hammatt, October 1, 1822, Bryant and Sturgis (Boston, MA) Records, vol. 10: Letterbook 1818–1829, Baker Library Historical Collections, Harvard Business School (Vol. 10: Letterbook hereafter cited as Bryant and Sturgis Letterbook). Distressed by the state of trade in the islands, and feeling cut off from American society, John C. Jones sent a letter of distress to his employers, confiding that if another were not sent to replace him, soon, "I shall become savage myself." John C. Jones to Marshall and Wildes, January 1823, MS AmW 63.

28. When Babcock was unjustifiably "turned out" by his employers Marshall and Wildes, Hammatt commented at length in his journal regarding Babcock's worth to the concern: "he has doubtless been of the most essential service to Marshall's interest here, and has in fact done all the business of the house—he has made the bargains, selected the wood with his own hands, traveled through the islands from mountains to shore, and possesses more influence with the chiefs, and especially with Krymakoo, than any other resident in the islands." Charles Hammatt, *Ships, Furs, and Sandalwood: A Yankee Trader in Hawaii 1823–1825*, ed. Sandra Wager-Wright (Honolulu: University of Hawai'i Press, 1999), 22.

29. John C. Jones to Marshall and Wildes, August 15, 1823, MS AmW 63.

30. John C. Jones to Josiah Marshall and Captain Dixey Wildes, May 31, 1823, MS AmW 63.

31. John C. Jones to Josiah Marshall and Captain Dixey Wildes, May 31, 1823, MS AmW 63.

32. To date little work has been done on the details of this supposed "debt" in the 1820s—no exact tabulation of debts accrued to individual chiefs, no detailed assessments of what is owed, even when US warships are pressed to collect on those "debts." Part of the work that needs to be done is an assessment working backward from the 1840s when consolidation of "debt" became a concern of the kingdom under the constitution.

33. William Gibson attempted to assess the transformation of Hawaiian society as a result of the Northwest Coast fur trade in terms of "degeneration," and "deculturization." Rather than drawing on English- and Hawaiian-language sources to tell a story of how society was transformed, the historiography on early nineteenth-century trade in Hawai'i tends to focus on decline, degeneration, and the loss of cultural stability and authenticity, mirroring the standard themes of contemporary native narrations of the same period. Gibson, *Otter Skins*, 284–291.

34. The numbers and types of goods and vessels, as well as the amount of sandalwood "debt" incurred, is aggregated from various New England merchant records, including the Bryant and Sturgis Letterbook. Bryant and Sturgis (Boston, MA) Records, 1801–1872, Baker Business Historical Collections, Harvard University; and Josiah Marshall Letters and Accounts, MS AmW 64, Houghton Library, Harvard University.

35. Peabody Museum of Salem, *One Hundredth Anniversary of the Building of "Cleopatra's Barge" 1816–1916: Catalog of the Commemorative Exhibition* (Salem, MA: Peabody Museum, 1916), 10.

36. Several sources note that Liholiho agreed to pay eight thousand piculs of sandalwood for the barge, equivalent to $90,000 in the Canton market. The amount seems outrageous, considering that it is estimated that it cost wealthy Salem merchant George Crowninshield $50,000 to build originally. Peabody Museum of Salem, *The Hawaiian Portion of the Polynesian Collections in the Peabody Museum of Salem: Special Exhibition, August–November, 1920* (Salem, MA: Peabody Museum, 1920), 52. See also W. D. Alexander, "The Story of Cleopatra's Barge," *Papers of the Hawaiian Historical Society*, no. 13 (Honolulu: Hawaiian Gazette Company, 1906), 28–29.

37. Charles Bullard to Mes. James P. Sturgis & Co., July 3, 1821, Charles B. Bullard Letterbook, transcription, 1821–1823, Massachusetts Historical Society.

38. Bullard to Sturgis & Co., July 3, 1821, Bullard Letterbook, Massachusetts Historical Society.

39. Bullard to Sturgis & Co., July 3, 1821.

40. Bullard to Sturgis & Co., July 3, 1821.

41. Bullard to Sturgis & Co., July 3, 1821.

42. Bullard to Sturgis & Co., July 3, 1821.

43. Charles Bullard to Mess. Bryant and Sturgis, October 13, 1821, Bullard Letterbook, Massachusetts Historical Society.

44. Bullard to Bryant and Sturgis, October 13, 1821, Bullard Letterbook, Massachusetts Historical Society.

45. Bullard to Bryant and Sturgis, October 13, 1821.

46. Bryant and Sturgis to Charles Hammatt, October 1, 1822, Bryant and Sturgis Letterbook.

47. A perplexing difficulty therefore arises in the sources, since by Hammatt's account the balance owed for the barge was 480 piculs, of which 1,520 had already been collected by his arrival on the scene in May 1823. Secondary source accounts insist that the barge was sold for 8,000 piculs, or $90,000, a figure not supported by Hammatt's journal, the agent in charge of collection.

48. One of Charles Hammatt's first activities when he arrived in the islands in 1823 was to collect information from the ship captains and other merchant agents in Honolulu with regard to the state of trade and disposition of his concern. Hammatt found out from "various sources" that although Bullard blamed the chiefs for not providing the sandalwood for the barge, his conduct had been "prejudicial to the interest of his employers." Bullard had bought a "large adventure of his own," giving his goods preference to the detriment of the others. There were also reports that Bullard had refused to pick up two thousand piculs of wood that had been given in payment by the chiefs until he had completed selling off all his merchandise. Before half of the sales were complete, the *Cleopatra's Barge* was found to be rotten and the wood was then given to rival trader John C. Jones. Charles Hammatt Journal, May 18, 1823.

49. A laila, Olelo ihola kekahi kaikaina ona, o Kaikioewa "Eia no makou a pau na kaikaina ou, a me ke Alii au, a me ko haole. E waiho mai oe i huaolelo na makou, i lohe hoi ke Alii au a me na kaikuahine ou" (Then one of his [Kamehameha's] younger relations, Kaikio'ewa said, "Here we all are, those of the younger generation belonging to you, your chiefs,

and your foreigners. Leave a word for us, that the chiefs and your female relations may hear"). The importance of the final words Kamehameha had to impart to his alo aliʻi is highlighted here in Kaikioʻewa's request. Samuel Mānaiakalani Kamakau, "Ka Moolelo o Kamehameha I," *Ka Nupepa Kuokoa* (Honolulu, HI), September 14, 1867.

50. Kamakau, "Ka Moolelo o Kamehameha I," *Ka Nupepa Kuokoa*, September 14, 1867.

51. Bryant and Sturgis to Charles Hammatt, October 1, 1822, Bryant and Sturgis Letterbook.

52. John C. Jones to Josiah Marshall and Dixey Wildes, October 5, 1821, MS AmW 63.

53. Jones to Marshall and Wildes, October 5, 1821, MS AmW 63.

54. Jones to Marshall and Wildes, October 5, 1821.

55. Jones to Marshall and Wildes, October 5, 1821.

56. Samuel Mānaiakalani Kamakau, "Ka Moolelo o na Kamehameha no ka Noho Alii o Liholiho ma luna o ke Aupuni, a ua Kapa ia o Kamehameha," *Ka Nupepa Kuokoa*, February 1, 1868.

57. Jones to Marshall and Wildes, August 10, 1822, MS AmW 63.

58. Journal of the Sandwich Islands Mission, March 20, 1821, Sandwich Islands Mission Letters and Papers, October 23, 1819–January 14, 1824, American Board of Commissioners for Foreign Missions Pacific Islands Missions Records, ABC 19.1: Hawaiian Islands Mission, 1824–1909, Houghton Library, Harvard University. On his return in October 1821, see Josiah Marshall Letters and Accounts, October 5, 1821, MS AmW 64.

59. Hammatt, *Ships, Furs, and Sandalwood*, 49. On another occasion, Kālaimoku traveled to Kauaʻi to get people there to cut sandalwood. He chose to go to Kauaʻi rather than visit Kaʻahumanu, who was gravely ill, although many of the other aliʻi went to her bedside. In his stead he sent his wife, the chiefess Nāmahana.

60. Robert Ellwell to Josiah Marshall, October 10, 1821, MS AmW 63. Ellwell estimated that sandalwood might bring $5 a picul that season. John C. Jones to Josiah Marshall and Dixey Wildes, January 22, 1822, MS AmW 63.

61. Jones to Marshall and Wildes, October 5, 1821, MS AmW 63.

62. John C. Jones admitted as much: "they [the chiefs] will never again make the exertion they have this year, they will make no contracts but say if anything comes, that they want, they will buy it." Jones to Marshall and Wildes, November 20, 1821, MS AmW 63.

63. Jones maintained the habit of giving extravagant presents, suggesting to his employers in a letter of January 1823 that it would "be a good plan to send the King, Mr. Pitt (Kalaimoku) and Tamoree some valuable presents, it will go a great ways." Jones to Marshall and Wildes, January 1823, MS AmW 63.

64. Jones to Marshall and Wildes, July 6, 1821, MS AmW 63.

65. Jones regularly reports selling cargoes at "twice full" their worth.

66. Jones to Marshall and Wildes, January 1823, MS AmW 63.

67. Jones to Marshall and Wildes, July 6, 1821, MS AmW 63.

68. Jones to Marshall and Wildes, July 6, 1821.

69. The king had purchased a house frame, brig, and cargo five months earlier for 7,700 piculs. Jones to Marshall and Wildes, July 6, 1821, MS AmW 63; Jones to Marshall and Wildes, November 20, 1821, MS AmW 63.

70. Jones to Marshall and Wildes, March 9, 1823, MS AmW 63.

71. Jones to Marshall and Wildes, March 9, 1823.

72. Jones to Marshall and Wildes, March 9, 1823.

73. Charles Hammatt Journal, May 30, 1823.

74. Hammatt, *Ships, Furs, and Sandalwood*, 18.

75. Charles Hammatt Journal, June 17, 1823; also August 8 and 27, 1823; Hammatt, *Ships, Furs, and Sandalwood*, 19–20, 24–25, 28.

76. Jones often wrote to his employers expressing his desire to do right by them thereby maintaining a good reputation. See Jones to Marshall and Wildes, January 1823, MS AmW 63.

77. While much has been made of the influence of missionaries upon chiefly politics, comparatively little has been done to study merchant activity in relation to chiefly governance.

78. Rifkin,"Debt and the Transnationalization of Hawai'i," 43–66.

79. Dixey Wildes to Josiah Marshall, July 18, 1825, MS AmW 63.

Chapter 2

1. "Donation of Curiosities," *Boston Columbian Centinel*, August 28, 1790, p. 48.

2. "Donation," *Boston Columbian Centinel*, p. 48.

3. For further reading on this subject, see Joyce Chaplin, *Subject Matter: Technology, the Body, and Science on the Anglo-American Frontier, 1500–1676* (Cambridge, MA: Harvard University Press, 2001); also, Susan Scott Parrish, *American Curiosity: Cultures of Natural History in the Colonial British Atlantic World* (Chapel Hill: University of North Carolina Press, 2006).

4. Ward Safford to Jeremiah Evarts, May 13, 1816, American Board of Commissioners for Foreign Missions Archives, ABC 12.1: Letters from Agencies: General Series, 1821–1899, Houghton Library, Harvard University (hereafter cited as ABC 12.1). See also Charles Prentice, Joseph Harvey, and James Morris to Samuel Worcester, June 25, 1816, ABC 12.1, vol. 2; Charles Prentice, Joseph Harvey, and James Morris to Samuel Worcester, August 20, 1816, ABC 12.1, vol. 2.

5. Words like *heathen* appear in scare quotes in the first instance to mark a particular term as problematic and having a life shared across the cultural and social divide between Hawaiians and American missionaries and Christians. A word freighted with power and indigenous to its context, its original use must remain. James Merrell makes an important intervention for historians by drawing their attention to the loaded words deployed by scholars writing about American Indians; it is important for this work, however, to go beyond English-language constructions of history and point out how these words must have been received by those whose lives and societies were reconditioned and reformulated according to these introduced concepts. Furthermore, while seizing upon Merrell's important cautionary to our practice as Americanists, this work seeks to encourage historians to denaturalize their own approaches by engaging native-language archives where possible, so that the very categories of comparison may be recalibrated by the terms which were in play when encountered and settlement ensued, and so that we may account for a more robust view of the complexity that occurred during colonial settlement. James H. Merrell, "Second Thoughts on Colonial Historians and American Indians," *William and Mary Quarterly*, 3rd ser., 69, no. 3 (July 2012).

6. Samuel J. Mills to the President of the Prudential Committee of the Board of Commissioners for Foreign Missions, March 14, 1814, ABC 12.1, vol. 2.

7. Mills to President of the Prudential Committee, March 14, 1814, ABC 12.1, vol. 2; E. W. Dwight, *The Memoirs of Henry Obookiah* (New Haven, CT: Office of the *Religious Intelligencer*, 1818).

8. Mills to President of the Prudential Committee, March 14, 1814, ABC 12.1, vol. 2.

9. Samuel J. Mills, Chauncey Goodrich, and Ward Safford to Samuel Worcester, May 25, 1816, ABC 12.1, vol. 2.

10. Memorial of the Connecticut Committee on the Subject of a School for the Education of Heathen Youth (Charles Prentice, Joseph Harvey, and James Morris) to the ABCFM, August 20, 1816, ABC 12.1, vol. 2.

11. Connecticut Committee to ABCFM, August 20, 1816. See also "School for Heathen Youth," *Boston Recorder*, September 24, 1816, p. 155; American Board of Commissioners for Foreign Missions, *A Narrative of Five Youth from the Sandwich Islands Now Receiving an Education in This Country* (New York: J. Seymour, 1816), 44.

12. Connecticut Committee to ABCFM, August 20, 1816.

13. *Natives* is another term historians should deploy with multiple valences and meanings, as is true also of many Hawaiian words.

14. Connecticut Committee to ABCFM, August 20, 1816.

15. Connecticut Committee to ABCFM, August 20, 1816.

16. Connecticut Committee to ABCFM, August 20, 1816.

17. Connecticut Committee to ABCFM, August 20, 1816.

18. Also included in the list of prospective pupils were men from India and Africa and Jews from various parts of the "heathen world." Connecticut Committee to ABCFM, August 20, 1816.

19. Connecticut Committee to ABCFM, August 20, 1816.

20. Connecticut Committee to ABCFM, August 20, 1816.

21. Connecticut Committee to ABCFM, August 20, 1816.

22. ABCFM, *A Narrative of Five Youth.*

23. As early as the fall of 1815, a manuscript introducing the American public to the Hawaiian youths had been written by their Connecticut supporters and sent to Boston in hopes that it would be published and sold to raise funds for their education and upkeep. See Ward Safford to Jeremiah Evarts and Jedidiah Morse, May 13, 1816, ABC 12.1, vol. 2; Mills, Goodrich, and Safford to Worcester, May 25, 1816, ABC 12.1, vol. 2.

24. "Honourable Munificence," *Boston Daily Advertiser*, June 24, 1816; *Massachusetts Spy or Worcester Gazette*, June 15, 1816; *Alexandria (VA) Gazette*, June 15, 1816, Commercial and Political; *Middlebury (VT) National Standard*, June 26, 1816; "Religious Intelligence," *Middlebury Vermont Mirror*, June 26, 1816; *Dedham (MA) Gazette*, June 28, 1816; *Lexington (KY) Western Monitor*, July 5, 1816; *Farmer's Cabinet* (Amherst, NH), July 6, 1816; *Newark Centinel of Freedom*, July 16, 1816; *New Haven City Gazette*, July 17, 1816.

25. In providing citations to the various publications that carried and then subsequently reprinted an article or letter about Hawai'i, I am providing a view of the geographic range of circulation, as well as illustrating how news was circulated in religious and secular publications of the time. What becomes clear is that news items about the Sandwich Islands and these men were not always limited to Boston, or even to New England.

26. "Honourable Munificence," *Boston Daily Advertiser*, June 24, 1816.

27. Akua is a general term for a god or gods. The translation of Akua into a proper name illustrates one in a very long *history* of misunderstandings and misinterpretations, as Americans little acquainted with Hawai'i and Hawaiian people generated "news" about the Sandwich Islands. See"From the Religious Intelligencer," *Washington City Weekly Gazette*, July

20, 1816, p. 274: "The natives worship a God called Acooa." Americans compared themselves to Hawaiians by translating Hawaiian things into their own systems of valuation.

28. "Honourable Munificence," *Boston Daily Advertiser*, June 24, 1816.

29. "Honourable Munificence," *Boston Daily Advertiser*, June 24, 1816.

30. "Honourable Munificence," *Boston Daily Advertiser*, June 24, 1816.

31. "New Haven, June 1. Honourable Munificence," *Stockbridge (MA) Berkshire Star*, June 20, 1816, p. 2.

32. "To Tamoree, King of Atowy, One of the Sandwich Islands," *Norfolk (VA) American Beacon and Commercial Diary*, April 22, 1817, p. 3.

33. John A. Andrew, *Rebuilding the Christian Commonwealth: New England Congregationalists and Foreign Missions, 1800–1830* (Lexington: University Press of Kentucky, 1976).

34. Vaill's wording also suggests that Honoli'i's idol worship marks him as ignorant as a block of wood. "Owhyhees Now in Connecticut," *Boston Recorder*, July 17, 1816.

35. "Owhyhees Now in Connecticut," *Boston Recorder*, July 17, 1816.

36. The spirit of missions was something converts like Honoli'i could experience and in turn practice upon fellow natives. The phrase also applied to the feeling that the benevolent American public could catch, and also embody through meetings of missionary associations and prayers. Finally, the spirit of missions was something that could be supported by Christian donations, as also the term for operations that missionaries undertook to spread the gospel and civilization throughout the heathen world.

37. "Owhyhees Now in Connecticut," *Boston Recorder*, July 17, 1816.

38. "Owhyhees Now in Connecticut," *Boston Recorder*, July 17, 1816.

39. "Owhyhees Now in Connecticut," *Boston Recorder*, July 17, 1816.

40. *Middlebury (VT) Christian Messenger*, January 20, 1819, pp. 1–2. By 1817, Nālimahauna (Nahlemah-hownah) had lived in Massachusetts for twelve years, since the age of about fourteen, while George Prince Kaumuali'i (Tamoree), who had been in the United States since the age of five, retained little recollection of Hawaiian language. Dwight, *Memoirs of Henry Obookiah*, 76.

41. ABCFM, *A Narrative of Five Youth*, 32–33.

42. American Board of Commissioners for Foreign Missions, *Report of the American Board of Commissioners for Foreign Missions, Compiled from Documents laid before the Board, at the Seventh Annual Meeting, which was held at Hartford, (Con.) Sept. 18. 19. 20, 1816* (Boston: Samuel T. Armstrong, 1816), 3, 12.

43. ABCFM, *Report of the American Board*. Excerpts from reports were republished verbatim in newspapers, and in this case, one week after the meeting had been convened. The *Boston Recorder* published a story about the school and told the public that in addition to two American Indians, one of the five Hawaiians is a "Prince, the son of a King of one of the Sandwich Islands." "School for Heathen Youth," *Boston Recorder*, September 24, 1816, p. 155. Readers would have read this news first in the *Recorder*, since the ABCFM *Report* was not published until October. Atowy or Atooi was the way Americans heard the Hawaiian 'O Kaua'i, the 'O being a particle marking the subject, the name of a person or place.

44. James Morris to the American Board of Commissioners for Foreign Missions, September 2, 1817, ABC 12.1, vol. 2; John Chauncey Pease and John Milton Niles, *A Gazetteer of the States of Connecticut and Rhode-Island* (Hartford, CT: W. S. Marsh, 1819), 229.

45. "Owhyheean Prince," *Boston Recorder*, October 29, 1816, p. 174.

46. "Owhyheean Prince," *Boston Recorder*, October 29, 1816.

47. "Owhyheean Prince," *Boston Recorder*, October 29, 1816.

48. "Owhyheean Prince," *Boston Recorder*, October 29, 1816.

49. It seems that George Prince Kaumualiʻi had fabricated this notion that it was Rev. Vaill's idea to name him George Prince, as he is listed as such on the muster roll of the ship *Wasp* in 1815.

50. In British circles, it had become a commonplace by this time for donors to ask that a specific child, according to its sex and mission field, be educated and clothed with their money. Donors would be given the power to choose the name that the child was to answer to. Very often donors named children after deceased relatives they sought to honor, and usually the child would bear the donor's surname. Relation to God, British citizens, and empire was engineered by this process through the fund-raising arms of the Foreign Mission movement. The Americans at the time were trying to educate the benevolent American republic about this practice.

51. "Captain Edes," *Boston Daily Advertiser*, vol. 15, no. 39, November 14, 1816, p. 2.

52. *Boston Recorder*; *Salem (MA) Gazette*, November 12, 1816; *Boston Daily Advertiser*; *Boston Repertory*, November 14, 1816; *New York Commercial Advertiser*; *New York Evening Post*, November 15, 1816; *New York Columbian*, November 16, 1816; *New York Courier*; *Baltimore Patriot*; *Newark Centinel of Freedom*; *Philadelphia Poulson's American Daily Advertiser*, November 18, 1816; *New Haven Connecticut Journal*, November 19, 1816; *Boston Weekly Messenger*, November 21, 1816; *Albany Advertiser*; *Washington City Gazette*, November 23, 1816; *Greenfield (MA) Franklin Herald*, November 26, 1816; *Massachusetts Spy or Worcester Gazette*, November 27, 1816; *Albany Advertiser*; *Reading (PA) Der Weltbothe*, December 4, 1816; *Washington, DC, Daily National Intelligencer*, December 7, 1816; *Norfolk (VA) American Beacon and Commercial Diary*, December 9, 1816; *Sunbury (PA) Nordwestliche Post*, January 3, 1817; *Alexandria (VA) Gazette and Daily Advertiser*, June 17, 1817.

53. *Boston Recorder*, November 12, 1816.

54. *Boston Recorder*, November 12, 1816; Letter of Samuel Worcester to the ABCFM, 1819, ABC 12.1.

55. "Sandwich Islands," *Boston Recorder*, November 26, 1816, p. 191.

56. Cotting petitioned the Massachusetts legislature for assistance for the boy, but his petition was ignored.

57. Letter to Tamoree, October 19, 1816, published in *Massachusetts Spy, or Worcester Gazette*, December 4, 1816.

58. "Sandwich Islands," *Boston Recorder*, November 26, 1816, p. 191. Reprinted in *New York Evening Post*, November 29, 1816; *Boston Recorder*, December 3, 1816 and January 13, 1817. This essay was also published in *Albany Daily Advertiser*; *Washington, DC, Daily National Intelligencer*, December 3, 1816; *Albany Daily Advertiser*; *Massachusetts Spy, or Worcester Gazette*; *Philadelphia Poulson's American Daily Advertiser*; *New York Spectator*, December 4, 1816; *Alexandria (VA) Gazette*; *Stockbridge (MA) Berkshire Star*; *Boston Yankee*; *Washington (KY) Union*, December 20, 1816; *Haverhill (MA) Merrimack Intelligencer*, December 21, 1816; *Chillicothe (OH) Weekly Recorder*, January 1, 1817; *Salem (MA) Gazette*, January 3 and 4, 1817; *Springfield (MA) Hampden Federalist*, January 23, 1817.

59. "Sandwich Islands," *Albany Advertiser*, no. 371, December 3, 1816, p. 2.

60. "Sandwich Islands," *Albany Advertiser*.

61. *Boston Recorder*, November 26, 1816; "Sandwich Islands," *Albany Advertiser*.

62. "Sandwich Islands," *Albany Advertiser*.

63. "For the American Daily Advertiser Prince Kummoree's Letter," *Philadelphia Poulson's American Daily Advertiser*, January 17, 1817. Also republished in *Middlebury (VT) Christian Messenger*, February 5, 1817.

64. "For the American Daily Advertiser," *Philadelphia Poulson's*; *Middlebury (VT) Christian Messenger*, 1817.

65. "For the American Daily Advertiser," *Philadelphia Poulson's*; *Middlebury (VT) Christian Messenger*, 1817.

66. "George Prince Tamoree," *Massachusetts Spy or Worcester Gazette*, vol. 44, no. 2280, December 18, 1816, p. 3.

67. "George Prince Tamoree," *Massachusetts Spy*.

68. "George Prince Tamoree," *Massachusetts Spy*.

69. "George Prince Tamoree," *Massachusetts Spy*.

70. "George Prince Tamoree," *Massachusetts Spy*.

71. All sources that quote the petition footnote a secondary source, and not the petition to the Massachusetts legislature of May 28, 1810. The petition is dated in May, but Cotting notes in his letter to the editor that the petition was made in the winter of 1811. Rowan himself was practicing a sort of artifice, since in his petition, he asked for remuneration for three years' boarding, education, and medicine for the boy, and that as he was "no longer able to continue" his attentions requested the legislature would "receive said lad and recover him to his native place, or dispose of him as you may deem proper."

72. "Obituary," *Concord (MA) Middlesex Gazette*, vol. 33, no. 1684, March 5, 1818, p. 3. Also republished in *Boston New-England Palladium and Commercial Advertiser*, vol. 46, no. 20, March 6, 1818, p. 2; *Boston Recorder*, vol. 3, no. 15, March 10, 1818, p. 3; *Middlebury (VT) Christian Messenger*, vol. 11, no. 15, March 11, 1818, p. 3.

73. "Obituary," *Middlesex Gazette*.

74. "Death of Obookiah. Communicated for the Recorder," *Boston Recorder*, vol. 3, no. 12, March 17, 1818, p. 46.

75. "Obituary," *Middlesex Gazette*.

76. "Obituary," *Middlesex Gazette*.

77. "Poetry: Obookiah's Grave," *Washington, DC, National Messenger*, vol. 1, no. 93, June 1, 1818, p. 4. Also republished in *Concord (NH) Observer*, vol. 1, no. 15, April 12, 1819, p. 4.

78. "Death of Obookiah," *Boston Recorder*, vol. 3, no. 12, March 17, 1818, p. 46.

79. Dwight, "Memoirs of Henry Obookiah," *Middlebury (VT) Christian Messenger*, December 9, 1818, p. 3; *Boston Recorder*, January 30, 1819, p. 19.

80. *Boston Christian Watchman and Baptist Register*, December 16, 1820, p. 4.

81. John Demos, *The Heathen School: A Story of Hope and Betrayal in the Age of the Early Republic* (New York: Vintage Books, 2014), 62–63.

82. *Mr. Humphrey's Sermon at the Ordination of the Missionaries Destined to the Sandwich Islands* (Boston: U. Crocker, 1819), 3–5.

83. *Humphrey's Sermon*, 10.

84. *Humphrey's Sermon*, 12.

85. *Humphrey's Sermon*, 12.

86. Dwight, *Memoirs of Henry Obookiah*; *Humphrey's Sermon*, 21–22.

87. Andrew, *Rebuilding the Christian Commonwealth.*

88. "Instructions of the Prudential Committee of the ABCFM to the Rev. Hiram Bingham and the Rev. Asa Thurston, Messrs. Daniel Chamberlain, Thomas Holman, Samuel Whitney, Samuel Ruggles, Elisha Loomis, John Honolii, Thomas Hopu, and William Kanui, of the Mission to the Sandwich Islands," *Instructions of the Prudential Committee of the American Board of Commissioners for Foreign Missions to the Sandwich Islands Mission* (Lahainaluna, HI: Press of the Mission Seminary, 1838), 22.

89. *Humphrey's Sermon,* 24.

90. *Humphrey's Sermon,* 24.

91. *Humphrey's Sermon,* 20.

92. *Humphrey's Sermon,* 22.

93. *Humphrey's Sermon,* 23–24.

94. *Humphrey's Sermon,* 17.

Chapter 3

Notes to epigraphs: Isa. 42:4 "He shall not fail nor be discouraged, till he set judgment in the earth, and the isles shall wait for his law." Hiram Bingham to Samuel Worcester, July 16, 1819, American Board of Commissioners for Foreign Missions, ABC 6: Candidate Department, Houghton Library, Harvard University.

1. "Journal of Hiram Bingham (Middlebury College), October 20, 1815," in *Selected Writings of Hiram Bingham (1814–1869), Missionary to the Hawaiian Islands: To Raise the Lord's Banner,* ed. Char Miller (Lewiston, NY: Edwin Mellen Press, 1988), 64–65.

2. "Bingham to Parents, November 27, 1816," *Selected Writings,* 68–69.

3. "Newspapers," *Bennington Vermont Gazette,* November 26, 1816.

4. "Bingham to Parents, November 27, 1816," *Selected Writings,* 72.

5. "Bingham to Parents, November 27, 1816," *Selected Writings,* 70.

6. "Bingham to Parents, November 27, 1816," *Selected Writings,* 70–71.

7. "Bingham to Parents, November 27, 1816," *Selected Writings,* 70–71.

8. "Communication," *National Advocate* (New York), June 16, 1817; "Boston Theater," *Boston Daily Advertiser,* October 25, 1816; "Boston Theater," *Boston Daily Advertiser,* November 14, 1816.

9. Sacred, not in the sense of God given, but sacralized and legitimated through American narratives of progress, or through the work of missionary hagiographers.

10. Edward Andrews, *Native Apostles: Black and Indian Missionaries in the British Atlantic World* (Cambridge, MA: Harvard University Press, 2013). Andrews makes this argument for the spread of missions in the British Atlantic world.

11. Lilikalā Kameʻeleihiwa, *Native Land and Foreign Desires: Pehea Lā e pono ai* (Honolulu: Bishop Museum Press, 1992), 22–23. While the translation above reflects the oral pattern in Hawaiian, another level of translation might render the phrase as "the past makes the future possible."

12. The sometimes forceful separation of Hawaiian people from moʻoʻōlelo Hawaiʻi (Hawaiian history and traditions) and ʻōlelo Hawaiʻi (Hawaiian language) and the replacement and erasure of these by Euro-American histories and English language over the twentieth century is, therefore, a particularly violent and slow process of settler colonialism that is still unfolding.

13. Such linguistic fluency is essential for any rigorous comparative history.

14. Gannaneth Obeysekere, *The Apotheosis of Captain Cook: European Mythmaking in the Pacific* (Princeton, NJ: Princeton University Press, 1992); Marshall Sahlins, *How "Natives" Think, About Captain Cook, for Example* (Chicago: University of Chicago Press, 1996). The Obeysekere debate about Captain Cook engaged questions of who could speak for natives in the writing of history. The debate garnered much notoriety, but one of the difficulties of the discussion is that neither of the scholars is fluent in Hawaiian language. Though the claim might be made that there are few sources from the period, the stature of the scholars involved legitimates the practice that one can write about the Hawaiian past, or encounter, without delving into the native-language "archive."

15. "Religious Intelligence," *Farmer's Cabinet* (Amherst, NH), April 14, 1821. The materials covered the period from October 23, 1819, to July 19, 1820.

16. "From the Boston Recorder, 23d Inst. Mission to the Sandwich Islands," *Newburyport (MA) Herald*, October 26, 1819. Also republished under the same title in *Hampden (MA) Federalist and Public Journal*, October 27, 1819; *Cooperstown (NY) Freeman's Journal*, November 1, 1819; *Norwich (CT) Courier*, November 3, 1819; *Farmer's Cabinet* (Amherst, NH), November 6, 1819. I list the different newspapers that ran stories about the mission to illustrate the geographical distribution of news about the Sandwich Islands Mission across the United States.

17. "From the Boston Recorder," *Newburyport (MA) Herald*, October 26, 1819.

18. Job 10:22.

19. American Board of Commissioners for Foreign Missions, *Instructions to the Missionaries About to Embark for the Sandwich Isles* (Boston: Crocker and Brewster, 1823).

20. *The Panoplist, and Missionary Magazine for the Year 1814*, vol. 10 (Boston: Samuel T. Armstrong, 1814), 148–149, 190–195.

21. "Mission to the Sandwich Islands," *New York Commercial Advertiser*, September 23, 1819; *Farmer's Cabinet* (Amherst, NH), September 25, 1819; and "Mission to the Sandwich Islands, the Isles Shall Wait for His Law," *Charleston (SC) Southern Evangelical Intelligencer*, October 16, 1819.

22. "The Isles Shall Wait for His Law" was published as a pamphlet, but was also picked up in several American newspapers. The newspaper version of the Worcester essay also listed supplies needed by the missionaries, along with places to drop off donations.

23. Acts 16:9 "And a vision appeared to Paul in the night; There stood a man of Macedonia, and prayed him, saying, Come over into Macedonia, and help us."

24. David L. Perry, "The Charge," in Heman Humphrey, *The Promised Land, A Sermon, Delivered at Goshen at the Ordination of the Rev. Messrs. Hiram Bingham and Asa Thurston as Missionaries to the Sandwich Islands, September 29, 1819* (Boston: S. T. Armstrong, 1819), 33–37.

25. "American Missions to the Cherokees," *Concord (NH) Observer*, January 11, 1819.

26. Perry, "The Charge."

27. ABCFM, *Instructions to the Missionaries*.

28. ABCFM, *Instructions to the Missionaries*.

29. In his ordination charge to Hiram Bingham and Asa Thurston, Rev. Perry noted as much, saying, "The ordinary aids and consultation of ministers in Gospel lands will be denied to you. The advice and Christian faithfulness of your brethren you cannot enjoy. You must therefore draw your support immediately from the infinite fountain, and be eminently men

of prayer. In that moral wilderness you must gather your manna daily or perish." Perry, "The Charge."

30. The congregation would be familiar with this story, as it was published multiple times. "Honourable Munificence," *Boston Daily Advertiser*, June 24, 1816; *Massachusetts Spy or Worcester Gazette; Alexandria (VA) Gazette*, Commercial and Political, June 15, 1816; *Middlebury (VT) National Standard*, June 26, 1816; "Religious Intelligence," *Middlebury Vermont Mirror*, June 26, 1816; *Dedham (MA) Gazette*, June 28, 1816; *Lexington (KY) Western Monitor*, July 5, 1816; *Farmer's Cabinet* (Amherst, NH), July 6, 1816; *Newark Centinel of Freedom*, July 16, 1816; *New Haven City Gazette*, July 7, 1816.

31. *Boston Recorder*, October 23, 1819. The story of Hopu's address was also carried in the following publications: *Boston Daily Advertiser*, October 25, 1819; *New York Commercial Advertiser*, October 25, 1819; *Newburyport (MA) Herald*, October 26, 1819; *New York Spectator*, October 26, 1819; *Hampden (MA) Federalist and Public Journal*, October 27, 1819; *Cooperstown (NY) Freeman's Journal*, November 1, 1819; "Mission to the Sandwich Islands," *Newbury (VT) Christian Messenger*, November 2, 1819; *Norwich (CT) Courier*, November 3, 1819; *Farmer's Cabinet* (Amherst, NH), November 6, 1819; and *Charleston (SC) Southern Evangelical Intelligencer*, November 6, 1819.

32. *Boston Recorder*, October 23, 1819.

33. Members from the congregations of Park Street Church, Old South Church, and the church in Essex Street were reported to be in attendance, as well as "many members of churches in and out of town." *Boston Recorder*, October 23, 1819.

34. "Second Edition," *Boston Intelligencer*, October 23, 1819. The *Boston Intelligencer* provided, along with the news, a critical view of the Sandwich Islands Mission, noting, "The Mission, for the purpose of propagating the Gospel among the savages, may prove to be advantageous; though we imagine the expediency of carrying ladies among a wild and uncontrollable race, is at least problematical. Besides, it may be seriously enquired of the promoters of the Scheme whether they had not better look at home, and continue to promote their Domestic Missions, with Equal zeal and enthusiasm." The *New Hampshire Sentinel* stopped short of outright criticism by publishing only the first sentence regarding ladies, leaving out the sentence that called the mission a "scheme." "Departure of the Missionaries," *Keene New Hampshire Sentinel*, October 30, 1819.

35. The monthly concert of prayer had originated in Scotland in 1744 and had "been adopted by Jonathan Edwards with the idea that on a given day all good Christians would unite in their prayers for revival." The concert was taken up by the London Missionary Society in 1795 and the American missionary societies followed suit, dedicating the day to the unification of Christian concern in prayer on behalf of the missionary cause. Sandra Wagner-Wright, *The Structure of the Missionary Call to the Sandwich Islands 1790–1830: Sojourners Among Strangers* (San Francisco, CA: Mellen Research University Press, 1990), 81.

36. Another monthly concert of prayer occurred on February 7, 1820, in which the missionaries felt "united with our brethren in America and with the friends of Christ in Different lands." On this occasion, the parting counsels of Brothers Fisk and Parsons were read aloud as well. Journal of the Sandwich Islands Mission, American Board of Commissioners for Foreign Missions Archives, 1819–1824, ABC 19.1: Hawaiian Islands Mission, Houghton Library, Harvard University.

37. Journal of the Sandwich Islands Mission, December 15, 1819, ABC 19.1.

38. Journal of the Sandwich Islands Mission, January 25, 1820, ABC 19.1.

39. Journal of the Sandwich Islands Mission, November 24, 1819, ABC 19.1; also "Hiram Bingham to Amos Bingham, 02 January 1820," *Selected Writings*, 153–154.

40. Journal of the Sandwich Islands Mission, November 30, 1819, ABC 19.1.

41. Journal of the Sandwich Islands Mission, March 26, 1820, ABC 19.1.

42. Daniel Chamberlain Journal, March 26, 1820, American Board of Commissioners for Foreign Missions Archives, 1819–1824, ABC 19.1: Hawaiian Islands Mission, Houghton Library, Harvard University.

43. *Connecticut Courant*, April 10, 1821, http://infoweb.newsbank.com.

44. *Connecticut Mirror*, April 9, 1821; *Connecticut Courant*, April 10, 1821; *Boston Missionary Herald*, April 1821; *New Hampshire Sentinel*, April 14, 1821, http://infoweb.newsbank.com. (Note: this article was published and republished many times.) Inoah was the missionary rendering of 'ai noa, or the practice of eating free of kapu (restriction). Periods of 'ai noa were observed following the death of high-ranking ali'i, in the space preceding the installment of a new chief. The battle between Kekuaokalani's and Liholiho's forces led by the warrior chief Kālaimoku was the decisive end to the 'ai kapu and also of official state religion. For an in-depth treatment of what led up to the battle and struggle for power within this extended family of ali'i, see Samuel Mānaiakalani Kamakau, *Ke Kumu Aupuni: He Mo'olelo Hawai'i no Kamehameha Ka Na'i Aupuni a me Kāna aupuni i ho'okumu ai* (Honolulu: Ahahui 'Ōlelo Hawai'i, 1996), 189–191, 204–217.

45. Journal of the Sandwich Islands Mission, March 30, 1820, ABC 19:1. *Marae* is a word used in variation in Tahiti, Cook Islands, Tonga, and Aotearoa. The Hawaiian word for this kind of sacred structure or place is *heiau*.

46. "Sandwich Mission," *Connecticut Mirror*, April 9, 1821, http://infoweb.newsbank.com. Emphasis added.

47. Speech was conduct and conduct was speech. Jane Kamensky, *Governing the Tongue: The Politics of Speech in Early New England* (New York: Oxford University Press, 1997), 5.

48. "I ka 'ōlelo nō ke ola, i ka 'ōlelo nō ka make"—Proverb. (In speech there is life, in speech death.)

49. Various definitions of the term *'a'apo* emphasize the speed with which information or knowledge is apprehended or received readily in the *na'au*, "guts/mind." 'A'apo is also translated as "one who learns quickly." What is not described is the process of learning, moving from the image of being captured in the hands or arms, but really by the ears and tongue. Once grasped, knowledge was stored in the na'au or guts, rather than the brain.

50. 'A'apo is also translated as "ready scholar."

51. Applying the term *mana* to the words of Euro-Americans removes their activity from received contexts and interpretively asserts a different ontology over the Euro-American actors in this chapter. If this seems like a strange application to readers, consider that it is commonplace to interpret Hawaiian actions through the filter of Euro-American epistemes and ontologies.

52. "Sandwich Mission," *Connecticut Mirror*, April 9, 1821, http://infoweb.newsbank.com.

53. *Boston Missionary Herald*, April 1821, p. 111.

54. Even when historians are disagreeing with the claim, they still see fit to repeat it. See Theodore Morgan, *Hawaii: A Century of Economic Change 1778–1876* (Cambridge, MA: Harvard University Press, 1948), 86.

55. Perry Miller, *Errand into the Wilderness* (Cambridge, MA: Belknap Press of Harvard University Press, 1956), 15.

56. Miller, *Errand into the Wilderness*, 114; Isa. 40:3; Mark 1:3.

57. Miller, *Errand into the Wilderness*, 112.

58. Missionary claims about the loss of 'ai kapu—namely, that the Hawaiian people were living in a religious vacuum and that this was linked to a weakness in governance or absence of law—have been largely repeated by historians writing about Hawai'i. From this economic history on Hawai'i came the unequivocal and yet all too familiar claim, "The bulk of the work of discrediting and disintegrating the old religious system had already been done during the four decades of visits by explorers and traders before them: the Islands were a religious vacuum." Theodore Morgan, *Hawaii: A Century of Economic Change, 1778–1876* (Cambridge, MA: Harvard University Press, 1948), 86.

59. Hawaiian historian Samuel Mānaiakalani Kamakau used the word *ho'ohiolo* (to tumble down, to cast down, collapse, falling) to describe the end of the 'ai kapu. The translation commonly used for the ending of the kapu in English is "overthrow." This is a good word if used in its "to knock or throw down" sense, or as "to cast down." In Hawaiian the term *ho'ohiolo* does not have the "overturning" (*hulihia*) sense of overthrow that the English word carries. Also, because of the freighted meaning of the term *overthrow* in Hawaiian historiography as being connected to the loss of the kingdom under Lili'uokalani, historians should perhaps revisit the efficacy and deployment of this term in relation to the 'ai kapu. Although the two moments in history are marked by radical governmental transformation and revolution, the tempting telos of Hawaiian historiography that reads the loss of the nation in 1893 back onto the 1820s should be resisted at all costs. For examples of this telos as it surprisingly emerges in the writings of contemporary Hawaiian scholars, see Haunani Kay Trask, *From a Native Daughter: Colonialism and Sovereignty in Hawai'i* (Monroe, ME: Common Courage Press, 1993); Noenoe Silva, *Aloha Betrayed: Native Hawaiian Resistance to American Colonialism* (Durham, NC: Duke University Press, 2004); Jonathan Kay Kamakawiwo'ole Osorio, *Dismembering Lāhui: A History of the Hawaiian Nation to 1887* (Honolulu: University of Hawai'i Press, 2002).

60. I mean sense in terms of logic and thinking, but also intuition and feeling, as an emphasis on sensory and affect.

61. The original phrase Kamakau uses is "He kapu ke kanaka na ke alii." Samuel Mānaiakalani Kamakau, "Ka Moolelo o Kamehameha I," *Ka Nupepa Kuokoa* (Honolulu), September 14, 1867.

62. A much more sophisticated reading of Hawaiian power needs to delve into the genealogies of the chiefs, the kapu that each inherited, and the lands and waters that they had responsibility for.

63. Kamakau, "Ka Moolelo o Kamehameha I," *Ka Nupepa Kuokoa* (Honolulu), February 16, 1867.

64. Rather than this kind of action reflecting a "structure of the conjuncture," as Marshall Sahlins has famously formulated, Hawaiians also had recent memory and a history within which their activities made sense. A more challenging test of this theory will come when a critical mass of anthropologists and historians are capable of reading and interpreting Hawaiian-language source materials as the basis for future scholarship. See Marshall Sahlins, *Islands of History* (Chicago: University of Chicago Press, 1985).

65. The kuhina nui that served the kingdom after Ka'ahumanu's death were all high-ranking chiefly women. These women perhaps wielded power that men could not, being the bridge connecting female and male power. More research needs to be done on the role these female kuhina played in governance and adjudication, in crafting, upholding, and maintaining law in the kingdom. Political anthropologist S. Lee Seaton suggests that kuhina is a Hawaiianization of the English title "queen." The doubling of this signification may have meaningfully struck the ears and consciousness of Hawaiian chiefs and subjects. S. Lee Seaton, "The Hawaiian 'kapu' Abolition of 1819," *American Ethnologist* 1 (February 1974): 196.

66. I'm playing here on the meanings of *malu*: as both shade and protection—that is, a "product" of correct chiefly rule. Malu means shade, protection, shelter, and the placement of kapu, which chiefs provide subjects and akua provided the people.

67. Much has been made in translation and within the literature on the 'ai kapu about the "forbidden" or "off-limits" nature of kapu. I would suggest that another way of understanding kapu as a naturalized practice within Hawaiian society would be to think of kapu as "order," or as imposing "order" or being "orderly." The emphasis on the forbidden nature of the 'ai kapu may have arisen because these interpretations have taken on the primary ideas emphasized by the mission, or other Western interpreters of 'ai kapu as inherently repressive and tyrannical and therefore indicative of a faulty system of governance. According to Samuel Mānaiakalani Kamakau, "The 'ai kapu was a law among the chiefs and people, not because of being put to death for eating things that were kapu, but in order to distinguish between things permissible to people and the things that were sacred to the gods" (my translation). "He kanawai no hoi ka ai kapu i na alii a me na makaainana. aole no ka make i ka ai ana i na mea i hookapu ia, no ka mea, he okoa no na mea i lahui ia, a he okoa no hoi ka mea i laa no ke akua." Samuel Mānaiakalani Kamakau, "Na Hana Kaulana. Ka Pau ana o Na kapu, a me Ka Noa Ana o Ka Ai Kapu," *Ka Nupepa Kuokoa* (Honolulu), October 5, 1867. Kamakau's interpretation, therefore, emphasizes the orderly function of 'ai kapu in society, over and above prohibition or punishment.

68. This kapu was classed as a kapu akua by Kamakau, which he explained in his article, "Na Hana Kaulana. Ka Pau Ana o Na kapu, a me Ka Noa Ana o Ka Ai kapu," *Ka Nupepa Kuookoa* (Honolulu), October 5, 1867. See also "Ka Hoomana Kahiko, Number 29. Na kapu Kahiko o Hawaii Nei, Ke Kumu o Na kapu, Ke kapu o Na Alii," *Ka Nupepa Kuokoa* (Honolulu), November 5, 1865.

69. My emphasis differs from the bias of missionary writings, which claimed that Hawaiians were living without gods or religion. Missionary interpretations of the casting down of 'ai kapu could not be divorced, in their thinking, from their idea of their purpose in the islands. In other words, the actions of Hawaiians were not, for the missionaries, independent of God's plan. However, while the state religious practice of the ali'i in heiau was destroyed, the religious observance of other kinds of religious practice, especially among the maka'āinana, persisted.

70. The shifting between heiau observance in agricultural and fishing temples and ceremonial observance in those dedicated to war, politics, and government demarcated the division between seasons, labor, and religious orientation over the course of every year.

71. Kapu regulating people's access to fish and other foodstuffs were still in force; some of these kapu were even enshrined in the first Hawaiian Constitution of 1840.

72. This phrase would have a particularly profound meaning and resonance to Hawaiians, in relation to the prominence of 'ōlelo (spoken words) in Hawaiian society. It was the

ʻōlelo of the chiefs that constituted the "law" governing society in a society where mana was a vocal point of rule.

73. One traditional example of this orientation to time can be found in Sybil Bingham's letter about the overturning of kapu: God's "piercing eye, surveys things past present and to come as one eternal NOW . . . surely this is the Lord's doing." Sybil Bingham to Misses Atwater and Mosely, November 24, 1816, Bingham Family Papers, Hawaiian Mission Children's Society, Box 2.

74. American Board of Commissioners for Foreign Missions, *Instructions of the Prudential Committee of the American Board of Commissioners for Foreign Missions to the Sandwich Island Mission* (Lahainaluna, HI: Press of the Mission Seminary, 1838) 22.

75. Journal of the Sandwich Islands Mission, March 30, 1820, ABC 19.1.

76. A few titles focusing on missionary wives discuss the role of women in mission. Hawaiians, however, in the Grimshaw text, seem to play a supportive, if not outright incidental, role. See Patricia Grimshaw, *Paths of Duty: American Missionary Wives in Nineteenth-Century America* (Honolulu: University of Hawaiʻi Press, 1989); Mary Zwiep, *Pilgrim Path: The First Company of Women Missionaries in Hawaii* (Madison: University of Wisconsin Press, 1991).

77. Questions arise which will not be resolved here about Kālaimoku's name, which was also rendered quite commonly "Kalanimoku." According to Hiram Bingham, *Kalanimoku* meant "rent heaven." *Moku* means "cut, severed, amputated or broken in two, to cut and divide." *Lani*, or "heaven," is a common epithet for chief. Hiram Bingham, *A Residence of Twenty-One Years in the Sandwich Islands, or The Civil, Religious, and Political History of Those Islands* (Hartford, CT: H. Huntington, 1847), 12.

78. "Philadelphia, February 12," *Providence Gazette and Country Journal*, February 28, 1791.

79. A fanciful, highly fictionalized three-part pantomime depicting the death of Captain James Cook at the hand of the natives of "Owhyee" played to audiences in Europe and America during the late 1790s.

80. Daniel Chamberlain Journal, April 1, 1820, ABC 19.1.

81. The missionaries had recently discussed the matter of the "common stock of property" belonging to the group while aboard the *Thaddeus*. The issue had been raised, and eight rules formally adopted by the mission family dealing with the "business of buying and selling among the Sandwich Islanders." The missionaries were also worried about potential abuses to the "sacred fund" that had been donated by the Christian public for their common use. The serious discussion was probably sparked by the behavior of Dr. Thomas Holman; he and his wife had their own ideas about how they would profit from the services he tendered to other foreigners while residing in the islands. Journal of the Sandwich Islands Mission, March 23, 1820, ABC 19.1.

82. Daniel Chamberlain Journal, April 1, 1820, ABC 19.1.

83. Journal of the Sandwich Islands Mission, April 1, 1820, ABC 19.1.

84. Journal of the Sandwich Islands Mission, April 2, 1820, ABC 19.1; "First Sabbath at the Islands," *Boston Missionary Herald*, April 1821, p.115. Note the passage of time between the date of the letter and its published appearance in the *Missionary Herald*.

85. In Hawaiian, kapu is a state that an object or person inhabits or achieves. Although Bingham reported ruins, Hawaiians who entered the enclosure were not fixated on the

destruction of objects. Stepping within the formerly dedicated space, they were quite literally *hehi*, trampling or "treading," in a place they were not accustomed to entering. The term *hehi* was another way to say a person was flouting or breaking a kapu.

86. Journal of the Sandwich Islands Mission, April 4, 1820, ABC 19.1.

87. John Young was the boatswain of the American ship *Eleanora*, under Capt. Simon Metcalf, which was engaged in the China trade. Young had been taken captive by Kamehameha in 1790 and had become one of his most trusted haole advisers. Young was married to chiefesses of high rank, thereby securing his allegiance and service to the government through family connection.

88. Journal of the Sandwich Islands Mission, April 4, 1820, ABC 19.1.

89. Journal of the Sandwich Islands Mission, April 4, 1820, ABC 19.1.

90. Journal of the Sandwich Islands Mission, April 4, 1820, ABC 19.1.

91. Journal of the Sandwich Islands Mission, April 4, 1820, ABC 19.1.

92. Journal of the Sandwich Islands Mission, April 11, 1820, ABC 19.1; also "Petition to Settle at Woahoo," *Boston Missionary Herald*, April 1821.

93. Journal of the Sandwich Islands Mission, April 11, 1820, ABC 19.1.

94. Cox's Hawaiian name was Keʻeaumoku. He was a brother of Kaʻahumanu and governor of the island of Maui at the time of the mission's arrival.

95. Journal of the Sandwich Islands Mission, April 11, 1820, ABC 19.1. For conventional treatments of the arrival of the missionaries that privilege missionary agency, especially the "energy, tough-mindedness, self-righteousness, and censoriousness of Rev. Bingham," see Gavan Daws, *Honolulu: The First Century: The Story of the Town to 1876* (Honolulu: Mutual Publishing, 2006), 39; also Arrell Morgan Gibson, *Yankees in Paradise: The Pacific Basin Frontier,* completed with the assistance of John S. Whitehead (Albuquerque: University of New Mexico Press, 1993), 272–274. Gibson called Hiram Bingham "physically tough" and of "strong will and acute intellect." Moreover, in Gibson's treatment, Bingham simply "chose Honolulu as the center for the American Board mission."

96. Journal of the Sandwich Islands Mission, April 10, 1820, ABC 19.1; also "Dance of the Natives," *Boston Missionary Herald*, April 1821.

97. "Bingham to Parents, November 27, 1816," *Selected Writings*, 72.

98. Journal of the Sandwich Islands Mission, April 10, 1820, ABC 19.1; *Boston Missionary Herald*, April 1821.

99. The ʻaha ʻōlelo, or chiefly council, has not received much attention by scholars, primarily because of the focus on "great men" like Kamehameha. At this time, the ʻaha was composed of the high chiefs governing each island.

100. Journal of the Sandwich Islands Mission, April 10, 1820, ABC 19.1; also "The Application Formally Made," *Boston Missionary Herald*, April 1821.

101. Journal of the Sandwich Islands Mission, April 10, 1820, ABC 19.1.

102. Journal of the Sandwich Islands Mission, April 12, 1820, ABC 19.1; "First Settlement of the Gospel in Owhyhee," *Boston Missionary Herald*, April 1821.

103. "Mission to the Sandwich Islands Introductory Remarks," *Boston Missionary Herald*, May 1821, p. 129.

104. "Introductory Remarks," *Boston Missionary Herald*, May 1821.

105. Journal of the Sandwich Islands Mission, May 10, 1820, ABC 19.1.

106. Journal of the Sandwich Islands Mission, May 10, 1820, ABC 19.1.

107. Journal of the Sandwich Islands Mission, May 10, 1820, ABC 19.1.

108. Journal of the Sandwich Islands Mission, May 10, 1820, ABC 19.1.

109. Liholiho had requested that Thomas Hopu, Doctor Holman, and his wife, as well as one minister stay in Kona, Hawai'i. Rev. Asa Thurston and his wife Lucy stayed in Kailua, while Rev. Hiram Bingham and his wife Sybil went on to O'ahu.

110. Boki also decided where the houses could be built. The missionaries asked for a particular plot to build upon, but he denied their request, saying that the land belonged to farmers.

111. More scholarship needs to be done to track the American ships involved in various trading efforts in the Pacific during this period.

112. Daniel Chamberlain Journal, October 2, 1820, ABC 19.1.

113. Daniel Chamberlain Journal, October 9, 1820, ABC 19.1.

114. Daniel Chamberlain Journal, April 8, 1820, ABC 19.1.

115. Instructions of the Prudential Committee, 22.

116. Journal of the Sandwich Islands Mission, July 14, 1820, ABC 19.1; "State of the Mission at Kirooah," *Boston Missionary Herald*, June 1821.

117. "Assemblage from Distant Parts of the World," *Boston Missionary Herald*, May 1821.

118. "Assemblage," *Boston Missionary Herald*, May 1821.

119. On drudgery, see "Dedication of the House," *Boston Missionary Herald*, August 1821, p. 246; also "Report of the Prudential Committee," *Boston Missionary Herald*, March 1822, p. 66.

120. "Civilities of Commodore Vassilieff," and "Michael Vassilieff to Rev. Mr. Bingham. Dec. 19, 1821," *Boston Missionary Herald*, February 1823, p. 41. The sum was generous enough that almost a decade later, portions of the donation that had been held in reserve were still being used to purchase timber to build a schoolhouse for educating ali'i and native teachers. "Schools, Training for Native Teachers," *Boston Missionary Herald*, September 1830, p. 281.

121. The *Missionary Herald* of 1821 carried regular updates from the removed mission fields of Bombay, Ceylon, and Palestine. It also carried news of the US missions to Cherokee and Choctaw.

122. Bingham, *A Residence of Twenty-One Years in the Sandwich Islands.*

123. Three of the first five ministers, Hiram Bingham, William Richards, and Asa Thurston, graduated from Andover Theological Seminary, while Charles Stewart and Artemas Bishop graduated from Princeton Theological Seminary.

124. *American Baptist Magazine, and Missionary Intelligencer* (Boston: James Loring, and Lincoln and Edmands, 1823).

125. The charge given at the ordination of Hiram Bingham and Asa Thurston, the first ministers to the Sandwich Islands in 1819, came to a close reinforcing this idea: "We now have consecrated you to God and to the heathen. You are, henceforth, dead to the world, dead to the refinements of civilized society, and the endearments of social ties to the bosom of your native land. Our eyes are shortly to behold you no more!"

126. "Mission to The Sandwich Islands," *American Baptist Magazine, and Missionary Intelligencer* (Boston: James Loring, and Lincoln and Edmands, 1823).

Chapter 4

Note to epigraph: Hoapili to Kaahumanu, October 24, 1827, Non-Missionary Letters, 1820–1900, Hawaiian Mission Children's Society Library, Mission Houses Museum, Honolulu. The verb *ho'okamakama* literally means to make children. The development of this

Hawaiian term to mean the English "prostitution" is part of this historical evolution of Hawaiian law and governance.

1. Hoapili to Kaahumanu, October 24, 1827. Indeed, this is the only written evidence that I have found of the 1825 kapu prohibiting Hawaiian women from visiting ships for the purpose of prostitution. Kapu were not recorded, but written *about*. Foreign writers will note when an activity is "tabued," but the exact words and word order of prohibition were not retrievable to ears and memories untrained in Hawaiian political speech and utterance. The lack of a Hawaiian education made foreign writers suspect, if not outright poor, recorders of Hawaiian political discourse. Future work would continue to study kapu as a phenomenon that continued to operate over the course of the nineteenth century. The historiographic consensus regarding the end of kapu coupled with the inability of most scholars to interpret and place Hawaiian-language sources in historical context have long been obstacles to such work.

2. Another more common variation of this phrase is "ua ʻōlelo ʻia," meaning "it has been said."

3. "Mai loko mai o ka waha"—This phrase, usually glossed as "orally," misses the pedagogy that goes into passing down texts orally. The phrase refers to the passing on of memorized texts, rather than everyday wisdom imparted by elders.

4. Each aliʻi had his or her own messenger or messengers to convey their speech to a targeted audience. Missionaries wrote about messengers who were present for activities or ceremony in place of the aliʻi. See, for example, Clarissa Lyman Richards Journal, March 27, 1823, p. 34, Hawaiian Mission Houses Digital Archives, Typescript; Levi Chamberlain Journal, vol. 4, December 5, 1824–June 26, 1825, May 5, 1825, p. 39, Hawaiian Mission Children's Society Library (HMCSL), Honolulu, Digital Archives, Typescript.

5. ʻAʻapo "ready, one who has the facility to apprehend meaning quickly. One who is fast to learn, memorize, and repeat."

6. See the work of Māori historian Nepia Mahuika, whose dissertation illuminates the appropriative nature of "oral tradition," tracing its emergence as historiographic discursive category and the manner in which it disarticulates the full embodied nature of oral history (*kōrero tuku iho*). In this work, the genealogical, performative, and material aesthetic of Māori oral history changes over time as it moves between speech and print. The complex work of Hawaiian-language professor Hiapo Perreira gives structure to genres of Hawaiian speech and literature, *meiwi moʻokalaleo* (Hawaiian ethnoliterary devices) and *hualekikona* (lexical-terms), through in-depth study of Hawaiian oral-to-text works. See the rich body of work produced by John Charlot on the training of Hawaiian aural-oral intellectuals, and methods of close-reading Hawaiian oral-to-text works. Listening to textual sources recommends an approach that is applicable in any number of historical contexts in places where orality was and is still the primary medium of communication, even as writing is introduced. It is also a way of processing and understanding evidence as not only "content bearing," but also as elevating the importance of form and genre, and identifying hallmarks and oral formulaics in speech that an audience familiar with the Hawaiian language would have been attentive to at the time. Identifying form illuminates the historical context, one in which listeners would hear a phrase and understand that the words to follow were a royal decree. Nepia Mahuika, " 'Kōrero Tuku Iho': Reconfiguring Oral History and Oral Tradition" (PhD diss., University of Waikato, Hamilton, New Zealand, 2012), http://hdl.handle.net/10289/6293; Hiapo Perreira, "He Kiʻina Hoʻokuanaʻike Mauli Hawaiʻi ma ke Kālailai Moʻokalaleo," *Hūlili: Multidisciplinary Research on Hawaiian Well-Being* 9 (2013); John Charlot, *Classical Hawaiian Education:*

Generations of Hawaiian Culture (Lāʻie, HI: Pacific Institute, Brigham Young University, 2005).

7. Scholars might consider studying the relationship between speech, oral performance, and literacy in nineteenth-century Hawaiʻi. Based on the research and writings of John Charlot, kuʻualoha hoʻomanawanui, Kapali Lyon, Hiapo Perreira, Noenoe Silva, and Denise Noelani Arista, it seems clear that reading and writing do not replace the salience of speech in law and politics. Additionally, the way kānaka maoli continue to *haku* (compose) in Hawaiian oral genres late into the century—since these are published in *nūpepa* and manuscripts—also supports this argument of the persistence of speech forms in written and printed texts.

8. For far too long, scholars in Hawaiʻi have written about chiefly rule as tyrannical, despotic, and lacking in process. It is to be hoped that future scholarship can attend to the idea that rule through democracy is not the only historical political formation where deliberation, historical precedent, and consensus play an important role in governance.

9. Levi Chamberlain Journal, vol. 2, October 1, 1823, Hawaiian Mission Children's Society Library, Honolulu, Digital Archives, Typescript.

10. "Sandwich Island Mission—Journal—1819–1825," vol. 6, p. 576, Hawaiian Mission Houses Museum.

11. "He Mau Kanawai no ke ava o Honoruru, Oahu," Broadside Collection, Hawaiian Mission Children's Society Library, Mission Houses Museum, Honolulu.

12. Attending to the nuanced and layered meaning in diplomatic speech and writing illustrates the importance of Hawaiian source material to reshaping methods of reading the encounter between Euro-Americans and indigenous peoples in and between sources in Hawaiian and English.

13. Joseph Goodrich and Samuel Ruggles to Jeremiah Evarts, Corresponding Secretary, April 27, 1824, "Public Journal kept at Waiākea, Hawaiʻi," Joseph Goodrich and Samuel Ruggles to Jeremiah Evarts, Corresponding Secretary, April 27, 1824, Manuscript Collection, Hawaiian Mission Children's Society Library, Mission Houses Museum, Honolulu.

14. "The Sandwich Islands," *Missionary Herald*, vol. 22, 1826, p. 4.

15. Rev. William Richards to Jeremiah Evarts, August 9, 1825, ABC 19.1, American Board of Commissioners for Foreign Missions Pacific Islands Missions Records, 1819–1960, Houghton Library, Harvard University.

16. It is likely that the majority of these teachers were previously educated under kapu in Hawaiian intellectual and religious traditions and therefore were seasoned for further educational instruction.

17. "The Sandwich Islands," *Missionary Herald*, p. 4.

18. Joint Letter of the Mission to Jeremiah Evarts, October 7, 1826, ABCFM-Hawaii Papers, Houghton Library, Harvard University, 1820–1900, Hawaiian Mission Children's Society Library, Mission Houses Museum, Honolulu.

19. Rev. Charles Stewart and Rev. William Richards to Jeremiah Evarts, March 6, 1824, ABCFM-Hawaii Papers.

20. Stewart and Richards to Evarts, March 6, 1824, ABCFM-Hawaii Papers.

21. Richards and Stewart to Evarts, March 31, 1825, ABCFM-Hawaii Papers.

22. Richards and Stewart to Evarts, March 6, 1824, ABCFM-Hawaii Papers.

23. If there was any way that missionary policies interfered directly with Hawaiian politics, it was not over the kapu on prostitution, but the policy of marriage and sexual relations.

On June 28, 1824, an 'aha 'ōlelo was convened to discuss the "propriety" of Kauikeauoli Kamehameha III's marriage to Nāhi'ena'ena, his sister. Missionaries who were present registered their disapproval of the "incestuous" arrangement, although printer Elisha Loomis noted in his journal that "it is well known here that the Prince and Princess, for a considerable time past, have lived in a state of incest." Journal of Elisha Loomis, June 27, 1824, The Journal Collection, 1819–1900, Hawaiian Mission Children's Society Library, Mission Houses Museum, Honolulu. The category of incest has been applied by Euro-American scholars discussing marriage practices among the ali'i, often without explanations mediating against the negative connotations associated with the term in Euro-American Christian context.

24. I am using the word *practice* here to mean routinized and everyday behavior, not in the more politicized presentist sense, which elevates "practice" as traditional, in contradistinction to intellectual pursuits or projects imposed from the outside.

25. Rev. William Richards and Rev. Charles Stewart, Journal of the Lahaina Mission, February 2, 1825, ABC 19.1.

26. Richards and Stewart, Journal of the Lahaina Mission, March 23, 1825.

27. Charles Samuel Stewart, *Journal of a Residence in the Sandwich Islands, During the Years 1823, 1824, and 1825* (London: H. Fisher, Son, and P. Jackson, 1828), 261.

28. Marie Alohalani Brown, *Facing the Spears of Change: The Life and Legacy of John Papa 'Ī'ī* (Honolulu: University of Hawai'i Press, 2016).

29. "Certificates of several persons respecting Captain Buckle's purchasing a mistress to accompany him on a sea voyage," Note of Rev. Richards, November 9, 1827, ABCFM-Hawaii Papers.

30. "Certificates of several persons," Testimony of Namale, November 9, 1827, ABCFM-Hawaii Papers.

31. "Certificates of several persons," Testimony of David Malo, November 9, 1827, ABCFM-Hawaii Papers. Malo's testimony was given in English translation only.

32. "Certificates of several persons," Note of Rev. Richards, November 9, 1827, ABCFM-Hawaii Papers.

33. "Certificates of several persons," Testimony of Nāhi'ena'ena, ABCFM-Hawaii Papers. The exact date that the *Daniel IV* sailed from Lahaina is not clear, as none of the letters mention it.

34. "Certificates of several persons," Testimony of Hoapilikane, ABCFM-Hawaii Papers.

35. "Certificates of several persons," Testimony of David Malo, ABCFM-Hawaii Papers.

36. Alice Te Punga Somerville, *Once Were Pacific: Māori Connections to Oceania* (Minneapolis: University of Minnesota Press, 2012).

37. "Pehea la wau e pono ai i kou wahi" (my translation). The English gloss by Richards reads, "What is it right for me to do?" whereas my translation emphasizes a setting to rights by the actor in order to achieve a pono state. Pono refers to the person's ethical disposition, not simply to correct action. The rest of this testimony is recorded in English only. "Certificates of several persons," Testimony of Taua, ABCFM-Hawaii Papers.

38. "Ka Mana'o o ke ali'i" is another phrase that has a formal life in Hawaiian speech. In 1825, "Ka Manao o Nā Ali'i," the speeches of the ali'i delivered before the people on the subject of Christianity, was published. The title capitalized on the importance of the decisions of the ali'i, especially when rendered formally through speech.

39. "Certificates of several persons," Testimony of Nāhi'ena'ena, ABCFM-Hawaii Papers: "na kuu wahi kahu no, na Leoiki i koi ia mai e ka Haole e Kami Pala e holo pu i wahine

nana." The censure of female attendants by others, which Leoiki surely faced if she defied the will of Wahinepiʻo, could take a heavy toll. When Rev. Richards visited Taua during an illness on February 3, 1825, he found Halekiʻi, one of the favorite attendants of Nāhiʻenaʻena. When Richards asked why the woman was "away from her chief," Taua replied that the people were angry with her because "she did not wail according to their ancient custom at a recent funeral." Halekiʻi had grown tired of the excessive teasing and sought respite at Taua's home. Richards remarked in his journal that the girl was a good pupil and that she had "cast off all habits of immorality and strenuously opposes the evil practices of her associates. . . . They watch her night and day and if she attempts to retire she is so closely followed that she says herself, 'I am almost dead by being watched.' " Rev. Richards to Jeremiah Evarts, November 30, 1825, ABCFM-Hawaii Papers.

40. Richards to Evarts, November 30, 1825, ABCFM-Hawaii Papers.

41. Richards to Evarts, November 30, 1825, ABCFM-Hawaii Papers.

42. "Certificates of several persons," Testimony of Mikahela Kekauonohi, ABCFM-Hawaii Papers: "ua kuai ia mai nei ka o Leoiki e oe I ke kala kula!" I mai o Wahine Pio, "Oia ihola no—ua hewa wau—ua lilo aku ka wahine i ka haole—ua lilo mai ke kala iaʻu." Alaila i mai o Kalaimoku, "ua hewa loa oe—noʻu paha ua nei ka hewa make pu aku kou uhane mamuli o kou hewa." Richards' translation differs from my translation in that he chooses to translate "hewa" as "wicked," whereas I believe that hewa is a state in which other people hold each other accountable. Kālaimoku, unlike his sister Wahinepiʻo, had already begun a process of education and Christian self-introspection, which he hoped would make him an acceptable candidate for church membership.

43. "Certificates of several persons," Testimony of Harieta Nahienaena, ABCFM-Hawaii Papers (my translation).

44. The money was never claimed or spent by any of the chiefs; instead, the doubloons ended up in Rev. Richards' hands by 1827. "Certificates of several persons," Note of Rev. Richards, November 9, 1827, ABCFM-Hawaii Papers.

45. To apply kapu to transient foreigners would also make them subjects of Hawaiian history.

46. Journal of the Sandwich Islands Mission, November 10, 1824, ABC 19.1.

47. "Deposition of Mr. Richards," William Richards to Jeremiah Evarts, August 14, 1829, Sandwich Islands Mission: Letters and Papers, 1823–1830, vol. 2, ABC 19.1.

48. Keʻeaumoku was married to Nāmahana, daughter of Kekaulike, and their children Kaʻahumanu and Kaheiheimālie were two of several chiefly wives of Kamehameha.

49. Samuel Mānaiakalani Kamakau provides the words of Keʻeaumoku's final kauoha: " 'Aʻohe aliʻi e kipi i kō aupuni, hoʻokahi nō naʻe kipi nui o kō aupuni, ʻo kō wahine nō (Kaʻahumanu); a nui kō mālama, ʻaʻole e kipi ʻia kō aupuni." Ke Kumu Aupuni: Ka Moʻolelo Hawaiʻi no Kamehameha Ka Naʻi Aupuni a me kāna aupuni I hoʻokumu ai (Honolulu: ʻAhahui ʻŌlelo Hawaiʻi, 1996).

50. The term poʻolua (two-headed) denoted the offspring of two fathers, whereas punalua (double-spring) referred to persons engaged in sexual relations with more than one partner, as two men with one women, or two women who had sexual relations with the same man; also, wives of brothers or husbands of sisters (with no sexual privileges). Here I have adjusted the dictionary definitions of the term and replaced "husband" and "wife" with "man" or "woman," to lift the Christian bias that favored the idea that sexual relations could only occur

"legitimately" within marriage. The emphasis of the former, poʻolua rests perhaps upon a dual source of genealogy, and lineage, whereas the latter emphasizes sexual relations.

51. Marshall Sahlins suggests that "usurpation is typically marked, either as means or consequence, by the appropriation of the ranking woman of the deposed line: to produce a child not only tabu by mother-right but, as descendant at once of the usurper and the usurped, a child that synthesizes the contrasting qualities of rule, mana and tabu, in the highest form." Marshall David Sahlins, *Historical Metaphors and Mythical Realities: Structure in the Early History of the Sandwich Islands Kingdom* (Ann Arbor: University of Michigan Press, 1981), 12. However, in my formulation, it is the high-ranking aliʻi wahine who is appropriating the mana of the men to add to her alliances.

52. Samuel Mānaiakalani Kamakau, "Ka Moolelo o Kamehameha I: Ke au ia Kamehameha, mai ka A.D. 1797 a hiki i ka A.D. 1811. Kona hoi ana," *Ka Nupepa Kuokoʻa* (Honolulu), July 20, 1867.

53. Noenoe Silva is perhaps the first scholar to point out the politics behind "poetry." *Aloha Betrayed: Native Hawaiian Resistance to American Colonialism* (Durham, NC: Duke University Press, 2004). The sheer number of chants that touch upon the genealogies and lives of these aliʻi published in Hawaiian-language newspapers later in the nineteenth century require more scholarly attention.

54. The movement of oral into printed text requires that we continue to develop approaches and methods to historicize their production and refine our interpretations in order to submit them to rules of evidence that comport with or are consonant with Hawaiian modes of producing and reproducing various genres and their conventions. Scholars cannot assume, for example, that a text published in the mid-nineteenth century was composed at or near the time of its publication. Indeed, a significant number of these published chants in multiple genres were composed and performed (their primary purpose!) much earlier.

55. Don Francisco de Paula Marin Journal, October 17, 1821, in Ross H. Gast, *Don Francisco de Paula Marin: The Letters and Journal of Francisco de Paula Marin*, ed. Agnes C. Conrad (Honolulu: University Press of Hawaiʻi for the Hawaiian Historical Society, 1973).

56. See Sally Engle Merry, *Colonizing Hawaiʻi: The Cultural Power of Law* (Princeton, NJ: Princeton University Press, 2000), 63–76. Merry considers the *kapu law* of 1820s as "religious law" and the "adoption of Anglo-American law" as one process.

57. T. W. Van Metre, G. G. Huebner, and D. S. Hanchett, "The Trade with Non-Contiguous Possessions," *History of Domestic and Foreign Commerce of the United States* (Washington, DC: Carnegie Institution of Washington, 1915), 101–103.

58. Don Francisco de Paula Marin Journal, April 22, August 21, November 1, 1822.

59. "Notice," Mission Press, Oʻahu, March 8, 1822, Broadside Collection, Hawaiian Mission Children's Society Library, Mission Houses Museum, Honolulu.

60. Bryant and Sturgis to Captain Charles Preble, September 29, 1822, Bryant and Sturgis Letterbook, Bryant and Sturgis (Boston, MA) Records v. 10, Baker Library Historical Collections, Harvard Business School.

61. I have not been able to locate a copy of this publication. While it is included in Forbes' *Hawaiian National Bibliography*, Mr. Forbes also notes that he did not see a copy of the handbill. David W. Forbes, *Hawaiian National Bibliography*, vol. 1, *1780–1830* (Honolulu: University of Hawaiʻi Press, 1999), 401.

62. *Missionary Herald*, July 1825, p. 210.

63. *Missionary Herald*, July 1825, p. 210.

64. Spectator [pseud.], "Good Devised," Sandwich Islands Mission, March 31, 1824, Broadside Collection, 1820–1853, Hawaiian Mission Children's Society Library, Mission Houses Museum, Honolulu.

65. "Good Devised," Broadside Collection, HMCSL.

66. "Good Devised," Broadside Collection, HMCSL.

67. "Good Devised," Broadside Collection, HMCSL.

68. "The Suppression of Vice," Mission Press, November 5, 1824, Broadside Collection, Hawaiian Mission Children's Society Library, Mission Houses Museum, Honolulu.

69. "Suppression of Vice," Broadside Collection, HMCSL.

70. "Suppression of Vice," Broadside Collection, HMCSL.

71. "Suppression of Vice," Broadside Collection, HMCSL.

72. "Suppression of Vice," Broadside Collection, HMCSL.

73. "Suppression of Vice," Broadside Collection, HMCSL.

74. "Suppression of Vice," Broadside Collection, HMCSL.

75. "Suppression of Vice," Broadside Collection, HMCSL.

76. "Suppression of Vice," Broadside Collection, HMCSL.

77. Loomis Journal, April 28, 1825, Journal Collection, HMCSL.

78. Loomis Journal, August 6, 1825, Journal Collection, HMCSL.

79. Loomis Journal, April 28, 1825, Journal Collection, HMCSL.

80. Loomis Journal, April 28, 1825, Journal Collection, HMCSL.

81. Levi Chamberlain Journal, April 28, 1825, ABC 19.1.

82. Loomis Journal, April 29, 1825, Journal Collection, HMCSL.

83. Loomis Journal, April 29, 1825, Journal Collection, HMCSL.

84. By order of His Majesty, "Notice," March 8, 1822, Broadside Collection, Hawaiian Mission Children's Society.

85. "He Mau Kanawai no ke ava o Honoruru, Oahu," Broadside Collection, Hawaiian Mission Children's Society Library, Mission Houses Museum, Honolulu.

86. The first published government document was the 1822 "Notice," which was given to missionary printer Elisha Loomis by Liholiho's secretary John Rives on March 8, 1822. "Notice," Broadside Collection, Hawaiian Mission Children's Society Library, Mission Houses Museum, Honolulu.

87. "He Mau Kanawai," Mission Houses Museum.

88. It may be that the oral nature of kapu has confused historians who are unfamiliar with how orally based societies make rules and preserve the peace among their peoples. The assumption that law must be written or published in order to be binding may have contributed to the misapprehension that the mission was the supplier of law to Hawaiians lacking a robust system of regulation since the casting down of the 'ai kapu.

89. The first such rules, published under the name "kānāwai," were promulgated on June 2, 1825, as "He mau kanawai no ke awa Honoruru, Oahu."

90. Kapu would not be incorporated into any published code of laws until the publication of the 1840 constitution and laws. *Ke Kumukānāwai a me nā Kānāwai o ko Hawai'i Pae 'Āina* (Honolulu, O'ahu: s.n., 1841).

91. Levi Chamberlain Journal, December 21, 1823, ABC 19.1; also *Missionary Herald*, vol. 22, 1826, p. 240.

92. Evidence of the strength and persistence of oral tradition can be found in the voluminous pages of Hawaiian newspapers, as Hawaiian writers from many different backgrounds published stories, histories, chants, prayers, and genealogies that had been preserved and passed down over the centuries. The persistent publication over the course of the nineteenth century of orally performed genres of chant also point to the richness of Hawaiian oral tradition and innovation.

93. Eliab Grimes to Josiah Marshall, June 7, 1825, Josiah Marshall Letters and Accounts, MS AmW 63, Houghton Library, Harvard University.

94. Captain Rutter to Josiah Marshall, August 16, 1825, MS AmW 63. This contention of the decline of the Hawaiian labor force as missionary induced worsened over the following year. John C. Jones, agent for Marshall and Wildes and the US consul in the islands, wrote, "All business, all occupations, all labour, all amusement, have ceased and religion the most absurd and unreasonable stalks throughout this land, spreading desolation and misery. . . . Nothing but the sound of the church going bell is heard from the rising to the setting sun, and religion is cramm'd down the throats of these poor simple mortals whilst certain famine and destruction are staring them in the face . . . their conduct is infamous, degrading and revolting to any sense of right and justice." John C. Jones to Josiah Marshall, August 16, 1825, MS AmW 63.

95. Richards to Evarts, August 14, 1829, ABCFM-Hawaii Papers.

96. Richards to Evarts, November 30, 1825, ABCFM-Hawaii Papers.

97. "Instructions of the Prudential Committee of the ABCFM to the Rev. Hiram Bingham and the Rev. Asa Thurston, Messrs. Daniel Chamberlain, Thomas Holman, Samuel Whitney, Samuel Ruggles, Elisha Loomis, John Honolii, Thomas Hopu, and William Kanui, of the Mission to the Sandwich Islands," *Instructions of the Prudential Committee of the American Board of Commissioners for Foreign Missions to the Sandwich Islands Mission* (Lahainaluna, HI: Press of the Mission Seminary, 1838).

98. In a letter to Corresponding Secretary Jeremiah Evarts, Richards had been informed "in the autumn of 1825" by the chiefs of Maui that "there had been a tabu laid, prohibiting females from visiting ships for the purpose of prostitution." Richards claimed that he "did not know whether the tabu existed on the other islands or not." Richards to Evarts, August 14, 1829, ABCFM-Hawaii Papers.

99. Richards to Evarts, November 30, 1825, ABCFM-Hawaii Papers.

100. Richards to Evarts, November 30, 1825, ABCFM-Hawaii Papers.

101. Richards to Evarts, November 30, 1825, ABCFM-Hawaii Papers.

102. Richards to Evarts, November 30, 1825, ABCFM-Hawaii Papers.

103. Richards to Evarts, November 30, 1825, ABCFM-Hawaii Papers.

104. Richards to Evarts, November 30, 1825, ABCFM-Hawaii Papers.

105. Richards to Evarts, November 30, 1825, ABCFM-Hawaii Papers.

106. Richards to Evarts, November 30, 1825, ABCFM-Hawaii Papers.

107. Richards to Evarts, November 30, 1825, ABCFM-Hawaii Papers.

108. Loomis Journal, October 11, 1825, Journal Collection, HMCSL.

109. Loomis Journal, October 11, 1825, Journal Collection, HMCSL.

110. Loomis Journal, October 11, 1825, Journal Collection, HMCSL; also Richards to Evarts, November 30, 1825, ABCFM-Hawaii Papers.

111. Richards to Evarts, November 30, 1825, ABCFM-Hawaii Papers.

112. Loomis Journal, October 11, 1825, Journal Collection, HMCSL.

113. The journal of Elisha Loomis for the same day provides an alternative wording of what the sailors said, albeit within the same spirit: "The sailors insisted that they must have their girls and would seize and carry them off by force." Loomis Journal, October 4, 1825, Journal Collection, HMCSL.

114. Levi Chamberlain Journal, October 4, 1825, ABC 19.1.

115. The missionaries settled on Honolulu, Oʻahu, benefited from the presence of the highest-ranking ruling chiefs in the islands, Kaʻahumanu and Kālaimoku, whose word could quickly mobilize an armed native populace.

116. Don Francisco de Paula Marin Journal, October 19, 1825.

117. Loomis Journal, October 25, 1825, Journal Collection, HMCSL.

118. Of course, since kapu has not been extensively studied by scholars as "precedent," it is difficult to determine if this was the first time foreigners revolted against Hawaiian rule.

Chapter 5

1. Kapu were imposed (*kau*) and removed (*hemo*). When kapu was removed, which was the general state or nature of things, the context was transformed intrinsically in some way from kapu to noa. When a kapu was ended, it was also appropriate to say "pau ke kapu," or "the kapu is ended." The very nature of kapu as legal construct was temporary, not permanent. Rather than focusing upon "impermanence" as a site of weakness, however, it is the flexibility of restrictions and the nature of kapu to be directly responsive to context that should be considered in terms other than "strength" or "weakness" and not, yet again, in distinction to legal formations or constructions from the West, which always seek to legitimate the Western as normative and therefore inevitable. For the phrase "Noa ke Kapu" see "Ka Moolelo Kaao o Hiiaka-i-ka-Poli-o-Pele," *Kuokoa Home Rula* (Honolulu), March 11, 1910.

2. Models for legal transformation in Hawaiʻi are wanting or simplistic, relying on binary arguments of "missionary influence" or "agency" rather than focusing on chiefly governing strategies, the work of chiefly counselors, modes of deliberation, and social institutions for ordering behavior. Sally Engle Merry, *Colonizing Hawaiʻi: The Cultural Power of Law* (Princeton, NJ: Princeton University Press, 2000).

3. Religion scholar John Charlot has written extensively on the pedagogy of training experts, the oral/aural dissemination of knowledge, and the significance of specific turns of phrase in Hawaiian speech. See John Charlot, *Classical Hawaiian Education: Generations of Hawaiian Culture* (Lāʻie, HI: Pacific Institute, Brigham Young University, 2005).

4. One of the main reasons for this oversight on the part of historians stems from the categories of comparison that they have traditionally employed to discuss this period. Historians tend to distinguish between three groups—chiefs, missionaries, and merchants—without going into further detail regarding governing structures among Hawaiians. Ralph Kuykendall is one of the few historians who has mentioned the council of chiefs, but he does not write about the inner workings of the ʻaha ʻōlelo, its composition, the frequency with which it met, or the manner in which it deliberated. Sally Engle Merry, who has written about the imposition of Western law in Hawaiʻi, does not touch upon the existence of the ʻaha ʻōlelo at all in her work. Kuykendall, *The Hawaiian Kingdom 1778–1854*, vol. 1 (Honolulu: University of Hawaiʻi Press, 1980); Merry, *Colonizing Hawaiʻi: The Cultural Power of Law* (Princeton, NJ: Princeton University Press, 2000). The following standard books consulted on this period

also overlook the significance of the ʻaha ʻōlelo entirely: Harold Whitman Bradley, *The American Frontier in Hawaiʻi: The Pioneers, 1789–1843* (Stanford, CA: Stanford University Press, 1942); Gavan Daws, *Shoal of Time: A History of the Hawaiian Islands* (New York: Macmillan, 1968); Daws, *Honolulu: The First Century: The Story of the Town to 1876* (Honolulu: Mutual Publishing, 2006); Jonathan Kay Kamakawiwoʻole Osorio mentions the ʻaha ʻōlelo in his book but does not go into depth regarding its significance during this period. Osorio, *Dismembering Lāhui: A History of the Hawaiian Nation to 1887* (Honolulu: University of Hawaiʻi Press, 2002).

5. "January 17, 19, 1826," in *Journal of Stephen Reynolds*, ed. Pauline N. King (Honolulu: Ku Paʻa, 1989).

6. Journal of Stephen Reynolds, January 24, 1826.

7. Journal of Elisha Loomis, January 27, 1826, The Journal Collection, 1819–1900, Hawaiian Mission Children's Society Library (HMCSL), Mission Houses Museum, Honolulu.

8. Loomis Journal, February 1, 1826, Journal Collection, HMCSL. What was perhaps more shocking was the revelation later that day from a Hawaiian teacher who informed Loomis that "Capt. P. Had applied to a girl" in Loomis' school to "live with him."

9. Journal of Stephen Reynolds, February 20, 1826.

10. Loomis Journal, February 21, 1826, Journal Collection, HMCSL.

11. The extract from a letter by Rev. Mr. Richards that not only the crew were guilty, but that the captain of the *Dolphin* was an instigator and accessory in this outrage. N. Whiting, "Late Outrage at the Sandwich Islands," *Religious Intelligencer* (New Haven, CT), January 6, 1827.

12. Loomis Journal, February 21, 1826, Journal Collection, HMCSL.

13. Loomis Journal, February 21, 1826, Journal Collection, HMCSL.

14. Loomis Journal, February 21, 1826, Journal Collection, HMCSL.

15. Journal of Stephen Reynolds, February 21, 1826.

16. Loomis Journal, February 21, 1826, Journal Collection, HMCSL.

17. Journal of Stephen Reynolds, February 21, 1826.

18. In Hawaiian, the name *Honolulu* literally means calm bay or harbor. Levi Chamberlain Journal, February 22, 1826, The Journal Collection, 1819–1900, Hawaiian Mission Children's Society Library, Mission Houses Museum, Honolulu.

19. Loomis Journal, February 22, 1826, Journal Collection, HMCSL.

20. Loomis Journal, February 22, 1826, Journal Collection, HMCSL.

21. Loomis Journal, February 21, 1826, Journal Collection, HMCSL.

22. Chamberlain Journal, February 21, 1826, Journal Collection, HMCSL.

23. Loomis Journal, February 21, 1826, Journal Collection, HMCSL.

24. The unnamed chief in this excerpt is probably Kaʻahumanu.

25. Loomis Journal, February 21, 1826, Journal Collection, HMCSL.

26. N. Whiting, "Late Outrage at the Sandwich Islands," *Religious Intelligencer* (New Haven, CT), January 6, 1827.

27. Whiting, "Late Outrage," *Religious Intelligencer*.

28. Whiting, "Late Outrage," *Religious Intelligencer*.

29. It is going to take a lot of work to sift through precontact moʻolelo, chants, missionary records, and legal documents and to build a compendium of kapu to identify precedent and delve deeper into its construction. The Hawaiian-language textual archive transforms the nature of our work, shifting our focus from paradigms, "historical metaphors," and "structures of conjuncture" to consider the words spoken and subsequently written and published by Hawaiians *and* foreigners as empirical evidence.

30. D [pseud.], "Extract of a letter from Mrs. Bingham to a friend in Springfield, Mass. dated Oahu March 1, 1826, giving an acount of the late shameful outrage by the crew of the Dolphin, an American vessel," *Religious Intelligencer* (New Haven, CT), December 23, 1826, p. 466.

31. Loomis Journal, February 24, 1826, Journal Collection, HMCSL.

32. "Letter Extract from Richards," *Religious Intelligencer* (New Haven, CT), January 6, 1827.

33. "Extract of a letter from Mrs. Bingham," *Religious Intelligencer* (New Haven, CT), December 23, 1826, p. 466.

34. "Extract of a letter from Mrs. Bingham," *Religious Intelligencer*.

35. Loomis Journal, February 27, 1826, Journal Collection, HMCSL.

36. Loomis Journal, February 27, 1826, Journal Collection HMCSL; "Extract of a letter from Mrs. Bingham," *Religious Intelligencer* (New Haven, CT), December 23, 1826, p. 466.

37. Loomis Journal, February 26, 1826, Journal Collection, HMCSL.

38. Loomis Journal, February 26, 1826, Journal Collection, HMCSL.

39. Loomis Journal, February 26, 1826, Journal Collection, HMCSL.

40. Chamberlain Journal, October 22, 1827, Journal Collection, HMCSL.

41. Chamberlain Journal, February 28, 1826, Journal Collection, HMCSL.

42. Loomis Journal, February 28, 1826, Journal Collection, HMCSL.

43. Journal of Stephen Reynolds, March 13, 1826.

44. Journal of Stephen Reynolds, March 6, 12, 16, 18, 1826.

45. Journal of Stephen Reynolds, March 19, 1826.

46. Journal of Stephen Reynolds, March 20, 1826.

47. The sensational eroticization of Hawaiian women's bodies and behavior from the first fifty years of contact (1778–1828) that has been accepted as "true" makes the refusal of sex or sexualization in more recent times legitimate grounds for denativizing Hawaiian people, necessitating further inquiry.

48. Chamberlain Journal, April 1, 1826, Journal Collection, HMCSL.

49. Loomis Journal, February 21, 1826, Journal Collection, HMCSL.

50. Loomis Journal, February 21, 1826, Journal Collection, HMCSL.

51. Chamberlain Journal, March 11, 1826, Journal Collection, HMCSL.

52. *Religious Intelligencer* (New Haven, CT), December 23, 1826.

53. Chamberlain Journal, April 1, 1826, Journal Collection, HMCSL.

54. Journal kept at Lahaina, Maui, by William Richards, June 13, 1826, The Journal Collection, 1819–1900, Hawaiian Mission Children's Society Library, Mission Houses Museum, Honolulu.

55. Journal kept at Lahaina, Maui, by William Richards, June 13, 1826.

56. Journal kept at Lahaina, Maui, by William Richards, June 13, 1826.

57. Journal kept at Lahaina, Maui, by William Richards, June 13, 1826.

58. Perhaps it is also best to consider Hawaiian legality in its own historical context, since without this we cannot begin to understand the foundations upon which Hawaiian precedents were constructed. Kapu as a juridical category has been interpreted according to Euro-American legal structures, which are usually assumed to be superior regardless of historical context, precedent, or application. Because it has always been assumed that kapu post-1819 is nonexistent, here again it is necessary to suggest a place where reading broadly in English-

and Hawaiian-language sources to craft a taxonomy of kapu would be useful. A research approach to rebuild the fabric of ontology and epistemology up from sources, in order to understand text, we need to build contexts.

59. David Malo to Mr. and Mrs. Elisha Loomis, December 11, 1827, Missionary Letters, 1820–1900, Hawaiian Mission Children's Society Library, Mission Houses Museum, Honolulu.

60. Hoapili to Ka'ahumanu, October 24, 1827, Non-Missionary Letters, HMCSL. "A holo malu iho nei ka wahine e hookamakama o Nkoko a me Mikapako, aole au i ike i ka inoa o kahi mau wahine" (Several women went off secretly for the purpose of prostitution, Nakoko and Mikapako I do not know the names of some of the women) (my translation). *Ho'okama-kama* literally means "to act as if to cause children."

61. Hoapili to Ka'ahumanu, October 24, 1827, Non-Missionary Letters, HMCSL. "alaila nonoi aku au i ke alii moku ia Kapena Kalaka e hoihoi mai i ka wahine, aole e ae mai, hoomaewa ia mai kou olelo" (Then I asked the commander of the ship, Captain Clark to return the women, he did not consent, instead ridiculed my words) (my translation).

62. Hoapili to Ka'ahumanu, October 24, 1827, Non-Missionary Letters, HMCSL. "E hana wale no oukou, aole e pono, aole pela Pelekane, aole no oukou e pono ka aua i ka wahine i ka Pelekane: o ka wahine no i hele ma ka hewa mai aua oukou o hiki mai ka manuwa pau loa oukou i ka luku" (my translation). The English translation for the last phrase reads, "a man of war will come and destroy you all." According to Rev. William Richards' account, Hoapili had demanded "for three days" that the women be returned. Richards to Evarts, December 6, 1827, ABCFM-Hawaii Papers, Houghton Library, Harvard University, 1820–1900, Hawaiian Mission Children's Society Library, Mission Houses Museum, Honolulu.

63. Hoapili to Ka'ahumanu, October 24, 1827, Non-Missionary Letters, HMCSL.

64. Hoapili to Ka'ahumanu, October 24, 1827, Non-Missionary Letters, HMCSL. "Piha loa keia aina i ka moku, noa Maui nei, o wela loa, aohe kauhale. Ua makaukau kuu mokku e kii mai ia oukou I keia po."

65. Hoapili to Ka'ahumanu, October 24, 1827, Non-Missionary Letters, HMCSL (my translation). Historians writing about these years of outrage have never published the words of these ali'i in their assessment of these events, even if they have drawn upon the translated sources to inform their work. Juri Mykannen, *Inventing Politics: A New Political Anthropology of the Hawaiian Kingdom* (Honolulu: University of Hawai'i Press, 2003). Emphasis added.

66. Hoapili to Ka'ahumanu, October 24, 1827, Non-Missionary Letters, HMCSL.

67. Richards to ABCFM, December 6, 1827, ABCFM-Hawaii Papers. Emphasis added.

68. Richards to ABCFM, December 6, 1827, ABCFM-Hawaii Papers.

69. Richards to ABCFM, December 6, 1827, ABCFM-Hawaii Papers. His letter is a long report that Richards compiled for the ABCFM regarding the attack, which constituted the third "outrage" against the missionaries that began on October 23, 1827. In his letter, Richards includes copies of letters he wrote and those he received from Levi Chamberlain, Richard Charlton, and Captain William Buckle.

70. None of the three different accounts of this outrage, Hoapili's, Malo's, or Richards', provides any information about which of the Maui chiefs were present at this meeting. Because their names are omitted from the correspondence, Boki and Ka'ahumanu were not present, and Kālaimoku had passed away in February of this year. Had Boki or Ka'ahumanu been in Lahaina, they would have figured largely into the accounts of what had transpired.

71. Hoapili to Ka'ahumanu, October 24, 1827, Non-Missionary Letters, HMCSL. "Uwaoia makou e Mika Rikeke." The English translation provided reads, "We were persuaded to yield by Rev. Richards." *'Uwao*, however, has more of the sense of reconciliation, intercession, and arbitration, indicating the participation of more than one party, whereas the English translation emphasizes Richards' persuasion of Hoapili and the chiefs only.

72. Richards to Chamberlain, September 18, 1827, Missionary Letters, HMCSL.

73. Richards to Chamberlain, September 18, 1827, Missionary Letters, HMCSL.

74. Richards to Chamberlain, September 18, 1827, Missionary Letters, HMCSL. "Club Law: the use of the club to enforce obedience; physical force as contrasted with argument; law or rule of the physically stronger," *Oxford English Dictionary*, 2nd Edition (Oxford: Oxford University Press, 1989), s.v. "Club Law."

75. Richards to Chamberlain, September 18, 1827, Missionary Letters, HMCSL.

76. Richards to Chamberlain, September 18, 1827, Missionary Letters, HMCSL.

77. See Jeremiah Evarts to Levi Chamberlain, June 11, 1827, ABCFM-HEA Papers, 1820–1920, Hawaiian Mission Children's Society Library, Mission Houses Museum, Honolulu. "I should say here that all the exposures, which we have made hitherto, of the outrages at the islands, have been made after much deliberation and the most entire conviction that they ought not to be longer withheld from the public eye. . . . Such exposures the Committee are determined to make in case nothing else will ensure the better behavior of such others as visit and dwell at the islands."

78. Richards to Evarts, December 6, 1827, ABCFM-Hawaii Papers.

79. Richards to Evarts, December 6, 1827, ABCFM-Hawaii Papers. The name of the newspaper is never mentioned in any of the sources.

80. Richards to Evarts, December 6, 1827, ABCFM-Hawaii Papers.

81. Richards to Evarts, December 6, 1827, ABCFM-Hawaii Papers.

82. Richards to Evarts, December 6, 1827, ABCFM-Hawaii Papers.

83. Richards to Evarts, December 6, 1827, ABCFM-Hawaii Papers.

84. Richards to Evarts, December 6, 1827, ABCFM-Hawaii Papers.

85. Richards to Evarts, December 6, 1827, ABCFM-Hawaii Papers. Chamberlain Journal, October 27, 1827, Journal Collection, HMCSL.

86. Richards to ABCFM, December 6, 1827, ABCFM-Hawaii Papers; Chamberlain Journal, October 27, 1827, Journal Collection, HMCSL.

87. Elisha Loomis to Jeremiah Evarts, August 7, 1827, Missionary Letters, HMCSL.

88. Elisha Loomis to Jeremiah Evarts, August 7, 1827, Missionary Letters, HMCSL.

89. Malo to Loomis, December 11, 1827, ABCFM-Hawaii Papers.

90. Malo to Loomis, December 11, 1827, ABCFM-Hawaii Papers.

91. Malo to Loomis, December 11, 1827, ABCFM-Hawaii Papers.

92. Chamberlain Journal, October 27, 1827, Journal Collection, HMCSL; Malo to Loomis, December 11, 1827, ABCFM-Hawaii Papers.

93. Chamberlain Journal, November 2, 1827, Journal Collection, HMCSL.

94. *Mā* is a word that is indicative of the group of persons always known to frequent the company of a particular chief. Making up the retinue of each ali'i would be other minor ali'i from that island, those connected by marriage, or those adopted into a chiefly family. It might also include some of the members of a chief's alo ali'i.

95. Chamberlain Journal, November 3, 1827, Journal Collection, HMCSL.

96. Richards to Chamberlain, September 18, 1827, Missionary Letters, HMCSL.

97. Richards to Chamberlain, September 18, 1827, Missionary Letters, HMCSL.

98. Richard Charlton to William Richards, November 13, 1827, in William Richards to Jeremiah Evarts, December 6, 1827, ABCFM-Hawaii Papers. See also Chamberlain Journal, November 2, 1827, Journal Collection, HMCSL.

99. Charlton to Richards, November 13, 1827, in Richards to Evarts, December 6, 1827, ABCFM-Hawaii Papers.

100. Richards to Charlton, November 14, 1827, included in Richards to ABCFM, December 6, 1827, ABCFM-Hawaii Papers.

101. Richards to Charlton, November 14, 1827, included in Richards to ABCFM, December 6, 1827, ABCFM-Hawaii Papers.

102. Charlton to Richards, November 14, 1827, in Richards to Evarts, December 6, 1827, ABCFM-Hawaii Papers.

103. Richards to Charlton, November 15, 1827, in Richards to Evarts, December 6, 1827, ABCFM-Hawaii Papers.

104. Richards to Evarts, December 6, 1827, ABCFM-Hawaii Papers.

105. "November 6, 1827," *Journal of Stephen Reynolds*, ed. Pauline N. King (Honolulu: Ku Pa'a, 1989).

106. Samuel Mānaiakalani Kamakau, *Ke Aupuni Mo'i* (Honolulu: Kamehameha Schools Press, 2001), 40.

107. "E ko Maui mau ali'i, aloha 'oukou. Inā e ki'i aku 'o Kāpena Bākala, Kāpena Kalaka a me kanikela Beritania I ke kumu a 'oukou 'ea, e mālama 'oukou iā 'oukou iho, a mai 'au'a 'oukou i ke kumu 'oukou, e ho'oku'u mai nō, he haole nō, he haole namu, na lākou nō ia e hana, aia ko 'oukou hewa 'o ka 'uao wale aku iā lākou." Kamakau, *Ke Aupuni Mō'ī*, 40.

108. *Ki'i* "to seek for sexual ends." The translators of *Ruling Chiefs* suggest that Ka'ahumanu was compelled by force to sleep with Kanihonui. Samuel M. Kamaku, *Ruling Chiefs of Hawai'i,* (Honolulu: Kamehameha Schools Press, 1961); however, sexual liaisons between older chiefly women and younger generations of men were a Hawaiian cultural norm.

109. "Ma nā 'āina hea o ka honua nei i ho'āhewa 'ia ai ka mea ha'i a ho'āpono 'ia ka mea hana hewa?" Kamakau, *Ke Aupuni Mō'ī*.

110. "No ke aha lā e ho'āhewa 'ia ai 'o Mr. Rikeke, ka mea ha'i a e ho'āpono 'ia ai ho'i 'o Kapena Bakala, ka mea nāna i hana hewa aku iā Mr. Rikeke?" Kamakau, *Ke Aupuni Mō'ī*. It is worth it to note here that although Richards wrote a letter, Malo in this account is portrayed as having used the word *ha'i*, spoke, emphasizing speech over the medium of writing.

111. Richards to Evarts, December 6, 1827, ABCFM-Hawaii Papers.

112. Richards to Evarts, December 6, 1827, ABCFM-Hawaii Papers.

113. Richards to Evarts, December 6, 1827, ABCFM-Hawaii Papers.

114. Richards to Evarts, December 6, 1827, ABCFM-Hawaii Papers.

115. Richards to Evarts, December 6, 1827, ABCFM-Hawaii Papers.

116. Richards to Evarts, December 6, 1827, ABCFM-Hawaii Papers. This may have been true of Hoapili, but there were other high chiefs like Kuakini, the ali'i governor of Hawai'i, who were fluent speakers of English and could read and write.

117. Richards to Evarts, December 6, 1827, ABCFM-Hawaii Papers. It is unclear who attended this 'aha 'ōlelo, as none of the sources provide names, save for proof of their individual attendance. Stephen Reynolds notes on that day that he "went with many others up to the

Chiefs, to hear Mr. Richards make his defence. He did not make his appearance till many of the Chiefs were gone." Journal of Stephen Reynolds, November 26, 1827.

118. Richards to Evarts, December 6, 1827, ABCFM-Hawaii Papers.

119. Richards to Evarts, December 6, 1827, ABCFM-Hawaii Papers.

120. Richards to Evarts, December 6, 1827, ABCFM-Hawaii Papers.

121. Richards to Evarts, December 6, 1827, ABCFM-Hawaii Papers.

122. Richards to Evarts, December 6, 1827, ABCFM-Hawaii Papers.

123. Richards to Evarts, December 6, 1827, ABCFM-Hawaii Papers.

124. Richards to Evarts, December 6, 1827, ABCFM-Hawaii Papers.

125. Richards to Evarts, December 6, 1827, ABCFM-Hawaii Papers.

126. Richards to Evarts, December 6, 1827, ABCFM-Hawaii Papers.

127. Richards to Evarts, December 6, 1827, ABCFM-Hawaii Papers.

128. Richards to Evarts, December 6, 1827, ABCFM-Hawaii Papers. Emphasis added.

129. William Richards to Captain William Buckle, November 27, 1827, included in Richards to Evarts, December 7, 1827, ABCFM-Hawaii Papers.

130. Richards to Buckle, November 27, 1827, included in Richards to Evarts, December 7, 1827, ABCFM-Hawaii Papers.

131. Buckle to Richards, November 28, 1827, in Richards to Evarts, December 7, 1827, ABCFM-Hawaii Papers.

132. Buckle to Richards, November 28, 1827, in Richards to Evarts, December 7, 1827, ABCFM-Hawaii Papers.

133. Buckle to Richards, November 28, 1827, in Richards to Evarts, December 7, 1827, ABCFM-Hawaii Papers.

134. Buckle to Richards, November 28, 1827, in Richards to Evarts, December 7, 1827, ABCFM-Hawaii Papers.

135. Richards to Evarts, December 7, 1827, ABCFM-Hawaii Papers.

136. Chamberlain Journal, December 1, 1827, Journal Collection, HMCSL.

137. Chamberlain Journal, December 7, 1827, Journal Collection, HMCSL.

138. Chamberlain Journal, December 7, 1827, Journal Collection, HMCSL.

139. Chamberlain Journal, December 8, 1827, Journal Collection, HMCSL.

140. Richards to Evarts, December 7, 1827, ABCFM-Hawaii Papers.

141. Chamberlain Journal, December 8, 1827, Journal Collection, HMCSL.

142. Chamberlain Journal, December 8, 1827, Journal Collection, HMCSL.

143. Chamberlain Journal, December 8, 1827, Journal Collection, HMCSL.

144. Chamberlain Journal, December 8, 1827, Journal Collection, HMCSL.

145. Chamberlain Journal, December 8, 1827, Journal Collection, HMCSL.

146. King Kauikeaouli, "He Olelo no ke Kanawai," December 8, 1827, Broadside Collection, HMCSL (my translation).

147. "He Olelo no ke Kanawai," Broadside Collection, HMCSL.

148. Chamberlain Journal, December 14, 1827, Journal Collection, HMCSL.

149. David Malo to Mr. and Mrs. Loomis, December 11, 1827, ABCFM-Hawaii Papers, Houghton Library, Harvard, 1820–1900. This letter exists only in translation and is located in the missionary journals collection. Malo's original Hawaiian-language letter has not been found.

Afterword

1. "It is not my desire however to have it [his association with the board] dissolved at the present juncture, when it appears to me there is uncommon necessity for unity of action, not only in missionaries, but in all the friends of missionary freedom. My firm conviction is that there are weighty reasons, reasons far more weighty than there have been at any previous period for continuing my connection with the Board." William Richards, "Report to the Sandwich Islands Mission," May 1, 1839, Hawaiian Mission Children's Society Library, Mission Houses Museum, Honolulu.

2. "June 4th to 20th, 1838," *The Revised Minutes of the Delegate Meeting of the Sandwich Islands Mission* (Honolulu: Mission Press, 1839), 7.

3. Richards, "Report," May 1, 1839.

4. Richards, "Report," May 1, 1839.

5. Richards, "Report," May 1, 1839.

6. Richards, "Report," May 1, 1839. Emphasis added.

7. Davida Malo to Kaahumanu II and Mataio, August 18, 1837, Series 402 (Chronological File), FO & Ex, Hawai'i State Archives, Honolulu. Emphasis added.

8. Malo to Kaahumanu II and Mataio, August 18, 1837.

9. In Ralph Kuykendall's translation (*The Hawaiian Kingdom 1778–1854* [Honolulu: University of Hawai'i Press, 1980], 1:153) of the passage, he uses "great nation" where I have used "large" to match the parallel construction above it, referring to the size of the fishes, and not their eminence.

10. Iosepa Keohokaua, "Ka Moolelo no Davida Malo," *Ka Elele Hawaii* (Honolulu), May 15, 1854.

11. For details on how the "system of laws" was written and Richards' thoughts on the process, see Richards, "Report," May 1, 1839.

12. General Records—Journals and Minutes Records of the Legislature 222–2, May 8, 1845, Hawai'i State Archives, Honolulu.

Appendix

1. Nogelmeier, *Mai Pa'a i Ka Leo: Historical Voice in Hawaiian Primary Materials, Looking Forward and Listening Back* (Honolulu: Bishop Museum Press, 2010), 2, 96.

INDEX

Numbers in italics refer to figures.

"heathens," 54, 57, 75, 81, 128; conversion of, 95; education of, 58, 61, 63; Hawaiians compared to heathens in the Bible, 114; influence of ship captains and sailors on, 158; missionary project and, 171; as problematic term, 254n5; sexual intercourse with, 163

heiau (temples), 16, 104, 107; destruction of, 108–109; marae ("moraeah") as variant, 102, 105, 262n45; of Puʻukohola, 114, 115

helu genre/practice, 15

"He Mau kānāwai no e ava Honoruru, Oahu" [Regulations for the Port of Honolulu, Oʻahu] (Kālaimoku, 1825), 165, 166, 167–168

hewa (transgression), 139, 148, 149, 194, 195, 271n42

historiography, 121, 126; "canon" texts of, 6, 244n9; colonial, 245n11; "fatal impact" thesis, 7; focus on social decline and degeneration, 251n33; languages and, 8, 12; "missionary influence" thesis, 86, 137, 245n19, 275n2; telos of "overthrow," 263n59

history, 6, 8, 11, 92; Captain Cook's "discovery" and, 4, 5; genealogies and, 15, 17, 27; missionary narratives and, 73, 86; newspapers and, 89; between orality and writing, 10, 13; spoken word and, 87. See also moʻolelo

Hoapili, 143, 144, 149, 203; "affair of the haole" council and, 209–211; John Palmer "outrage" and, 194–199, 206, 215; on Leoiki's "purchase," 211; letter to Kaʻahumanu, 133, 134–135; mā (retinue) of, 204

Holman, Dr. Thomas, 118, 265n81, 267n109

Holmes, Oliver, 164

Holmes, Polly, 164, 165

Honoliʻi (Honoree), John, 56, 60, 69, 102; ABCFM promotional narrative about, 62; conversion narrative of, 65–66; at Park Street Church, 98; return to Hawaii, 80; on US merchant ships, 61

Honolulu, 120–121, 126, 140, 170; merchant agents stationed at, 26; "outrages" by sailors in, 173–174; printing press set up in (1822), 114–115; whaleships visiting, 156. See also Dolphin, USS, "outrage" by sailors of

"Honourable Munificence" (article, 1816), 62–64

Hopu (Hopoo), Thomas, 56, 57, 60, 77; ABCFM promotional narrative about, 62; conversion narrative of, 63, 65; introduction to Liholiho, 115; in Kona, 267n109; ʻŌpūkahaʻia's death and, 76; in pulpit of Park Street Church, 97–98; as replacement for ʻŌpūkahaʻia, 97; return to Hawaii, 80, 99–100, 102; as translator, 115; on US merchant ships, 61

human sacrifice, 53, 94, 104, 114

Humphrey, Rev. Heman, 79–83

Hunnewell, James, 102

hurahura (hula) dancing, 144, 145

Hydaspe (ship), 161–163

"idolatry," 103, 104, 105, 144

ʻĪʻī, John Papa, 145

imperialism, 52

India, 94, 97

Indians, American, 61, 81, 82; Cherokee, 97, 267n121; Choctaw, 97, 267n121; Hawaiians compared to, 114; Protestant evangelizing of, 91, 94; Wampanoag, 95, 116

Ingraham, Captain Joseph, 53

J. and T. H. Perkins (Boston firm), 23

John Palmer (English whaleship), "outrage" by, 194–206, 215, 278nn69–70

Jones, John C., 31–32, 38, 250n19, 251n27; concern for reputation with employers, 50, 254n76; on Hawaiians civilized through trade, 33–34; on Kaumualiʻi as chiefly customer, 43–44; merchant–missionary conflict and, 274n94; on missionaries as obstacle to trade, 47; relations with Hawaiian chiefs, 32–33; reports to employers on chiefly politics, 42; on ships purchased by chiefs, 36; on vicious competition in sandalwood market, 45

Kaʻahumanu, 25, 26, 36, 117, 210, 222, 253n59; "affair of the haole" council and, 204, 207, 208–209, 210; ʻai noa and, 107; Charlton's threats and, 203; chiefly influence of, 250n19; chiefs' debts to merchants and, 34; Christian conversion of, 144; code of laws and, 218; debate on sending Kuakini to England and, 216–217; events leading to Dolphin "outrage" and, 180–182, 183, 186, 187; genealogy of, 152; John Palmer "outrage" and, 194, 198–199; Jones's description

Liholiho Kamehama II, 4, 25, 42, 107, 140,
216; as *ali'i nui* (high chief), 221; American
intentions toward Hawai'i and, 117; cost of
merchants' goods and, 46, 47; death of,
182; drunken "frolicks" of, 43, 48; end of
'ai kapu and, 262n44; failed *Cleopatra's
Barge* deal and, 38–39; fleet of ships
amassed by, 35–36, 252n36; genealogy of,
21; as king of the Sandwich Islands, 26;
missionaries' introduction to, 115–116;
Notice on unruly sailors (1822), 157,
273n86; on power of *palapala* (reading and
writing), 123–124; rift with high chiefs, 48;
settlement of missionaries in Hawai'i and,
267n109
Lili'uokalani, 263n59
Linnekin, Jocelyn, 243n5
literacy, 102, 168, 225, 233; coexistence with
orality, 168; high rate among Hawaiians
(1840), 86; as new priority for the *ali'i*, 168;
"oral tradition" and, 13
London Missionary Society (LMS), 80, 82,
96, 97, 147, 261n35
Lono (god), 109
Lonoikamakahiki, 16
Loomis, Elisha, 120, 141, 270n23; *Dolphin*
"outrage" and, 180–181, 183, 187, 188, 189,
191, 276n8; on "purchase" of Hawaiian
women by ship captains, 164–165; on sailors' "outrages," 174, 275n113
Lyon, Kapali, 269n7

Magee, Captain James, 53
Mahuika, Nepia, 268n6
maka'ainana (commoners, non-ali'i subjects), 5, 72, 79, 87; authority of the *ali'i*
and, 137; end of *'ai kapu* and, 105, 107; in
Lahaina, 143; law and social relations with
ali'i, 175, 176, 185, 194; literacy among, 168
mālama 'āina (caring for the land), 24
Malo, David, 36, 146, 147, 220, 222, 246n25;
advice in form of prophecy, 225; "affair of
the *haole*" and, 208–209; on *ali'i* and relations with other nations, 223–225; on
Charlton's threats, 203
malu (shelter, protection), 107, 148, 192, 212,
226, 264n66
mana (spiritual power), 3, 13, 145, 213, 243n4;
genealogical chants and, 16; of Ka'ahumanu, 153, 154; Kamehameha I's harnessing of, 20; *kapu* and, 154; *palapala* (reading

and writing) associated with, 123–124; poli-
tics of, 27–29; in words of Euro-Ameri-
cans, 103, 262n51
maoli (Hawaiian, indigenous), 10, 12, 176, 225;
body politic, 176; historians, 12; *kapu* and,
185
Marin, Don Francisco de Paula, 156, 174, 180
Marquesa Islands, 23
Marshall, Josiah, 29
Marshall and Wildes (New England firm),
31–32, 35, 38, 44, 168, 169, 251n28
Masters, Captain, 32
Maui, 26, 120, 139, 195, 200, 266n94
Mayhew, Thomas, 95
McKinzie, Edith, 248n32
Meek, Captain Thomas, 38
mele (song), 176, 231
Memoirs of Henry Obookiah, The (ABCFM,
1818), 77–78
merchant agents, 8, 10, 20, 91, 127, 225;
authority of the *ali'i* and, 137; chiefly debts
to, 44, 45; consumer goods brought to
Hawaiian Islands, 41; as debt collectors, 31;
demand for a Hawaiian "national" debt,
51; doubt thrown on missionary narratives
by, 215; grievances against missionaries,
169; inflation of prices by, 46, 49; knowledge of chiefly politics and power, 26; letters to merchant houses in America, 121;
limited knowledge of chiefly politics, 44,
49, 50; missionaries' dependence on, 122;
missionaries resented by, 47; pleasure-
seeking by, 30; sandalwood trade and, 9,
11; security in governance and, 111; supercargoes, 31
Merrell, James, 254n5
Merry, Sally Engle, 275n4
Michener, James, 90
Middle Church (New Haven, Conn.), 171
Mikabako, 194–195, 278n60
Mills, Samuel, 56–58, 127
missionaries, 4, 5, 20, 214–215; arrival in
Hawai'i (1820), 9, 100, 105; authority of the
ali'i and, 137; background of, 12; claimed
absence of religion among Hawaiians, 105,
264n69; "common stock of property" of,
265n81; Congregationalist, 2, 80; construction of authority of, 126; conviction of cultural superiority, 66; dependence on
merchants, 122; encounters with visiting

"Suppression of Vice, The" (broadside, 1824), 159, 161–163
Suter, Captain John, 36, 37, 38

Tabernacle Church (Salem, Mass.), 93
Tahiti, 94, 97, 116, 147
Tamaamaah or Tamahamaha. *See* Kamehameha I
Tamoree (Kaumuali'i), George Prince, 46, 253n63; ABCFM promotional narrative about, 62, 67–75; adoption of "George Prince" name, 69, 72, 257n49; Hawaiian language forgotten by, 67, 70, 72, 256n40; letters to father, 72, 74; at Park Street Church, 98; return to Hawaii, 80; sent as boy to America, 55–56; on US merchant and navy ships, 56, 61, 67
Tappan, William B., 130
Taua, 147–148, 271n39
Thaddeus (ship bringing missionaries to Hawai'i), 41, 99, 100, 101, 117; chiefs' meeting on board (1820), 111–112; in Liholiho's fleet, 36; Sabbath observance on deck of, 115
Thames (ship with second company of missionaries), 129, 161–163
theater, 65, 89–90, 118
Thompson, Alpheus B., 180
Thurston, Rev. Asa, 79, 93, 115, 118, 267n125; at Andover Theological Seminary, 267n123; in Kailua, 267n109
time, ordering of, 109–110, 265n73; before and after Christian conversion, 147; climate of Hawai'i versus Protestant sense of time, 123; "old system" and "new system," 223

ua 'ōlelo kākou ("it has been said"), 133, 136, 268n2
Unitarianism, 89
United States, early republic, 18, 185, 221; Indian Removal of Five Nations, 245n15; lack of interest in colonizing Hawai'i, 94–95; museums stocked with curiosities of maritime travels, 53–54, 60; Navy warships, 56, 67, 191; popular curiosity about Hawai'i and the Pacific, 55; post-colony political status, 104; westward expansion, 52, 94–95

Vaill, Rev. William S., 64–66, 69–70
Vancouver, Captain George, 19, 248n2
Vassilieff, Commodore Michael, 125, 126

Wahinepi'o, 140, 143–145, 220, 222; Christianity and, 271n42; Leoiki's "purchase" by Captain Buckle and, 145, 146–150, 164, 179, 193
"Wake, Isles of the South!" (hymn, Tappan), 130
Wākea (male god), 108
War of 1812, 23, 56
Wasp (US warship), 56, 257n49
Wayland, Francis, 222
whalers/whaling ships, 9, 55, 91, 122, 145–147; doubt thrown on missionary narratives by, 215; expansion of Pacific whaling fleet, 109, 156; schedule of arrivals in Hawaiian ports, 110
White, Alfred, 122
Whitney, Samuel, 120, 142
Wildes, Captain Dixey, 29–30, 50
Williams, Dr., 124
Winship, Captain Jonathan, 23
Winship, Captain Nathaniel, 23, 120
women, Hawaiian: *'ai kapu* rules and, 107–108; children from unions with sailors, 163, 164; exotic qualities desired by sailors, 170–171; *John Palmer* "outrage" and, 194–195, 198, 199, 278nn60–62; sensational sexualization of, 277n47; sexual abuse of, 190; sexual encounters with foreign men, 1, 9, 11, 14; transformation of Hawaiian law/governance and, 220; usurpation by appropriation of high-ranked woman, 153, 271n51. *See also* prostitution, *kapu* against
women, missionary and "civilized," 111, 170
Worcester, Rev. Samuel, 93, 94, 96–97, 129; departure of first missionaries to Hawai'i and, 99; as mission corresponding secretary, 100; official letter to Kamehameha, 115
writing, 13–14, 86, 122–123; essential to Sandwich Island Mission, 92–93; as tool of Christianization of "heathens," 75. *See also palapala* (reading and writing)

Young, John, 115, 117, 123, 266n87

ACKNOWLEDGMENTS

'A'ole pau ka 'ike i ka hālau ho'okahi

All knowlege is not found in one school

E nā akua, nā 'aumakua, nā lālani o nā ali'i,
e o'u mau kūpuna, a i nā kumu o ka wā ma mua a i kēia
wā e holo nei.

My journey to bring this book to completion began decades ago with the intellectual spark and guidance of many kumu (teachers). In seeking after knowledge, I have been guided by these authoritative words that were passed down to us: 'a'ole pau ka 'ike i ka hālau ho'okahi. My intellectual mo'okū'auhau has grown mana (branches) into scholarly training in Hawaiian religion, language, and literature, and American history.

My first appreciation is for those kumu who trained me in Hawaiian oral traditions through performance. I am deeply indebted to Robert Manuhaokalani Gay, Pōmaika'i Gaui, and John Keolamaka'āinanaokalanio-kamehameha'ekolu Lake for teaching me the importance of the beauty and strength of language, kumu who trained my memory and ear and helped me to find my voice. It is due to the perseverence of such kumu in keeping oral historical traditions of Hawaiian prayer, chant, and dance alive and vibrant that those of us belonging to succeeding generations have been able to travel the path of our ancestors. The training I received in mele and oli was fortified by the profound knowledge of kūpuna (elders) and experts from our community. Working with Edith McKinzie on the Hawaiian-language newspaper indexing project and Rubellite Kawena Johnson on the kanikau (laments) project opened up vistas on Hawaiian-language print culture and intellectual traditions that remain fathomless, ever offering scholars opportunities for future study. They taught me how to translate, how to present my findings before the community, how to speak like a woman, a native scholar, and how to tell mo'olelo.

Although finding one's voice is important in any language, the ability to hear is equally significant. The first voices that I understood in Hawaiian were gently imbued with the sound of the soughing waves of Miloliʻi and the crisp rustle of hala leaves. The voices of ʻAnakala Eddie Kaanaana and Tūtū Lilia Wahinemaikaʻi Hale brought me to the consciousness of Hawaiian language, a moment of birth that I will never forget. Their voices remain with me still, a gift for which I will ever be deeply thankful and blessed.

I am indebted to the many Hawaiian-language kumu for developing within me the ability to speak ma ka ʻōlelo Hawaiʻi; to these esteemed kumu I offer my aloha: Malia Melemai, Hauʻoli Victorino, Lalepa Koga, Kalani Akana, Kalani Whittaker, Kaleikoa Kaʻeo, Laiana Wong, and Puakea Nogelmeier. To Lalepa Koga I owe special thanks for his support and insightful discussions with me on the subjects of war, politics, and genealogy, and for introducing me to my first Hawaiian history ma ka ʻōlelo makuahine.

I am fortunate to have worked with Friedrich Seifert and John Charlot, my mentors through both my BA and MA in religion at the University of Hawaiʻi at Mānoa. From these biblical scholars, I learned the art and patience of close-reading and close-hearing a text, which is at the foundation of my approach to historical sources. I am indebted to Professor Charlot still for his material support for this book and the many hours he spent reading and commenting on chapters over years of writing and revision.

When you are from an island, personal commitments and support run deep, and here in the form of a helu or listing are the many people to whom I give my mahalo. To the hui of kānaka maoli scholars, intellectuals, and creatives who have sustained me with food, friendship, debate, discussion, and aloha over the course of these years, I also give my respect and thanks: Hokulani Aikau, Malia Akutagawa, Rosie Alegado, Lōkahi Antonio, Nanea Armstrong, Tammy Hāʻiliʻōpua Baker, Kamanamaikalani Beamer, Kaʻeo Bradford, Leah Caldeira, David Chang, Robert Kealoha Domingo, Māhealani Dudoit, Mehanaokalā Hind, Kelikokauaikekai Hoe, kuʻualoha hoʻomanawanui, Ioane Hoʻomanawanui, Analu Kameʻeiamoku Josephedis, Kalani Kaanaana, Lilikalā Kameʻeleihiwa, Bryan Kamaoli Kuwada, Leslie Keahiloa Lang, Joshua Iwikauikauakukuiʻāikeawakea Lake, Renee Pualani Louis, Kealiʻi Makekau, Kawika McKeague, Kalae Miles-Davis, Jonathan Kamakawiwoʻole Osorio, Hiapokeikikāne Perreira, Aaron Salā, Kimo Silberstein, Noenoe Silva, Ty Tengan, Kamehaʻililani Waiau, Kamoaʻe Walk, Laʻakea Yoshida, and Terry Kanalu Young.

Much aloha for Judy Dente, Yvette Lee, and Suzanne Finney for your friendship and nurturing spaces for children, and for work. Aloha to David Goldberg and Adolph Yago for being on watch during the homestretch.

My hālau have become my family, nurturing and insistent that I continue in my commitments, abetting my educational and intellectual pursuits. My aloha to Kumu Sam ʻOhukaniʻohiʻa Gon III and Kalama Cabigon, whose love of word play and translation always kept my wit and tongue sharp. Aloha to ka ʻōpū hālaualiʻi John Mahiʻai Cummings and wife Adaline, who housed, fed, and cared for me and my family whenever we unexpectedly turned up. Aloha for Kumu Māhealani Wong, to whom I owe a particular debt of thanks for her twinship and her aloha for my family over these many years, kuʻu aloha mau a mau.

This book would not have been the same were it not researched, formulated, and written in transit. My thanks to the families who have taken me in and supported my work on both sides of the Atlantic. Mahalo to Kateia and Karl Burrows, who opened their home to me when I did research in London. Aloha nui to Richard and Mia Chase, who hosted the weekly Friday night supper club, which provided my family a loving home away from home. Thanks to the Friday night regulars, Mark Bernstein and Linda Thorsen, Al and Theresa Jacobson, and Aaron Chase for lively conversation and kind attentions, and for your patience in listening to the progress of the work. A debt of gratitude is owed to Jason Baird and Jessie Little Doe Baird for accepting us as part of your extended family over these many years. We have been blessed by the vibrancy of Wampanoag life and language in Mashpee and Aquinnah. Life that you shared with us while we were many miles and many years away from our own home. Your friendship and aloha have meant much to us over the years, *he aloha mau.*

This book benefited from long conversations with generous colleagues who have assisted me along the way to improve chapters and present papers at conferences or for publication. Mahalo to Randy Akee, Alexis Antracoli, Yoni Appelbaum, Jessie Little Doe Baird, David Chang, Ashley Cohen, Kevin Quinn Doyle, Joanna Frang, Claire Gherini, Mishuana Goeman, Brett Graham, Don Johnson, Doug Kiel, Shane Landrum, Adam Lewis, R. Zamora Linmark, Pippa Koch, Rob McGreevy, Dan Taulapapa McMullin, Lyra Monteiro, Mairin Odle, Lachlan Paterson, Matt Pehl, Anne Marie Reardon, Sarah Rodriguez, David Soll, Alice Te Punga Somerville, Derek Taira, Matthew Uiagalelei, and Will Walker.

For their service at all hours, via email, text, or social media, mahalo to my diligent colleagues, Keola Donaghy, Kapali Lyon, and Kale Langlas, who read my work with eyes and ears trained to great attention to detail regarding Hawaiian orthography and translation and who offered up their suggestions for further research in Hawaiian-language sources. I am also the grateful beneficiary of the steady encouragement of writer and researcher David Forbes, whose vast knowledge of archival holdings touching on Hawai'i is certainly unparalleled.

These scholars read every word of manuscript and offered up their own work to assist me in thinking through my own travails, for them I have a few more words of thanks and aloha to offer in return. I have great regard for Adria Imada, whose excellent scholarship on Hawaiian history has deeply inspired me. Adria's insightful comments on multiple drafts and her conversations with me grew as our friendship has. Her insights and expertise have improved this work immensely, *aloha and mahalo nui*. To Judy Kertész, who watched over my development from application to graduation, whose intelligence, and perceptions of the fraught nature of writing native history in America have been a beacon for my own intellectual development, *aloha nui*. To Laura Lehuanani Yim, I owe a particular debt of thanks. Her support and dedication to this project and to my work as a scholar over the course of many, many years has made worlds of difference, *ku'u aloha palena 'ole*.

At Brandeis University, I was accepted into a nurturing community of scholars and mentors whose lessons and example I am still growing toward. My aloha to Mary Baine Campbell and Michael Willrich for their interest in Hawai'i's literary and legal history. Special mahalo to David Hackett Fischer, who introduced my ear to the artful eloquence of American national history, and to David Engerman and Damon Salesa, special mentors to me and my work, *ku'u aloha nui*. Mahalo to my colleagues at the University of Hawai'i at Mānoa whose support made this work possible. Leonard Andaya, Cristina Bacchilega, Sue Carlson, David Hanlon, Vilsoni Hereniko, Peter Hoffenberg, Craig Howes, Morris Lai, Matthew Lauzon, Alexander Mawyer, Suzanna Reiss, and Lee Siegel. Mahalo to my haumāna who have helped me to experience truly what it is to be a kumu. For teaching me and sharing their own rising insight into mo'olelo Hawai'i as this book was being birthed, my aloha to Shirley Buchanan, Suzanne Corley, Noah Dolim, Makanani Sala, Sarah Tamashiro, and Catherine Ulep.

At the forefront of the work are the many people who care for the sources and who assisted me in locating materials and navigating their important collections at a number of institutions, including the Andover-Harvard Theological, Baker, Harvard Law-School, Widener, and Houghton Libraries of Harvard University, the Goldfarb and Farber libraries at Brandeis University; the Massachusetts Historical Society in Boston; the James Duncan Phillips Library of the Peabody-Essex Museum in Salem, Massachusetts; Boston Public Library Archives; the New York Public Library; the Bancroft Library at the University of California; the School of Oriental and Asian Studies at the University of London; and the National Archives and Public Records Office at Kew. Thanks to Peggy Bendroth at the Congregational Historical Society for sharing historic Congregational Boston with me on a walking tour. At the New Bedford Whaling Museum Research Library, my thanks go out to Maritime curator, Michael Dyer and especially to Jan Keeler for sharing her expertise in Pacific Maritime and whaling records, and for opening her home to me and my family. Special thanks to former administrative director and librarian of the Hawaiian Historical Society, Barbara Dunn, and members of her staff, and Ipo Santos-Bear for their assistance. My heartfelt thanks and aloha to Kanani Reppun, former head archivist at the Hawaiian Mission Children's Society Library, whose active interest in this project and expertise made this book possible. Thanks to John Barker at the Hawaiian Mission Children's Society Archives for his support of this project, Jennifer Higa at the Hawaiian Historical Society, and Jason Kapena Achiu at the Hawai'i State Archives. Together, these institutions and their staffs have provided the essential material that made this project possible, and I remain indebted to them.

This work received financial and material support in all stages of its growth that has allowed it to blossom and thrive. While at Brandeis, I was supported by the Irving and Rose Crown Fellowship. Research was generously sustained by the Mellon Hawai'i Fellowship and the work of Matt Hamabata at the Kohala Center. The Charles Eastman Fellowship at Dartmouth College saw the project through its final stages; thanks are due to Bruce Duthu, Colin Calloway, Dale Turner, Vera Palmer, and Melanie Benson-Taylor for their support and discussions concerning the work. The support I received for research and writing resulted in my receiving the Allan Nevins Prize from the Society of American Historians, and I am thankful for their generous support of my work. Later work on the manuscript was sustained by a grant of uninterrupted research leave from UH Mānoa funded by the Mellon Sawyer Fellowship, the McNeil Center on Early American Studies at the University of Pennsylvania, and the Woodrow Wilson Minority Faculty Fellowship.

In each new place, I was blessed to have interlocutors, colleagues who read and respected my work and supplied incisive comments on the manuscript. In their presence and learning from their guidance, I was always engaged and frequently in awe—mahalo nui to Chris Capozzola, David Eng, David Kazanjian, Theodore Jun Yoo, and Gayatri Spivak. The work has certainly been shaped by the comments and suggestions I received on the manuscript from Edward Gray, Ann Fabian, and Rebecca McLennan; and to Daniel Richter, who generously gave his time to discuss the work with me on several occasions, many thanks for giving me the space, intellectual community, and audience it needed to grow, *aloha nui*. I am grateful for the support given to the project by Brian Delay, and indebted to Robert Lockhart, whose kind counsel and patience have always left me feeling supported, and who lifted the work up whenever I have spoken with him, *he aloha nui ka'u nou*.

From my acceptance at Brandeis through the present day, Jane Kamensky remains an amazing mentor and role model, providing a secure foundation for my development as an American historian. Jane has fostered me through intellectual and personal growing pains, imparting to me an appreciation and regard for the discipline of history and my role within it. Jane's keen intellect, and narrative prowess have provided me with an excellent example of who a historian and writer is and what she does, setting a high bar of excellence to which I have just begun to aspire. He lālā au no ku'u kumu.

Finally, it is with a full heart that I thank my 'ohana, for without their efforts and sacrifices, this book would not have been possible. As a person enamored of words, I find that mine are not sufficient to equal the aloha of my parents Rose and Vince Arista who supported me through every phase of my education, and who care for our sons Hi'iakalehuakaulei and Ka'ulawena during my long absences in pursuit of this mo'olelo. Hi'ia and Ka'ula, thank you very much for your aloha, patience, and understanding. My husband Chad Hashimoto's affection for me has revealed itself in every aspect of this book's production: from home-cooked meals, to reading stories to children crying for their mother, long agonizing conversations, bearing the kaumaha of this history even as he held me up, through the years of separation our relationship has endured, he aloha. He has read every word I have written and edited every page I have produced. I never say or show enough what it means to have his malu over me, I ku'u kāne kai kahu i ke ahi, ke aloha mau i kēia ao a i ke ao e hiki mai ana.